Douglas Biber's new book extends and refines the research and methodology reported in his ground-breaking *Variation across speech and writing* (1988). In it he gives a linguistic analysis of register in four widely differing languages: English, Nukulaelae Tuvaluan, Korean, and Somali. Using the Multi-Dimensional analytical framework employed in his earlier work, Biber carries out a principled comparison of both synchronic and diachronic patterns of variation across the four languages. Striking similarities as well as differences emerge, allowing Biber to predict for the first time cross-linguistic universals of register variation. This major new work will provide the foundation for the further investigation of cross-linguistic universals governing the patterns of discourse variation across registers, and will be of wide interest to any scholar interested in discourse, register, and the linguistic correlates of orality and literacy.

Dimensions of register variation

Dimensions of register variation
A cross-linguistic comparison

Douglas Biber
Northern Arizona University

CAMBRIDGE
UNIVERSITY PRESS

Published by the Press Syndicate of the University of Cambridge
The Pitt Building, Trumpington Street, Cambridge CB2 1RP
40 West 20th Street, New York, NY 10011–4211, USA
10 Stamford Road, Oakleigh, Melbourne 3166, Australia

First published 1995

Printed in Great Britain at the University Press, Cambridge

A catalogue record for this book is available from the British Library

Library of Congress cataloguing in publication data

Biber, Douglas.
Dimensions of register variation: a cross-linguistic comparison /
Douglas Biber.
      p.   cm.
Includes index.
ISBN 0 521 47331 4 (hardback)
1. Register (Linguistics) 2. Contrastive linguistics. I. Title.
P302.815.B53 1995
306.4' 4–dc20   94–17041   CIP

ISBN 0521 47331 4 hardback

EBF

Contents

Figures

Tables

Acknowledgments

I have been greatly helped in writing the present book by numerous friends and colleagues. I owe a special debt to the previous PhD students who have completed dissertation projects within the Multi-Dimensional framework at the University of Southern California: Niko Besnier, who studied register variation in Nukulaelae Tuvaluan; Yong-Jin Kim, who studied register variation in Korean; Mohamed Hared, who collaborated with me over several years to study register variation in Somali (as well as standardization processes in Somali for his dissertation research); and Dwight Atkinson, who studied the historical development of Medical Prose and Science Prose in English. The present cross-linguistic investigation, which is based on a synthesis of these previous studies together with my own previous work, would not have been possible without the efforts of these colleagues.

In addition, several of the research studies reported in the following pages have been carried out in collaboration with Ed Finegan. Besides being a co-author and my best critic, Ed has continued to freely offer his friendship, advice, and encouragement.

Much of the research reported here has been generously supported by grants from the National Science Foundation. Work on register variation in Somali was funded by Grant BNS-8811720 and Grant BNS-9096258 (PI: Doug Biber; Research Assistant: Mohamed Hared). Work on the ARCHER project, analyzing diachronic register variation in English, was funded by Grant BNS-9010893 (Co-PIs: Doug Biber and Ed Finegan; Research Assistants: Dwight Atkinson, Randi Reppen, Ann Beck, Jena Burges, Dennis Burges). In addition, these projects have been supported by supplemental university-internal grants from the University of Southern California and Northern Arizona University.

Several colleagues have read and commented on earlier drafts of the present book. Suzanne Romaine read the entire manuscript and raised a number of important issues that required attention; Ed Finegan provided especially detailed comments on the initial chapters of the book. Bill Grabe and Randi Reppen also provided useful comments and discussions on various parts of the book.

In addition, I am grateful to several colleagues at Northern Arizona University for their friendship and stimulating interactions relating to discourse and language use: Susan Carkin, Susan Conrad, Susan Foster-Cohen, Bill Grabe, Joan Jamieson, Mary McGroarty, Randi Reppen, Fredricka Stoller. Susan Foster-Cohen has been especially encouraging and supportive during her tenure as Chair of the English Department at NAU.

Finally, I owe thanks on a more personal level: to Randi Reppen, for her companionship over the last year; and to Teresa, David, and Martha Biber, for their patience and understanding while I was working on various parts of this study (including periods while I was away on extended trips overseas).

Abbreviations

COMP	complement
DECL	declarative
DIR	directional (particle)
DRV	derivational (suffix)
FM	focus marker
FOC	focus
FRM	framing (relative pronoun)
HON	honorific
IMP	impersonal (particle)
INTERR	interrogative
LOC	locative
NEG	negative (marker)
OBJ	object
OPT	optative (marker)
PST	past (tense)
Q	question
QM	question marker
REFLEX	reflexive
REL	relative
SUBJ	subject
TOP	topic

1   Introduction

1.1   Registers, dialects, and linguistic variation

Variability is inherent in human language: a single speaker will use different linguistic forms on different occasions, and different speakers of a language will say the same thing in different ways. Most of this variation is highly systematic: speakers of a language make choices in pronunciation, morphology, word choice, and grammar depending on a number of non-linguistic factors. These factors include the speaker's purpose in communication, the relationship between speaker and hearer, the production circumstances, and various demographic affiliations that a speaker can have.[1] Analysis of the systematic patterns of variation associated with these factors has led to the recognition of two main kinds of language varieties: *registers*, referring to situationally defined varieties, and *dialects*, referring to varieties associated with different groups of speakers.

In the present book, *register* is used as a cover term for any variety associated with particular situational contexts or purposes. Although register distinctions are defined in non-linguistic terms, there are usually important linguistic differences among registers as well. In many cases, registers are named varieties within a culture, such as novels, letters, editorials, sermons, and debates. Registers can be defined at any level of generality: for example, academic prose is a very general register, while methodology sections in psychology articles are a much more highly specified register.

Two main kinds of dialects are commonly distinguished in linguistics: *geographic dialects* are varieties associated with speakers living in a particular location, while *social dialects* are varieties associated with speakers belonging to a given demographic group (e.g., women versus men, or different social classes). Most recent dialect studies have used a comparative approach to study social dialects, describing the linguistic patterns of variation across social groups in major urban centers such as New York City, Norwich, Belfast, and Montreal.

Although linguistic differences among geographic and social dialects have been more extensively studied, it turns out that the linguistic differences

1

among the registers within a language are in many ways more noteworthy. When speakers switch between registers, they are doing different things with language – using language for different purposes and producing language under different circumstances. Many language choices are functionally motivated, related to these differing purposes and production circumstances, and thus there are often extensive linguistic differences among registers. In contrast, dialect differences are largely conventional and therefore less fundamental in nature. Regardless of any dialect differences, speakers using the same register are doing similar communicative tasks; therefore, in most basic respects the characteristic language features used in a given situation are similar across speakers.

To illustrate, text samples 1.1 and 1.2 compare conversations recorded in a working-class (WC) family and a middle-class (MC) family (in the city of Bristol, England).

Text sample 1.1: Working-class conversation

   A: I probably yeah. I probably need two cards.
   B: Right. ⟨unclear⟩ . . .
   C: Nat you gotta have a bath my love it's what . . . twenty-five to nine darling.
   B: ⟨unclear⟩ like ⟨unclear⟩. Two different ones.
   A: That's a lovely. Any
   C: Envelope.
   A: Any envelopes. Any envelopes with them Nat?
   B: Yep. Get you one now. . . .
   C: Nat said her envelopes don't stick very well.
   A: Don't it?
   B: What?
   A: ⟨unclear⟩
   C: Yeah. Do you hear her get off the bed then?
   A: Mm.
   B: What?
   C: Lady jumped off the bed. She heard us come in. . . . There's cake in the fridge Nat.
   B: I bet he don't eat it.
   C: I don't know. He don't eat a lot of cake do he?
   B: He eats all my cake though.

Text sample 1.2: Middle-class conversation

   A: You should be going to bed now.
   B: No I don't wanna go to bed.

```
A:  Come on. . . .
C:  [laugh]
A:  [laugh] . . . Come on, bed! . . .
C:  Don't swear at me my dear.
B:  I'm not swearing at you. I just pointed upwards. To go up . . .
    the stairs . . .
A:  We'll be up in a minute. . . .
C:  Brush your teeth.
B:  I've already done that. I'm coming I'm coming . . . ooh . . .
    parents!
A:  Kids!
B:  Parents! . . .
A:  Okay.
C:  You'd better take her lamp upstairs out of the way as well
    because that's, remember that's a present. It's gotta be wrapped
    up.
A:  It's got to be wrapped up. Yeah.
C:  I know she's picked it out but [laugh]
A:  [laugh] . . .
C:  I ordered a skirt this morning as well.
A:  Right.
C:  A navy blue pleated one.
A:  Mhm. So you want . . . it'll probably come as black and white
    spotted
C:  Yeah.
```

The only obvious dialect marker in these two text samples is the use of *do* with a third person singular subject in the WC conversation (*he don't eat it. He don't eat a lot of cake do he?*) Because dialect markers such as these are often highly stigmatized, a relatively rare occurrence of a few features can serve as an important indicator of dialect differences.

Overall, though, the most striking aspect of comparison between text samples 1.1 and 1.2 is the extent of sameness. Situationally, the two conversations are very similar in their production circumstances, primary purposes, and interactiveness. Both conversations are spoken (rather than written), and they are produced on-line, with the words and grammatical organization being assembled on the spot as the conversation unfolds. There is little time to plan ahead, and virtually no opportunity to edit afterwards. In addition, both conversations are personal and directly interactive. Conversational partners express their own personal attitudes, feelings, and concerns, and they interact with one another to build a shared discourse jointly. These characteristics are tied to conversation as a register and are thus not affected by dialect considerations.

The contextual characteristics shared by these two conversations have important linguistic correlates. For example, the on-line production circumstances of both conversations result in generally short sentences, with many utterances not being structurally complete sentences at all (assuming the traditional concept of a grammatical sentence). These latter include simple responses (*right, what?, okay, yeah*) as well as utterances that build on the shared physical context to supply missing information (e.g., *Any envelopes*; *A navy blue pleated one*). Both conversations also have numerous contracted forms, such as *it's, that's, don't, I'm, we'll*. In addition, many of the referents in both conversations are not explicitly identified, so that hearers must rely on the context for understanding (e.g., *Do you hear her get off the bed then? I bet he don't eat it. I know she's picked it out*). The interactive nature of conversation further results in linguistic similarities between these two texts. For example, both conversations have frequent references to *I* (the speaker) and *you* (the addressee). Similarly, there are frequent direct questions and directives in both (e.g., *Don't it? What? Do you hear her . . .? Nat you gotta have a bath*; *You should be going to bed now*; *Brush your teeth*); these constructions would not be appropriate without a specific addressee (*you*).

The fundamental nature of register variation can be further illustrated by comparing the above two conversational samples to a text representing written, informational prose. Text sample 1.3 below is taken from a science textbook.

Text sample 1.3: Science textbook

A system of equations that provides an accurate and physically satisfactory representation of an experimental system can be cumbersome, and even complicated and of high order, so solutions may often only be obtained as numerical approximations to solutions. Thus the numerical solutions themselves may be considered to be approaching an equilibrium or periodic solution.

The contextual characteristics of this science text are strikingly different from those of the conversational texts. The science text is written, carefully planned, edited, and revised. It is produced by an author who does not overtly refer to himself in the text. The production is not interactive; the text is addressed to a large audience of scientists, but these addressees are never directly referred to. The primary purpose of the text is to present information about non-linear science, as opposed to the (inter)personal purposes of conversational participants from both dialects in text samples 1.1 and 1.2.

Due to the influence of these contextual factors, the linguistic characteristics of the science text are dramatically different from those of the conversational texts. The sentences of the science text are all grammatically complete, and many of them are quite long and grammatically complex. None of the reduced or interactive linguistic characteristics common in conversation occurs in this text. However, science texts do contain numerous linguistic characteristics rarely found in conversation. In text sample 1.3, these characteristics include technical vocabulary (e.g., *numerical approximations, equilibrium, periodic solution*), complex noun phrase constructions (e.g., *A system of equations that provides an accurate and physically satisfactory representation of an experimental system*), and passive constructions (e.g., *solutions may often only be obtained, solutions . . . may be considered*).

The extensive linguistic differences between the conversational texts (from both dialects) and this science text reflect the fundamental influence of register, associated with contextual differences in production circumstances, purpose, interactiveness, etc. Because these contextual factors operate across dialects, a full understanding of the associated patterns of register variation is essential to any comprehensive analysis of language use in a speech community.

The present book takes these considerations one step further, investigating the extent to which register factors operate in similar ways across languages and cultures. Register variation is widely considered to be intrinsic to all cultures. For example:

each language community has its own system of registers . . . corresponding to the range of activities in which its members normally engage (Ure 1982: 5)

register variation, in which language structure varies in accordance with the occasions of use, is all-pervasive in human language (Ferguson 1983: 154)

no human being talks the same way all the time . . . At the very least, a variety of registers and styles is used and encountered (Hymes 1984: 44)

Given the ubiquity of register variation, analysis of the linguistic patterns across registers is of central importance for both the linguistic description of particular languages and the development of cross-linguistic theories of language use. Hymes (1984: 44) argues that the analysis of register variation – 'verbal repertoire' in his terms – should become the major focus of research within linguistics:

[the] sociolinguistic perspective . . . has the possibility of taking the lead in transforming the study of language, through developing and consolidating the systematic study of verbal repertoire.

The abilities of individuals and the composite abilities of communities cannot be understood except by making 'verbal repertoire', not 'language', the central scientific notion. To do so requires a mode of description in linguistics which can address the organization of linguistic features in styles, that is, in ways which cut across the standard levels of linguistic structure.

The present study, by comparing the patterns of register variation across four quite different languages and cultural settings, provides a major step towards these goals.

1.2   Introduction to previous research on register

Interest in register analysis can be traced back to the merging of situational, social, and linguistic descriptions by anthropological linguists such as Boas, Sapir, Malinowski, Whorf, Bloomfield, and Firth during the first half of the twentieth century. These observers typically focused on non-western languages and cultures, and occasionally examined language in different social contexts. Two important early studies focusing on situated language are Malinowski's (1923) discussion of the 'context of situation' and Firth's (1935) elaboration of that concept. Early in the century, Boas established the value of collecting and analyzing natural texts, and that became accepted practice for linguists such as Sapir, Kroeber, and Bloomfield. Predating the early studies of social dialect variation in the mid-1960s, researchers such as Ferguson, Gumperz, Halliday, and Hymes examined linguistic variation across social situations and communicative uses, as well as across speaker groups.

In the late 1950s and the early 1960s, a number of papers and books appeared describing particular registers of various languages and the ways in which linguistic form is influenced by communicative purpose and the context of situation. These include studies by Ferguson on 'high' and 'low' diglossic varieties and on baby talk, by Gumperz on the range of 'argots' used in rural South Asian villages, by Brown and Gilman on the role of second person pronouns in relationships of 'power' and 'solidarity', by Brown and Ford on American English address terms, by Leech on press advertising and on the language of poetry, and by Crystal and Davy on conversation, unscripted commentary, newspaper reporting, legal documents, and the language of religion. Hymes (1964), Pride and Holmes (1972), and Giglioli (1972) have collected many valuable papers from this period.

Over the last thirty years, there have been an increasing number of register studies undertaken by scholars in linguistics, communication, rhetoric, education, anthropology, and other related disciplines. Atkinson and Biber (1994) survey these studies, grouping them into four major categories: synchronic descriptions of a single register; diachronic descriptions tracing the evolution of a single register; synchronic descriptions of the patterns of variation among multiple registers; diachronic descriptions tracing changes in the patterns of variation among multiple registers. Register studies also differ in the linguistic characteristics chosen for analysis, the use of quantitative and/or qualitative methodologies, and the language studied.

Section 1.2.1 surveys the terminological differences found in previous register studies, while section 1.2.2 briefly surveys previous studies of a single register (both synchronic and diachronic). Then in sections 1.3 and 1.4, I turn to previous research on register variation, which provides the immediate background to the present study.

1.2.1   Terminology in register studies: *register, genre, style, sublanguage*, and *text type*

The term *register* is used in the present book as a general cover term for situationally defined varieties. This usage is similar to that of sociolinguists such as Ure (1982), Ferguson (1983, 1994), and Hymes (1984). For example:

the register range of a language comprises the range of social situations recognized and controlled by its speakers – situations for which appropriate patterns are available (Ure 1982: 5)

register variation 'is the linguistic difference that correlates with different occasions of use'. (Ferguson 1994: 16)

Register distinctions are defined in non-linguistic terms, by differences in purpose, interactiveness, production circumstances, relations among participants, etc. For this reason, particular registers can be more-or-less constrained in their linguistic characteristics: for example, experimental psychology articles are highly constrained in their linguistic characteristics, while novels employ a wide range of differing linguistic configurations. Thus, register analyses must describe the extent of linguistic variability within a register, in addition to the typical linguistic characteristics of the register. (*Text types* differ from *registers* in that they are defined in linguistic rather than situational terms – see below.)

Registers can be defined by situational characteristics at any level of generality. Halliday (1988: 162) also notes this fact, stating that registers 'can be identified at any delicacy of focus'. There can be major differences among registers specified at different levels of generality. At one extreme, very general registers such as speech and writing are defined only by reference to their physical mode; at the other extreme, highly specified registers such as methodology sections in psychology articles are defined in terms of their physical mode, production circumstances, intended audience, micro-purpose, topic, etc. In the present study, register differences are assumed to define a continuous space of variation;[2] thus, no attempt is made here to identify discrete register levels or to propose separate terms for varieties at different levels of generality (cf. Biber 1994).

Readers should be aware, however, that there is no general consensus within sociolinguistics concerning the use of *register* and related terms such as *genre* and *style*. A few writers (e.g., Trudgill 1974; Wardaugh 1986) restrict the term *register* to refer only to occupational varieties, such as computer programmer talk or auto mechanic talk. Several other researchers attempt to make a theoretical distinction between *register* and *genre*. Ventola (1984) and Martin (1985) refer to register and genre as different 'semiotic planes': genre is the 'content-plane' of register, and register is the 'expression-plane' of genre; register is in turn the 'content-plane' of language. Martin (1985) and Couture (1986) both describe registers as comprising particular configurations of the contextual categories of field, tenor, and mode (proposed by Firth and Halliday). Martin (1985: 250) further states that 'genres are how things get done', listing poems, narratives, expositions, lectures, recipes, manuals, appointment making, service encounters, and news broadcasts as examples of genres.

Gregory and Carroll's (1978: 64) and Couture's (1986:80) characterization of register – 'language in action' – is similar to Martin's characterization of genre. In contrast, Couture (p. 80) characterizes genre as 'conventional instances of organized text'. As examples of registers, Couture lists the following: the language used by preachers in sermons; the language used by sports reporters in giving a play-by-play description of a football game; and the language used by scientists reporting experimental research results. Genres include both literary and non-literary text varieties; for example, short stories, novels, sonnets, informational reports, proposals, and technical manuals.

Ferguson (1994) also attempts a theoretical distinction between *registers* and *genres*. *Register* variation is associated with 'a communication situation that recurs regularly in a society', while *genre* variation is associated with 'a message type that recurs regularly in a society' (pp. 20–21). Examples of registers cited by Ferguson include sports announcer talk and cookbook recipes, while chat, conversation, directions in a strange town, love-letters, newspaper articles, and obituaries are given as examples of genres.

The IPrA Survey of Research in Progress (Nuyts 1988) uses a number of different terms. The survey exemplifies terms in a hierarchical presentation rather than explicitly defining the terms. At a high level of generality, the survey distinguishes between *language varieties* and *discourse types*. *Register* is considered to be a language variety, along with *dialect, argot, slang*, and *jargon*; examples of registers in this framework include aviation language, journalese, legalese, literary language, religious language, scientific language, technical language, and mythical language. The survey identifies two major discourse types: *conversation types* and *text types*. Conversation types include adult–child, classroom, interview, dinner, meeting, narrative, and courtroom. Text types include advertisement, comic strip, essay, joke, legal text, letter, literature, message, monologue, narrative, obituary, report, and summary.

In all these discussions, the distinction between register and genre tends to be quite abstract and vague. In practice, it is difficult to decipher the empirical correlates of these supposedly discrete categories, or to determine whether a particular variety should be classified as a register, a genre, or some other text category. For this reason, the present study uses only the term *register* as the general cover term associated with all aspects of variation in use.

The term *sublanguage* (Kittredge and Lehrberger 1982; Grishman and Kittredge 1986) has been used within computational linguistics to refer to 'a subsystem of language that . . . [is] limited in reference to a specific subject domain'; each sublanguage is claimed to have its own 'distinctive grammar' (Grishman and Kittredge 1986: ix). Sublanguages are quite restricted; for example, analyses of sublanguages have focused on medical articles about lipoprotein kinetics (Sager 1986) and Navy telegraphic messages (Fitzpatrick, Bachenko, and Hindle 1986).[3]

Finally, the term *style* has perhaps been used for a wider range of concepts than any of the other terms. Crystal and Davy (1969) use the term in a similar way to the use of register here; Joos (1961) similarly uses the term style to refer to registers at a high level of generality. Labov (1972) uses style to refer to language production under circumstances that require differing amounts of attention to speech (e.g., reading word lists versus an interview). More commonly, style has been treated as a characteristic way of using language. This usage often has an evaluative sense, as when writing handbooks discuss writing with style (which carries the implication that many people write without style). With regard to literary language, style in this sense has been studied as a characteristic of particular genres, particular periods, particular authors, and even particular texts (see discussion in Leech and Short 1981). A similar notion of style has been used to study conversational interactions, where each culture can be described as having a distinctive *communicative style* (e.g., Tannen 1984a, b).

In my own previous studies, I have used the term *genre* as a general cover term, similar to my use of *register* in the present book (e.g., Biber 1988; Biber and Finegan 1989a). In Biber (1988: 68), I describe *genres* as 'text categorizations made on the basis of external criteria relating to author/speaker purpose' and 'the text categories readily distinguished by mature speakers of a language; for example . . . novels, newspaper articles, editorials, academic articles, public speeches, radio broadcasts, and everyday conversations. These categories are defined primarily on the basis of external format' (Biber 1989: 5–6). In practical terms, these categories are adopted because of their widespread use in computerized language corpora. The use of the term *register* in the present book corresponds closely to *genre* in these earlier studies.

In contrast, the term *text type* has been used in my own previous analyses to refer to text categories defined in strictly linguistic terms (Biber 1989). That is, regardless of purpose, topic, interactiveness, or any other non-linguistic factors, text types are defined such that the texts within each type are maximally similar with respect to their linguistic characteristics (lexical, morphological, and syntactic), while the types are maximally distinct with respect to their linguistic characteristics. After the text types are identified on formal grounds, they can be interpreted functionally in terms of the purposes, production circumstances, and other situational characteristics shared by the texts in each type. A comparison of text types in English and Somali is presented in chapter 9.

1.2.2 Previous studies of a single register

Studies of a single register have three major components: description of the situation in which the register is used; description of the linguistic characteristics of the register; and analysis of the functional or conventional associations between the situational and linguistic features. These relationships are schematized below:

$$\text{SITUATIONAL FEATURES} \longleftrightarrow \begin{array}{c} \text{FUNCTIONS} \\ \text{and} \\ \text{CONVENTIONS} \end{array} \longleftrightarrow \text{LINGUISTIC FORMS}$$

These relationships are bidirectional, with situational characteristics influencing the choice of linguistic form, while the choice of linguistic features in turn helps to create the situation. Positing a functional association does not entail a one-to-one mapping between form and function. Rather, the mapping across form–function–situation often comprises complex many-to-many kinds of relations.

Associations between form and situation can be motivated either by functional communicative requirements or by simple conventions. Functionally motivated patterns can be related to a number of situational characteristics, such as the physical setting, the extent of shared context or background knowledge, the degree of interactiveness, the production circumstances, the primary purposes or communicative goals of participants, and the social relations among participants. Finegan (1982) illustrates form-function associations in his analysis of common linguistic features (e.g., pronouns, imperatives, passives) in last wills and letters of transmittal; Zwicky and Zwicky (1980) cite the use of past participle modifiers and 'tasty adjectives' as examples of conventional features of American restaurant menus. Ferguson (1983) describes both types of association in his analysis of baseball game broadcasts.

Most studies of a single register focus on a specialized kind of language. Early studies of this type include the following: Mellinkoff (1963), which describes the characteristic lexical and grammatical features of legal language; Ferguson (1964), which describes the typical linguistic characteristics of baby talk; and Leech (1966), which provides a comprehensive register description of advertising language. More recently, Ferguson (1983) has investigated the distinctive situational and linguistic characteristics of radio sportscasting; Heath and Langman (1994) have undertaken a related description of the sports coaching register; Bruthiaux (1994) presents a register analysis of personal advertisements in the *LA Weekly*; and Jucker (1992) provides a book-length treatment of syntactic variation in British newspapers.

There have been fewer diachronic studies of single registers, and these usually focus on the evolution of some professional variety (science or legal prose). For example, Hiltunen (1990) traces the evolution of legal prose in English from 635 AD to the present. Halliday (1988) analyzes syntactic changes in English scientific prose (in physics), from the fourteenth century onward. Bazerman (1984, 1988) uses several different methodological approaches to describe experimental science articles and presents two diachronic analyses: a rhetorical analysis of the *Philosophical Transactions of the Royal Society* from the years 1665–1800, and a register analysis of historical change in spectroscopic articles from the journal *Physical Review* from the years 1893–1980. Similar to synchronic studies of single registers, diachronic studies include both detailed linguistic analyses and descriptions of the salient situational characteristics. These diachronic studies show how historical change in the characteristic linguistic features of a register is closely tied to changes in the perceived purposes or primary audience of a register.

1.3   Previous research on register variation

The study of register can also be approached from a variationist perspective. Register variation studies compare the linguistic characteristics of two or more registers, usually using quantitative techniques to isolate linguistic similarities and differences among registers. Most previous studies of register variation have compared registers varying along a single situational parameter, such as formality, attention paid to speech, extent of planning, or physical mode. The following subsections survey previous synchronic and diachronic studies of register variation, as well as register studies of non-western languages and computational analyses of sublanguages. Section 1.4, then, is devoted to studies adopting the Multi-Dimensional approach to register variation.

1.3.1 Previous synchronic studies of register variation along a single situational parameter

Comparisons of spoken and written registers have been the most common type of variation study. These studies have generally relied on quantitative methods to analyze differences in the relative distributions of surface linguistic features, such as adjectives, nominalizations, passives, and various clause types.

An early study comparing spoken and written registers is Blankenship (1962), which analyzed the lectures and published writing of public figures, focusing on linguistic features marking complexity (such as sentence length and passives). In a more elaborate study, Blankenship (1974) compared six spoken and written registers with respect to a wide variety of linguistic features, including word length, sentence length, type-token ratio, adjectives, and prepositions.

In an influential series of articles, Chafe (1982; Chafe and Danielewicz 1986) compared four spoken and written registers: dinner-table conversations, personal letters, lectures, and academic papers. These registers were analyzed with respect to linguistic characteristics from two functional/linguistic parameters: integration/fragmentation and involvement/detachment. The parameter of integration/fragmentation was realized by linguistic features such as nominalizations, participles, and attributive adjectives versus clause co-ordination; the parameter of involvement/detachment was realized by linguistic features such as first-person pronouns versus passives.

Tannen (1982a) compared spontaneous conversational narratives and elicited written versions of the same story, with respect to discourse phenomena such as the use of repetition, parallelism, and structural elaboration. Chafe and Tannen (1987) survey the extensive literature comparing spoken and written registers.

Another closely related parameter of variation is the distinction between planned and unplanned discourse described by Ochs (1979). This study compares unplanned, spoken narratives versus planned, written narratives on the same topic. Linguistic features analyzed include referent deletion, differing uses of demonstratives and definite articles, and active and passive voice.

Finally, a number of register variation studies have been directed towards analysis of the differences between restricted and elaborated codes (building on the theoretical framework developed by Bernstein). These studies typically involve comparisons across social groups as well as comparisons across registers. For example, Rushton and Young (1975) compared three written registers across working-class and middle-class groups of students: imaginative descriptive writing, opinionative discursive writing, and technical explanatory writing. This study focused primarily on syntactic characteristics, such as complex nominal modifiers, passives, WH subordinators, and deeply embedded clauses. Poole and Field (1976) use a factor analysis to compare interviews and written personal essays by working-class and middle-class undergraduates; linguistic features analyzed include mean sentence length, subordinate clauses, adjectives, adverbs, passives, and pronouns.

1.3.2   Previous diachronic studies of register variation

There have been far fewer studies dealing with diachronic register variation, that is, the analysis of the changing relations among registers across time. Such studies are essential for a complete understanding of the processes of language standardization, modernization, and adaptation. In most previous linguistic studies, language change is treated as a mechanical process influenced only by language-internal (rather than social/situational) factors. Further, languages are usually treated as if they were homogeneous constructs uniformly affected by diachronic developments. However, recent studies show that a register perspective is crucial to a complete understanding of the processes of language development and change: that linguistic change interacts in complex ways with changing patterns of register variation.

Romaine's (1980, 1982) 'sociohistorical' approach shows how structural changes enter a language in particular registers and subsequently evolve at different rates in different registers. This approach is based on analysis of the relative frequency of forms across registers from different historical periods. Romaine (1980) traces the development of WH relative clause markers in Scots English, analyzing the alternation among relative clause markers in registers such as verse play, narrative prose, epistolary prose, and record prose; this study shows how WH relative clause markers first entered the language in the most complex literate registers.

Kytö and Rissanen (1983), Rissanen (1986), Kytö (1986, 1991), Nevalainen (1986), and Nevalainen and Raumolin-Brunberg (1989) adopt Romaine's sociohistorical approach to study the patterns of historical syntax in early British and American English. For example, Rissanen (1986) describes the differing development of periphrastic *do* in formal written registers (e.g., chronicles) versus speech-based registers (e.g., sermons and records of meetings). Devitt (1989a, b) also uses this approach to analyze the influence of register variation on historical processes of standardization in Scots English and American English. She considers five registers (private records, private correspondence, official correspondence, religious treatises, and public records) and shows how linguistic features such as present participle inflections and relative pronouns were standardized at different rates in different registers.

While these empirical studies are important for their analysis of the interplay between language change and register variation, they do not provide comprehensive analyses of the changing patterns of register variation in a language. Other recent programmatic articles, however, have noted the importance of overall changes in the register system of a language and have called for comprehensive historical analysis of these developments. For example:

> The register range of a language is one of the most immediate ways in which it responds to social change. The difference between developed and undeveloped languages (Ferguson, 1968) is fundamentally one of register range, and language contact, which contributes to language development ... is mediated by particular registers ... This issue is concerned with both the pressures that make for change and the way in which these changes are realized linguistically. (Ure 1982: 7)

> [one of the two main tasks requiring attention within sociolinguistics at present is] the description and analysis of the organization and change of verbal repertoires in relation to the main processes of societal evolution of our time (Hymes 1984: 44–45)

Section 1.4.2 below surveys studies that extend the Multi-Dimensional approach in ways that enable such comprehensive analyses of the changing relations among registers in a language.

1.3.3   The study of register variation in non-western languages

Most studies of register variation have dealt with Indo-European languages, with English receiving by far the most attention. There have, however, been a few studies of register variation in non-western languages. For example, Duff (1973) compares oral and written stories in the Arawakan language Amuesha, finding differences in discourse organization, explicitness (e.g., the use or omission of temporal markers), and noun phrases. Deibler (1976) compares letters and conversations in Gahuku, a Papua New Guinean language, with respect to such features as contractions, shortened verbs, imperatives, and sentence length. Hurd (1979) presents a comparative description of a traditional legend, a personal narrative, and a procedural text in the Papua New Guinean language Nasioi, based on analysis of repetitions, grammatical reductions, conjunctions, and vocabulary selection.

Clancy (1982) and Tannen (1984a) compare spoken and written narratives about the 'pear film'. Clancy presents a comparison of Japanese spoken and written narratives, focusing on referential choice (full NP, pronoun, or zero), word order, and relative clause types. Tannen compares spoken and written narratives in Greek and English, showing how Greeks in both modes and speakers in both languages tended to be more interpretive. Li and Thompson (1982) compare the characteristics of written classical Chinese with spoken and written modern Mandarin, focusing on zero anaphora, clause length, and the presence of grammatical morphemes. Chafe (1982) includes a comparison of conversational and ritual Seneca texts, briefly describing ways in which ritualistic language is more integrated and detached (more structural elaboration, and frequent impersonal constructions), while conversational language is more fragmented and involved (e.g., frequent evidentials related to emphasis or hedging).

Even fewer studies undertake diachronic register analyses of non-western languages. Romaine (1994) provides one of the few existing historical descriptions of register development in a non-western language. This study documents the early development of sports reportage in Tok Pisin, as it emerged as a distinct register in the newspaper *Wantok*. Hared (1992) adopts Romaine's earlier sociohistorical approach to analyze the historical changes in three Somali press registers over the first seventeen years of their history (1972–89). This study shows how the complementary processes of standardization and modernization interact with register factors in influencing the course of linguistic change.

Most of the studies cited above are restricted in scope, analyzing relatively few registers with respect to relatively few linguistic characteristics. In large part, these restrictions are due to the difficulties of fieldwork in many non-western languages. That is, the lack of previous grammatical and functional descriptions makes it difficult to decide which linguistic features to study, and it is often a time-consuming and labor-intensive job to compile a large corpus of texts from a non-western language. There have, however, been three comprehensive studies of register variation in non-western languages: analyses of Korean, Nukulaelae Tuvaluan, and Somali using the Multi-Dimensional approach. These studies, which provide the basis for the cross-linguistic comparisons in the present book, are introduced in section 1.4.3 below.

1.3.4   Computational analyses of sublanguages

Researchers in computational linguistics concerned with issues of linguistic variation have focused on the computational analysis of *sublanguages*, highly specified registers of a language that operate within specific domains of use with restricted subject matter. Many sublanguage studies have compared varieties across languages, making them especially relevant to the purposes of the present book.

Sublanguages are usually taken from science and technology domains and are restricted to a particular topic. Examples of sublanguages analyzed to date include scientific journal articles on lipoprotein kinetics (Sager 1986), Navy telegraphic messages (Fitzpatrick, Bachenko, and Hindle 1986), weather reports (Lehrberger 1982), aviation maintenance manuals, and stock market reports (Kittredge 1982). Because they are so restricted in purpose and topic, sublanguages are much more systematic in structure and meaning than the language as a whole; thus computational systems for applied natural-language processing can achieve greater success when they are designed specifically for texts from a single sublanguage.

As noted above, research on sublanguages is particularly relevant to the present investigation because some of these studies are explicitly cross-linguistic: for example, Lehrberger (1982) and Kittredge (1982) discuss the use of sublanguage grammars as the basis for information retrieval and automatic translation between English and French. The kinds of issues raised in these studies are directly related to the issues investigated here. For example, Lehrberger (1982: 105) raises the following questions:

1   To what extent do corresponding sublanguages in different languages have similar characteristics?

2   Are there groups of sublanguages that have grammatical characteristics in common?

3   Are there systematic patterns underlying the evolution of sublanguages, associated with scientific developments and cultural changes?

Kittredge (1982) differs from most sublanguage studies in that it explicitly adopts a variationist perspective, comparing the extent and kinds of variability within and across sublanguages. Further, Kittredge compares the extent of sublanguage variability cross-linguistically, presenting highly interesting and provocative conclusions such as:

'the written style of English and French tended to be more similar in specialized technical texts than in general language texts' (1982: 108).

'parallel sublanguages of English and French are much more similar structurally than are dissimilar sublanguages of the same language. Parallel sublanguages seem to correspond more closely when the domain of reference is a technical one' (1982: 108).

'purpose of text and semantic domain have a powerful influence on text and sentence structure' (1982: 135).

With respect to structural characteristics, shared purpose is much more important than shared semantic domain, and in fact, a 'common semantic domain has little to do with structure at the sentence or text level' (1982: 135). Thus, recipes, aviation manuals, and other kinds of manuals or assembly instructions show strong structural similarities, while English weather bulletins and weather synopses show important structural differences even though they share the same semantic domain.

'One is therefore drawn to conclude that English and French technical texts show the strongest parallels because the text purpose is more similar here than in descriptive texts . . . Most of the unexpected structures one finds in a sublanguage text can be associated not so much with a shift in semantic domain as with a shift (usually quite temporary) in the attitude which the text producer takes towards his domain of discourse' (1982: 135).

Questions needing additional research identified by Kittredge include:

1   What are the parameters of sublanguage complexity?

2   How does the 'professionalization' of a sublanguage affect the rigidity of its style? In less professionalized (e.g., colloquial) sublanguages, which lack recognized norms, is there considerably less consistency of structure and any greater 'distance' between English and French style?

3   How do the constraints of sublanguage semantics and pragmatics influence sentence structure and text structure? Can structural resemblances between semantically different sublanguages be related to similarities of text purpose?

4   How are the boundaries of a sublanguage determined? To date, most sublanguages chosen for analysis have tended to be quite restricted. To what extent do the same generalizations hold as more general kinds of registers are analyzed?

The present study investigates similar research questions, but it adopts a quite different analytical approach. First, the registers investigated here are defined at a higher level of generality than typical sublanguages (e.g., academic prose as a general register versus scientific journal articles on lipoprotein kinetics as a restricted sublanguage). Further, the present study distinguishes between registers, defined on the basis of situational characteristics, and text types, defined on the basis of linguistic characteristics. Both of these points are discussed further in chapter 9.

More importantly, the Multi-Dimensional approach used here attempts to be comprehensive in coverage, with respect to both linguistic and non-linguistic characteristics. From a linguistic perspective, most sublanguage studies (and most register studies generally) attempt to identify the few linguistic characteristics that are 'distinctive' for a register. In contrast, the cross-linguistic comparisons here are comprehensive in that they are based on a representative range of linguistic features in each language, with the analyses based on the systematic co-occurrence patterns among features (see chapter 2).

With respect to non-linguistic characteristics, most sublanguage studies have focused only on the influence of topic, although Kittredge (1982) also emphasizes the importance of purpose. In contrast, the present study investigates the importance of a large number of non-linguistic characteristics, including interactiveness, production circumstances, and personal stance, in addition to communicative purpose.[4] In sum, the cross-linguistic analyses presented here are more comprehensive, as well as more macroscopic, than the kinds of analyses typically included in sublanguage studies. In chapters 7 and 10, I discuss the extent to which these Multi-Dimensional analyses can be used to provide a theoretical framework for the more microscopic investigations required for sublanguage research.

1.4   Introductory overview of the Multi-Dimensional approach to register variation

Although there have been a large number of previous register studies adopting a comparative perspective, there have been few attempts to provide a comprehensive analysis of register variation in a language. Rather, most previous studies have compared only a restricted range of registers varying along a single situational parameter. The Multi-Dimensional (MD) approach to register variation – the analytical approach adopted in the present book – was developed to fill this gap.

MD analyses describe the relationships among the full range of registers in a language, with respect to multiple linguistic parameters of variation. As shown in later chapters, the MD approach also enables motivated register comparisons across languages. The following subsections briefly introduce previous MD studies, while fuller theoretical and methodological descriptions of the MD approach are given in chapters 2 and 5 respectively.

1.4.1   Multi-Dimensional studies of synchronic register variation in English

The MD approach to register variation was originally developed by Biber (1984c, 1985, 1986, 1988) for comparative analyses of spoken and written registers in English. Methodologically, the approach uses computer-based text corpora, computational tools to identify linguistic features in texts, and multivariate statistical techniques to analyze the co-occurrence relations among linguistic features, thereby identifying the underlying *dimensions* of variation in a language. The analytical goal of the MD approach is to provide comprehensive descriptions of the patterns of register variation having two components: (1) identification of the underlying linguistic parameters, or *dimensions*, of variation; and (2) specification of the linguistic similarities and differences among registers with respect to those dimensions.

Dimensions are defined by distinct groupings of linguistic features that co-occur frequently in texts. Dimensions are identified statistically by a factor analysis, and they are subsequently interpreted in terms of the communicative functions shared by the co-occurring features. Interpretive labels are posited for each dimension, such as 'Involved versus Informational Production', 'Narrative versus Non-narrative Concerns', and 'Explicit versus Situation-Dependent Reference'.

Two primary motivations for the MD approach are the assumptions that: (1) generalizations concerning register variation in a language must be based on analysis of the full range of spoken and written registers; and (2) no single linguistic parameter is adequate in itself to capture the range of similarities and differences among spoken and written registers. The approach thus requires analysis of numerous spoken and written registers with respect to numerous linguistic features. In earlier synchronic MD analyses of English (e.g., Biber 1986, 1988), approximately 500 texts from twenty-three registers were analyzed, including face-to-face conversations, interviews, public speeches, broadcasts, letters, press reportage, official documents, academic prose, and fiction. Linguistic features analyzed in these studies include lexical features (e.g., type–token ratio, word length, hedges, emphatics), grammatical features (e.g., nouns, prepositional phrases, adjectives), and syntactic features (e.g., relative clauses, adverbial clauses).

Registers can be compared along each dimension. Two registers are similar along a dimension to the extent that they use the co-occurring features of the dimension in similar ways. MD analyses show that registers are often similar along one dimension but quite different along other dimensions.

The early MD studies of English have been extended in several ways. Biber (1988) gives the fullest account of the methodology and a synchronic analysis of the relations among spoken and written registers; Biber and Finegan (1986) and Biber (1989) analyze the linguistically well-defined *text types* of English (i.e., text varieties which are maximally similar in terms of their linguistic characteristics; see chapter 9); Biber (1990, 1993a, b, c, 1994) and Biber and Finegan (1991) elaborate on methodological considerations; Biber (1987, 1991) considers specialized registers of English (British versus American writing, primary-school reading materials); Biber and Finegan (1994a) analyze the patterns of variation across subsections within medical research articles (viz., Introduction, Methodology, Results, and Discussion); and Biber and Finegan (1988, 1989b) and Biber (1992a, b) consider specialized linguistic domains (stance, discourse complexity, and referential strategies).

Two of the major conclusions of these synchronic MD studies of English are that: (1) no single dimension of variation is adequate in itself to account for the range of similarities and differences among registers – rather, multi-dimensional analyses are required; and (2) there is no absolute difference between spoken and written language – rather, particular types of speech and writing are more or less similar with respect to different dimensions.

1.4.2   Multi-Dimensional studies of diachronic register variation in English

The MD approach has also been used to study diachronic patterns of register variation in English. These studies use the dimensions identified and interpreted in Biber (1988) to trace the development of registers across time periods. Biber and Finegan (1989a, 1992, 1994b) study the development of English written registers from 1650 to the present with respect to three linguistic dimensions. The 1989a study traces the development of fiction, essays, and letters; this study interprets the observed patterns of change relative to the changing purposes and readership of written texts. The 1992 study adds an analysis of dialogue in drama and dialogue in fiction to the 1989 description. Finally, the 1994b study uses the framework developed in these previous studies to compare the written styles of particular eighteenth-century authors (Swift, Defoe, Addison, and Johnson) across different registers.

In addition, two studies by Atkinson use the MD approach to trace the evolution of professional registers in English. Atkinson (1992) combines a multi-dimensional approach with a detailed analysis of rhetorical patterns to study the development of five subregisters of medical academic prose from 1735 to 1985, focusing on the *Edinburgh Medical Journal*. Atkinson (1993) employs a similar integration of multi-dimensional and rhetorical methodologies to analyze the evolution of scientific research writing, as represented in the *Philosophical Transactions of the Royal Society of London* from 1675 to 1975. Chapter 8 of the present book integrates these previous MD studies (by Biber, Finegan, and Atkinson) to provide a more comprehensive picture of diachronic register variation in English.

1.4.3   Multi-Dimensional studies of register variation in non-western languages

Three MD studies of register variation in non-western languages have been completed to date: Besnier's (1986, 1988) analysis of Nukulaelae Tuvaluan; Kim's (1990; Kim and Biber 1994) analysis of Korean; and

Biber and Hared's (1992a, b, 1994) analysis of Somali. Taken together, these studies provide the first comprehensive investigations of register variation in non-western languages.

The first MD study of a non-western language was undertaken by Besnier (1986, 1988) on Nukulaelae Tuvaluan. This study analyzes the characteristics of seven spoken and written registers (e.g., conversations, political meetings, private-setting speeches, sermons, letters) with respect to three underlying linguistic dimensions of variation ('Attitudinal versus Authoritative Discourse', 'Informational versus Interactional Focus', 'Rhetorical Manipulation versus Structural Complexity'). As in the MD analyses of English registers, each dimension represents a distinct grouping of linguistic features that co-occur frequently in texts, reflecting shared communicative functions.

The second MD analysis of a non-western language, carried out by Kim (1990; Kim and Biber 1994), was even more ambitious, analyzing the relations among twenty-two spoken and written registers in Korean. This study identified five major dimensions of variation: 'Informal Interaction versus Explicit Elaboration', 'Discourse Chaining versus Discourse Fragmentation', 'Stance', 'Narrative Concern', and 'Honorification'.

Finally, Biber and Hared (1992a) study the relations among twenty-six spoken and written registers in Somali with respect to five major dimensions of variation: 'Structural Elaboration: Involvement versus Exposition', 'Lexical Elaboration: On-Line versus Planned/Integrated Production', 'Argumentative versus Reported Presentation of Information', 'Narrative versus Non-Narrative Discourse Organization', and 'Distanced, Directive Interaction'. Biber and Hared (1992b, 1994) extend this MD analysis of Somali to study historical change following the introduction of native-language literacy in 1973. The 1992b study compares the range of register variation found before 1973 (when only spoken registers existed) with that found immediately after 1973 (among spoken *and* written registers). The 1994 study traces the evolution of seven press registers from 1973 to 1989, analyzing the historical evolution of written registers in their initial periods of development.

These studies of Korean, Nukulaelae Tuvaluan, and Somali, together with the earlier MD analyses of English, provide the basis for the cross-linguistic investigations of register variation in the present book.[5]

1.5   The importance of cross-linguistic studies of register variation

The present study investigates patterns of register variation from a cross-linguistic perspective, addressing the extent to which the underlying dimensions of variation and the relations among registers are configured in similar ways across languages. Given the research gaps identified above – with relatively few comprehensive studies of register variation in English and very few studies of register variation in non-western languages – it will come as no surprise that there have been essentially no previous cross-linguistic investigations of register variation. Similarly, since there have been few diachronic analyses of register variation in any language (western or not), it is not surprising that there have not been previous cross-linguistic diachronic comparisons of register variation. However, there are at least four reasons why such cross-linguistic studies (both synchronic and diachronic) are needed at the present time.

First, as the following chapters show, there are highly systematic similarities in the patterns of register variation across languages, suggesting the operation of underlying form–function associations tied to basic aspects of human communication. The four languages analyzed here show striking similarities in their basic patterns of register variation, as reflected by:

the co-occurring linguistic features that define the dimensions of variation in each language;

the functional domains represented by those dimensions; and

the linguistic/functional relations among analogous registers.

The cultural and linguistic diversity among these four languages raises the possibility that some of these shared patterns will turn out to reflect universals of register variation. Assuming that all languages comprise a range of registers, the analysis of these shared patterns of register variation is central to any comprehensive theory of cross-linguistic typology and universals.

Second, diachronic comparisons of register variation across languages are crucial to a broad range of theoretical issues, including the general mechanisms of historical change, the processes of language standardization and modernization, and the influence of literacy on language change. In particular, the following chapters show that languages as diverse as English and Somali have undergone similar patterns of evolution following the introduction of written registers. These similarities again raise the possibility of universals of register variation, in this case relating to the historical development of written registers in response to pressures of modernization and language adaptation.

Third, cross-linguistic analyses of register variation are needed as a basis for on-going research in computational linguistics (e.g., analyzing bilingual text corpora to develop computational systems for machine translation). As noted above, related research in this area has focused on the analysis of sublanguages. Studies such as Kittredge (1982) have found that technical sublanguages can be more similar cross-linguistically than disparate sublanguages within the same language. However, there are

several unresolved issues in sublanguage research, many of which relate
to the overall linguistic characterization of sublanguages and the question
of how the range of sublanguages relate to one another within and across
languages. The following chapters show that such issues can be addressed
in the MD approach.

Finally, cross-linguistic analyses of register variation are essential for the
development of comprehensive text typologies. As chapter 9 shows, the text
categories that are well defined linguistically (i.e., the *text types*) are remark-
ably similar across languages, when compared within the multi-dimensional
space of each language.

The analyses in chapters 4–7 show that the MD approach is particularly well suited to cross-linguistic comparisons because it is based on
the co-occurrence patterns that are well represented in each language,
reflecting the communicative functions that are well represented in the
corresponding culture. Comparisons based on individual linguistic features
cannot address these issues. As Hymes predicted in 1974, 'it is essential to
isolate the dimensions and features underlying taxonomic categories. These
features and dimensions, more than particular constellations of them, will be
found to be universal, and hence elementary to descriptive and comparative
frames of reference' (p. 41). The analyses in chapters 7–9 show that there
are indeed strong similarities in the underlying dimensions of English,
Nukulaelae Tuvaluan, Korean, and Somali. Future research is required
to determine which of these shared patterns reflect underlying universals
of register variation.[6]

1.6   Overview of the present study

The present study synthesizes earlier MD analyses of register variation in
four quite different languages: Biber's (1986, 1988; Biber and Finegan
1989a) analysis of English; Besnier's (1986, 1988) analysis of Nukulaelae
Tuvaluan; Kim's (1990; Kim and Biber 1994) analysis of Korean; and
Biber and Hared's (1992a,b, 1994) analysis of Somali.[7] The study explicitly
compares the patterns of register variation across languages, addressing the
extent to which there are cross-linguistic similarities with respect to:

1   the co-occurrence patterns among linguistic features, and the ways
     in which features function together as underlying dimensions;
2   the synchronic relations among registers;
3   the diachronic patterns of change within and among registers;
4   the text types that are well defined linguistically.

The four languages analyzed here complement one another in several
respects. From a strictly linguistic point of view, these languages are
from four quite different language families: English from Indo-European,

Tuvaluan from Austronesian, Korean from Altaic, and Somali from the Cushitic subfamily of Afroasiatic. They are notably different in their geographic locations, as well as in their cultural and religious associations. Geographically, the specific variety of English used for the present study is spoken in England, and it thus represents a major European language with millions of speakers. Tuvaluan represents the opposite extreme: the variety studied here is spoken on the central Pacific atoll of Nukulaelae, which has only about 310 inhabitants. Korean represents one of the major Asian languages, with approximately 65 million speakers. And Somali represents one of the major languages of Africa, spoken by approximately 5 million inhabitants of the countries of Somalia, Djibouti, Ethiopia, and Kenya.

Culturally, these four groups range from the primarily urbanized speakers of English and Korean, to the mixed urbanized and rural speakers of Somali (ranging from city-dwellers to nomadic camel-herders), to the traditional fishing/gathering/farming culture of Nukulaelae Tuvaluan. Religion plays a central role in the daily lives of speakers from two of these cultural groups: Christianity in Nukulaelae Tuvaluan and Islam in Somali; thus, speech events in these cultures almost always contain some reference to God or other religious associations. Religion plays a less central role in the English and Korean cultures.

These languages also differ with respect to their status: English is spoken in many countries around the world, it has a long history of literacy and standardization, and it has an extremely broad range of spoken and written registers; Nukulaelae Tuvaluan represents the other extreme in that it has very few speakers, restricted primarily to a single atoll in the Pacific, a relatively short history of literacy, only two written registers, and a generally restricted range of spoken registers. Korean is spoken primarily in Korea, but it has a long history of literacy and presently has a wide range of spoken and written registers with well-established uses. Finally, Somali is spoken in four countries of East Africa (with some official status in two of those countries), but it is not well known outside of those countries. It has a very short history of literacy, although at present it has a wide range of spoken and written registers.

Overall, the languages considered in the present investigation represent four quite different language types and social situations. Obviously any attempt to identify cross-linguistic universals of register variation must be based on a larger sample of languages. The goal here is more modest: to investigate the possibility of such universals, to identify and interpret the generalizations concerning register variation that hold across these four languages, and to explore the utility of the MD approach for such analyses. Although the sample of languages is small, the investigation here can be regarded as a relatively strong test of these research questions. That is, given the extreme linguistic, sociocultural, and situational differences across the four languages considered here, any marked cross-linguistic similarities in the patterns of register variation can be interpreted as reflections of basic communicative functions shared cross-culturally, indicating the potential for cross-linguistic universals (or at least universal tendencies) governing the patterns of register variation.

1.7   Outline of the remainder of the book

Chapter 2 further develops two of the themes introduced in the present chapter: it describes the analytical requirements of comprehensive studies of register variation, and it presents a more detailed theoretical introduction to the MD approach. In chapter 3, I outline the important cultural and social aspects of the four language situations included in the study. This chapter also includes a brief description of the social history of literacy in each case, as well as situational descriptions of the registers represented in each language. Chapter 4 illustrates the difficulties involved in cross-linguistic register comparisons based on individual linguistic features. The chapter compares three registers in English and Somali with respect to selected individual linguistic features, showing that conclusions differ considerably depending on the structural level used for comparison. Chapter 4 concludes with a brief discussion of how the MD approach provides a solution to the methodological indeterminacy of cross-linguistic comparisons based on individual features.

Chapter 5 summarizes the methodology used for MD studies and describes the text corpora, tagging programs, linguistic features, and statistical procedures used in the analysis of each of the four languages. Chapter 6 then presents and interprets the four MD analyses of register variation. For each dimension in each language, this chapter describes the set of co-occurring linguistic features grouped on the dimension, the similarities and differences among registers with respect to the dimension, and the functional underpinnings.

Chapter 7 presents the heart of the book: a cross-linguistic comparison of the patterns of register variation from several perspectives. First, the dimensions themselves are compared across the four languages, with respect to both the sets of co-occurring linguistic features and their underlying communicative functions. The strongest similarities exist for those dimensions that serve similar functions; in many cases these dimensions are represented cross-linguistically by structurally similar sets of linguistic features, and they define similar relations among spoken and written registers.

The analysis in chapter 7 further shows that it is possible for communicative functions to be given different prominence in two languages; for example, two dimensions might be clearly distinguished in one language but conflated in a second language. Several dimensions are represented in all four languages and are thus potential candidates for universal status. Other dimensions are shown to reflect the particular communicative demands of a given culture and language. An overall comparison of the multi-dimensional space for each language shows that dimensions are differently salient depending on the importance of particular functional domains in the four cultures.

In addition, chapter 7 compares the dimensions in each language from a structural perspective, showing that many communicative functions have quite similar structural bases in these four languages. Finally, this chapter compares selected registers across the four languages, showing that there are similar multi-dimensional characterizations associated with characteristics of the physical situation, while there are linguistic differences associated with different particular communicative purposes. The conclusion to chapter 7 discusses the theoretical implications of these observed cross-linguistic patterns.

Chapters 8 and 9 are more specialized, comparing only English and Somali. Chapter 8 focuses on diachronic register variation, comparing the evolution of written registers in English and Somali. Despite important differences in their social histories – English with a long history of written registers, in contrast to the extremely compressed history of written registers in Somali – there are notable patterns of similarity in the development of written registers in the two languages. Chapter 9 then compares the text typologies of English and Somali. For this analysis, the register distinctions are set aside, and cluster analysis (a multivariate statistical technique) is used to identify the text types that are linguistically well defined in each language. In this chapter, it is shown that certain text types are linguistically well defined in both languages, while others appear to be distinctive. As in chapter 8, these patterns are discussed relative to the differing functional priorities of English and Somali.

In conclusion (chapter 10), I briefly summarize the main points of the study, describe related on-going research, and identify a number of research issues that require further investigation.

The book also includes two appendices, presenting brief grammatical descriptions of the linguistic features used in the analyses of Korean and Somali. Appendix I on Korean is written by Yong-Jin Kim, adapted from his 1990 dissertation; appendix II on Somali is written by Mohamed Hared and myself.

2 The comprehensive analysis of register variation

2.1 Requirements of a comprehensive analytical framework for studies of register variation

A comprehensive analysis of register variation in a language must be based on an adequate sampling of registers, texts, and linguistic features:

1 *registers*: the full range of the registers in the language should be included, representing the range of situational variation;
2 *texts*: a representative sampling of texts from each register should be included;
3 *linguistic features*: a wide range of linguistic features should be analyzed in each text, representing multiple underlying parameters of variation.

Although there have been many important register studies, few previous analyses of register variation are comprehensive in this sense.

The restrictions of previous research, and the need for more comprehensive analyses, have been noted by several scholars. Characterizing the state of research in 1974, Hymes notes that 'the fact that present taxonomic dimensions consist so largely of dichotomies – restricted vs. elaborated codes, ... standard vs. non-standard speech, formal vs. informal scenes, literacy vs. illiteracy – shows how preliminary is the stage at which we work' (1974: 41). This state of affairs was still largely true in the 1980s. Thus, Schafer (1981: 12) finds it 'frustrating' that although previous studies 'are based on texts produced in particular circumstances by only a few subjects ... speaking and writing in only one situation, this doesn't prevent researchers from offering their results as accurate generalizations of universal difference between speaking and writing'. And Tannen (1982a: 1) writes that:

Linguistic research too often focuses on one or another kind of data, without specifying its relationship to other kinds. In order to determine which texts are appropriate for proposed research, and to determine the significance of past and projected research, a perspective is needed on the kinds of language and their interrelationships ... discourse analysis needs a taxonomy of discourse types, and ways of distinguishing among them.

Specifically, an analytical framework for comprehensive register studies should provide tools for analysis of the linguistic characteristics of registers, analysis of the situational characteristics of registers, and analysis of the functional and conventional associations between linguistic and situational characteristics.

1   A comprehensive framework should enable analysis of all salient linguistic characteristics of registers, including specification of the co-occurrence relations among the linguistic features themselves. As Crystal and Davy (1969: 13) put it: 'A definitive book on English stylistics would provide a specification of the entire range of linguistic features entering into the definition of what we have been calling a variety of language, as well as a theoretical framework capable of accounting for them'.

Two major types of linguistic characterization can be distinguished. First, there are *register markers*, which are distinctive linguistic features found only in particular registers: for example, the 'count' (balls and strikes) is a linguistic routine found only in broadcasts of baseball games (Ferguson 1983: 165–67). Second, registers are distinguished by *register features*, that is, differing quantitative distributions of core linguistic features (e.g., nouns, pronouns, subordinate clauses). A comprehensive framework should include a specification of the full range of such features, as well as mechanisms for analyzing the relations among features in terms of their patterns of co-occurrence and alternation.

2   A comprehensive framework should enable a complete situational characterization of individual registers, as well as a precise specification of the similarities and differences among registers. Frameworks for the situational characterization of registers have been proposed by Hymes (1974), Duranti (1985), and Biber (1988, 1994).

3   A comprehensive framework should provide formal apparatus to specify the relationship between situational characteristics and linguistic characteristics, as mediated by communicative functions and conventions. Such mechanisms should be able to cope with the continuous nature of register variation. In the multidimensional approach, this requirement is met through the analysis of linguistic co-occurrence patterns, as described in section 2.3 below.

2.2   Linguistic features used for register analyses

Register markers – distinctive indicators of a register – are relatively rare. Many registers are restricted topically, making individual lexical items possible candidates as register markers: for example, the terms *home run* and *inning* are likely to occur in texts about baseball games. In practice, though, lexical choice itself does not typically distinguish a register. Thus the term *home run* could easily occur in a baseball game broadcast, a newspaper article, a personal letter, or a romance novel, among other registers. Grammatical routines, on the other hand, can sometimes serve as distinctive register markers; for example, the phrase *the count is two and one* would provide a fairly distinctive marker of a baseball game broadcast (see Ferguson 1983).[1] Most registers, though, are not reliably distinguished by the presence of register markers.

In contrast, register features are core lexical and grammatical characteristics found to some extent in almost all texts and registers. Register features are pervasive indicators of register distinctions because there are often large differences in their relative distributions across registers. In fact, many registers are distinguished only by a particularly frequent or infrequent occurrence of a set of register features.

Any linguistic feature having a functional or conventional association can be distributed in a way that distinguishes among registers. Such features come from many linguistic classes, including: phonological features (pauses, intonation patterns), tense and aspect markers, pronouns and pro-verbs, questions, nominal forms (nouns, nominalizations, gerunds), passive constructions, dependent clauses (complement clauses, relative clauses, adverbial subordination), prepositional phrases, adjectives, adverbs, measures of lexical specificity (once-occurring words, type–token ratio), lexical classes (hedges, emphatics, discourse particles, stance markers), modals, specialized verb classes (speech act verbs, mental process verbs), reduced forms (contractions, *that*-deletions), co-ordination, negation, and grammatical devices for structuring information (clefts, extraposition).

A comprehensive linguistic analysis of a register requires consideration of a representative selection of linguistic features. Analyses of these register features are necessarily quantitative, because the associated register distinctions are based on differences in the relative distribution of linguistic features. Register markers can be analyzed using qualitative methods, because the mere presence of the marker serves to identify a register. In contrast, register features must be analyzed using quantitative methods, because it is the relative frequency of the feature that serves to identify a register.

2.3   Co-occurrence in register analyses

On first consideration, it seems unlikely that the relative distribution of common linguistic features could reliably distinguish among registers. In fact, individual linguistic features do not provide the basis for such distinctions. However, when analyses are based on the co-occurrence and alternation patterns within a group of linguistic features, important differences across registers are revealed.

The importance of linguistic co-occurrence has been emphasized by linguists such as Firth, Halliday, Ervin-Tripp, and Hymes. Brown and Fraser (1979: 38–39) observe that it can be 'misleading to concentrate on specific, isolated [linguistic] markers without taking into account systematic variations which involve the co-occurrence of sets of markers'. Ervin-Tripp (1972) and Hymes (1974) identify 'speech styles' as varieties that are defined by a shared set of co-occurring linguistic features. Halliday (1988:162) defines a register as 'a cluster of associated features having a greater-than-random . . . tendency to co-occur'.

The notion of linguistic co-occurrence has been given formal status in the Multi-Dimensional approach to register variation, where different co-occurrence patterns are analyzed as underlying *dimensions* of variation. In this approach, the co-occurrence patterns comprising each dimension are identified quantitatively, rather than on an *a priori* functional basis. That is, based on the actual distributions of linguistic features in a large corpus of texts, statistical techniques (specifically factor analysis) are used to identify the sets of linguistic features that frequently co-occur in texts. The methods used to identify these co-occurrence patterns are fully described in chapter 5.

It is not the case, though, that quantitative techniques are sufficient in themselves for analyses of register variation. Rather, qualitative techniques are required to interpret the functional bases underlying each set of co-occurring linguistic features. The dimensions of variation have both linguistic and functional content. The linguistic content of a dimension comprises a group of linguistic features (e.g., nominalizations, prepositional phrases, attributive adjectives) that co-occur with a high frequency in texts. Based on the assumption that co-occurrence reflects shared function, these co-occurrence patterns are interpreted in terms of the situational, social, and cognitive functions most widely shared by the linguistic features. That is, linguistic features co-occur in texts because they reflect shared functions. A simple example is the way in which first- and second-person pronouns, direct questions, and imperatives are all related to interactiveness. Contractions, false starts, and generalized content words (e.g., *thing*) are all related to the constraints imposed by real-time production. The functional bases of other co-occurrence patterns are less transparent, so that careful qualitative analyses of co-occurring features in particular texts are required to interpret the underlying functions. The functional interpretations of the four MD analyses considered in the present study are given in chapter 6.

2.4   Register as a continuous construct

One of the main distinguishing characteristics of the framework developed here is that it treats register as a continuous rather than discrete construct. From a linguistic perspective, this means that the focus of analysis is on the relative distribution of common linguistic features, in terms of the patterns of co-occurrence and alternation. Registers are not equally well defined in their linguistic characteristics. Some registers (e.g., legal documents) have well-defined norms so that there is relatively little variation among the texts within the register; other registers (e.g., academic prose) are less specified linguistically, so that there are considerable differences among texts within the register (see Biber 1988: chapter 8; Biber 1990). Similarly from a situational perspective, registers are distributed across a continuous range of variation, and they can be defined at different levels of generality (see Biber 1994). It is important to recognize these differences in register comparisons since they determine in part the extent to which any two registers are comparable.

2.5   Corpus linguistics and the computational analysis of register variation

Although automated analyses using computers are not absolutely necessary for comprehensive register analyses, the use of computers does greatly facilitate such analyses. In fact, given that comprehensive analyses require large text samples from many registers, analyzed for a wide range of linguistic features, it is not really feasible for an individual to undertake such a study without the aid of computers.

Currently there are very large computer-based text *corpora* available – systematic text collections that represent a domain of use within a language. Numerous software tools have been developed to process these text collections, enabling (semi-)automatic linguistic analyses. These tools include:

concordancing programs, which provide lists of the occurrences of some key word and its surrounding context;

large on-line dictionaries, which can provide many kinds of information about individual words: their grammatical category, the relative probabilities of grammatical categories for ambiguous items, and word senses;

part-of-speech taggers, which assign grammatical categories to words in texts, using rules that depend on the surrounding context, or using probabilistic information;

morphological analyzers, which determine the grammatical category of unknown words based on identifiable affixes;

syntactic analyzers and parsers, which identify various syntactic constructions and determine their boundaries;

simple counting programs, which compile frequency counts for various
linguistic features in texts.

The advantages of corpus-based analysis include:

1   The adequate representation of naturally occurring discourse, including representative text samples from each register. Thus, corpus-
based analyses can be based on long passages from each text, and
multiple texts from each register.

2   The adequate representation of the range of register variation in a
language; that is, analyses can be based on a sampling of texts from
a large number of spoken and written registers.

3   The (semi-)automatic linguistic processing of texts, enabling analyses
of much wider scope than otherwise feasible. With computational
processing, it is feasible to entertain the possibility of a comprehensive linguistic characterization of a text, analyzing a wide
range of linguistic features. Further, once the software tools are
developed for this type of analysis, it is possible to process all
available on-line texts.

4   Much greater reliability and accuracy for quantitative analyses of
linguistic features; that is, computers do not become bored or tired
– they will count a linguistic feature in the same way every time it is
encountered.

5   The possibility of cumulative results and accountability. Subsequent
studies can be based on the same corpus of texts, or additional
corpora can be analyzed using the same computational techniques.
Such studies can verify the results of previous research, and findings
will be comparable across studies, building a cumulative linguistic
description of the language.

There are currently numerous computer-based corpora generally available, and the amount of corpus-based research is steadily increasing. Taylor,
Leech, and Fligelstone (1991) survey thirty-six English machine-readable
corpora (including information on the availability of each), while Altenberg
(1991) has compiled a bibliography of approximately 650 studies based on
the major text corpora.

Among the English corpora, the Brown Corpus, Lancaster–Oslo–Bergen
Corpus, and London–Lund Corpus are the best known. The Standard
sample of Present-Day American English (the Brown Corpus for short),
which was completed in 1964, was the first large computer-based text corpus
for any language. Work on this corpus began in 1962 at Brown University,
supervised by Nelson Francis and Henry Kučera. A tagged version of this
corpus, in which each word is marked for its grammatical category, was

completed in 1979 (see Francis and Kučera 1979, 1982). This corpus was designed to provide a representative selection of published written texts in American English. Defining the universe of texts as the collection of books and periodicals published in 1961 in the Brown University Library and the Providence Athenaeum, texts were randomly selected from fifteen major registers (e.g., press reportage, press editorial, popular lore, learned and scientific writings, general fiction, science fiction, humor). Texts are about 2,000 words in length, and the entire corpus comprises 500 texts, or a total of approximately 1 million words of running text. Details on the specific texts included in the corpus are given in Francis and Kučera (1979).

In 1978, a parallel corpus of British English was completed, providing a broad sample of written texts published in Britain in 1961. Work on this corpus was carried out at three sites: the University of Lancaster, the University of Oslo, and the Norwegian Computing Centre for the Humanities at Bergen, and thus the corpus is known as the LOB (Lancaster–Oslo–Bergen) Corpus. This corpus has the same basic design as the Brown Corpus: the same fifteen registers, and 500 texts of about 2,000 words each. The LOB corpus manual (Johansson, Leech, and Goodluck 1978) describes the corpus as a whole and provides specifics on the particular texts included. In the case of the LOB Corpus, books were randomly selected from the 1961 publications listed in *The British National Bibliography Cumulated Subject Index, 1960–1964* (which is based on the subject divisions of the Dewey Decimal Classification system), and periodicals and newspapers were randomly selected from the publications listed in *Willing's Press Guide*, 1961. A tagged version of the LOB Corpus became available in the late 1980s.

These two corpora of written texts are complemented by the London–Lund Corpus of Spoken English (Svartvik and Quirk 1980; Svartvik 1990). Based on the spoken texts in the Survey of English Usage compiled at University College London (supervised by Randolph Quirk), this corpus was subsequently computerized at Lund University (supervised by Jan Svartvik). The London–Lund Corpus includes 100 spoken British English texts of about 5,000 words each. The total corpus contains approximately 500,000 words, representing six major spoken registers: private conversations, public conversations (including interviews and panel discussions), telephone conversations, radio broadcasts, spontaneous speeches, and prepared speeches.

Other important English corpora include the Helsinki Diachronic Corpus of English, the Birmingham (COBUILD) Corpus, the Longman/Lancaster English Language Corpus, the British National Corpus, and the Data Collection Initiative. There are also several text collections for other European languages. Engwall (1992) provides a brief survey of French language corpora, including the *Trésor de la langue française*, a collection of literary works totaling well over 70 million words. There are also numerous Swedish language computer-based text collections. Gellerstam (1992) describes eighteen different Swedish corpora, which together comprise more than 20 million words of text from a wide range of spoken and written registers. The SUC corpus is a comprehensive Swedish corpus with a similar design to the Brown Corpus. The Danish–English–French Corpus in Contract Law (Faber and Lauridsen 1991) is a parallel corpus, containing a carefully stratified selection of texts relating to contract law for these three languages.

There are far fewer computer-based corpora of non-western languages, and the three corpora of spoken and written registers used for the present study are among the most comprehensive of these: the corpus of Nukulaelae Tuvaluan compiled by Niko Besnier, the corpus of Korean compiled by Yong-Jin Kim, and the corpus of Somali compiled by the present author and Mohamed Hared. These text collections are described in chapters 3 and 5.

2.6   Theoretical overview of the Multi-Dimensional approach to register variation

The Multi-Dimensional approach to register variation (elsewhere referred to as the Multi-feature/Multi-dimensional approach) was used in the analysis of all four languages considered here. The approach was first used in Biber (1984c, 1985, 1986) and then developed more fully in Biber (1988). Since this approach provides the basis for the present book, I provide a theoretical overview here. Methodological aspects are discussed in detail in chapter 5, and the MD analyses of all four languages are presented in chapter 6.

Some of the general characteristics of the MD approach are:

1   It is corpus-based, depending on analysis of a large number of naturally occurring texts.

2   It is computer-based in that it depends on automated and interactive analyses of linguistic features in texts. This characteristic enables distributional analysis of many linguistic features across many texts and text varieties.

3   The research goal of the approach is the linguistic analysis of texts, registers, and text types, rather than analysis of individual linguistic constructions.

4   The importance of variationist and comparative perspectives are assumed by the approach. That is, the approach is based on the assumption that different kinds of text differ linguistically and functionally, so that analysis of any one or two text varieties is not adequate for conclusions concerning a discourse domain (e.g., speech and writing in English).

5   The approach is explicitly multidimensional. That is, it is assumed

that multiple parameters of variation will be operative in any discourse domain.

6 The approach is quantitative. Analyses are based on frequency counts of linguistic features, describing the relative distributions of features across texts. Multivariate statistical techniques are used to analyze the relations among linguistic features and among texts.[2]

7 The approach synthesizes quantitative and qualitative/functional methodological techniques. That is, the statistical analyses are interpreted in functional terms, to determine the underlying communicative functions associated with each distributional pattern. The approach is based on the assumption that statistical co-occurrence patterns reflect underlying shared communicative functions.

8 The approach synthesizes macroscopic and microscopic analyses. That is, macroscopic investigations of the overall parameters of linguistic variation, which are based on analysis of the distribution of many linguistic features across many texts and registers, are complemented by detailed analyses of particular linguistic features in particular texts.

As noted above, several sociolinguists have emphasized the centrality of linguistic co-occurrence for analyses of registers, genres, or text types (e.g., Ervin-Tripp 1972; Hymes 1974; Brown and Fraser 1979; Halliday 1988). Surprisingly, despite these theoretical discussions, few empirical investigations are based on the analysis of co-occurring linguistic features. Rather the norm has been to compare varieties with respect to a few apparently unrelated linguistic features, with no analysis of the relations among the linguistic characteristics.[3] In part, this shortcoming is due to the fact that the empirical identification of co-occurrence patterns has proven to be quite difficult.

The few researchers who have recognized the importance of co-occurrence relations, such as Chafe (1982; Chafe and Danielewicz 1986) and Longacre (1976), have been forced to resort to their intuitions to posit basic groupings of co-occurring features. Chafe thus identifies two parameters – integration/fragmentation and detachment/involvement – and posits a number of linguistic features associated with each parameter. Longacre also identifies two underlying parameters – projected time and temporal succession – and posits a group of features associated with each. These studies are important in that they recognize the need for analyses based on the co-occurrence relations in texts, and they attempt to identify basic sets of co-occurring linguistic features.

In fact, a large number of comparative sociolinguistic investigations identify a basic dichotomy among registers and propose a set of linguistic features associated with the dichotomy, thus giving at least implicit recognition to the importance of co-occurrence relations. Studies of this type include the following: Ferguson (1959) on 'high' and 'low' diglossic varieties; Bernstein (e.g., 1970) on restricted and elaborated codes; Irvine (1984) on formal and informal registers; Ochs (1979) on planned and unplanned discourse; and numerous studies on speech versus writing.

There are three major theoretical differences between the MD approach and these earlier investigations of register variation. First, apart from the Chafe and Longacre frameworks, most studies have analyzed linguistic variation in terms of a single parameter, suggesting that there is a single basic situational distinction in language (e.g., formality or attention paid to speech) and that all other distinctions are derivative. In contrast, MD studies have demonstrated that no single parameter or dimension is adequate in itself to capture the full range of variation among registers in a language. Rather, different dimensions are realized by different sets of co-occurring linguistic features, reflecting different functional underpinnings (e.g., interactiveness, planning, informational focus and explicitness).

A related difference is that most previous studies have assumed that register variation can be analyzed in terms of simple, dichotomous distinctions, so that varieties are either formal or informal, planned or unplanned, etc. Empirical investigations do not support the existence of such dichotomous distinctions, however. Rather, registers differ from one another by being more or less formal, more or less planned, more or less interactive, etc.; and MD studies have shown that there is a continuous range of linguistic variation associated with each of these distinctions. The dimensions used in MD studies are thus quantitative, continuous parameters of variation, and each dimension is able to distinguish among a continuous range of texts or registers. For this reason, dimensions can be used to analyze the *extent* to which registers are similar (or different).

Finally, in the MD approach dimensions are identified empirically using quantitative statistical techniques, providing a solution to the methodological problem of identifying the salient co-occurrence patterns in a language. There is no guarantee that groupings of features proposed on intuitive grounds actually co-occur in texts: for example, neither Longacre's parameters (see Smith 1985) nor Chafe's parameters (see Redeker 1984) accurately describe sets of linguistic features that actually co-occur regularly in English texts. In contrast, the statistical techniques used in MD studies provide a precise quantitative specification of the co-occurrence patterns among linguistic features in a corpus of texts.

The use of quantitative techniques, however, does not replace the need for qualitative/functional analysis. Rather, the co-occurrence patterns defining each dimension are identified using quantitative/statistical techniques, but the shared functions underlying these co-occurrence patterns must be determined through qualitative analyses of particular texts.

The studies of the four languages considered in the present book show that the MD approach enables comprehensive comparative analyses of the registers within a language. In contrast, most earlier register variation studies had restricted research designs: they typically analyzed only a few registers (and a few texts), with respect to a few, selected linguistic features, and with no empirical investigation of the co-occurrence relations among features. Even though such studies do not provide an adequate research basis for global generalizations concerning the patterns of register variation in a language, global conclusions are commonly presented in a confident manner. As a result, the conclusions of earlier studies have often been contradictory (see Biber 1986; 1988: chapter 3). These contradictions can be reconciled when the full range of registers, linguistic features, and dimensions are considered together in a comprehensive analysis of register variation.

Similarly, the present book shows that conclusions concerning cross-linguistic register differences cannot be based on analysis of individual linguistic features or pairwise comparisons of selected registers. To an even greater extent than for register comparisons within a language, adequate cross-linguistic comparisons must be based on prior analyses of the co-occurrence patterns among linguistic features in each language. As chapter 4 shows, cross-linguistic register comparisons based on individual features are doomed to failure due to indeterminacy concerning the appropriate level of structure to be used in the analysis. The main point here is more basic: even if it were methodologically possible to compare registers across languages with respect to individual features, such comparisons would not provide the basis for general conclusions concerning the cross-linguistic patterns of register variation – for this purpose, a multidimensional analysis incorporating the full range of linguistic features is required.

3 Sociocultural description of the four language situations

As noted in chapter 1, the four languages analyzed in the present study differ in nearly every conceivable way: in their geographic locations, language families, cultural settings, social histories, and characteristic speech events and literacy events. The present chapter provides further details about these differences. While it is not intended as a complete ethnography of the language situations, the chapter does provide sufficient background to interpret the sociolinguistic patterns described in following chapters.

Several of the differences among these four languages can be related to a continuum of institutional development, comprising considerations such as the synchronic range of written registers, the social history of literacy, the range of spoken registers, the number of speakers, and the extent to which the language is associated with a bounded community in a particular geographic location. English is near one extreme of this continuum, having a long history of literacy, a very wide range of both spoken and written registers, a very large number of speakers, and a wide distribution as both a first and second language across many countries. Nukulaelae Tuvaluan is near the opposite extreme on this continuum: it has a relatively short history of literacy, very few written registers, few spoken registers, few speakers, and a speech community that is restricted primarily to a single atoll in the Pacific.

Korean and Somali are intermediate along this continuum, and they also show that these characteristics are not perfectly correlated. Korean is relatively similar to English in many respects: it has a very long history of literacy and a wide range of both spoken and written registers, but it has a relatively short history of widespread, popular literacy; it has fewer speakers than English; and it has a distribution restricted primarily to language use in Korea (plus immigrant communities in various cities around the world). Finally, Somali has an extremely short history of literacy, but at present it has a much wider range of spoken and written registers than Nukulaelae Tuvaluan (although a smaller range than either English or Korean). It has many more speakers than Tuvaluan but fewer than Korean, although the extent of its geographic distribution is similar to Korean.

In one important regard, the four languages considered here are similar to one another: the development of written registers in each of these languages has been influenced by contact with other major languages. Latin and French were used for institutional and academic written registers over several centuries in England, preceding and co-existing with the development of English written registers. Similarly, Chinese written registers were used over a long period in Korean society preceding and co-existing with the development of Korean written registers. In Somali culture, Arabic was used for written religious texts over a period of centuries, while, more recently, Italian and English were used for written institutional registers. The transition to Somali written registers occurred abruptly in the early 1970s. Finally, Samoan was used for written registers in Tuvaluan society until recently. Thus, in each of these four languages, the linguistic characteristics of written registers (and probably institutional spoken registers as well) has been influenced to some extent by pre-existing foreign models. Even in this regard, though, the social differences among the four language situations are striking: the foreign models are adopted from different languages in each case, representing different language families and cultures having quite different literacy traditions.

Thus, the four languages analyzed here represent four strikingly different language types and situations. As such, a comparison of the patterns of register variation across these languages provides a solid foundation for initial cross-linguistic generalizations. Given this background, the following sections will provide brief descriptions of each language situation.

3.1   English

The particular variety of English studied here is British English, although the register differences between the American and British dialects are minor when considered from a cross-linguistic perspective (based on the comparison in Biber 1987). British culture, to the extent that it makes sense to describe it as a single entity, is quite heterogeneous relative to Korean, Tuvaluan, and Somali culture. (This is even more the case if we consider all English-speaking cultures.) British speakers of English represent numerous ethnic groups, religious backgrounds, geographic regions, occupations, social classes, and educational backgrounds. Thus, perhaps the most important characteristic of British culture relative to the other three groups considered here is its diversity.

English is from the Indo-European language family, and although it has a wide international distribution, it is taken here to represent a European language and culture. English as a language has evolved in numerous ways to serve the complex institutional needs of British society and the former British colonies.

English has been written since the seventh century, although it was not until after the decline of the Norman influence around 1300 that English writing began to be widely used (Smith 1992). Before that time, Latin and French were used for most institutional and academic written functions. Although Latin continued to be used into the sixteenth century, the domains of English writing have been gradually extended since *c.* 1300 to include government, law, theology, academia, and public domains such as the press and entertainment.

Numerous written and spoken English registers evolved over this period of late Middle English and early Modern English, to meet the communicative demands of developing institutions in central government, legal affairs, commerce, education, social welfare, information dissemination, etc. This period also witnessed the development of literary writing. These texts were written primarily in verse until fictional and non-fictional prose became more popular in the late seventeenth and early eighteenth century.

English written registers thus have a quite long history relative to the other languages included in the present study. Nearly all of the written registers included here have been in continuous existence since the early eighteenth century, and many of them can be traced back considerably further. As described in Biber and Finegan (1989a) and Finegan (1992), the seventeenth century witnessed the rise of experimental science and a general preference for rationalism over emotionalism. For the first time, writers were using English as much as Latin (Fowler 1987: 124), and new genres such as the scientific expository essay, biography, and history began to appear in English. English press reportage, editorials, and modern fiction can also be traced back to this general period. Other registers, such as drama and letters, can be traced back much earlier and were already well established by the seventeenth century.

The literate reading public in England and the United States was also growing during the eighteenth century. Before that time, literacy was primarily restricted to the aristocracy, who had the leisure to pursue intellectual activities. The eighteenth century, however, witnessed an increase in popular, middle-class literacy in English. Although it is difficult to assess literacy levels in earlier periods, there was clearly a marked expansion of the general reading public during the eighteenth century. Laqueur (1976: 255) notes that 'perhaps as many as 60% of men in England by 1754 and 40% of the women could sign the marriage register and there is evidence that an even higher proportion were probably able to read'. Based on self-reports, by the year 1800, male adults in England claimed 62 percent literacy, in Scotland 62 percent, and in New England 90 percent (Clifford 1984: 475).

In addition, the eighteenth century produced writers such as Defoe and Richardson, who were from the middle class themselves and addressed themselves primarily to middle-class readers. Periodicals such as *The Spectator* and *The Tatler* began to appear in the early eighteenth century, and the first modern magazine (*Gentleman's Magazine*) appeared in 1731 (Abrams *et al.* 1979: 1735). This popular press was primarily informational, with essays and articles about politics, science, and philosophy as well as local scandal and gossip. These periodicals had substantial circulations. Addison, in the March 12, 1711 edition of *The Spectator*, estimates that there were 3,000 copies of the paper distributed every day, and twenty readers of each copy. By the late eighteenth century a large number of books, tracts, almanacs, and magazines were in widespread circulation among ordinary people (Cook-Gumperz 1986: 21).

This extension of literacy to the middle class was not uniformly welcomed in the eighteenth century, since writers such as Swift, Pope, and Johnson remained distinctly aristocratic in their subject matter and intended audience. However, by the nineteenth century, the shift towards a popular literacy began to be widely accepted as the norm. Mass schooling reinforced the already widespread popular literacy (Cook-Gumperz 1986; de Castell and Luke 1986). Fictional genres such as the novel and short story became well established and were widely read by the general public. These trends continued into the modern period, so that literacy became nearly universal in the United States and England. Thus at present, English readers have a wide range of backgrounds and interests, and a large body of literature has been written for this general reading public.[1]

Today there is a very large range of registers in English, although no study has actually catalogued the various types. Two examples can be given to illustrate the extent of register diversification in English. One is Basso's (1974) taxonomy of letters in English, which includes eighteen types, including thank-you letters, love letters, and poison-pen letters under the general category of personal letters, and business letters, letters of recommendation, and letters of resignation under formal letters. The second example is the corpus of contract law described in Faber and Lauridsen (1991), which includes six major text categories (statutes, *travaux préparatoires*, judgments, contracts, legal textbooks, articles in law journals) and twenty-four different thematic categories (with headings such as 'formation and validity of contracts', 'legal effects of contracts', and 'breach of contract'). These examples illustrate the wide range of register differences in English even within highly restricted domains of language use.

Given that the totality of registers in English has never been fully documented, it is not currently possible to build a corpus including texts

Table 3.1 *Written registers of English used in the present study (all except letters from the LOB Corpus)*

Press
  National/provincial
  Daily/Sunday
  Reportage
    Political, sports, society, spot news, financial, cultural
  Editorials
    Institutional, personal, letters to the editor
  Reviews

Religion
Skills, trades and hobbies
Popular lore
Biographies

Official documents
  Government documents (reports, acts, treaties, etc.)
  Foundation and industry reports
  College catalogue

Academic prose
  Natural sciences
  Medicine
  Mathematics
  Social and behavioral sciences
  Political science, law, education
  Humanities
  Technology and engineering

Fiction
  General
  Mystery
  Science
  Adventure
  Romance
  Humor

Letters
  Personal
  Professional
  Recommendation

from all registers. However, it is important to represent as wide a range of variation as possible. In earlier multidimensional studies, this was accomplished through the use of two of the large computer-based text corpora described in chapter 2: the LOB Corpus and the London–Lund Corpus. Table 3.1 shows the range of written register distinctions used in

Table 3.2 *Spoken registers of English used in the present study (from the London–Lund Corpus)*

Face-to-face conversation
Telephone conversation
   Between equals, business associates, disparates
Public conversations, debates, and interviews
Broadcasts (radio)
   Sports
   Non-sports
Spontaneous speeches
   Court cases
   Dinner speech
   Radio essays
   Speeches in House of Commons
Prepared speeches
   Sermons
   University lectures
   Court cases
   Political speeches
   Popular lecture

earlier MD studies; apart from the letters, these are all from the LOB Corpus. Table 3.2 shows the range of spoken registers included in earlier MD studies.

The register distinctions used here include several of the subcategories in the LOB and London–Lund Corpora as well as all of the major categories (e.g., within press reportage, spot news versus sports reportage versus financial reportage; within academic prose, natural science versus humanities prose). There are other registers of English that could be included in a comprehensive study: for example, most kinds of unpublished writing (apart from letters) are not included; these include personal writing to oneself (notes or diaries), memos, and various kinds of printed writing (e.g., leaflets, brochures, advertisements, instruction sheets). However, the registers that are included represent a wide range of speech and writing in English, and thus they provide an adequate database for the purposes here: to identify the dimensions of variation in English and compare the patterns of register variation cross-linguistically.

3.2   Korean

Korean is similar to English in having a wide array of spoken and written registers, and literacy has been an integral part of Korean culture for centuries. However, it was only recently (the end of the nineteenth century) that a native Korean literacy was fully implemented. The following summary is based on Kim (1990: chapter 2).

Until the fifteenth century, all Korean writing used Chinese characters. Since these characters are meaning-based, readers needed to learn many characters to be literate, and there were thus few literates during this time. In the fifteenth century, a Korean alphabet using a sound-based system, *Hangul*, was developed. This system was not readily accepted, however, and until the end of the nineteenth century, *Hangul* was regarded as a script only for women, used mostly for personal letters and translations of classical Chinese literature. In 1894, that situation changed when the government of Korea stipulated that all laws were to be written primarily in *Hangul*. Shortly thereafter, newspapers and magazines began to appear that adopted the *Hangul*-only policy.

Western-type schools were introduced in the early twentieth century, and these taught *Hangul* as a school subject for the first time in Korea's history. In the 1920s, then, there was an intensive period of literary innovation that introduced genres such as the novel, poems, and literary criticism using *Hangul*. A *Hangul* translation of the Bible was also completed during this time. The combination of these developments firmly established a popular, native literacy in Korea. More recently, many writers have been educated primarily in *Hangul* and thus written Korean is continuing to develop a greater proportion of native Korean vocabulary and more native-like syntax.

Culturally, hierarchical order and harmony in human relationships are regarded as central virtues in Korea, due to the influence of Confucian thinking. These virtues are realized linguistically as well as interactionally. Special terms of address (pronouns and personal names) and speech levels are used to mark the relation between speaker and hearer, and honorific infixes are used to mark the relation between the speaker and referents in a sentence. The so-called speech levels are especially interesting; these are sentence-final verbal suffixes, marking four levels of deference–condescension and distinguishing between formal and informal styles. As Kim (1990: 28ff.) notes, most previous research on speech levels has focused exclusively on spoken usage, and thus we know little about the use of these forms in written registers. They are required, however, in both speech and writing.

Kim (1990) includes twelve written registers and ten spoken registers in his study, summarized below:

Written registers
Newspaper reportage
Newspaper editorials
Novels
Literary criticism

College textbooks
Legal and official documents
Popular writing
Personal essays
Suasive essays
Political statements
Editorial letters
Personal letters

Spoken registers
Private conversation
Public conversation
Edited, published conversation drama
News broadcasting
Television documentary
Sportscast
Unscripted public address
Scripted public address
Folktale

The typical situations and purposes associated with each register are described in Kim (1990: chapter 2), and details about the particular texts collected for each register are given in Kim (1990: section 3.2.1). As in the analysis of English, the registers included are not exhaustive, but they do represent most of the range of register variation in Korean.

Among the spoken registers, there are four types of dialogue: face-to-face private conversations, public conversations, published conversations, and television drama. Private conversations are natural interactions among friends or peers, ranging over several topics. Public conversations are tape-recorded from a professional seminar, radio and television talk shows, and a parliamentary hearing. These are all more topic-focused than the private conversations, plus they are conducted in the presence of a third-party audience. Published conversations are interviews printed in monthly magazines; these have been edited and thus do not represent verbatim speech. Finally, television drama also represents an edited kind of conversation, in this case reflecting the writer's perception of speech. These last two registers were included to investigate the relation between verbatim and edited private and public conversations.

News broadcasting includes both radio and television reportage. In earlier periods, this register was almost always scripted, with announcers reading the texts prepared by reporters. More recently, though, reporters have begun to present the news live, so that a much greater proportion of reportage is not scripted. Similarly, television documentaries are a relatively recent development in Korean. These typically involve a narrator plus several other interviewed participants, who describe aspects of the natural environment or cultural heritage of Korea. Sportscasts in Korean seem relatively similar to those in English. There is usually an announcer, who describes the play-by-play action, and a commentator, who presents analyses of the actions or overall situation. In television sportscasting, there is less need to report every action since the audience can observe for themselves. Broadcast discussions of sports occur primarily during live sporting events in Korea, in contrast to the situation in the United States and England, where there are numerous other radio and television shows summarizing and analyzing recent sporting events.

Public speeches have a short history in Korea, where they are restricted primarily to cultural activities adapted from western cultures, such as political speeches and Christian sermons. Traditionally, the Confucian virtue of modesty has discouraged people from developing fluent public-speaking skills, and the credibility of a fluent public speaker is often questioned. At present, Christian ministers are among the most fluent public speakers, often giving spontaneous speeches, while politicians tend to rely on reading carefully written texts. Both kinds of speeches are included in the study of Korean: planned, unscripted presentations, such as sermons, wedding addresses, and a spontaneous church prayer, as well as scripted presentations, including written sermons and presidential addresses.

Finally, the telling of folktales has become quite rare in Korea, but it has a long and well-established history. Most of the folktale texts in this study were collected and transcribed by the Academy of Korean Studies. The folktales were told by experienced story tellers, with local villagers and the researcher as a live audience.

Among the written varieties, two newspaper registers are included: report-age and editorials. Newspaper reportage is primarily narrative, recounting past events; editorials are institutional statements of opinion. Both registers deal with a wide range of subjects (international affairs plus numerous domestic issues relating to society, politics, finance, and sports).

Novels is used as a cover term for fictional works of varying length. As noted above, this register evolved in the early part of the twentieth century; previous fictional texts were primarily folktales or Chinese classical texts. Korean novels are similar to English novels in that they can combine discourse of many different types, including narration, description, dialogue, and even exposition. Literary criticism became popular around the same time as the modern Korean novel, but it differs notably from novels in being a type of academic, expository prose.

College textbooks are also academic, but they are written with a didactic

purpose. They are typically expository, but historical texts include considerable narrative portions, and texts in fields such as statistics or engineering can
include considerable segments of procedural discourse. The category of legal
and official documents includes various laws, regulations, and other official
documents, such as the constitution of Korea, an international commercial
treaty, regulations for a high-school alumni association, and the platform
statement for a political party.

Popular writing refers to periodical articles written for the general public.
The texts included in Kim's study tend to be descriptions of various Korean
traditions. Personal essays are also written for general readers, presenting
personal reflections on a writer's past experiences. Suasive essays are more
didactic, presenting educational information relating to religion, marriage,
and other cultural or social concerns. Political statements are overtly persuasive, reflecting a long tradition within Korean culture fostering the open
expression of political opposition, even when it entails great personal risk.
During the 1980s, such written statements became relatively common as
greater freedom of speech was tolerated. These statements are overt protests
against existing practices, often adopting an angry tone. They deal with issues
relating to existing political systems, social and economic justice, national
education, agriculture, and religion.

Finally, two kinds of letters are included in the Korean study. The first,
editorial letters, are taken from question-and-answer columns in magazines;
these typically deal with personal, legal, or health problems. The second,
personal letters, are addressed to friends or relatives; these are truly
interactive and personal in nature, and impressionistically they have many
characteristics that are typical of speech.

3.3   Nukulaelae Tuvaluan

Nukulaelae is a small atoll of the Tuvalu group in the Central Pacific. Rather
than analyzing the register patterns found in Tuvaluan as a whole, Besnier
(1986, 1988) focused on the atoll of Nukulaelae, to represent a situation of
restricted literacy. That is, although there is a relatively extensive range of
spoken and written Tuvaluan registers used on the national level (associated
with the central government, the press, etc.), only a restricted range of
registers is used on the atoll of Nukulaelae. Although literacy is highly
valued on Nukulaelae – the island can claim a history of literacy that began
around 1860 and an adult literacy rate of essentially 100 percent – there are
only two major written registers in widespread use and a relatively limited
number of spoken registers as well. The following description is based on
Besnier (1986, 1988).

The speech community on Nukulaelae is small, ranging between 300 and

350 speakers. The atoll has been isolated for most of its history, and even now the main contact with the outside world is through a government ship that arrives about once a month. The first recorded contact with the western world was in 1821, when a ship stopped by the atoll.

Literacy and Christianity were both introduced to Nukulaelae around 1860, and they have remained closely associated to the present time. A lay deacon from Manihiki island was beached involuntarily on Nukulaelae in 1861, and over the few months of his residency he taught the basics of Christianity, reading, and writing. Samoan missionaries then began arriving in 1865, bringing more hymnals and Bibles.

Given this history, Samoan was the primary language of literacy until recently. (Samoan was also the official language of the Ellice Islands, the colonial predecessor to Tuvalu, until 1931.) Initially, literacy activities on Nukulaelae were restricted to reading the Bible and other Christian materials. However, by the 1880s there were reports that Nukulaelae residents were prolific letter writers. In addition, deacons and preachers write sermons and sermon notes, and some island residents use writing for personal notes and records.

The two written registers analyzed in Besnier's study represent the only types of continuous written discourse in Nukulaelae Tuvaluan: personal letters and scripted sermons. Personal letters are typically written to relatives on other islands of Tuvalu or elsewhere. These can have multiple purposes, including the expression of affect towards the addressee, various requests and responses (especially relating to financial concerns), and the conveyance of local and personal news. Written sermons are produced by lay deacons, although often sermons are based only on notes or an outline. Even when these are written as continuous prose, many preachers improvise during delivery. Only texts representing continuous discourse were included in Besnier's study. Sermons explain scripture readings and deal with traditional Christian topics. They are an atypical speech event on Nukulaelae in that they often involve exhortations, and even accusations, in contrast to other public interactions where directives and confrontation are avoided if possible.

Given that oral interaction is much more prevalent on Nukulaelae than written communication, it might be surprising that the range of spoken registers is restricted relative to languages such as English and Korean. However, it seems to be the case that the proliferation of written registers is accompanied by a proliferation of spoken registers. Thus, in highly literate societies, language use in institutional domains such as government, law, commerce, education, academia, and the press has resulted in the development of specialized written registers as well as associated spoken registers.

Besnier analyzes five spoken registers for Nukulaelae, although two of these (maneapa speeches and private-setting speeches) are distinguished primarily by their settings, and another one (radio broadcasts) was a one-time occurrence. These five spoken registers are listed below, as well as the two written registers, included in the analysis of Nukulaelae Tuvaluan.

Informal conversations
Political meetings
Maneapa speeches
Private-setting speeches
Radio broadcasts
Personal letters
Scripted sermons

The first spoken register is conversation. Most conversations on Nukulaelae are multi-party rather than dyadic, and they cover a wide variety of topics. The conversations recorded by Besnier were typically set in a cooking hut, involving interactions among men and women of various ages.

Political meetings are recorded from sessions of the local Council of Elders, where issues such as island-internal conflicts and community cohesion are discussed. Only selected male elders can participate in these meetings, and the interactions are highly circumspect towards one another.

Maneapa speeches are also delivered spontaneously by male elders, but they differ from speeches at political meetings in that they are addressed to the entire island community during feasts and dances in the maneapa (community house). Maneapa speeches can be entertaining and witty, and they can also include announcements, expression of appreciation to certain members of the community, narratives with pointed morals relating to current events in the community, and exhortations to maintain community traditions and practices. Private-setting speeches are similar to maneapa speeches except that they are delivered in private homes during family events, such as weddings and funerals. Apart from setting, the main differences between maneapa and private-setting speeches relate to their overall structure (which is more formalized for maneapa speeches), the specificity of topics (expected to focus on the event at hand in private-setting speeches), and the use of teasing and joking (less common in private-setting speeches).

Finally, the radio broadcast included in Besnier's study represents a unique event, in which the national radio station recorded local residents of Nukulaelae debating whether pastors should be allowed to stand for parliamentary election. Although this speech event was experimental in nature, it was not completely foreign to Nukulaelae islanders in that debates had previously been aired on the radio. In addition, the debate was similar in some respects to local political meetings. Major differences from political meetings involved the much wider intended audience, participation by young men in addition to elders, greater preplanning of the speeches, discussion of a topic that was relatively removed from local concerns, and a very direct, sometimes accusatory, expression of opinion.

3.4   Somali

Somali is a Cushitic language spoken by approximately 5 million inhabitants of the countries of Somalia, Djibouti, Ethiopia, and Kenya. Somalia is one of the few African countries in which nearly 100 percent of the population share the same mother tongue. The following description, which is based on Biber and Hared (1992a, b, 1994), depicts the patterns of language use in Somalia as they existed in 1989. The current (1993–94) language situation in Somalia is probably quite different – especially regarding the production and distribution of written registers – because of the extensive fighting and collapse of central government institutions.

Similar to the Nukulaelae situation, the early history of literacy in Somalia is closely associated with religion. When indigeneous Somali literacy was introduced, however, it was not primarily used for religious purposes, differing from the continuing association between religion and literacy in Nukulaelae Tuvaluan.[2]

Arabic language literacy accompanied the introduction of Islam to Somalia, which was well established on the coast of East Africa by the tenth century. Traditionally, a high percentage of Somalis have been able to read Arabic in the sense that they can decode and pronounce the words. These skills are taught in village Quranic schools, where children memorize the letters of the Arabic alphabet and also memorize much of the Quran. There are few children, however, who learn to read Arabic with understanding, and an even smaller proportion who learn to write Arabic prose.

More recently, English and Italian literacies were introduced during the colonial period. Schools using Italian were established in the southern part of Somalia, while schools using English were established in the north. Relatively few children were able to attend these schools, however, with the proportion becoming even smaller with higher levels of education.

There was no widely accepted written tradition for Somali itself before 1972,[3] when the government of Somalia named it as the official language. Before that time, Arabic, Italian, and English were used for official purposes. In a short time after 1972, however, there were many official and professional varieties of writing in Somali, including dictionaries, grammars, textbooks, newspapers, histories, biographies, storybooks, letters, and government documents. Interestingly, written Somali has not replaced Arabic in the religious domain, because the Quran is considered untranslatable and Arabic is preferred for related writings on Islam.

The history of Somali literacy began abruptly on October 21, 1972, when Siyaad Barre, the president of Somalia, announced the development of a new standardized orthography for Somali and declared that Somali would be the sole official language of state, bureaucracy, and education. This proclamation was implemented in short order. For example, mass literacy campaigns were conducted from October 1972 to January 1973, and from July 1974 to February 1975. During these periods, all students in the last two years of primary school and the first year of secondary school were recruited as literacy instructors. In all, approximately 15,000 instructors (including many civil servants and police and army officers) were active during these periods, some of them even traveling with nomadic villages. Within a very short period of time, there was a national newspaper (*Xiddigta Oktoobar*) and two periodical news magazines (*Waaga Cusub* and *Codka Macalinka*) in Somali. Folk stories, a number of non-fiction pamphlets, and government memos also appeared quickly in Somali, while textbooks and longer fictional or historical works began appearing after two or three years. Several studies describe the social processes involved in the introduction of mass literacy to Somali society (Andrzejewski 1974; Laitin 1977; Geshekter 1978; Mezei 1989). Ali and Gees (1979), Andrzejewski (1978, 1979), Galeb (1979) and Hared (1992) further document overt language-planning efforts to extend the lexical stock of Somali in order to make it suitable for use in institutional domains such as education, politics, and mass media.

In the 1970s, most writers of Somali were administrators, teachers, and journalists who had previously been educated in Italian or English. By the early 1980s, however, writers who had been educated in Somali began to enter the workforce. The introduction of an indigenous writing system made literacy and schooling more accessible for all Somalis and thus decreased the social distance between educated, urban adults and non-educated, rural adults. For example, according to the statistics in Nelson (1982), primary-school enrollments in the country as a whole increased from 35,306 in 1968–69 to 263,751 in 1978–79 (for both males and females). Education for females lagged behind males, but it showed a similar increase: from 7,937 in 1968–69 to 95,200 in 1978–79.

As a result of these trends, a relatively large number of young adults in urban areas participate in modern Somali culture as consumers of literacy; the number of literates is much lower in rural areas due to economic pressures. (Literacy rates are also much lower among older adults.) There are few actual producers of written texts, however. All published Somali texts are produced in the capital city of Mogadishu by educated journalists, government employees, teachers, and fiction writers. Government employees in other cities also produce unpublished memos and official letters, while the production of written texts by non-professionals is restricted primarily

Table 3.3 *Written registers used for the analysis of Somali*

A. Press (*wargeysyada*)
   News reportage (*war*)
   Editorial (*faallo*)
   Letters to the editor (*ra'yiga iyo aqoonta*)
   General-interest articles (*maqaal guud*)
   Announcements (*iidheh iyo ogeysiis*)
   Serial story (*taxane sheeko*)
   Sports review (*faaqidaadda ciyaaraha*)

B. Government Documents (*qoraalo dawladeed*)
   Memos (*wareegto*)
   Political pamphlets (*qoraal barabagaandha*)
   Published political speeches (*khudbad siyaasadeed*)

C. Personal adult writing (*qoraalo dadweyne*)
   Letters (*warqad*)
   Applications or petitions (*arji*)

D. Educational/academic texts (*qoraalo waxbarasho*)
   High-school textbooks (*buug dugsiyada sare*)
   Theses (*teesooyin*)
   Academic essays (*qoraal cilmiyeed*)

E. Literature (*suugaan*)
   General fiction (*sheeko mala-awaal*)
   Folklore stories (*sheeko-xariir*)

F. General writings (*qoraalo guud*)
   Historical writings (*qoraal tariikheed*)
   General-knowledge books (*qoraal aqoon-guud*)
   Book introductions (*arar*)
   Analytical articles (*maqaal gaar*)

to personal letters, and occasional petitions and notes. (Most petitions are written by professional petition writers for members of the lay public.)

Table 3.3 summarizes the written registers included in the corpus of Somali texts. These represent a fairly exhaustive sampling of Somali writing, including all available written registers and all available texts for some categories. Written texts were collected from three time periods, 1973–74 (the initial period of Somali literacy), 1977–79 (a middle period when written registers had become fairly well established), and 1988–89 (representing the most recent period).[4]

The press registers are probably the best developed written registers in Somali. Somali newspapers have been in continuous existence since January 1973. In 1989 there was both a daily paper (*Xiddigta Oktoobar*) and a weekly (*Ogaal*). Several registers from newspapers are included in the Somali study.

News reportage (*war*), taken from the front page of the papers, are articles reporting on current events. Only articles written by the Somali news agency (SONNA) are included in this register; acknowledged translations of articles written by international news agencies (such as Reuters or the Associated Press) were systematically excluded. Institutional editorials (*faallo*) are taken from a titled editorial page. These are commentaries with no acknowledged author, discussing a current event or situation and typically arguing in support of the official government position. Some example topics are the retreat of the Soviets from Afghanistan, the Somali business situation and problems with the black market, and an agreement between Ethiopia and Somalia to stop border fighting. The situational characteristics of *ra'yiga dadweynaha*, 'the opinion of the people', changed considerably from 1973 to the current period. In all periods, these texts were published on a separate, titled page of the newspaper. In earlier periods, these were true letters to the editor, written by interested readers of the paper concerning local and nationalistic issues (such as family responsibility, the administration of local town governments, the importance of economic progress, and the repair of the city sports stadium). In the current period, though, this page was renamed *ra'yiga iyo aqoonta* 'opinion and knowledge'. These are invited editorials and articles, written by experts on specialized topics such as the economy, international relations, and Somali culture and history.

Iidheh iyo ogeysiis are announcements and notices, presented in a special section of the newspaper. These include announcements about meetings and public events (e.g., new plays, new books, the opening of a new shop or hotel), as well as notices to individuals (e.g., a summons to appear in court or to pay an electricity bill). *Faaqidaadda ciyaaraha* are sports reviews that appear regularly; these present relatively in-depth discussion of current sports news, including biographies, discussion of recent tournaments, and analysis of particular games.

Finally *maqaal guud* and *maqaal gaar* are more informational articles that appear on the inside pages of newspapers but do not have their own titled sections. *Maqaal guud* are general interest articles, on topics such as general health, the value of friendship, the danger of using drugs, AIDS, respecting your neighbor, and problems with hair dyes. These are addressed to a wide audience and discuss a topic in relatively superficial terms. In contrast, *maqaal gaar* are longer and more analytical, dealing with more specialized issues relating to international relations, politics, economics, social problems, scientific discoveries, the environment, etc.

Government documents were relatively difficult to collect due to security concerns. Memos (*wareegto*) are official statements of policy written by a governmental office or institution for distribution to other offices. Although these were relatively common, they were generally unavailable to us because they were regarded as politically sensitive. The memos in this study were rescued from a back storage closet at Lafoole College (part of the Somali National University). In contrast, it was easy to buy political propaganda pamphlets (*qoraal barabagaandha*) and booklets of published political speeches (*khudbad siyaasadeed*) in the central market, although few of these were published in recent years. Both types of pamphlets are distributed by the government on topics such as the advantages of socialism and the contributions of the Revolution to the development of the country. The pamphlets tend to be more historical and analytical than the speeches. The political speeches were attributed to the then-president of Somalia (Maxamed Siyaad Barre), but they were written (and often read) by members of his staff.

Personal letters (*warqad*) were collected from friends and relatives of Hared in Mogadishu. Writers of these letters come from various educational backgrounds and ages, including both males and females. The letters are truly personal, being addressed to close relatives or friends. Petitions (*arji*) are personal but official in purpose. They are addressed to an individual in an official capacity to present personal appeals, such as requests for a leave or transfer from a job, a passport, a loan, or housing.

High-school textbooks (*buug dugsiyada sare*) are samples taken from the only textbook series in the country. Text samples are included from books on biology, chemistry, physics, geography, history, and Somali literature. Academic prose (*qoraal cilmiyeed*) actually combines two subregisters: published academic essays and theses. The essays are taken from two collections of academic papers (apparently the only two such collections). The first book focuses on *qaad* (a mild narcotic chewed in East Africa), dealing with biological, chemical, medical, economic, and social issues. The second is from a collection of essays on cultural and linguistic aspects of Somali. Academic theses are required for many of the bachelor's degrees at Somali National University. The theses (*teesooyin*) used for this study are from the schools of Political Science and Lafoole College (the teacher-training faculty). Theses can be written in Italian, English, or Somali, but most recent theses in these two colleges are written in Somali.

The category *sheeko mala-awaal* 'imaginative stories' also combines two subregisters: short novels and serial stories published in the newspaper. Recent novels could be bought in the central market but were relatively few in number; episodes of serial stories were printed in many issues of the daily national newspaper. Fiction has changed in purpose since 1973. Earlier works of fiction addressed serious issues relating to Somali national identity or social development, while most recent fiction presents variations on a love theme (a country girl comes to the city, falls in love, and has various adventures). *Sheeko-xariir* 'silk (i.e. entertaining) stories' are booklets

Table 3.4 *Spoken registers used for the analysis of Somali*

A. Conversation and story-telling (*sheekayn*)
       Spontaneous narratives (*sheeko*)
       Non-narrative conversation (*hadal caadi*)

B. Speeches (*hadal jeedin*)
       University lectures (*cashar jaamcadeed*)
       Conference lectures (*lakjar*)
       Sermons (*wacdi*)
       Quranic exposition (*tafsiir*)

C. Spontaneous radio broadcasts (*hadal raadiyo*)
       Live sports broadcasts (*ciyaar-tebin*)

D. Formal interaction and meetings (*hadal shir*)
       Committee meetings (*shir guddi*)
       Family meetings (*shir qoys*)
       Discussions following lectures (*falanqo lakjar*)

of traditional folk stories. These were relatively common immediately after the introduction of Somali literacy, as an aid to beginning readers, but few were published in the 1980s.

The final type of written register collected for Somali was *goraala guud* 'general writings'. As with some of the other categories, these were more common in earlier periods, including general interest booklets on personal hygiene, agriculture, etc., as well as more specialized historical and biographical books on famous Somali leaders and events. None of these booklets has been published in recent years, however. Book introductions were also included as a type of general writing. These occur in most books (fiction and non-fiction), labeled either as *arar* or *hordhac*. They correspond to introductions and prefaces in English books. *Arar* and *hordhac* present the background to a book, including some or all of the following: a summary of the book, a history of the writing of the book, the reasons why the book was written, why it is important, and sometimes acknowledgments (although these are often in a separate section).

Table 3.4 presents the spoken registers used in Biber and Hared's study of Somali. These represent a wide range of urban spoken registers but do not include traditional nomadic varieties.

Two conversational registers are included: *hadal caadi* 'plain conversation' and *sheeko* 'stories'. These both represent face-to-face interactions among friends or relatives, the normal pastime in the evenings. Conversational narratives are monologues that describe past events, either the personal experiences of the narrator or stories about other participants. Conversations include discussions of the day's events, jokes, and other casual forms of interaction.

Two types of lectures were collected: from the university and from an academic conference. *Cashar jaamcadeed* are university lectures given by teachers at the Somali National University on philosophy, political economy, political science, history, geography, and biology. The borrowed term *lakjar* is used for academic conference lectures, in this case given at the Fourth International Congress of Somali Studies in Mogadishu (June 1989). Academic lectures (apart from teaching in the university) are a rare speech event in Somali. Even in the present case, Somali participants in the congress were originally instructed to deliver their talks in either Italian or English for the sake of foreign participants. However, when many foreign visitors canceled their trips due to political instability, most Somali participants decided to deliver their talks in Somali, enabling investigation of this evolving register. *Falanqo lakjar* are taken from the discussions after the lectures at this same conference. These were often lengthy and quite confrontational, and participants seemed to enjoy the discussions as much as the lectures.

There are two different kinds of religious monologues common in Somali: *wacdi* and *tafsiir*. *Wacdi* are presented in the mosque every Friday at the weekly Islamic service; they include explanations of the Quran and Hadith (Islamic traditional law), discussion of present-day implications, and spiritual exhortations. *Tafsiir* occur publicly on Thursday nights, but they can occur in private settings any night of the week. These tend to be more didactic, again focusing on explanations of the Quran or Hadith. They can be given in a mosque or in the courtyard of a house.

In the 1970s and early 1980s, it was fairly common for public sporting events to be covered by radio broadcasts. In the late 1980s, though, sporting events became less common, as did broadcasts of those events. Sports broadcasts (*ciyaar-tebin*) involve several reporters taking turns describing the action on the playing field and adding background information. Only one sports broadcast was recorded for the Somali study, covering a soccer game combined with a marathon race. All other kinds of radio broadcasts were read from scripted texts, and these were thus not included in the study.

Finally, spoken interactions in two further kinds of meetings were analyzed for Somali. The first, *shir guddi*, is a formal committee meeting. These meetings routinely occur in various government offices. The actual meetings recorded were taken from the regular staff meetings of the newspaper *Ogaal*. Other meetings of this type are scheduled for some special purpose and are thus more formal in nature. Text samples of this type were taken from a special meeting with representatives from UNICEF and the Government Ministries of Health, Education, and Information, to develop strategies for improving the health habits of women and their children during pregnancy and immediately after birth. In contrast, family meetings (*shir qoys*) are more intimate and less structured planning sessions to discuss various financial and (inter)personal issues. The particular texts for this register were collected during a single meeting of Hared with his family.

3.5   The influence of language contact in the four language situations

The descriptions in the preceding sections identify extensive social/cultural differences in the four language situations studied here. However, in one regard the four situations are similar: literacy first entered each of these cultures through contact with a foreign language. As a result, it is likely that the evolution of native written registers in each of these language situations has been influenced by pre-existing foreign models.

In England, Latin and French were widely used for written registers over a period of centuries before English became the dominant language for written purposes. Native English speakers were reluctant to use English for written registers, because they believed that it was not sufficiently prestigious and that it lacked the terminology and structural devices required to discuss institutional and academic subjects. Korea was similarly dominated by Chinese literacy until native Korean written registers became the norm in the current century.

On Nukulaelae, literacy was first introduced through the language Rarotongan. However, Samoan quickly became the dominant language used for written registers; shortly after 1865, nearly all writing on Nukulaelae was done in Samoan. The dominant use of Tuvaluan for written purposes is a very recent development.

Finally, Arabic, Italian, and English have all been used for written registers in Somalia: Arabic over a period of centuries for religious purposes; Italian and English over the last century for governmental and educational purposes. As described above, it was only in 1972 that the country underwent a radical transition to native Somali written registers.

Thus, in all four language situations, written registers were typically produced in foreign languages before native-language literacy became the norm. Comparative, empirical research is required to determine the ways in which this contact with other languages influenced the development of literacy in each case. However, it is likely that these pre-existing foreign written registers were used to some extent as models for comparable native written registers, at least over the early course of their evolution.

3.6   Summary

This chapter has briefly described the language situation for each of the four languages included in the present study, including a brief history of literacy and a description of the spoken and written registers included for analysis. As noted above, these four languages represent quite different linguistic and cultural types. In some cases, there are comparable registers across the four languages: for example, all four have conversations, personal letters, and speeches, and all except Nukulaelae Tuvaluan have fiction, press reportage, and textbook/academic prose. However, in their social histories, cultural organizations, and linguistic resources, these four languages are notably different. Given this diversity, the present database enables a relatively strong test of the claim that there are systematic cross-linguistic patterns of register variation.

The central issue in an investigation of this type is the extent to which registers are similar cross-linguistically in their linguistic characteristics. Such an analysis requires a prior determination of the appropriate bases of comparison: which registers are actually comparable cross-linguistically, and what linguistic characteristics should be used for those comparisons? Chapter 4 shows that these issues cannot be adequately addressed based on comparisons of individual registers with respect to particular linguistic characteristics. Rather, a multidimensional framework, based on the parameters of variation that are well represented within each language, is required.

4 The linguistic bases of cross-linguistic register comparisons: a detailed quantitative comparison of English and Somali registers

4.1 Introduction

One of the key issues in cross-linguistic register analyses is choosing the units of analysis and determining to what extent they are actually comparable. This is relevant both to the registers chosen for analysis and to the linguistic characteristics considered. In the present chapter, these issues are illustrated through a detailed comparison of English and Somali registers.[1]

Throughout the analyses in this book, a quantitative, distributional approach is adopted to describe the linguistic characteristics of registers. These distributional patterns are interpreted functionally, based on previous research which shows that the preferred linguistic forms of a register are those that are best suited functionally to the situational demands of the variety (see, e.g., Chafe 1982; Finegan 1982; Ferguson 1983; Janda 1985; Biber 1988). For example, the situational demands of conversation are very different from those of an academic paper, and therefore the characteristic linguistic forms of these registers will be markedly different. Thus, consider the relative frequencies of first-person pronouns, second-person pronouns, and nouns in these two registers, presented in table 4.1.

Both first- and second-person pronouns are tied directly to the communicative situation in their meaning: first-person pronouns are used to refer to an actively 'involved' addressor, while second-person pronouns require a specific addressee in order to be felicitous. In contrast, nouns generally refer to third-person entities and can refer to either concrete objects or abstract concepts; nouns are the primary bearers of referential meaning in a text (apart from deictic, pronominal references to the immediate physical context).

In conversation, both the addressor and the addressee are actively involved, directly interacting with one another and expressing their own personal thoughts and feelings. For this reason, conversation has frequent references to 'you' (the specific addressee) and 'I' (expressing the personal thoughts, feelings, and activities of the speaker). For similar reasons, conversations have relatively infrequent nouns. Conversational participants have

Table 4.1 *Mean frequencies of first- and second-person pronouns in two English registers (per 1,000 words of text; taken from Biber 1988: 255, 264)*

	Conversations	Academic prose
1st person pronouns	57.9	5.7
2nd person pronouns	30.8	0.2
Nouns	137.4	188.1

primarily interactive, involved purposes, rather than abstract, informational purposes, and therefore conversations have few nouns relative to other registers.

In contrast, academic prose does not have a specific individual addressee, writers of academic prose do not usually have involved or interpersonal purposes, but they do have highly informational purposes. Academic prose articles are written to a bounded but unknown audience, and there is little possibility for direct interaction between addressor and addressee. Further, the writer's purpose typically focuses on the information being presented rather than his or her own personal feelings or activities. For these reasons, there is a functional dispreference for first- and second-person pronouns in academic prose, coupled with a notable preference for nouns. The pronoun 'you' is very rarely used because there is no individual that it can refer to, and 'I' is dispreferred because of the emphasis on the information itself rather than the personal feelings of the author. With respect to first-person pronouns, these functional preferences have become conventionalized in some types of academic prose, so that direct references to the author are avoided even when the writer is expressing his or her own personal thoughts or activities. For similar reasons, nouns are particularly common in academic prose, because of the high emphasis on referential information.

This example illustrates an important characteristic of register variation: that the distribution of linguistic forms across registers is systematic because it is functionally motivated. That is, preferred and dispreferred linguistic forms correspond to the communicative demands of different registers.[2]

A central working hypothesis of this book is that there are some communicative functions that are marked in all languages, and that registers can therefore be compared cross-linguistically with respect to the linguistic features serving those functions. For example, interactiveness, personal involvement, and the focused presentation of referential information might be candidates for universal communicative functions. Other communicative functions are not equally important in all languages, and these will serve to mark the distinctiveness of particular languages.

A second hypothesis might be assumed to follow from the above hypothesis: to the extent that a linguistic feature is the same structurally in two languages, it will share similar communicative functions and be distributed in similar ways across the languages. However, the present chapter shows that this hypothesis is not workable without modification; that, rather, entire systems of linguistic features must be compared to reliably represent the underlying functions of each language.

Comparisons of linguistic features across languages can exhibit four different structural/functional relations:

1   Structurally similar features are distributed in similar ways across comparable registers in two languages, and they are functionally similar.

2   Structurally similar features are distributed in different ways across comparable registers in two languages. This distribution can have two different underlying sources:
   (a) the registers being compared across the two languages are in fact different with respect to one or more of their situational/communicative characteristics; or
   (b) the linguistic features being compared fill different roles when considered relative to their respective grammatical systems, and they thus serve different communicative functions.

3   Structurally different linguistic features are distributed in similar ways across comparable registers in two languages, and they are functionally similar.

4   Structurally different features in two languages are distributed in different ways across two languages, and they are functionally different.

The fourth kind of relation above involves comparisons that are not motivated on either structural or functional grounds (such as comparing past tense verbs in one language to second-person pronouns in a second language). This possibility is thus uninteresting theoretically and so is not pursued further here.

The first kind of relation identified above involves the opposite kind of comparison: one that is motivated on both structural and functional grounds. These comparisons are obviously important, but because they are not problematic, they also are not considered further here.

In contrast, both the second and the third kind of relation identified above involve comparisons that are problematic, being motivated on either structural or functional grounds, but not both. It turns out that comparisons of this type are common cross-linguistically, and therefore it is essential to develop analytical approaches for these cases. The present chapter investigates these two kinds of comparative relations through a comparison of press editorials, fictional narratives, and personal letters in English and Somali.

First, the chapter compares the distributions of first- and second-person pronouns across the two languages. These features are similar structurally and functionally in the two languages, yet they are distributed differently. These differences can be attributed to the registers themselves: the extent to which appeal to an inclusive 'we' is appropriate in editorials, and the extent to which dialogue is used to support the story-line in fictional narrative.

Second, the chapter compares the distributions of passive constructions in English and impersonal constructions in Somali. In this case, although the features are quite different structurally across the two languages, the analyses here indicate that these features are similar functionally and thus are distributed similarly across registers.

The most serious problems for cross-linguistic comparisons arise in cases where apparently similar linguistic features are in fact different when considered relative to the full range of options in their respective grammatical systems. This situation is illustrated through a comparison of relative clause constructions in the two languages. These forms serve quite different roles relative to the range of related structural options in the two languages, and thus they have quite different distributions. The investigation of relative clauses leads to a comparison of preverbal particles in Somali and prepositional phrases in English, which in turn leads to an overall comparison of nominal and verbal modifiers in the two languages.

Although these latter comparisons, which are not at all atypical for cross-linguistic analyses, can be justified on structural grounds, they are shown to be inadequate as comparisons of functional equivalents, with respect to either grammatical or communicative functions. Register analysts are thus left in need of some reliable basis for cross-linguistic comparisons. The conclusion of the present chapter argues that underlying dimensions of variation, based on stable linguistic co-occurrence patterns, provide such a basis.

4.2   The text samples

Three registers of Somali and English are compared for the purposes of this chapter: editorials from daily newspapers, narratives from book-length fictional stories, and personal letters between friends or relatives. In Somali, these registers are referred to as *faallo* (editorials), *sheeko mala-awaal* (imaginative stories), and *warqad* (letters).[3] All three registers are described in chapter 3.

Faallo refers specifically to a kind of political commentary which appears regularly in Somali newspapers. Ten faallo from 1989 editions of the weekly newspaper *Ogaal* were analyzed here; these are institutional editorials, with no acknowledged author. The faallo texts are compared to the twenty-seven English editorials analyzed in Biber (1988). These were written in the year 1961 in British newspapers such as the *Daily Herald, The Guardian*, and *The Times*. These texts include institutional editorials, personal editorials (with an acknowledged author), and letters to the editor.

The term *sheeko* is used to refer to written fictional narratives.[4] The sheeko samples in this comparison are taken from twelve short books, which represent all of the Somali fiction published in the years 1985–89. These texts are compared to the twenty-nine general fiction texts analyzed in Biber (1988).

Finally, *warqad* are personal letters; ten letters written to relatives or close friends during the years 1986–89 are analyzed here. These are compared to the six English personal letters analyzed in Biber (1988).[5]

In most respects, the situational characteristics of the corresponding English and Somali registers are quite similar. Somali faallo and English editorials are similar in being informational and persuasive in purpose; they tend to be societal, institutional, and relatively abstract in content; they are addressed to a large, potentially unbounded audience; writer and readers share little personal background knowledge; and there is little possibility of interaction between writer and reader (although it is sometimes possible for a reader to reply with a 'letter to the editor'). Sheeko/fiction are similar to the faallo/editorials in audience characteristics and degree of interactiveness, but they differ in that their purpose is not persuasive or primarily informational, and their topics are typically concrete descriptions of events (and situations). In addition, sheeko/fiction can include extensive dialogue. Warqad/letters differ from these other registers in that they are directed to a specific individual who shares considerable personal background knowledge with the writer; they are directly interactive; and they are concerned primarily with interpersonal relationships, personal concerns, and concrete topics, rather than the conveyance of abstract or institutional information.

There are some important situational differences between the analogous registers in these two languages, however. In particular, the register pairs sometimes differ in their specific purposes and topics, and there are also some differences in audience and interactiveness. These differences can be used to account for some of the cross-linguistic differences discussed below.

4.3   Normalization of frequency counts to a common basis for cross-linguistic comparisons

An analytical problem that arises in quantitative cross-linguistic comparisons concerns the need for a common basis for text counts. In the analyses of this chapter, all frequency counts are normalized to a common basis of 1,000 words of text.[6] Thus, no matter how long a particular text is, normalized frequency counts are comparable across texts.

However, because grammatical 'words' are not necessarily equivalent cross-linguistically, an additional adjustment is required for cross-linguistic comparisons of frequency counts. In particular, words in Somali tend to be more complex morphologically than words in English, and thus they incorporate more aspects of meaning. For example, definite articles, possessive pronouns, and demonstrative pronouns are all regularly suffixed onto the noun that they modify in Somali, while these are represented as separate words in English. To illustrate the extent of these differences, the following Somali text passage from a faallo can be compared to its English translation: the original Somali passage consists of approximately eighty words, while the English translation requires approximately 110 words (depending on the particular translation and method of counting words).

Text sample 4.1: Somali faallo

Dhinaca   keenista   daawada   iyo qaybinteedaba,
the side (of) the-bringing (of) the medicine and even their distribution

dhibaatooyinka   ka jira   waxaa ka   mid ah daawo
the problems (which) at exist what   from one is medicine (which)

boorso lagu   sido oo   aan la   ogeyn waxa ay ka
purse 'they'-with carry and (which) not 'they' know   what it from

sameysan tahay, cidda   sameysay iyo waxa ay tarto
made   is,   people-the (who) made (it) and what it does

toona, oo   si xaaraan ah   dalka   u soo galeysa,
neither and (that) way forbidden being country-the into   enters

taasoo   aynnu ognahay khasaarooyinka   wax-yeellada
that one (which) we   know   losses-the (which) damages-the

caafimaad leh ee   bulshadeenna ka soo   gaara.
health   have and (which) society-our from towards reaches

Qorsheyntii   qaybinta   daawooyinka
planning-the (of) distributing-the (of) medicine-the (of)

dalkana   waxa ku guuleystay   geddisley   yaryar
country-the-and what with succeeded (was) traders (which) small

ah oo   ku sugan waxa loogu   yeero farmashiyayaasha,
are and (which) in are   what 'they'-in call   pharmacies

guul-darradaas   iyo marin-habaabintaas waxa dhaliyay
victory-without-that and path-misleading-that what caused (was)

ka-gaabinta   xil-gudashadii
from-becoming-short-the (of) responsibility-fulfilling-the (which)

looga   baahnaa Wakaaladda   ASPIMA.
'they'-from-to needed   agency-the (of) ASPIMA

Translation
With respect to importing medicine and distributing it, the problems that exist include medicine carried in a purse [i.e. sold on the
blackmarket], which it is not known what it is made of, the people who
made it, or what it does, and which enters the country in a forbidden
way; that one [i.e. the medicine] which has known problems, which
include health damages that come from it to our society. And what
has succeeded in planning the distribution of the medicine of the
country is the small traders who are in the so-called 'pharmacies';
what caused that failure and that deception was the lack of fulfillment
of responsibility which was needed from the agency of ASPIMA.

As illustrated by this passage, frequency counts can differ cross-linguistically
simply because they have been normed to a different grammatical basis. From
a survey of Somali sentences and English translations, this factor seems to be
about 3:4 between these two languages; that is, on average it takes around 100
words in English to express a Somali sentence of seventy-five words. Given this
difference, a straight comparison of frequencies normed per 1,000 words would
provide considerably more opportunities for constructions to occur in Somali
than in English. To account for this difference, Somali frequency counts are
reduced by a factor of 0.75 in the present chapter.

For example, first-person pronouns occur on average 44.3 times per
1,000 words in Somali sheeko (fiction), while in English fiction, first-person
pronouns occur on average only 32.0 times per 1,000 words. From this
comparison, it appears that these pronouns are more frequent in Somali
sheeko than in English fiction. However, the above discussion shows that
1,000 words of text are not truly comparable in the two languages: that
1,000 words of English text corresponds to approximately 750 words of
Somali text. Because of this difference, a comparison of text counts normed
to 1,000 words essentially bases the Somali counts on an extra 250 words in
relation to the English counts. The 0.75 transformation applied to the Somali
counts adjusts for this difference. The effect of this transformation is to base
Somali counts on 750 words of text, in comparison to an equivalent text basis
of 1,000 words in English.

Table 4.2 *Mean frequency of pronouns per 1,000 words*

Somali normalized counts					
	Faallo 1972	Faallo 1989	Sheeko 1972	Sheeko 1989	Warqad 1989
1st person pronouns	23.5	5.1	15.0	44.3	104.3
2nd person pronouns	2.6	0.8	6.4	18.2	56.2
Somali counts adjusted (3:4) to English word basis					
	Faallo 1972	Faallo 1989	Sheeko 1972	Sheeko 1989	Warqad 1989
1st person pronouns	17.7	3.9	11.3	33.2	78.2
2nd person pronouns	1.9	0.6	4.8	13.6	42.1
English normalized counts					
	Editorials		Fiction		Letters
1st person pronouns	11.2		32.0		62.0
2nd person pronouns	1.6		11.1		20.2

4.4   Distributional comparison of linguistic features in Somali and English

4.4.1   'Interactive' features: first- and second-person pronouns

The first example considered here is the distribution of first- and second-person pronouns. In Somali, these classes include independent and dependent pronouns (Saeed 1987: 161–64), and both English and Somali include subject and object forms. (See appendix II for a grammatical description of pronouns in Somali.) The functional interpretation of these linguistic features is relatively straightforward, with first-person pronouns being used for self-reference and second-person pronouns being used for interlocutor-reference. However, as table 4.2 shows, there are interesting differences in the distribution of these forms, both across registers and across languages.

To more fully account for these differences, table 4.2 includes frequency counts for faallo and sheeko in an earlier historical period (1972–74), which represents the initial development of written communication in Somali. As can be seen from table 4.2, both faallo and sheeko have changed considerably in their use of first- and second-person pronouns, suggesting that these registers themselves have undergone functional/conventional shifts.

In the case of faallo, the 1972 register is similar to English editorials, using a moderate number of first-person pronouns (and few second-person pronouns). Applying the 3:4 adjustment to first-person pronouns (shown in the middle portion of table 4.2), a Somali frequency count of 23.5 converts to a count of 17.7, which is relatively close to the English frequency count of 11.2. In both the English editorials and the 1972 Somali faallo, these pronouns were nearly all plural in number, representing a collective presentation of opinion; for example

Text sample 4.2: Somali faallo

Dharka   aynu qaadanno, cuntada   aynu cunno,
clothes-the (that) we   wear   food-the (that) we   eat

baabuurta   aynu fuullo, alaabta   wax
vehicles-the (that) we   ride   material-the (that) something

lagu   dhisto, iyo boqolkiiba siddeetan waxyaabaha kale
'they'-with build   and 100-each   eighty (of) things-the   other

oo   aynu ku isticmaallo, waxaa laga   keenaa   dibedda.
which we   in use   where 'they'-from bring (is) outside

'The clothes that *we* wear, the food that *we* eat, the vehicles that *we* ride on, the materials used for building, and 80 percent of the other things that *we* use, are brought from outside (the country).'

Text samples 4.3–4.4: English editorials

4.3 The real question is what we should put to the Soviet Government as a basis for talks . . .

4.4 Who will speak up for Belgium? Who else but Britain. We have fought beside Belgium . . . We are allies still.

In the Somali sample 4.2, which is typical of 1972 faallo, all first-person plural pronouns have inclusive meaning and thus the collective nature of the proposition is encoded grammatically (cf. the use of a plural first-person pronoun in text sample 4.1 above). In the English editorials, first-person pronouns are similarly used to refer to an inclusive 'we' (as in 3 and 4), emphasizing collective endeavors or beliefs. Thus 1972 Somali faallo and English editorials are similar in this regard.

Present-day faallo, however, are markedly different, using relatively few first-person pronouns (and almost no second-person pronouns). This shift seems to be primarily due to a change in purpose and appropriateness conventions. Previously it was considered appropriate to attribute beliefs to a collective 'we', as an appeal to the common experiences and goals of all readers: in contrast, present-day faallo focus more on a factual presentation of information with little reference to the (shared) experiences of readers and writer.

The situational and linguistic characteristics of sheeko have also shifted dramatically from 1972 to the present with regard to these linguistic features. The 1972 sheeko had few first- and second-person pronouns relative to English fiction, while the 1989 sheeko frequencies are quite close to English fiction. This change reflects a shift in the typical conventions of fictional style, from primarily narrative texts (in 1972) to the present-day practice of including considerable dialogue to support the narrative. Present-day sheeko are thus similar to English fiction in having considerable dialogue and thus considerable first- and second-person references.

Finally, letters and warqad are relatively similar with respect to their use of both first- and second-person pronouns.

Overall these patterns show:

1   1972 faallo are relatively similar to editorials in having a moderate use of first-person plural pronouns, used to emphasize solidarity between the writer and readers; present-day faallo have shifted linguistically, towards a more institutional presentation of opinion which uses few self-references.[7]

2   Present-day sheeko are similar to English fictional novels in including considerable dialogue, and thus considerable first- and second-person pronouns, to support the narrative; earlier sheeko were markedly different in that they included little dialogue and thus had few first- or second-person pronouns.

3   Warqad and letters are similar in their interactive nature, resulting in a frequent use of first- and second-person pronouns in both languages.

These features illustrate the case where linguistic forms serve similar communicative functions cross-linguistically; but frequency counts can differ across two languages due to specific differences in the purposes or appropriateness conventions of equivalent registers.

4.4.2   Impersonal constructions

A second type of cross-linguistic comparison is where the two languages have structurally distinct forms that are functionally similar. Somali impersonal constructions and English passives can be used to illustrate this case. In both languages, these constructions function to demote the agent of a clause.

Somali does not have a passive construction, but it does have an impersonal subject pronoun, *la*, which appears in preverbal position; for example:

Table 4.3 *Distribution of impersonal constructions and passives (per 1,000 words)*

Somali normalized counts			
	Faallo	Sheeko	Warqad
Impersonal *la*	28.8	17.7	13.2
Somali counts adjusted (3:4) to English word basis			
	Faallo	Sheeko	Warqad
Impersonal *la*	21.6	13.3	9.9
English normalized counts			
	Editorials	Fiction	Letters
Agentless passives	11.7	5.7	2.8
By-passives	0.8	0.2	0.0
Impersonal *they*	0.0	0.0	1.2
Total passive/impersonal constructions	12.5	5.9	4.0
Reduced passive postnominal clauses	2.9	0.7	0.2
Passive attributive adjectives	3.5	4.7	0.2
Total constructions with passive function	18.9	11.3	4.4

4.5   Sac baa la   arkay.
cow FOC 'they' saw
'"They" saw a cow.'

The closest equivalent to this construction in English is the impersonal 'they', which has no specific referent; for example:

4.6   'They' announced on the radio last night that . . .

These constructions in English are rare, especially in written registers, but they share several functional similarities with agentless passive constructions, which are often near-equivalent variants. For example, compare 4.6 above with 4.7 below:

4.7   It was announced on the radio last night that . . .

The impersonal construction in Somali also seems to share several discourse functions with the English passive. As table 4.3 shows, the Somali impersonal and English passive constructions (including impersonal 'they') have similar relative distributions across registers. (The impersonal 'they' in English occurs only in letters, and even there it is rare.) Thus in both languages,

impersonals/passives are most common in faallo/editorials; their frequency
in sheeko/fiction is about half the frequency of that in faallo/editorials; and
their frequency in warqad/letters is about 25 percent less than the frequency
in sheeko/fiction.

Impersonal constructions in Somali have at least four related but distinguishable functions.

A. To demote the agent, in order to suppress the source of information and
the role of the author in the assertion of information. Under this function,
the author uses *la* to present information as known or given, while avoiding
personal responsibility for the information; for example:

4.8   Diinta   islaamka *la*gama heli   karo in . . .
          religion-the Islam   'they' cannot find that
          'It cannot be found in Islam that . . .'

4.9   Waxaa *la*   isku   raacsan yahay in . . .
          what 'they' REFLEX-with agree   is   that
          'It is agreed that . . .'

B. To demote the agent because it is already known in the discourse context,
or because it is not salient in the flow of information; this is accompanied
by promoting a non-agent constituent to informational prominence. For
example:

4.10   Shalay   bannaanbax weyn ayaa *la*gu   sameeyey
          yesterday rally   big FOC 'they'-in made

          magaalmadaxda Muqdisho.
          city-capital-the   Mogadishu

          'Yesterday, it was a big rally that "they" made in the capital city
          of Mogadishu.'

The agent in this sentence is easily inferred from the discourse context as
being 'the adult residents of Mogadishu'. This agent is demoted by the
use of *la*, while the informational salience of *bannaanbax weyn* ('a big rally')
is emphasized by being fronted and marked with the focus particle *ayaa*;
shalay ('yesterday') is marked as topic by being moved to sentence-initial
position. Thus under this function, *la* works together with other grammatical
devices to demote the agent while giving informational prominence to other
elements.

C and D: these are special cases of the two major functions identified above,
both usually involving speech act verbs.

C. To demote the agent and/or source of speech act verbs, because the agent is not important in the discourse context; to avoid responsibility for the assertion; or as an indirect expression of doubt about the assertion. For example:

4.11 Waxaa *la*   yidhi beri buu   raacay   geel.
        what   'they' said   once FOC-he looked after camels.
        'It was said that he once looked after camels.'

4.12 Waxa lacagtii   *lagu*   shubay,   sida *la*   yidhi, nin
        what money-the 'they'-in deposited how 'they' said   man

        hantidiisa   baanka u taal.
        account-his bank   at it is

        'The money was deposited, it was reported, in a man's bank account.'

D. Naming for referential identification/elaboration: under this function, *la/loo* is used with a speech act verb or mental process verb to give the name or identity of a referent. For example:

4.13 dhulka *loo*   yaqaan   Ciid-Nugaaleed . . .
        land-the 'they' know (as) Ciid-Nugaaleed
        'the land known as Ciid-Nugaaleed'

4.14 balliga   *la*   yiraahdo Sacmadeeqo . . .
        waterhole-the 'they' call   Sacmadeeqo
        'the water-hole called Sacmadeeqo'

These functions are similar to the discourse functions identified for passive constructions in English. For example, Celce-Murcia and Larsen-Freeman (1983: 228–29) identify the following discourse functions of passive constructions in English:

1   to omit the agent when it is redundant;
2   to omit the agent when the writer wants to be tactful or evasive;
3   to give the appearance of objectivity without revealing the source of information;
4   to emphasize the receiver or result of an action;
5   to retain the same grammatical subject in successive clauses; that is, when the theme is given information, and the agent is new information.

These functional similarities can account for the similarity in the relative distributions of English passives and Somali impersonals. However, the absolute frequencies of these constructions are quite different, even after the adjustment for different word bases: Somali impersonal constructions are

approximately twice as common as the total English passive and impersonal
'they' constructions. Most of this difference is due to the fact that there are
constructions in English that function as passives but do not have an overt
passive auxiliary verb. These constructions are of two main types:

   1   reduced relative clauses, for example:

4.15   protests organized by the opposition

4.16   coursework required by the department

   2   past participles functioning as attributive adjectives, for example:

4.17   an organized protest

4.18   required coursework

In Somali, both of these types of construction would typically be represented
as impersonal constructions embedded in a relative clause. For example:

4.19   koorsada *la*yska   bahan yahay waa . . .
       course-the 'they'-from need   it   is
       'the course (which) "they" require' or 'the required course'

As table 4.3 shows, when these reduced passive constructions are added to
the English frequency counts, the absolute frequencies of passives in English
are more comparable to the frequencies of impersonals in Somali (although
they are still slightly less common).

   In sum, the comparison of English passive constructions and Somali
impersonal constructions illustrates the case where structurally different
features in two languages serve similar discourse functions and have similar
relative distributions across registers. This comparison further illustrates
the indeterminacy common in attempts to compare individual linguistic
features cross-linguistically. Thus, in the present case, it is not clear
whether Somali impersonals should be compared to English passives; or
passives plus impersonal 'they' constructions; or passives plus impersonals
plus reduced past participial relative clauses plus attributive adjectives with
a passive sense. The comparison is actually more complicated in that some
English past participles functioning as attributive adjectives are ambiguous
as to whether they represent a passive process (with an unspecified agent)
or a stative description. Stative adjectives in English do not correspond
to impersonals in Somali and thus should not be included in the present
comparison; rather, these forms correspond to stative attributive adjectives
in Somali. For example:

4.20   lugta jaban
       leg-the broken
       'the broken leg'

As the following section shows, such indeterminacy can be even more problematic when features from complex overlapping grammatical systems are compared.

4.4.3   Overlapping grammatical systems: relative clauses and preverbal case particles/prepositions

Both English and Somali have productive relative clause constructions, and on first consideration, it should be possible to directly compare these features cross-linguistically. Similarly, Somali preverbal case particles seem to be the obvious structural counterpart to English prepositions. The following sections show, however, that there are major cross-linguistic differences in the distribution of these features. A closer examination of these differences further shows that these features play quite different roles in their respective grammatical systems. As a result, an analysis framed at a much higher level of generality, comparing all nominal modifiers and all verbal modifiers, is required to identify the underlying similarities across the two languages.

4.4.3.1 Relative clauses

Relative clauses are extremely productive in Somali. Text sample 4.1 (above), in which relative clauses are marked by '(which)' in the English translation, illustrates the dense use of relative clauses in Somali informational prose. In fact, relative clauses provide the basis for most types of syntactic dependency in Somali; for example, clefts, various types of adverbial subordination, and attributive adjectives can all be analyzed as special cases of relativization (Saeed 1984, 1987).

The analysis here includes only traditional relative clauses, which modify a non-pronominal head noun phrase. It distinguishes between restrictive and 'framing' relative clauses, however. Restrictive relatives have no overt relative pronoun in Somali. They function to specify the identity of intended referents as well as adding elaborating details. For example:

4.21 Xaalidii *deriskeena   ahayd* buugta   *ay sheegaysaa*   waa
         Hali-the neighbor-our was   books-the she is talking about are

         buugtii   Cali
         books-the Ali

         'The Hali who was our neighbor, the books that she is talking about are the books of Ali.'

'Framing' relative clauses, on the other hand, set a discourse frame for the following proposition. These clauses are marked by the conjunction *oo*.

When they have a pronominal head, these are typically temporal in nature, as in the following example:

4.22 Isag*oo quraacanaya*   ayey   u timid.
he   eating-breakfast FOC-she to came
'While he was eating breakfast, she came to him.'

Framing relative clauses with lexical head nouns, as in 4.23, can provide a temporal setting, or they can function as non-restrictive referential clauses:

4.23 Asli *oo huruda* baa waxaa toosiyey   Cali.
Asli sleeping   FOC what   awakened (was) Ali
'While Asli was sleeping, Ali awakened her.'

The discourse functions of these clauses need much fuller investigation. The present analysis follows Saeed (1987) and counts *oo* clauses with pronominal heads as a separate category (framing relatives); all relative clauses with lexical heads are combined.

The conjunction *oo* can also be used to co-ordinate relative clauses, as in 4.24 (from text sample 4.1 above).[8]

4.24 geddisley   *yaryar ah* oo   *ku sugan waxa loogu*
traders (which) small are and (which) in are   what 'they'-in

yeero farmashiyayaasha
call   pharmacies

'traders [[who are small] and [who are in so-called pharmacies]]'

It is further possible to distinguish between two categories of restrictive relative clause. The first category consists only of a head noun phrase followed by an identificatory noun phrase and the verb *ah* 'to be,' whereas the second category has a full embedded clause. For example:

NP NP *ah* relatives:

4.25 siyaasadda *hantiwadaagga ahi*
politics-the socialism   being
'the politics which is socialism'

4.26 wafdi   *Soomaali ah*
delegation Somali   being
'a delegation which is Somali'

Full clause relatives:

4.27 buugta   *ay sheegaysaa*
books-the she is talking about
'the books that she is talking about'

4.28   halgan *uu ku   hagaajinayo   noloshiisa*
struggle he with is making better life-his
'a struggle with which he is making his life better'

A textual analysis of these two classes of restrictive relative clause suggests the following difference in discourse function: *ah* relative clauses are typically used to specify the identity of a referent; they add only the minimum amount of information required for explicit identification, without elaborating details. Full clause relatives, on the other hand, seem to add elaborative information in addition to specifying the intended referent; for example, in 4.28 the relative clause identifies the particular struggle and adds some information concerning its influence.

There are also several structural options available in the English relative clause system. The analysis here distinguishes between *that* relative clauses and WH relative clauses, and within WH relatives, it distinguishes between restrictive and non-restrictive clauses. The analysis also includes a count for relative clauses with no overt relative pronoun.

The frequencies of these relative clause categories are given in table 4.4. As with the comparisons of pronouns and passives/impersonals, relative clauses in Somali and English show parallel distributional patterns across registers: faallo/editorials use the most relative clauses, sheeko/fiction have intermediate frequencies, and warqad/letters have the fewest relative clauses of these three registers. There is a striking difference between Somali and English in the absolute frequencies of these constructions, though. Even after the adjustment for different word bases, relative clause constructions are more frequent in Somali by many orders of magnitude: faallo has an overall average of 65.4 relative clauses per 1,000 words compared to only 9.2 in English editorials; sheeko has 47.8 versus only 5.1 in fiction; warqad has 32.0 versus only 2.1 in letters. Thus, despite the obvious structural similarities between relative clause constructions in Somali and English, the distribution of these features indicates that they are serving very different functions in the two languages.

4.4.3.2 Preverbal case particles/prepositions

In Somali there are no prepositions or postpositions. Rather, all case relations are marked by a series of preverbal case particles (see Biber 1984a, 1992c; Saeed 1987). For example,

4.29   Cabdi ninka   buu   dhagax ku tuuray.
Abdi man-the FOC-he rock   at he threw
'Abdi threw a rock at the man.'

Table 4.4 *Mean frequency distribution of relative clauses (per 1,000 words)*

Somali normalized counts	Faallo	Sheeko	Warqad
NP relative clause	54.4	42.1	27.8
NP NP *ah*	24.6	16.3	11.4
DEM *oo* relative clause	4.3	0.2	0.7
PRO *oo* relative clause ('framing')	4.8	5.2	2.7
Somali counts adjusted (3:4) to English word basis	Faallo	Sheeko	Warqad
NP relative clause	40.1	31.6	20.8
NP NP *ah*	18.5	12.2	8.6
DEM *oo* relative clause	3.2	0.1	0.5
PRO *oo* relative clause ('framing')	3.6	3.9	2.1
Total relatives	65.4	47.8	32.0
English normalized counts	Editorials	Fiction	Letters
that relative clauses, restrictive	1.8	0.7	0.5
WH relative clauses			
restrictive	5.4	2.1	1.1
non-restrictive	1.9	2.2	0.3
Relative clauses with			
no relative pronoun	0.1	0.1	0.2
Total relatives	9.2	5.1	2.1

4.30 Cali geela buu   guriga   Faduma u-ga   eriyey.
Ali   camels FOC-he house-the Faduma for-from chased
'Ali chased some camels away from the house for Faduma.'

As these example sentences show, Somali case particles are translated as prepositions in English.[9] (Saeed [1987: 185ff.] actually labels this grammatical category 'prepositions.') The major correspondences are as follows:

    u   to, for
    ku   in, into, on, at, with (by means of)
    ka   from, away from, out of
    la   (together) with

Thus on the surface, Somali preverbal case particles and English prepositions appear to be comparable linguistic features.

However, the frequency counts for these features, given in table 4.5, show a fundamental cross-linguistic difference: while the absolute frequencies are similar across the two languages, the relative distribution across registers is

Table 4.5 *Mean frequency distribution of preverbal particles/prepositions (per 1,000 words)*

Somali normalized counts			
	Faallo	Sheeko	Warqad
Preverbal particles	121.2	136.1	132.5
Somali counts adjusted (3:4) to English word basis			
	Faallo	Sheeko	Warqad
Preverbal particles	90.9	102.1	99.4
English normalized counts			
	Editorials	Fiction	Letters
Total prepositions	116.3	92.8	72.0

strikingly different. In English, editorials show by far the highest frequency of prepositions, fiction shows a moderate frequency, and letters have the lowest frequency. This pattern is in marked contrast to the distribution of preverbal case particles in Somali. Sheeko has the most frequent case particles followed by warqad. Surprisingly, faallo – which are much more informational than either sheeko or warqad – use preverbal case particles least frequently. Overall, despite the translation equivalence of English prepositions and Somali preverbal case particles, the distributional patterns seen in table 4.5 show that these features are serving quite different functions in the two languages. The following section provides a partial explanation of these differences.

4.4.3.3 Comparison of nominal modifiers and verbal modifiers

In Somali, preverbal case particles mark the relations of various indirect objects to the verb, and they are therefore part of the larger grammatical system of verbal modifiers. In contrast, English prepositional phrases can be either verbal modifiers or nominal modifiers. For example, contrast the grammatical function of the phrase *on the chalkboard* in the following two sentences:

4.31   The instructor wrote on the chalkboard.

4.32   The note on the chalkboard was entertaining.

In 4.31, the prepositional phrase *on the chalkboard* is functioning as an adverbial phrase modifying the verb *wrote*. In 4.32, though, the prepositional phrase is functioning as a postnominal modifier, and it can actually be rephrased as a complete relative clause as in 4.33:

4.33   The note that was on the chalkboard was entertaining.

English prepositional phrases functioning as nominal modifiers are actually more comparable to Somali relative clauses than to Somali preverbal case particles. For this reason, it makes sense to divide English prepositional phrases into verbal modifiers versus nominal modifiers for the sake of comparison. Table 4.5 shows that prepositional phrases as nominal modifiers are considerably more frequent than relative clauses in English. In addition, this table includes participial postnominal clauses, since these constructions also function as nominal modifiers. For example:

4.34   The instructor ⟨who was⟩ writing on the chalkboard . . .

4.35   The note ⟨which was⟩ written on the chalkboard . . .

These constructions are full relative clauses if the bracketed material is included, but they are postnominal participial clauses with equivalent meanings if the relative pronoun and copula are omitted. Finally, attributive adjectives are prenominal modifiers that add only a descriptive qualifier.

In Somali, there are only two main structural options available for nominal modification: relative clauses and attributive adjectives. Similar to relative clauses, attributive adjectives occur in postnominal position, but without a verb. For example

4.36   halgan   adag
         struggle difficult
         'a difficult struggle'

4.37   ur   qudhmuun
         odor rotten
         'a rotten odor'

When the complete systems of nominal modifiers are compared across Somali and English, the distributional patterns are quite similar.[10] Thus, table 4.6 shows that the relative distribution of noun modifiers across registers is the same in both languages. English shows a higher overall frequency, especially in editorials versus faallo, because of the extremely high frequency of attributive adjectives plus frequent prepositional phrases as noun modifiers. Somali, on the other hand, greatly favours full relative clauses but has somewhat lower overall frequencies.

In the same way, table 4.7 shows that the cross-language distributions are much more similar when Somali preverbal case particles are compared to only those English prepositional phrases that function as verbal modifiers (rather than to all prepositional phrases). Although the absolute frequencies of English prepositional phrases as verbal modifiers are considerably lower than Somali preverbal case particles, both of these features show the same

Table 4.6 *Mean frequency distributions of nominal modifiers (per 1,000 words)*

Somali normalized counts

	Faallo	Sheeko	Warqad
NP relative clause	54.4	42.1	27.8
NP NP *ah*	24.6	16.3	11.4
DEM *oo* relative clause	4.3	0.2	0.7
PRO *oo* relative clause ('framing')	4.8	5.2	2.7
Attributive adjectives	29.3	28.1	19.5

Somali counts adjusted (3:4) to English word basis:

	Faallo	Sheeko	Warqad
NP relative clause	40.1	31.6	20.8
NP NP *ah*	18.5	12.2	8.6
DEM *oo* relative clause	3.2	0.1	0.5
PRO *oo* relative clause ('framing')	3.6	3.9	2.1
Attributive adjectives	22.0	21.1	14.6
Total N modifiers [see fn. 9]	87.4	68.9	46.6

English normalized counts

	Editorials	Fiction	Letters
that relative clauses, restrictive	1.8	0.7	0.5
WH relative clauses			
restrictive	5.4	2.1	1.1
non-restrictive	1.9	2.2	0.3
Relative clauses with			
no relative pronoun	0.1	0.1	0.2
Participial postnominal modifiers			
(past and present)	4.9	1.8	0.2
Prepositional phrases as			
noun modifiers	38.2	15.2	16.8
Attributive adjectives	74.4	50.7	44.2
Total nominal modifiers	126.7	72.8	63.3

relative distribution across registers: the highest frequencies in sheeko/ fiction, lower frequencies in warqad/letters, and the lowest frequencies in faallo/editorials.

In addition, adverbs and adverbial clauses function as verbal modifiers in both languages. In Somali, there is no derivational process to form adverbs, and adverbial clauses are much more frequent than simple adverbs. In English, on the other hand, general adverbs are extremely frequent. When all verbal modifiers are considered together, both the absolute frequencies and the distribution across registers are quite similar cross-linguistically.

Table 4.7 *Mean frequency distributions of verbal modifiers (per 1,000 words)*

Somali normalized counts	Faallo	Sheeko	Warqad
Preverbal particles	121.2	136.1	132.5
Adverbial phrases	2.3	0.5	1.4
Adverbial clauses	14.0	24.6	21.1
Somali counts adjusted (3:4) to English word basis	Faallo	Sheeko	Warqad
Preverbal particles	90.9	102.1	99.4
Adverbial phrases	1.7	0.4	1.1
Adverbial clauses	10.5	18.5	15.8
Total verb modifiers	103.1	121.0	116.3
English normalized counts	Editorials	Fiction	Letters
Prepositions as verb modifiers	44.1	56.2	45.8
Adverbs	60.4	74.1	80.7
Adverbial clauses	4.5	5.0	9.6
Total verb modifiers	109.0	135.3	136.1

This section has identified both important differences as well as striking similarities between English and Somali. With respect to individual linguistic features, there are notable differences both in the relative distribution across registers and in the absolute frequencies of features. Further, there are overall differences in the allocation of grammatical resources: Somali favors clausal constructions, such as relative clauses and adverbial clauses; English favors phrasal and lexical modifiers, such as prepositional phrases, attributive adjectives, and adverbs. However, when complete grammatical systems are compared – such as the complete systems of noun modification and verb modification – the distribution of forms is more similar cross-linguistically, both in relative terms across registers and in absolute frequencies.

4.5   Summary of the chapter findings

This chapter has explored cross-linguistic register comparisons across Somali and English with respect to particular linguistic features. The analyses have shown that, within each language, there are major linguistic differences among registers, and those differences are associated with different communicative functions and conventions. One of the main purposes of the chapter has been to examine the sources of cross-linguistic register differences. These can be due to:

1   a comparison of analogous registers that actually differ in their communicative purposes or appropriateness conventions – illustrated from the differences in the use of first-person pronouns between faallo and editorials, caused by different register conventions;

2   a comparison of linguistic features that appear to be structurally equivalent but are in fact grammatically and functionally different – illustrated from the comparison of Somali preverbal case particles (which mark only verbal modifiers) with English prepositions (which mark both verbal and nominal modifiers);

3   a comparison of equivalent features that serve different roles in their respective grammatical systems – illustrated from the comparison of relative clauses in Somali and English. (Relative clauses are the major device used for noun modification in Somali, but much less important than attributive adjectives and prepositional phrases as nominal modifiers in English.)

In addition, the chapter has shown that in some cases structurally different features can serve similar grammatical and discourse functions cross-linguistically, resulting in similar distributions across registers (illustrated from the comparison of English passives and Somali impersonal constructions).

In certain respects, the extent of cross-linguistic similarities across registers is striking. In particular, the relative distribution of forms across registers was quite similar across the two languages (while the absolute frequencies showed stronger differences). The major exception was the comparison of Somali preverbal case particles and English prepositions, which were distributed in quite different ways across registers. In this case, a closer analysis showed that prepositions belong to two quite distinct classes – verbal modifiers and nominal modifiers – and that only the former class is grammatically and functionally comparable to Somali case particles. Overall, though, the relative patterns of variation across registers were strikingly similar cross-linguistically.

While there were greater differences in the absolute frequencies between English and Somali, it was further found that absolute frequencies are relatively similar cross-linguistically when complete grammatical/functional systems are compared. Examples of this type are the comparisons of all nominal modifiers, all verbal modifiers, and all agent-demoting forms between Somali and English. However, even at this level, the comparisons are problematic. First, quantitative comparisons must be normalized to a common 'word' basis in each language. In addition, there continue to be unresolved issues concerning the range of features to include in a given grammatical system. In the present analyses, these include the role of stative constructions in the comparison of Somali impersonals and English passives, and the place of genitive constructions in the analysis of nominal modifiers.

In sum, when cross-linguistic register comparisons are based on individual linguistic features, the register analyst is faced with tantalizingly interesting findings coupled with fundamental doubts concerning the appropriate methodologies to use.

4.6   Textual dimensions as a basis for cross-linguistic register comparisons

As noted above, some of the cross-linguistic analyses presented in this chapter have isolated interesting points of comparison. The cumulative effect, however, has been to raise serious questions about the feasibility of any analytical approach based on comparison of particular linguistic features. That is, analyses based on individual features necessarily entail a high degree of uncertainty concerning the appropriate level of structure to be used for comparisons, and very different conclusions can be reached depending on the structures analyzed. In fact, there is no independent criterion that can be used to determine the appropriate level of comparison.

For example, it was shown that relative clauses are much more common in Somali than in English. However, if the comparison is extended to include English constructions that function as reduced relative clauses – participial postnominal modifiers and prepositional phrases functioning as postnominal modifiers – the difference between the two languages is reduced (although the comparable structures are still considerably more common in Somali). Further, if attributive adjectives are also included, so that the comparison is between all nominal modifiers in the two languages (rather than just relative constructions), the frequencies in English are considerably higher. A further extension of this analysis could also include genitive constructions. None of these comparisons should be considered the correct one; all four of them can be justified on structural grounds. Rather, the main conclusion is that comparisons based on individual linguistic features do not provide a reliable basis for cross-linguistic generalizations.

In the present chapter, these problems have been illustrated through a comparison of two languages. Such issues are even more problematic for comparisons across multiple languages, which would quickly become stuck in a quagmire of decisions regarding the appropriate structures to be included in the analyses.

An alternative approach, adopted in the present book, is to base cross-linguistic comparisons on a prior Multi-Dimensional analysis of each language. Dimensions are particularly well suited to cross-linguistic comparisons because they have their basis in the functions that are well-represented within each language/culture, rather than depending on some externally imposed set of structural criteria.

Although the Multi-Dimensional approach was originally developed for analyses of register variation within a single language, it also provides a powerful analytic tool for cross-linguistic analysis. In particular, the use of dimensions provides a solution to the problem of identifying the appropriate linguistic units to be used for cross-linguistic comparisons. Linguistically, each dimension comprises a set of linguistic features that co-occur frequently in texts; functionally, each dimension reflects a grouping of forms that serve common situational and communicative purposes. The following chapters show that some of these communicative functions appear to be basic to all four cultures and languages investigated here, and thus corresponding dimensions are found in all four languages. Other functions, however, are differently important in various cultures, and the dimensions corresponding to these functions are not equally well represented in all languages.

There are three specific advantages to the use of dimensions for cross-linguistic analyses of register variation:

1 The functional interpretation of dimensions has greater reliability, and greater claims to validity, than the interpretation of individual features. This is because the functional interpretation of each dimension depends on an assessment of the *shared* functions among the set of co-occurring linguistic forms; thus, it is less dependent on the functional interpretation of any individual feature.

2 For quantitative comparisons, the use of dimensions obviates the need to determine the appropriate word basis of each language and to normalize frequency counts to different bases. As discussed in chapter 5, dimensions are based on standardized frequency counts. (Statistical standardization transforms frequency counts to a scale representing their frequency relative to the range of variation for each feature – see chapter 5.) Standardized counts enable meaningful comparisons across linguistic features, across registers, and across languages. Thus, the issue of different normalization bases does not arise.

3 Most importantly, dimensions provide a natural solution to the problem of identifying comparable linguistic structures across languages. That is, dimensions are by definition the functionally important linguistic parameters of variation represented structurally in each language. To the extent that the same functions are realized linguistically across two languages, the corresponding dimensions are comparable. In contrast, there is no basis for claiming that individual linguistic structures defined at some arbitrary

structural level – such as relative clauses, versus all clausal nominal modifiers, versus all clausal and phrasal nominal modifiers – are similarly well defined functionally.

The use of dimensions in effect cancels the requirement that the 'same' linguistic feature be compared cross-linguistically. That is, dimensions can be functionally equivalent across two languages but comprise structurally different linguistic features, depending on the grammatical resources of the language in question. In this case, the cross-linguistic comparison depends on prior language-internal analyses to identify the salient dimensions and to interpret them functionally.

The use of dimensions enables a relatively straightforward assessment of the extent to which two languages are similar in their patterns of register variation. Once the MD analysis of each language is completed, the building blocks for cross-linguistic comparisons are already in place. In particular, three kinds of cross-linguistic relationships are identifiable using MD analyses:

1   a dimension has an approximate one-to-one correspondence functionally across two languages;
2   a dimension in language A collapses multiple functions that are salient in language B, and the single dimension in the first language thus corresponds to two or more dimensions in the second language;
3   a salient function in culture A is minimally relevant in culture B, and thus language A has a dimension not represented in language B.

All three of these possibilities are illustrated in chapters 6–7.

In sum, the use of dimensions provides a solid basis for cross-linguistic analyses of register variation, by identifying the functional parameters that are well represented within each language and then using those parameters for comparison. The following chapters will show the strength of this approach through a cross-linguistic analysis of English, Tuvaluan, Korean, and Somali.

5 Methodology

5.1 Overview of methodology in the Multi-Dimensional approach

The four languages compared in the present book have each been analyzed using the MD approach, following the same methodological steps:

1 Texts were collected, transcribed (in the case of spoken texts), and input into computer. The situational characteristics of each spoken and written register were noted during data collection.
2 Grammatical research was conducted to identify the range of linguistic features to be included in the analysis, together with functional associations of individual features.
3 Computer programs were developed for automated grammatical analysis, to 'tag' all relevant linguistic features in texts.
4 The entire corpus of texts was tagged automatically by computer, and all texts were post-edited interactively to insure that the linguistic features were accurately identified.
5 Additional computer programs were developed and run to compute frequency counts of each linguistic feature in each text of the corpus.
6 The co-occurrence patterns among linguistic features were analyzed, using a factor analysis of the frequency counts.
7 The 'factors' from the factor analysis were interpreted functionally as underlying dimensions of variation.
8 Dimension scores for each text with respect to each dimension were computed; the mean dimension scores for each register were then compared to analyze the salient linguistic similarities and differences among spoken and written registers.

In the present chapter, I discuss each of these methodological steps for each of the four languages. I first briefly describe the text corpora, linguistic features, and computational/statistical techniques used in the MD analysis of each language. Then, in section 5.7, I discuss more general theoretical issues relating to the selection and representativeness of texts and linguistic features in MD analyses.

5.2   The text corpora

The first requirement for the MD analyses of all four languages was to compile a representative text corpus. This task was relatively easy for the synchronic register analysis of English: large corpora of present-day spoken and written English texts were already in existence. However, there were no pre-existing text collections available for the synchronic analyses of Nukulaelae Tuvaluan, Korean, and Somali, or for the diachronic analyses of English and Somali. Thus these MD analyses required extensive preliminary work to identify the salient register distinctions in each case, collect texts from each register, transcribe spoken texts, and enter all texts into a computer. The discussion in sections 5.2.1–5.2.4 briefly presents the corpora for each of the four languages; a fuller discussion of the speech and writing situations represented by these corpora is given in chapter 3.

5.2.1   English

The MD analysis of English presented here actually synthesizes the results of several previous studies. The synchronic analysis of English registers, discussed in chapters 6 and 7, is based on the results of Biber (1988), using the LOB Corpus and London–Lund Corpus. The text type analysis presented in chapter 9, based on the results of Biber (1989), similarly uses the LOB and London–Lund Corpora. In contrast, the diachronic analysis of English register variation, presented in chapter 8, incorporates the findings of several earlier studies: Biber and Finegan (1989a, 1992, 1994b), Biber, Finegan, and Atkinson (1994), Biber et al. (1994), and Atkinson (1992, 1993). Each of these studies is based on a different subcorpus of texts, described below.

For the synchronic MD analyses of English, the task of building a suitable text database was relatively easy, because such corpora were already in existence. In particular, the Brown Corpus, LOB Corpus, and London–Lund Corpus (referred to as LL below), were readily available for this purpose. These corpora are introduced in chapter 2 (section 2.5).

The synchronic MD analyses of English are based on the LOB and LL Corpora. They do not use the Brown Corpus to avoid the confounding influence of dialect differences between British English (in the LOB and LL Corpora) and American English (in the Brown Corpus).[1] The selection of texts used in these studies is summarized in table 5.1.[2]

Table 5.2 summarizes the combined corpus used for the diachronic MD analysis of English in chapter 8. The subcorpus of essays, fiction, and personal letters was compiled by Biber and Finegan for their 1989 study. The texts in this subcorpus represent a convenience sample of

Table 5.1 *Composition of the synchronic corpus of English spoken and written registers. (Based on Biber 1988: table 4.2)*

Register	Number of texts	Approximate number of words
Written texts (categories 1–15 from the LOB corpus)		
1 Press reportage	44	88,000
2 Editorials	27	54,000
3 Press reviews	17	34,000
4 Religion	17	34,000
5 Skills and hobbies	14	30,000
6 Popular lore	14	30,000
7 Biographies	14	30,000
8 Official documents	14	28,000
9 Academic prose	80	160,000
10 General fiction	29	58,000
11 Mystery fiction	13	26,000
12 Science fiction	6	12,000
13 Adventure fiction	13	26,000
14 Romantic fiction	13	26,000
15 Humor	9	18,000
16 Personal letters	6	6,000
17 Professional letters	10	10,000
Total written	340	670,000
Spoken texts (from the London–Lund corpus)		
18 Face-to-face conversation	44	115,000
19 Telephone conversation	27	32,000
20 Public conversations, debates, and interviews	22	48,000
21 Broadcast	18	38,000
22 Spontaneous speeches	16	26,000
23 Planned speeches	14	31,000
Total spoken	141	290,000
Total corpus	481	960,000

well-known authors. The subcorpus of dialogue in drama and dialogue in fiction is also based on a convenience sample of well-known authors, compiled by Tony Greblick at the University of Southern California; this subcorpus was analyzed in Biber and Finegan (1992). The subcorpus of medical research writing was compiled by Atkinson for his 1992 study; this subcorpus comprises ten text samples from the *Edinburgh Medical Journal* at about forty-year intervals, beginning in 1735. The subcorpus of

Table 5.2 *Composition of the historical corpus of English (Based on Biber and Finegan 1989a, 1992; Atkinson 1992, 1993; Biber et al. 1994)*

A. Seventeenth century
    Essays (12 texts): Bacon, Browne, Burton, Butler, Dryden, Hobbes, Locke,
        Mather, Newton, Sprat, Temple
    Fiction narrative (5 texts): Behn, Bunyan
    Letters (9 texts): Strype, Oxinden, Peyton
    Dialogue in drama (4 texts): Congreve, Dryden, Jonson, Shakespeare
    Dialogue in novels (4 texts): Behn, Bunyan, Greene, Nashe
    Scientific research articles from the *Philosophical Transactions of the
        Royal Society of London* (10 texts from 1675)

B. Eighteenth century
    Essays (18 texts): Addison, Boswell, Burke, Cooper, Defoe, Johnson,
        Mandeville, Paine, Pope, Steele, Swift
    Fiction (8 texts): Austen, Defoe, Fielding, Johnson, Swift
    Letters (6 texts): Gray, Jefferson, Junius, Walpole
    Dialogue in drama (4 texts): Gay, Goldsmith, Home, Sheridan
    Dialogue in novels (4 texts): Burney, DeFoe, Fielding, Smollett
    Medical research articles from the *Edinburgh Medical Journal* (10 texts
        from 1735; 10 texts from 1775)
    Scientific research articles from the *Philosophical Transactions of the
        Royal Society of London* (10 texts from 1725; 10 texts from 1775)
    Legal opinions from the Pennsylvania Supreme Court (12 texts; 1750–99)

C. Nineteenth century (to 1865)
    Essays (10 texts): Darwin, Dickens, Emerson, Macaulay, Melville, Mill, Poe,
        Whitman
    Fiction (7 texts): Dickens, Hawthorne, Kingsley, Melville, Mill, Poe
    Letters (6 texts): Dickens, Keats, Lamb, Lincoln, Melville
    Dialogue in drama (7 texts): Boucicoult, Robertson, Taylor, Gillette,
        Jefferson, Ritchie, Smith
    Dialogue in novels (6 texts): Austen, Dickens, Hardy, Hawthorne, Melville,
        Stowe
    Medical research articles from the *Edinburgh Medical Journal* (10 texts
        from 1820; 10 texts from 1864)
    Scientific research articles from the *Philosophical Transactions of the
        Royal Society of London* (10 texts from 1825; 10 texts from 1875)
    Legal opinions from the Pennsylvania Supreme Court
        (22 texts: 1800–99)

scientific research writing was compiled by Atkinson in conjunction with the ARCHER project (see below). This subcorpus consists of ten text samples from the *Philosophical Transactions of the Royal Society of London,* selected at fifty-year intervals beginning in 1675; the subcorpus is analyzed in Atkinson (1993). Finally, the subcorpus of legal opinions, which has not previously been

Table 5.2 (*cont.*)

D. Modern (since 1865)
    Essays (11 texts): Arnold, Crane, Gosse, Hemingway, L. Huxley, Lawrence,
        Orwell, Twain, Woolf
    Fiction (13 texts): Harte, Hemingway, Lawrence, Lewis, Orwell, Steinbeck,
        Twain, Woolf
    Letters (10 texts): Hemingway, Steinbeck, Twain, Woolf
    Dialogue in drama (9 texts): Coward, Maugham, Pinter, Shaw, Miller, O'Neill,
        Rice, Williams, Wilde
    Dialogue in novels (10 texts): Forster, Twain, Stevenson, Joyce, Lawrence,
        Woolf, Dreiser, Hemingway, Mitchell, Steinbeck
    Medical research articles from the *Edinburgh Medical Journal* (10 texts
        from 1905; 10 texts from 1945; 10 texts from 1985)
    Scientific research articles from the *Philosophical Transactions of the
        Royal Society of London* (10 texts from 1925; 10 texts from 1975)
    Legal opinions from the Pennsylvania Supreme Court (23 texts; 1900–90)

    Total historical texts: 360 (*c.* 700,000 words)

analyzed, comprises ten text samples collected for each fifty-year period from the records of the Pennsylvania Supreme Court, beginning in 1750. This subcorpus is taken from the ARCHER corpus (see Biber, Finegan, and Atkinson 1994; Biber *et al.* 1994), which has been compiled as part of an NSF project investigating diachronic register variation in English.[3] Altogether, the combined diachronic corpus considered here contains 360 texts, ranging from approximately 1,000 to 4,000 words in length, for a total of approximately 700,000 words.

5.2.2 Nukulaelae Tuvaluan

The composition of the corpus for Nukulaelae Tuvaluan, developed by Besnier (1988), is summarized in table 5.3. This corpus comprises a total of 222 texts taken from two written and five spoken registers: personal letters, religious sermons, informal conversations, political meetings, maneapa speeches, private-setting speeches, and radio broadcasts. On average, texts are approximately 700 words long, and the complete corpus contains nearly 153,000 words of running text. The texts for two registers – political meetings and radio broadcasts – were taken from a single speech event.

5.2.3 Korean

The composition of the Korean corpus developed by Kim (1990) is summarized in table 5.4. This corpus is similar in size to the Nukulaelae Tuvaluan

Table 5.3 *Composition of the corpus for Nukulaelae Tuvaluan. (Based on Besnier 1988 table 1)*

Register	Number of texts	Approximate number of words
Written texts		
Personal letters	70	31,829
Religious sermons	51	35,947
Spoken texts		
Informal conversations	12	23,390
Political meeting*	19	17,194
Maneapa speeches	34	21,999
Private-setting speeches	22	13,666
Radio broadcast*	14	8,746
Total corpus	222	152,771

Note: *All texts in these registers produced in a single speech event

Corpus, although it is much broader in scope. There are a total of 150 texts in the corpus, split almost evenly between twelve written registers and ten spoken registers. Written registers include newspaper reportage, editorials, novels, college textbooks, official documents, suasive essays, and personal letters; spoken registers include private and public conversations, television dialogue, broadcast news, sports broadcasts, and public speeches. Texts are about 900 words long on average, and the total corpus is nearly 136,000 words in length.

5.2.4 Somali

The composition of the Somali corpus developed by Biber and Hared is presented in tables 5.5 and 5.6. This corpus, which includes both a synchronic and a diachronic component, is larger than the corpora for Tuvaluan and Korean, including roughly the same number of texts as the corpus of English (although texts are shorter, being about 1,000 words on average). The corpus has about the same range of registers as the corpora of English and Korean. The tagged written corpus has 413 texts from 23 registers. Texts were collected from three time periods since the introduction of literacy: 1973–74, 1978–80, and 1987–89. Written registers are taken from seven major domains of use: press, government documents, personal adult writing, educational/academic texts, literature, general writings, and scripted radio broadcasts.

The most recent period is the best represented in the written corpus,

Table 5.4 *Composition of the Korean corpus of spoken and written texts. (Based on Kim 1990 table 3.4)*

Register	Number of texts	Approximate number of words
Written texts		
1 Newspaper reportage	6	6,000
2 Newspaper editorial	6	4,000
3 Novels	10	10,500
4 Literary criticism	5	4,000
5 College textbooks	6	6,500
6 Legal and official documents	10	10,000
7 Popular writing	7	7,000
8 Personal essays	5	5,000
9 Suasive essays	7	7,000
10 Political statements	7	6,000
11 Editorial letters	5	3,000
12 Personal letters	6	4,500
Total written corpus	80	73,500
Spoken texts		
1 Private conversation	10	8,500
2 Public conversation, verbatim-transcribed	8	7,000
3 Public conversation, edited for magazines	5	4,000
4 Television drama	6	6,500
5 Broadcast news	5	4,000
6 Television documentary	5	4,000
7 Television sportscast	5	4,000
8 Public speeches, unscripted	9	8,000
9 Public speeches, scripted	7	7,000
10 Folktale	10	9,000
Total spoken corpus	70	62,000
Total corpus	150	135,500

since these texts were used to analyze the Somali dimensions of variation, providing a synchronic baseline for subsequent analyses of diachronic change. Thus nearly half the texts in the written corpus are from the 1987–89 period. It was more difficult to locate texts from the earlier two periods, and thus the representation is less complete.[4]

Spoken texts were collected from ten registers representing four major domains: conversation and interactive story-telling, speeches (and other monologues), spontaneous radio broadcasts, and formal interactions and meetings. A total of 121 spoken texts have been tagged (approximately

Table 5.5 *Composition of the Somali corpus of written texts, by historical period. (Based on Biber and Hared 1992a, b)*

Register	Number of texts in each period: 1973	1979	1988	Total tagged texts
A. Press (*wargeysyada*)				
News reportage (*war*)	11	10	14	35
Commentary (*faallo*)	11	10	10	31
Letters to the editor (*ra'yiga iyo aqoonta*)	10	10	5	25
General interest articles (*maqaal guud*)	16	16	17	49
Analytical articles (*maqaal gaar*)	10	10	11	31
Announcements (*iidheh iyo ogeysiis*)	10	10	10	30
Serial story (*taxane sheeko*)	7	7	7	21
Sports review (*faaqidaadda ciyaaraha*)	7	7	8	22
B. Government documents (*qoraalo dawladeed*)				
Memos (*wareegto*)	11	(3)	10	21
Political pamphlets (*qoraal barabagaandha*)	(3)	(7)	3	3
Published political speeches (*khudbad siyaasadeed*)	(11)	(1)	5	5
C. Personal adult writing (*qoraalo dadweyne*)				
Letters (*warqad*)	–	2	10	12
Applications or petitions (*arji*)	(3)	–	8	8
D. Educational academic texts (*qoraalo waxbarasho*)				
High-school textbooks (*buug dugsiyada sare*)	–	–	10	10
Theses (*teesooyin*)	–	(10)	10	10
Academic essays (*qoraal cilmiyeed*)	–	–	10	10
E. Literature (*suugaan*)				
General fiction (*sheeko mala-awaal*)	10	8	12	30
Folklore stories (*sheeko-xariir*)	8	–	4	12
F. General writings (*qoraalo guud*)				
Historical writings (*qoraal tariikheed*)	–	6	–	6
General-knowledge books (*qoraal aqoon-guud*)	5	7	–	12
Book introductions (*arar*)	(4)	(5)	5	5
G. Scripted radio broadcasts (*qoraalo raadiyo*)				
News commentary (*faallo war*)	–	–	11	11
Informational programs (*barnaamij*)	–	–	14	14
Total tagged written texts (texts in parentheses are not tagged)	116	103	194	413
Total written texts (Approximate number of words: 480,000)	139	129	215	483

Table 5.6 *Composition of the Somali corpus of spoken texts. (Based on Biber and Hared 1992a, 1992b)*

Register	Number of texts
A. Conversation and story-telling (*sheekayn*)	
Spontaneous narratives (*sheeko*)	20
Non-narrative conversation (*hadal caadi*)	21
B. Speeches (*hadal jeedin*)	
University lectures (*cashar jaamcadeed*)	10
Conference lectures (*lakjar*)	10
Sermons (*wacdi*)	10
Quranic exposition (*tafsiir*)	10
C. Spontaneous radio broadcasts (*hadal raadiyo*)	
Live sports broadcasts (*ciyaar-tebin*)*	10
D. Formal interactions and meetings (*hadal shir*)	
Committee meetings (*shir guddi*)	11
Family meetings (*shir qoys*)*	9
Discussions following lectures (*falanqo lakjar*)	10
Total spoken texts	121
(Approximate number of words: 120,000)	

Note: *Texts for these registers were recorded from a single speech event

120,000 words), although the complete spoken corpus is considerably larger. Only a single sports broadcast and family meeting were recorded for the study, so multiple text samples were taken from these events.

5.3   Linguistic features

A second preliminary task required for each language was to identify the linguistic features to be used in the analyses. The goal here was to be as inclusive as possible, identifying all linguistic features that might have functional associations (including lexical classes, grammatical categories, and syntactic constructions). Thus any feature associated with particular communicative functions, or used to differing extents in different text varieties, was included in the studies. Issues associated with the grouping of linguistic forms into feature classes are discussed further in section 5.7.4. Occurrences of these features are counted in each text of the corpus, providing the basis for all subsequent statistical analyses.

The sections below present summaries of the linguistic features used in the four languages. In the case of English, the identification of functionally important linguistic features was relatively easy due to the large body of previous research studies. These background studies include previous comparisons of spoken and written texts (see, e.g., the survey by Chafe and Tannen 1987), functional studies of particular linguistic features (e.g., Thompson 1983; Altenberg 1984), and descriptive grammars of English (especially Quirk *et al.* 1985). Functional studies relating to the English linguistic features analyzed here are discussed in Biber (1988: appendix II).

In the other three languages, linguistic features were selected on the basis of existing grammatical descriptions, exploratory analyses of texts from different registers, and analogy to functionally relevant features in English. For Nukulaelae Tuvaluan, the primary grammatical source was compiled by Besnier himself (Besnier 1989b). For Korean, Kim relied on standard grammars such as H. Lee (1989) and Nam and Ko (1988). Biber and Hared relied primarily on Saeed (1984, 1987) as the standard grammatical descriptions for Somali (cf. Biber 1992c). It is not possible to present complete structural descriptions of these languages here, but appendices are included at the end of the book that provide fuller descriptions of the linguistic features used in Korean and Somali.

5.3.1 Linguistic features of English

Based on a survey of previous research, the sixty-seven linguistic features listed in table 5.7 were identified as potentially important in English. This table organizes features according to sixteen major grammatical and functional categories:
1 tense and aspect markers;
2 place and time adverbials;
3 pronouns and pro-verbs;
4 questions;
5 nominal forms;
6 passives;
7 stative forms;
8 subordination features;
9 prepositional phrases, adjectives, and adverbs;
10 lexical specificity;
11 lexical classes;
12 modals;
13 specialized verb classes;
14 reduced forms and discontinuous structures;
15 co-ordination;
16 negation.

Table 5.7 *Linguistic features used in the analysis of English*

A. Tense and aspect markers
    1 Past tense
    2 Perfect aspect
    3 Present tense

B. Place and time adverbials
    4 Place adverbials (e.g., *above, beside, outdoors*)
    5 Time adverbials (e.g., *early, instantly, soon*)

C. Pronouns and pro-verbs
    6 First-person pronouns
    7 Second-person pronouns
    8 Third-person personal pronouns (excluding *it*)
    9 Pronoun *it*
    10 Demonstrative pronouns (*that, this, these, those* as pronouns)
    11 Indefinite pronouns (e.g., *anybody, nothing, someone*)
    12 Pro-verb *do*

D. Questions
    13 Direct WH questions

E. Nominal forms
    14 Nominalizations (ending in *-tion, -ment, -ness, -ity*)
    15 Gerunds (participial forms functioning as nouns)
    16 Total other nouns

F. Passives
    17 Agentless passives
    18 *by*-passives

G. Stative forms
    19 *be* as main verb
    20 Existential *there*

H. Subordination features
    21 *that* verb complements (e.g., *I said that he went.*)
    22 *that* adjective complements (e.g., *I'm glad that you like it.*)
    23 WH-clauses (e.g., *I believed what he told me.*)
    24 Infinitives
    25 Present participial adverbial clauses (e.g., *Stuffing his mouth with cookies, Joe ran out the door.*)
    26 Past participial adverbial clauses (e.g., *Built in a single week, the house would stand for fifty years.*)
    27 Past participial postnominal (reduced relative) clauses (e.g., *the solution produced by this process*)
    28 Present participial postnominal (reduced relative) clauses (e.g., *The event causing this decline was . . .*)
    29 *that* relative clauses on subject position (e.g., *the dog that bit me*)
    30 *that* relative clauses on object position (e.g., *the dog that I saw*)
    31 WH relatives on subject position (e.g., *the man who likes popcorn*)
    32 WH relatives on object position (e.g., *the man who Sally likes*)
    33 Pied-piping relative clauses (e.g., *the manner in which he was told*)

Table 5.7 *(cont.)*

34 Sentence relatives (e.g., *Bob likes fried mangoes, which is the most disgusting thing I've ever heard of.*)
35 Causative adverbial subordinator (*because*)
36 Concessive adverbial subordinators (*although, though*)
37 Conditional adverbial subordinators (*if, unless*)
38 Other adverbial subordinators (e.g., *since, while, whereas*)

I. Prepositional phrases, adjectives, and adverbs
    39 Total prepositional phrases
    40 Attributive adjectives (e.g., *the big horse*)
    41 Predicative adjectives (e.g., *The horse is big.*)
    42 Total adverbs

J. Lexical specificity
    43 Type–token ratio
    44 Mean word length

K. Lexical classes
    45 Conjuncts (e.g., *consequently, furthermore, however*)
    46 Downtoners (e.g., *barely, nearly, slightly*)
    47 Hedges (e.g., *at about, something like, almost*)
    48 Amplifiers (e.g., *absolutely, extremely, perfectly*)
    49 Emphatics (e.g., *a lot, for sure, really*)
    50 Discourse particles (e.g., sentence-initial *well, now, anyway*)
    51 Demonstratives

L. Modals
    52 Possibility modals (*can, may, might, could*)
    53 Necessity modals (*ought, should, must*)
    54 Predictive modals (*will, would, shall*)

M. Specialized verb classes
    55 Public verbs (e.g., *assert, declare, mention*)
    56 Private verbs (e.g., *assume, believe, doubt, know*)
    57 Suasive verbs (e.g., *command, insist, propose*)
    58 *seem* and *appear*

N. Reduced forms and dispreferred structures
    59 Contractions
    60 Subordinator *that* deletion (e.g., *I think [that] he went.*)
    61 Stranded prepositions (e.g., *the candidate that I was thinking of*)
    62 Split infinitives (e.g., *He wants to convincingly prove that . . .*)
    63 Split auxiliaries (e.g., *They were apparently shown to . . .*)

O. Co-ordination
    64 Phrasal co-ordination (NOUN *and* NOUN; ADJ; *and* ADJ; VERB *and* VERB; ADV *and* ADV)
    65 Independent clause co-ordination (clause-initial *and*)

P. Negation
    66 Synthetic negation (e.g., *No answer is good enough for Jones.*)
    67 Analytic negation (e.g., *That's not likely*)

Individual forms are grouped into feature classes on the basis of their shared discourse functions (see section 5.7.4 below). Fuller linguistic descriptions of these features are given in Biber (1988: appendix II).

5.3.2   Linguistic features used for Nukulaelae Tuvaluan

Besnier (1988) analyzes the forty-two linguistic features listed in table 5.8 for Tuvaluan. These features represent six major structural categories:

1   pronominal features;
2   nominal features;
3   verbal features;
4   adverbial features;
5   lexical features;
6   derived, compound, and complex clauses and discourse ties.

Besnier also notes that these features represent six major functional categories:

1   involvement and affect (e.g., first- and second-person pronouns, intensifiers);
2   'looser' and 'tighter' information packaging (e.g., focus marking, discourse linkers);
3   evidentiality (e.g., speech act verbs, mental process verbs);
4   structural complexity (e.g., subordinate clauses, nominalizations);
5   informational elaboration (e.g., prepositional phrases);
6   context dependence and interactiveness (e.g., pronouns, questions, quotes).

Many of these features have formal counterparts among the linguistic characteristics of English (e.g., pronouns, speech act verbs, relative clauses). Other Tuvaluan features, though, have no corresponding feature in English; these include the ergative case marker, which indicates high affect (Besnier 1988: 718), and the absolutive/contrastive case marker, which marks contrastive focus (Besnier 1986: 91). Similarly, there are English linguistic features that have no counterpart in Tuvaluan, including passive constructions, perfect aspect, and progressive aspect.

5.3.3   Korean

Table 5.9 lists the fifty-eight linguistic features that Kim analyzed for Korean. These are grouped into eleven major categories indicating their discourse function:

1   lexical elaboration;
2   syntactic complexity;

Table 5.8 *Features used in the analysis of Tuvaluan*

Pronominal features
1 First person singular pronouns *au* or *aku*
2 Second person pronouns *koe* (singular), *koulua* (dual), *koutou* (plural)
3 Third person pronouns *ia* (singular), *laaua* (dual), *laatou* (plural)
4 First person inclusive pronouns *taaua* (dual), *taatou* (plural)
5 First person exclusive pronouns *maaua* (dual), *maatou* (plural)
6 All-purpose anaphoric pronoun *ei*

Nominal features
7 Definite/specific noun phrase
8 Non-specific indefinite noun phrase
9 Anaphoric noun *mea* 'thing, entity, etc.'
10 Possessive noun phrase
11 First person demonstratives *teenei* (singular), *konei* (non-singular)
12 Second person demonstratives *teenaa* (singular), *konaa* (non-singular)
13 Third person demonstratives *teelaa* (singular), *kolaa* (non-singular)
14 Sentence-initial nominal focus marker *ko*
15 Ergative/high-agentivity/high-affect case marker *nee*
16 Absolutive/contrastive case marker *a*
17 Prepositional phrases (with *i* 'at, on, in,' *ki* 'to', etc.)
18 Possessive noun phrases (with *a* 'alienable,' *o* 'inalienable')

Verbal features
19 Non-past tense marker *e*
20 Past tense marker *ne*
21 Inchoative aspect marker *koo*
22 Durative aspect marker *koi*
23 Precautionary mood marker *maa/mana/mane*, etc.
24 Existential verbs *isi, i ai* 'there is', etc.

Adverbial features
25 Hedges *kaati* 'perhaps', *nee* 'tag question', *fua* 'just', etc.
26 Intensifying adverbs *eiloa* 'indeed, very,' *faeola* 'very, constantly', etc.

Lexical features
27 Speech act verbs *muna* 'say', *taku* 'tell', etc.
28 Mental process verbs *maafaufau* 'think', *taaofi* 'hold an opinion', etc.
29 Word length (in phonemes)
30 Type–token ratio (of the first 500 words of text)

Derived, compound, and complex clauses and discourse ties
31 Direct question-word questions
32 Direct yes–no questions
33 Direct quotes (in number of quoted words)
34 Nominalized verbs (suffixed with -V*ga*)
35 Ratio of raised noun phrases to total raising constructions
36 Relative clauses
37 Resultative/summative/reinforcing conjuncts *teenei laa* 'thus', etc.
38 General subordinators *o*, *kee*, etc.

Table 5.8 (*cont.*)

39 'Because' subordinators *me, i te mea*, etc.
40 Conditional clauses
41 Clausal and phrasal coordinators *kae* 'and, but,' *mo* 'and, with'
42 Discourse linkers *ia* 'well,' etc.

3   information structure;
4   situation markers;
5   sociolinguistic indicators;
6   cohesion markers;
7   tense/aspect markers;
8   sentence types;
9   verb types;
10   stance markers;
11   other features.

Some of these categories do not have corresponding categories in English or Tuvaluan: for example, 'speech levels' and formality are marked structurally by several forms in Korean (informal postpositions, formal conjuncts, level 1 formal sentence endings), as are related phenomena indicating the relationship between speaker and hearer (e.g., honorifics, humble expressions). Information structure and cohesion markers are also well-developed structural categories in Korean: for example, topic markers identify a word as topical, while subject markers identify a word as the focus of information. The various conjuncts in Korean (explanative, conditional, etc.) are sentence-initial connectors marking logical relations in texts, while the verbal connectors (explanative, conditional, etc.) are clitics that attach to verbs and combine two clauses in a single sentence. Brief linguistic descriptions of these features are provided in appendix I.

5.3.4 Somali

The linguistic features used by Biber and Hared for the analysis of Somali are listed in table 5.10. In all, sixty-five features were analyzed, representing eleven major categories:

1   dependent clauses;
2   main clause and verbal features;
3   nominal features;
4   pronouns;
5   adjectival features;

Table 5.9 *Features used in the analysis of Korean*

Lexical elaboration
 1 Attributive adjectives
 2 Derived adjectives (*-uj, -cek(in)*)
 3 Manner or degree adverb
 4 Place adverb or noun
 5 Time adverb or noun
 6 Plural marker
 7 Possessive marker
 8 Informal postposition (*hako*)
 9 Formal conjunct
10 Contractions
11 Total nouns

Syntactic complexity
12 Long negation
13 Short negation
14 Relative clauses
15 Noun complementation
16 Verb complementation
17 Embedded or indirect questions
18 Non-finite complementation
19 Quotative complementation
20 Adverbial subordination
21 Sentence length

Information structure
22 Passives
23 Topic markers
24 Subject markers
25 *-ita* as copula

Situation markers
26 Demonstrative or exophoric co-reference
27 Endophoric co-reference
28 First-person personal pronouns
29 Second-person personal pronouns
30 Third-person personal pronouns

Sociolinguistic indicators
31 Honorifics
32 Humble expressions
33 Level 1 speech level – formal sentence ending

Table 5.9 (*cont.*)

Cohesion markers
34 Explanative conjuncts
35 Conditional conjuncts
36 Co-ordinative conjuncts
37 Adversative conjuncts
38 General discourse conjuncts
39 Explanative verbal connectors
40 Conditional verbal connectors
41 Co-ordinative verbal connectors
42 Adversative verbal connectors
43 General discourse verbal connectors

Tense/aspect markers
44 Non-past tense
45 Past tense
46 Progressive aspect

Sentence types
47 Direct questions
48 Imperatives
49 Declarative sentences
50 Fragmentary sentence

Verb types
51 Psychological verbs
52 Speech act verbs
53 Dynamic verbs

Stance markers
54 Hedges
55 Emphatics
56 Attitudinal expressions

Other features
57 Type–token ratio
58 Postposition/case-receivable noun ratio

  6 lexical classes;
  7 lexical choice;
  8 preverbal particles;
  9 reduced and interactive features;
 10 co-ordination;
 11 focus constructions.

There is a rich system of dependent clauses in Somali, built primarily on various kinds of relativization. Features such as the preverbal particles and the multiple distinctions among focus constructions have no

Table 5.10 *List of linguistic features used in the analysis of Somali*

Dependent clauses
  1 Total dependent clauses
  2 Conditional clauses
  3 Purpose clauses
  4 Concessive clauses
  5 Temporal clauses
  6 Framing clauses (similar to non-restrictive relative clauses)
  7 *ah* relative clauses (with a reduced copula and no object)
  8 Full relative clauses
  9 Verb complements (VERB + *in-*)
 10 Demonstrative relative clauses (with demonstrative pronoun as head; concludes a series of relative clauses)
 11 *ahaan* adverbials (e.g., *guud ahaan* 'being general = generally')

Main clause and verbal features
 12 Total main clauses
 13 Average t-unit length (main clause plus associated dependent clauses)
 14 Verbless clauses (with copula deleted)
 15 Independent verbs
 16 Imperatives
 17 Optative clauses (*ha* + VERB- 'let X do Y')
 18 Compound verbs
 19 Present tense (verbs and adjectives)
 20 Past tense (verbs and adjectives)
 21 Possibility modals (*kar-*)
 22 Future modals (*doon-*)
 23 Habitual modals (*lah-*)

Nominal features
 24 Common nouns
 25 Proper nouns
 26 Possessive nouns
 27 Nominalizations (e.g., *-nimo, -tooyo, -aan*)
 28 Verbal nouns (e.g., *-id, -in, -is*)
 29 Agentive nouns (*-e, -te, -to, -so*)
 30 Compound nouns
 31 *-eed* genitives

Pronouns
 32 First-person pronouns (e.g., *ani-, -aan, i* + VERB)
 33 Second-person pronouns (e.g., *adi-, -aad, ku* + VERB)
 34 Third-person pronouns (e.g., *isa-, iya-, -uu, -ay*)

Adjectival features
 35 Derived adjectives (*-(s)an*)
 36 Attributive adjectives
 37 Predicative adjectives

Table 5.10 (*cont.*)

Lexical classes
38 Stance adjectives (e.g., *jecel* 'love', *neceb* 'hate', *hilmaansan* 'forget';
these function as verbs)
39 Stance verbs (e.g., *garo* 'understand', *hilmaan* 'forget', *baq* 'become afraid')
40 Speech act verbs (e.g., *sheeg* 'say', *sharax* 'explain')
41 Time deictics (e.g., *maanta*, 'today', *marar* 'sometimes')
42 Place deictics (e.g., *hoos* 'under', *dib* + VERB 'behind')
43 Downtoners (e.g., *malaha* 'perhaps', *yara* 'just, a little')
44 Amplifiers (e.g., *aad* 'really, very', *shaki la'aan* 'without doubt')
45 Concession conjuncts (*hase yeeshee* 'however', *laakiin* 'however')
46 Reason conjuncts (*waayo* 'the reason (is)', *sidaas darteed* 'as a result')

Lexical choice
47 Word length
48 *hapax legomena* (number of once-occurring words in first 500 words)
49 Type-token ratio (number of different words in first 500 words)

Preverbal particles
50 Single case particles (*u* 'to, for,' *ku* 'in, on, at, by means of', *ka* '(away)
from', *la* 'together with')
51 Case particle sequences (e.g., *uga kaga*)
52 Impersonal particles (*la*)
53 Locative/directional particles (*sii, soo*)

Reduced and interactive features
54 Contractions
55 Yes/no questions (*ma* + VERB)
56 'what if' questions (*soo, sow*)
57 WH questions (*maxaa-* 'what')
58 Simple responses (e.g., *haa* 'yes', *haye* 'ok', *nacam* 'true')

Co-ordination
59 Clause/phrase co-ordination (*oo*)
60 Phrase co-ordination (*iyo*)
61 Contrastive clause co-ordination (*eh*)
62 Clitic topic (clause) co-ordination (*-na, -se*)

Focus constructions
63 *waa* focus markers
64 *baa* focus markers
65 *waxaa* clefts

---

direct counterparts in any of the other three languages; and, as with Tuvaluan and Korean, there are English features (such as passive constructions and perfect aspect) that have no direct counterpart in Somali. Brief linguistic descriptions of the Somali features are provided in appendix II.

5.3.5 Summary of linguistic structures

Although there are marked structural differences across these four languages, there are certain basic grammatical, discourse, and communicative functions that are represented in each of the linguistic inventories. These include features that mark:

structural elaboration and complexity;

lexical elaboration, complexity, and specificity;

place and time reference;

temporal organization of discourse (tense and aspect);

referential cohesion and explicitness;

evidentiality, affect, and stance;

hedging and emphasis;

interactiveness and involvement.

These functions have different structural correlates in the different languages, and they are not equally well developed grammatically. In addition, the following chapters will show that these functions are not equally salient across the languages, although some of them are represented in the dimensions of all four languages.

5.4   Computational tagging tools and frequency counts

Computational tools were developed for all four languages, to 'tag' the words in texts for various lexical, grammatical, and syntactic categories, and to compile frequency counts of linguistic features. The grammatical tagging used in these studies is richer than that used in the Brown and LOB Corpora, in that it marks the word classes and syntactic information required to automatically identify the linguistic features listed in the last section.

The original programs for English were written in PL/1 and used a large-scale dictionary together with a number of context-dependent disambiguating algorithms. The dictionary was complied from a sorted version of the Brown Corpus; it contained 50,624 lexical entries from the four major grammatical categories of noun, verb, adjective, and adverb. Grammatical ambiguities (e.g., *move* as noun and verb) were identified by the existence of multiple entries in the dictionary. Biber (1988: appendix II) provides a fuller description of this tagging program and the algorithms used to identify each linguistic feature.

Besnier developed the tagging program for Tuvaluan in Pascal, to run on desktop computers. This program relies primarily on context-dependent algorithms and does not use an on-line dictionary. In contrast, both the Korean tagging program (developed by Kim and Biber) and the Somali tagging program (developed by Biber) used on-line dictionaries together with context-sensitive disambiguating procedures. These programs, which were also written in Pascal, work in a cyclical fashion to build an on-line dictionary containing an entry for every word in the corpus.[5]

In each of the projects, additional computer programs tally frequency counts of each feature in each text. These counts are normalized to a common basis, to enable comparison across the texts within a language. (Counts are normed to their frequency per 1,000 words of text in the English, Korean, and Somali projects; they are normed per 500 words of text in the Tuvaluan project.[6] The procedure for normalization is described in Biber (1988: 75–76; see chapter 4, note 6).

Tables 5.11, 5.12, and 5.13 present summary descriptive statistics for the normalized frequencies of linguistic features in the corpora of English, Korean, and Somali. (Comparable data are not available for Tuvaluan.) These tables include the mean (or average) frequency for each linguistic feature in the entire corpus, the minimum and maximum frequencies (i.e., the minimum and maximum occurrences of that feature in any text of the corpus), the range (i.e., the difference between the minimum and maximum frequencies), and the standard deviation (a measure of variability; about 68% of the texts in the corpus have frequency scores within the range of plus or minus one standard deviation from the mean score).

Although these tables do not give the relative frequencies of features in different registers, they do enable general comparisons across features and across the languages. For example, nouns are a very common feature in all three languages, but they are considerably more common in Korean and Somali than in English (occurring on average over 300 times per 1,000 words in Korean and Somali, versus an average frequency of 180 in English). Other features are relatively rare, although again they are often not equally rare in the three languages. For example, relative clauses occur only about 5 times per 1,000 words on average in English (combining the five types), versus an average frequency of 28 in Korean, and an average frequency of 57 per 1,000 words in Somali (combining the three types). Second-person pronouns occur on average only 1.7 times per 1,000 words in Korean, with a maximum frequency of 27; this can be contrasted with the average frequencies of 9.9 in English and 14.3 in Somali, which both have maximum frequencies of over 70 second-person pronouns per 1,000 words. These kinds of comparisons can be interesting in raising the issue of why a certain feature should be notably more common in one language than another. They are not directly useful, however, in providing answers to such questions, reinforcing the conclusions of chapter 3. Thus, in the present analyses these frequency counts form the basis for subsequent statistical and linguistic analyses (described in

Table 5.11 *Descriptive statistics for the English corpus as a whole*

Linguistic feature	Mean	Minimum value	Maximum value	Range	Standard deviation
Past tense	40.1	0.0	119.0	119.0	30.4
Perfect aspect verbs	8.6	0.0	40.0	40.0	5.2
Present tense	77.7	12.0	182.0	170.0	34.3
Place adverbials	3.1	0.0	24.0	24.0	3.4
Time adverbials	5.2	0.0	24.0	24.0	3.5
First-person pronouns	27.2	0.0	122.0	122.0	26.1
Second-person pronouns	9.9	0.0	72.0	72.0	13.8
Third-person pronouns	29.9	0.0	124.0	124.0	22.5
Pronoun IT	10.3	0.0	47.0	47.0	7.1
Demonstrative pronouns	4.6	0.0	30.0	30.0	4.8
Indefinite pronouns	1.4	0.0	13.0	13.0	2.0
DO as pro-verb	3.0	0.0	22.0	22.0	3.5
WH questions	0.2	0.0	4.0	4.0	0.6
Nominalizations	19.9	0.0	71.0	71.0	14.4
Gerunds	7.0	0.0	23.0	23.0	3.8
Nouns	180.5	84.0	298.0	214.0	35.6
Agentless passives	9.6	0.0	38.0	38.0	6.6
BY passives	0.8	0.0	8.0	8.0	1.3
BE as main verb	28.3	7.0	72.0	65.0	9.5
Existential THERE	2.2	0.0	11.0	11.0	1.8
THAT verb complements	3.3	0.0	20.0	20.0	2.9
THAT adj. complements	0.3	0.0	3.0	3.0	0.6
WH clauses	0.6	0.0	7.0	7.0	1.0
Infinitives	14.9	1.0	36.0	35.0	5.6
Present participial adv. clauses	1.0	0.0	11.0	11.0	1.7
Past participial adv. clauses	0.1	0.0	3.0	3.0	0.4
Past prt. postnom. clauses	2.5	0.0	21.0	21.0	3.1
Present prt. postnom. clauses	1.6	0.0	11.0	11.0	1.8
THAT relatives: subj. position	0.4	0.0	7.0	7.0	0.8
THAT relatives: obj. position	0.8	0.0	7.0	7.0	1.1
WH relatives: subj. position	2.1	0.0	15.0	15.0	2.0
WH relatives: obj. position	1.4	0.0	9.0	9.0	1.7
WH relatives: pied pipes	0.7	0.0	7.0	7.0	1.1
Sentence relatives	0.1	0.0	3.0	3.0	0.4
Adv. subordinator – cause	1.1	0.0	11.0	11.0	1.7
Adv. sub. – concession	0.5	0.0	5.0	5.0	0.8
Adv. sub. – condition	2.5	0.0	13.0	13.0	2.2
Adv. sub. – other	1.0	0.0	6.0	6.0	1.1
Prepositions	110.5	50.0	209.0	159.0	25.4
Attributive adjectives	60.7	16.0	115.0	99.0	18.8
Predicative adjectives	4.7	0.0	19.0	19.0	2.6
Adverbs	65.6	22.0	125.0	103.0	17.6
Type-token ratio	51.1	35.0	64.0	29.0	5.2

Table 5.11 (cont.)

Linguistic feature	Mean	Minimum value	Maximum value	Range	Standard deviation
Word length	4.5	3.7	5.3	1.6	0.4
Conjuncts	1.2	0.0	12.0	12.0	1.6
Downtoners	2.0	0.0	10.0	10.0	1.6
Hedges	0.6	0.0	10.0	10.0	1.3
Amplifiers	2.7	0.0	14.0	14.0	2.6
Emphatics	6.3	0.0	22.0	22.0	4.2
Discourse particles	1.2	0.0	15.0	15.0	2.3
Demonstratives	9.9	0.0	22.0	22.0	4.2
Possibility modals	5.8	0.0	21.0	21.0	3.5
Necessity modals	2.1	0.0	13.0	13.0	2.1
Predictive modals	5.6	0.0	30.0	30.0	4.2
Public verbs	7.7	0.0	40.0	40.0	5.4
Private verbs	18.0	1.0	54.0	53.0	10.4
Suasive verbs	2.9	0.0	36.0	36.0	3.1
SEEM/APPEAR	0.8	0.0	6.0	6.0	1.0
Contractions	13.5	0.0	89.0	89.0	18.6
THAT deletion	3.1	0.0	24.0	24.0	4.1
Stranded prepositions	2.0	0.0	23.0	23.0	2.7
Split infinitives	0.0	0.0	1.0	1.0	0.0
Split auxiliaries	5.5	0.0	15.0	15.0	2.5
Phrasal coordination	3.4	0.0	12.0	12.0	2.7
Non-phrasal coordination	4.5	0.0	44.0	44.0	4.8
Synthetic negation	1.7	0.0	8.0	8.0	1.6
Analytic negation	8.5	0.0	32.0	32.0	6.1

the following sections), but they are not used for direct cross-linguistic comparisons.

5.5   Identification and interpretation of factors, illustrated through the English factor analysis

As described in chapter 2, co-occurrence patterns are central to MD analyses in that each dimension represents a different set of co-occurring linguistic features. The statistical technique used for identifying these co-occurrence patterns is known as factor analysis, and each set of co-occurring features is referred to as a *factor*. In a factor analysis, a large number of original variables (in this case the linguistic features) are reduced to a small set of derived, underlying variables – the factors. In the present section, I introduce the procedures for interpreting these factors as dimensions and using the dimensions to analyze the relations among registers. The following sections

Table 5.12 *Descriptive statistics for the Korean corpus as a whole. (Based on Kim 1990; table 4.1). Features are listed in the order used on table 5.9. (N = 150. Frequencies are normalized to a text length of 1,000 words)*

Features	Mean	Minimum	Maximum	Range	Standard deviation
ATTR-ADJ	16.98	0.0	55.89	55.89	9.37
DRV-ADJ	6.09	0.0	48.47	48.47	9.25
MANN-ADV	37.14	5.4	90.17	84.72	17.90
*PLACE-ADV	5.54	0.0	38.98	38.98	6.27
TIME-ADV	9.85	0.0	37.29	37.29	7.54
*PLURAL	8.24	0.0	37.43	37.43	7.26
POSSESSIVE	32.38	0.0	91.54	91.54	22.93
INFORML PP	1.92	0.0	18.28	18.28	3.77
FORMAL CNJ	3.75	0.0	37.13	37.13	5.54
CONTRCTNS	6.66	0.0	80.73	80.73	11.76
TOT NOUNS	307.03	181.0	532.82	351.82	74.29
*LONG-NEG	4.38	0.0	19.50	19.50	3.22
SHORT-NEG	7.05	0.0	46.76	46.76	7.78
REL CLS	28.02	0.9	66.85	65.88	14.03
NP COMP	7.48	0.0	28.79	28.79	5.42
VB COMP	18.28	1.1	42.84	41.70	9.04
EMBD QUES	2.33	0.0	17.86	17.86	3.02
NON-FINITE	6.39	0.0	31.29	31.29	4.44
*QUOT CLS	6.83	0.0	27.37	27.37	5.59
S LENGTH	19.90	3.6	79.64	75.94	11.42
PASSIVES	7.91	0.0	42.18	42.18	7.79
*TOPIC MRKR	24.54	1.2	49.87	48.62	9.96
SUBJ MRKR	44.36	4.0	96.81	92.77	16.11
COPULA	15.01	0.0	41.93	41.93	8.79
EXPHOR REF	13.25	0.0	83.08	83.08	12.06
ENPHOR REF	12.85	0.0	48.47	48.47	9.74
*1 PRS PRO	12.34	0.0	45.00	45.00	10.57
*2 PRS PRO	1.73	0.0	27.20	27.20	3.56
*3 PRS PRO	1.93	0.0	21.03	21.03	3.52
HONORIFICS	12.05	0.0	123.87	123.87	21.55
HUMBLE	3.12	0.0	37.23	37.23	6.63
FORMAL END	15.00	0.0	81.36	81.36	21.62
EXPL-CNJ	2.51	0.0	19.46	19.46	3.68
*COND-CNJ	0.32	0.0	4.52	4.52	0.71
*COORD-CNJ	1.31	0.0	11.79	11.79	1.97
ADVERS-CNJ	1.61	0.0	13.56	13.56	2.14
DISC-CNJ	1.22	0.0	14.00	14.00	2.31
EXPL-VB	7.02	0.0	52.30	52.30	8.44
COND-VB	6.95	0.0	28.07	28.07	5.84
COORD-VB	24.00	0.8	76.15	75.29	11.73
*ADVERS-VB	5.00	0.0	19.04	19.04	3.75

Table 5.12 (*cont.*)

Features	Mean	Minimum	Maximum	Range	Standard deviation
DISC-VB	4.19	0.0	30.30	30.30	5.95
ADV SUBORD	15.95	1.5	71.34	69.83	8.44
PRESNT TNS	28.50	1.9	71.30	69.34	16.54
PAST TENSE	21.15	0.0	64.00	64.00	16.71
*PROGRESIVE	4.59	0.0	27.21	27.21	4.83
QUESTIONS	10.36	0.0	110.27	110.27	21.40
*IMPERATIVE	1.95	0.0	16.51	16.51	3.33
DECLARATIV	46.97	13.4	107.10	93.65	18.10
S FRAGMENT	7.45	0.0	85.87	85.87	13.51
PRIVATE VB	8.74	0.0	35.38	35.38	6.42
*PUBLIC VB	6.03	0.0	38.03	38.03	5.92
ACTION VB	39.21	0.0	135.84	135.84	28.64
HEDGES	3.36	0.0	20.43	20.43	3.30
EMPHATICS	9.38	0.0	30.56	30.56	5.81
ATTITUDE	3.98	0.0	14.60	14.60	3.24
TYPE/TOKEN	56.98	37.2	72.25	35.00	6.56
P.P/CASE	66.55	40.0	87.54	47.54	11.66

Note: Features marked with * were dropped from the final factor analysis.

then present a more technical description of the factor analysis for each language. Biber (1988: chapter 5) presents a detailed description of factor analysis intended for linguists, and Gorsuch (1983) provides a good technical description.

Every linguistic feature has a certain amount of variability across the texts of a corpus – the feature will be relatively common in some texts and relatively rare in others: for example, table 5.11 shows that nouns in English range from a minimum of 84 occurrences per 1,000 words in some texts to a maximum of 298 occurrences per 1,000 words in other texts. The *variance* of a feature's distribution measures how dispersed values are across this total range of variation; that is, are most values close to the mean score (in this case 180.5), with only a few extreme values near the minimum and maximum, or are the scores widely scattered, with many texts having values near the minimum and maximum?

When considering a set of linguistic features, each having its own variance, it is possible to analyze the pool of shared variance, that is, the extent to which the features vary in similar ways. Shared variance is directly related to co-occurrence. If two features tend to be frequent in some texts and rare in other texts, then they co-occur and have a high amount of shared variance.

Table 5.13 *Descriptive statistics for the Somali corpus as a whole. (Features are listed in the order used on table 5.10)*

Linguistic feature	Minimum	Maximum	Mean	Standard deviation
Dependent clauses	30.7	182.3	108.4	29.6
Conditional adv. clauses	0.0	25.3	4.3	4.8
Purpose adverbial clauses	0.0	13.9	2.0	2.4
Concessive adv. clauses	0.0	9.4	0.8	1.4
Time adverbial clauses	0.0	32.0	7.3	5.4
Framing clauses	0.0	24.6	4.5	4.4
AH relative clauses	0.0	58.9	16.7	9.9
Full relative clauses	7.4	82.8	38.9	13.8
Verb complement clauses	0.0	48.0	16.6	10.2
TAASOO relative clauses	0.0	11.1	1.1	1.9
AHAAN adverbial clauses	0.0	8.8	1.6	1.9
Main clauses	14.5	202.8	84.9	44.0
T-unit length	4.9	69.0	16.1	9.9
Verbless clauses	0.0	19.4	3.9	3.6
Independent verbs	1.1	184.7	57.0	46.4
Imperatives	0.0	39.8	4.8	6.1
Optative clauses	0.0	11.6	2.1	2.3
Compound verbs	0.0	15.3	4.1	3.5
Present tense forms	43.1	229.9	137.4	34.8
Past tense forms	3.3	150.5	59.0	30.1
Possibility modals	0.0	23.6	4.9	4.2
Future modals	0.0	12.3	1.2	2.0
Habitual modals	0.0	25.9	1.7	3.1
Total other nouns	168.7	396.4	280.4	39.2
Proper nouns	0.0	206.0	32.6	28.8
Possessive nouns	2.9	79.3	18.5	11.2
Nominalizations	0.0	31.2	5.9	6.4
Verbal nouns	0.0	98.2	19.1	17.8
Agentive nouns	0.0	85.3	15.1	15.0
Compound nouns	0.0	66.6	16.9	15.7
-EED genitives	0.0	51.9	8.7	8.8
First-person pronouns	0.0	137.6	32.7	31.5
Second-person pronouns	0.0	73.1	14.3	16.2
Third-person pronouns	13.3	179.5	73.1	26.3
Derived adjectives	1.0	54.3	18.7	8.6
Attributive adjectives	3.3	53.9	23.0	9.2
Predicative adjectives	0.7	29.7	10.6	5.8
Stance adjectives	0.0	12.5	1.6	2.3
Stance verbs	0.0	40.2	13.4	7.8
Speech act verbs	0.0	79.3	13.3	9.6
Time deictics	0.0	33.3	9.7	6.5
Place deictics	0.0	39.5	10.1	6.0

Table 5.13 (*cont.*)

Linguistic feature	Minimum	Maximum	Mean	Standard deviation
Downtoners	0.0	14.9	1.8	2.3
Amplifiers	0.0	31.4	6.5	6.3
Concessive conjuncts	0.0	13.3	3.0	2.4
Reason conjuncts	0.0	9.9	1.7	1.9
Word length	4.3	6.2	5.2	0.4
Once-occurring words	23.0	58.0	39.7	6.0
Type-token ratio	38.0	69.0	55.1	5.0
Single case particles	41.6	122.9	83.3	13.4
Case particle sequences	0.0	33.8	12.8	6.2
Impersonal constructions	2.1	69.6	27.0	12.6
Directional particles	2.2	42.2	15.3	7.6
Contractions	10.6	182.6	76.1	43.7
Yes/no questions	0.0	28.1	4.5	6.6
'What if' questions (SOO)	0.0	7.3	0.4	1.0
WH questions	0.0	15.1	2.7	3.6
Simple responses	0.0	119.6	11.2	25.0
OO co-ordinators	7.9	77.6	29.1	10.3
IYO co-ordinators	0.0	58.0	22.8	10.5
EH co-ordinators	0.0	44.6	5.1	6.8
Clitic (-*NA*) coordinators	1.1	61.4	19.3	9.2
WAA focus markers	0.0	54.5	14.8	12.3
BAA focus markers	0.0	112.5	28.0	25.9
WAXAA clefts	3.2	59.1	23.1	10.7

Factor analysis attempts to account for the shared variance among features by extracting multiple factors, where each factor represents the maximum amount of shared variance that can be accounted for out of the pool of variance remaining at that point. (Thus, the second factor extracts the maximum amount of shared variance from the variability left over after the first factor has been extracted.)

Each linguistic feature has some relation to each factor, and the strength of that relation is represented by *factor loadings*. (The factor loading represents the amount of variance that a feature has in common with the total pool of shared variance accounted for by a factor.) For example, the factor loadings for the factor analysis of English are given in table 5.14. Factor loadings can range from 0.0, which indicates the absence of any relationship, to 1.0, which indicates a perfect correlation. The factor loading indicates the extent to which one can generalize from a factor to a particular linguistic feature, or the extent to which a linguistic feature is representative of the dimension underlying a factor. Put another way, the size of the loading

112   Methodology

Table 5.14 *Rotated factor pattern to identify the dimensions of variation in English (Promax rotation). Features are listed in the order used on tables 5.7 and 5.11)*

LX feature	Factor 1	Factor 2	Factor 3	Factor 4	Factor 5	Factor 6	Factor 7
PAST TENSE	−0.083	0.895	0.002	−0.249	−0.049	−0.052	0.021
PERFECTS	0.051	0.480	0.049	−0.016	−0.101	0.146	0.143
PRES TENSE	0.864	−0.467	−0.008	0.229	−0.006	0.011	0.011
PL ADV	−0.417	−0.060	−0.492	−0.094	−0.067	−0.018	−0.023
TM ADV	−0.199	−0.062	−0.604	−0.020	−0.290	0.116	−0.046
PRO 1	0.744	0.088	0.025	0.026	0.089	−0.008	−0.098
PRO 2	0.860	−0.043	−0.018	0.016	0.007	−0.168	−0.064
PRO 3	−0.053	0.727	−0.074	−0.018	−0.167	−0.076	0.138
PRO IT	0.706	−0.021	−0.038	−0.034	−0.038	0.022	0.060
PRO DEM	0.756	−0.166	−0.001	−0.108	0.004	0.306	−0.077
PRO ANY	0.618	0.046	0.011	0.085	−0.094	−0.085	−0.032
PRO DO	0.821	0.004	0.071	0.049	−0.057	−0.077	−0.056
WH-QUES	0.523	−0.024	0.117	−0.111	−0.032	0.036	−0.094
N-TION	−0.272	−0.237	0.357	0.179	0.277	0.129	−0.019
N-ING	−0.252	−0.127	0.216	0.177	0.087	−0.052	0.052
OTHER N	−0.799	−0.280	−0.091	−0.045	−0.294	−0.076	−0.213
AGLS-PASV	−0.388	−0.145	0.109	0.060	0.430	0.063	−0.057
BY PASV	−0.256	−0.189	0.065	−0.124	0.413	−0.089	−0.045
BE STATIVE	0.713	0.056	0.075	0.008	0.014	0.292	0.180
EX THERE	0.262	0.108	0.113	−0.124	−0.004	0.318	0.017
THAT VB CL	0.045	0.228	0.125	0.265	0.053	0.558	−0.122
THT ADJ CL	−0.124	0.066	−0.080	0.123	0.171	0.360	0.183
WH CL	0.467	0.143	0.221	0.032	−0.050	−0.044	−0.027
INF	−0.071	0.059	0.085	0.760	−0.274	−0.005	−0.074
ADV CL-ING	−0.211	0.392	−0.142	−0.076	0.268	−0.217	0.121
ADV CL-ED	−0.025	−0.154	0.029	−0.050	0.415	−0.142	−0.059
WHIZ -ED	−0.382	−0.336	−0.071	−0.137	0.395	−0.128	−0.103
WHIZ -ING	−0.325	−0.114	0.080	−0.169	0.212	−0.070	−0.093
THTREL SBJ	0.051	−0.036	0.021	0.019	−0.058	0.184	0.033
THTREL OBJ	−0.047	0.053	0.201	0.223	−0.125	0.457	−0.065
WHREL SUBJ	−0.087	−0.067	0.453	−0.027	−0.174	0.228	0.047
WHREL OBJ	−0.072	0.049	0.627	−0.060	−0.083	0.302	0.165
WHREL PIPE	−0.029	0.026	0.606	−0.144	0.046	0.280	0.192
SENT REL	0.550	−0.086	0.152	−0.118	−0.025	0.048	−0.041
ADV CL COS	0.661	−0.080	0.110	0.023	−0.061	0.078	−0.076
ADV CL CON	0.006	0.092	0.100	−0.071	0.010	−0.056	0.300
ADV CL CND	0.319	−0.076	−0.206	0.466	0.120	0.103	−0.007
ADVCL OTHR	−0.109	0.051	−0.018	0.008	0.388	0.102	0.109
PREP	−0.540	−0.251	0.185	−0.185	0.234	0.145	−0.008
ADJ ATTR	−0.474	−0.412	0.176	−0.055	−0.038	−0.064	0.299
ADJ PRED	0.187	0.076	−0.089	0.248	0.311	−0.012	0.210
ADVS	0.416	−0.001	−0.458	−0.020	−0.156	0.053	0.314
TYPETOKN	−0.537	0.058	0.002	−0.005	−0.311	−0.228	0.219

Table 5.14 (*cont.*)

LX feature	Factor 1	Factor 2	Factor 3	Factor 4	Factor 5	Factor 6	Factor 7
WRDLNGTH	−0.575	−0.314	0.270	−0.009	0.023	0.028	0.081
CONJNCTS	−0.141	−0.160	0.064	0.108	0.481	0.180	0.217
DOWNTONERS	−0.084	−0.008	0.021	−0.080	0.066	0.113	0.325
HEDGES	0.582	−0.156	−0.051	−0.087	−0.022	−0.145	0.096
AMPLIFIERS	0.563	−0.156	−0.028	−0.124	−0.124	0.225	−0.018
EMPHATICS	0.739	−0.216	0.015	−0.027	−0.188	−0.087	0.210
DISC PRTCLE	0.663	−0.218	−0.128	−0.029	−0.096	0.165	−0.140
DEMONSTRTV	0.040	−0.062	0.113	0.010	0.132	0.478	0.153
POS MODALS	0.501	−0.123	0.044	0.367	0.122	−0.022	0.115
NEC MODALS	−0.007	−0.107	−0.015	0.458	0.102	0.135	0.042
PRD MODALS	0.047	−0.056	−0.054	0.535	−0.072	0.063	−0.184
PUBLIC VB	0.098	0.431	0.163	0.135	−0.030	0.046	−0.279
PRIVATE VB	0.962	0.160	0.179	−0.054	0.084	−0.049	0.106
SUASIVE VB	−0.240	−0.035	−0.017	0.486	0.051	0.016	−0.237
SEEM/APPEAR	0.054	0.128	0.160	−0.010	0.015	0.045	0.348
CONTRACTNS	0.902	−0.100	−0.141	−0.138	−0.002	−0.057	−0.032
THAT DEL	0.909	0.036	0.098	−0.059	−0.005	−0.178	−0.081
STRAND PREP	0.426	0.007	−0.124	−0.210	0.023	0.340	−0.100
SPLIT INF	DROPPED						
SPLIT AUX	−0.195	0.040	0.012	0.437	0.043	0.120	0.239
PHRS COORD	−0.253	−0.091	0.355	−0.066	−0.046	−0.324	0.126
CLS COORD	0.476	0.041	−0.052	−0.161	−0.139	0.218	−0.125
SYNTH NEG	−0.232	0.402	0.046	0.133	−0.057	0.176	0.110
ANLYTC NEG	0.778	0.149	0.017	0.125	0.019	0.001	0.037

reflects the strength of the co-occurrence relationship between the feature in question and the total grouping of co-occurring features represented by the factor.

As table 5.14 shows, each linguistic feature has some loading (or *weight*) on each factor.[7] However, when interpreting a factor, only features with salient or important loadings are considered. In the present analyses, features with loadings smaller than 0.35 are considered not important in the interpretation of a factor.[8] Thus for factor 1 on table 5.14, the salient loadings include PRES TENSE (0.864), PL ADV (−0.417), PRO 1 (0.744), PRO 2 (0.860), PRO IT (0.706), PRO DEM (0.756), PRO ANY (0.618), etc. Positive or negative sign does not influence the importance of a loading; for example, nouns (OTHER N), with a loading of −0.799, have a larger weight on factor 1 than first-person pronouns (PRO 1), with a loading of 0.744. Rather than reflecting importance, positive and negative signs identify two groupings of features that occur in a complementary pattern as part of the same factor. That is, when the features with positive loadings occur together frequently

Table 5.15 *Summary of the factorial structure for dimension 1 (factor 1) of the English study*

Dimension 1	
Private verbs	0.96
THAT deletion	0.91
Contractions	0.90
Present tense verbs	0.86
Second-person pronouns	0.86
DO as pro-verb	0.82
Analytic negation	0.78
Demonstrative pronouns	0.76
General emphatics	0.74
First-person pronouns	0.74
Pronoun IT	0.71
BE as main verb	0.71
Causative subordination	0.66
Discourse particles	0.66
Indefinite pronouns	0.62
General hedges	0.58
Amplifiers	0.56
Sentence relatives	0.55
WH questions	0.52
Possibility modals	0.50
Non-phrasal co-ordination	0.48
WH clauses	0.47
Final prepositions	0.43
(Adverbs	0.42)
Nouns	−0.80
Word length	−0.58
Prepositions	−0.54
Type−token ratio	−0.54
Attributive adjectives	−0.47
(Place adverbials	−0.42)
(Agentless passives	−0.39)
(Past participial postnominal clauses	−0.38)

in a text, the features with negative loadings are markedly less frequent in that text, and vice versa.

Table 5.15 presents only the features having salient loadings on factor 1 – that is, this table lists all features that have loadings greater than 0.35 on factor 1 (from table 5.14). The interpretation of a factor as a functional dimension is based on (1) analysis of the communicative function(s) most widely shared by the set of co-occurring features defining a factor, plus (2) analysis of the similarities and differences among registers with respect to the factor.

Factor interpretations depend on the assumption that linguistic co-occurrence patterns reflect underlying communicative functions. That is, particular sets of linguistic features co-occur frequently in texts because they serve related sets of communicative functions. In the interpretation of a factor, it is important to consider the likely reasons for the complementary distribution between positive and negative feature sets as well as the reasons for the co-occurrence patterns within those sets.

The procedure for factor interpretation can be illustrated through consideration of the co-occurring features on English factor 1, presented in table 5.15. A full interpretation of this dimension is given in chapter 6, including discussion of the defining features in several illustrative text samples.

The first step in the interpretation of a factor is to assess the functions shared by the co-occurring features. On factor 1, the interpretation of the features having negative loadings is relatively straightforward because they are relatively few in number. Nouns, word length, prepositional phrases, type–token ratio, and attributive adjectives all have negative loadings larger than $|0.45|$, and none of these features has a larger loading on another factor. High frequencies of all these features indicate an informational focus and a careful integration of information in a text. These features are associated with texts that have an informational focus and provide ample opportunity for careful integration of information and precise lexical choice. Text sample 5.1 illustrates these co-occurring linguistic characteristics in an academic article:

Text sample 5.1: Technical academic prose

> Apart from these very general group related aspects, there are also individual aspects that need to be considered. Empirical data show that similar processes can be guided quite differently by users with different views on the purpose of the communication.

This text sample is typical of written expository prose in its dense integration of information: frequent nouns and long words, with most nouns being modified by attributive adjectives or prepositional phrases (e.g., *general group related aspects, individual aspects, empirical data, similar processes, users with different views on the purpose of the communication*).

The set of features with positive loadings on factor 1 is more complex, although all of these features have been associated in one way or another with an involved, non-informational focus, related to a primarily interactive or affective purpose and on-line production circumstances. For example, first- and second-person pronouns, WH questions, emphatics, amplifiers, and sentence relatives can all be interpreted as reflecting interpersonal interaction and the involved expression of personal feelings and concerns.

Other features with positive loadings on factor 1 mark a reduced surface form, a generalized or uncertain presentation of information, and a generally 'fragmented' production of text; these include *that*-deletions, contractions, pro-verb DO, the pronominal forms, and final (stranded) prepositions. In these cases, a reduction in surface form also results in a more generalized, less explicit content. Text sample 5.2 illustrates the use of the linguistic characteristics that co-occur with positive loadings in a formal conversation (an interview):

Text sample 5.2: Formal conversation

    B: come in - come in - - ah good morning
    A: good morning
    B: you're Mrs Finney
    A: yes I am
    B: how are you - my name's Hart and this is Mr Mortlake
    C: how are you
    A: how do you do
    B: won't you sit down
    A: thank you - -
    B: mm well you are proposing - taking on - quite something Mrs Finney aren't you
    A: yes I am
    B: mm
    A: I should like to anyhow
    B: you know what you'd be going into
    A: yes I do

This text sample is typical of face-to-face interactions in showing frequent questions, first- and second-person pronouns, and other direct references to the immediate participants. The sample also illustrates the effects of on-line production, as reflected in frequent contractions and the use of general referring expressions (e.g., *taking on quite something*). The negative features grouped on factor 1 are notably absent in this text. There are few lexical nouns (as opposed to pronouns) in this interaction, and the ones that do occur are often part of formulaic expressions (e.g., *good morning*). There are also few attributive adjectives and prepositional phrases.

Overall, based on both positive and negative co-occurring linguistic features, factor 1 seems to represent a dimension marking affective, inter-actional, and generalized content (the features with positive loadings, above the dashed line in table 5.15) versus high informational density and exact informational content (the features with negative loadings, below the dashed line). Two separate communicative parameters seem to be represented here:

the primary purpose of the writer/speaker (informational versus involved), and the production circumstances (those enabling careful editing possibilities versus those dictated by real-time constraints). Reflecting both of these parameters, the interpretive label 'Involved versus Informational Production' can be proposed for the dimension underlying this factor.

This interpretation is supported by the characterization of registers with respect to the dimension. That is, it is possible to compute *dimension scores* for each text and to compare texts and registers with respect to those scores.

The frequency counts of individual linguistic features might be considered as scores that can be used to characterize texts (e.g., a noun score, an adjective score, etc.). In a similar way, *dimension scores* (or *factor scores*) can be computed for each text by summing the frequencies of the features having salient loadings on that dimension. In the English study, only features with loadings greater than $|0.35|$ on a factor were considered important enough to be used in the computation of factor scores. For example, the dimension 1 score for each text is computed by adding together the frequencies of private verbs, *that* deletions, contractions, present tense verbs, etc. – the features with positive loadings on factor 1 (from table 5.15) – and then subtracting the frequencies of nouns, word length, prepositions, etc. – the features with negative loadings.

In all four MD studies, frequencies are standardized to a mean of 0.0 and a standard deviation of 1.0 before the dimension scores are computed. This process translates the scores for all features to scales representing standard deviation units. Thus, regardless of whether a feature is extremely rare or extremely common in absolute terms, a standard score of $+1$ represents one standard deviation unit above the mean score for the feature in question. That is, standardized scores measure whether a feature is common or rare in a text relative to the overall average occurrence of that feature. The raw frequencies are transformed to standard scores so that all features on a factor will have equivalent weights in the computation of dimension scores. (If this process was not followed, extremely common features would have a much greater influence than rare features on the dimension scores.) The methodological steps followed to standardize frequency counts and compute dimension scores are described more fully in Biber (1988: 93–97).

Once a dimension score is computed for each text, the mean dimension score for each register can be computed. Plots of these dimension scores then allow linguistic characterization of any given register, comparison of the relations between any two registers, and a fuller functional interpretation of the underlying dimension. For example, consider figure 5.1, which plots the mean dimension scores of six English registers on dimension 1. The registers with large positive values (such as conversation), have high frequencies of present tense verbs, private verbs, first- and second-person

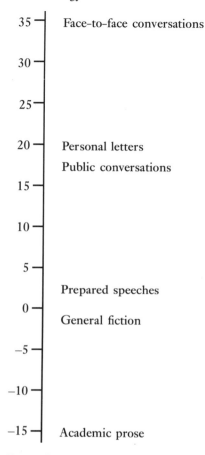

35 ─┤   Face-to-face conversations

30 ─┤

25 ─┤

20 ─┤   Personal letters
         Public conversations

15 ─┤

10 ─┤

5 ─┤

         Prepared speeches
0 ─┤
         General fiction

−5 ─┤

−10 ─┤

−15 ─┤   Academic prose

Figure 5.1 Mean scores of English dimension 1 for six registers. (Dimension 1: 'Involved versus Informational Production.') ($F = 111.9$, $p < 0.0001$, $r^2 = 84.3\%$)

pronouns, contractions, etc. – the features with salient positive weights on dimension 1. At the same time, registers with large positive values have markedly low frequencies of nouns, prepositional phrases, long words, etc. – the features with salient negative weights on dimension 1. Registers with large negative values (such as academic prose) have the opposite linguistic characteristics: very high frequencies of nouns, prepositional phrases, etc., plus low frequencies of private verbs, contractions, etc.

The relations among registers shown in figure 5.1 confirm the interpretation of dimension 1 as distinguishing among texts according to an involved versus informational production. Conversational texts are largely interactive and involved, since participants typically are not inclined to highly informational purposes, nor do they have time for careful, highly informational production. Conversations thus have frequent occurrences of present tense verbs, private verbs, first- and second-person pronouns, contractions, and the other positive features on dimension 1, coupled with relatively infrequent occurrences of nouns, prepositional phrases, long words, and the other negative features on dimension 1. Registers such as public conversations (interviews and panel discussions) are intermediate because they have a relatively informational purpose but participants are constrained by on-line production and actively interacting with one another. Finally registers such as academic prose are non-interactive but extremely informational in purpose, produced under highly controlled and edited circumstances.

The statistics given for F, p, and r^2 at the bottom of figure 5.1 show that dimension 1 is a strong predictor of register differences in English.[9] The F and p values give the results of an ANOVA, which tests whether there are statistically significant differences among the registers with respect to their dimension 1 scores. A p value smaller than 0.001 means that it is highly unlikely that the observed differences are due to chance (less than 1 chance in 1,000). The value for r^2 is a direct measure of importance. The r^2 value measures the percentage of the variance among dimension scores that can be predicted by knowing the register categories. In the case of dimension 1, 84.3 percent of the variation in the dimension scores of texts can be accounted for by knowing the register category of each text. These statistics show that dimension 1 is a significant as well as very powerful predictor of register differences in English. In the dimensional plots given in chapter 6, similar statistics are reported for each dimension in each language. All of these dimensions are significant predictors of register differences, and most of them are quite strong as well, with r^2 values over 50 percent.

The discussion of dimension 1 here has been necessarily brief, since it serves only to illustrate the interpretive process. A full interpretation, including discussion of dimension 1 features in text samples from several registers, is given in chapter 6.

Similarly, this process of interpretation can be followed for each dimension in each of the four languages. A joint consideration of all dimensions in a language then enables an overall analysis of the multidimensional patterns of register variation. Chapter 6 presents such analyses for each language, as the basis for the cross-linguistic comparisons in chapter 7.

The following sections of the present chapter summarize the technical details of the factor analyses in each language, providing further background

Table 5.16 *First eleven eigenvalues of the unrotated factor analysis for English.*
(Based on Biber 1988: table 5.1)

Factor number	Eigenvalue	Percentage of shared variance
1	17.67	26.8
2	5.33	8.1
3	3.45	5.2
4	2.29	3.5
5	1.92	2.9
6	1.84	2.8
7	1.69	2.6
8	1.43	2.2
9	1.32	2.0
10	1.27	1.9
11	1.23	1.9

information for interested readers. This information is not required to understand the analyses in chapter 6, however.

5.6   Summary of technical information concerning the factor analyses

5.6.1   English

The primary factor analysis for English (Biber 1988) has already been discussed above. There are a number of technical details that can be added, however. The first concerns the decision to extract seven factors. Factor analysis is an exploratory technique, and although the procedure provides precise estimates of the association between linguistic features and dimensions (the factor loadings), there is no mathematically exact method for determining the number of factors to be extracted. Rather, several indicators are compared to decide on the optimal solution.

First, the eigenvalues for each subsequent factor are considered (presented in a table or a 'scree plot'). Eigenvalues measure the additional amount of shared variance accounted for by each subsequent factor, and they can thus be used to indicate the point in the analysis where extracting additional factors contributes little additional information. Table 5.16 presents the eigenvalues for the first eleven factors in the factor analysis for English. The first factor accounts for the most shared variance by far: 26.8 percent. The second, third, and fourth factors also account for relatively large amounts of shared variance (8.1, 5.2, and 3.5 percent respectively), but the amount of additional shared variance accounted for by additional factors drops off after that point.

A second piece of information comes from a consideration of the factorial structure for each of the solutions. In the English analysis, solutions for 4, 5, 6, 7, and 8 factors were considered, to assess whether plausible interpretations were possible in each case. This whole process is guided by the general principle that it is better to extract too many factors than too few. Extracting too few factors can result in the loss of information, because the factorial structure will probably fail to represent some underlying constructs, and distinct constructs will probably be collapsed into single factors. In contrast, the main risk associated with overfactoring is that one or two factors will be uninterpretable; these factors can be discarded, with no adverse influence on the overall factorial structure. In the present case, these various considerations pointed to the seven-factor solution as optimal. Together, the seven factors accounted for approximately 52 percent of the total shared variance.[10]

An additional step in the analysis involves rotation of the factors. Because a principal factor analysis operates in such a way that the first factor extracts the maximum amount of variance, most features end up loading on this factor. In addition, most features will have relatively small, but not trivial, loadings on many factors in the initial factor solution. Both of these characteristics partially obscure the basic constructs underlying the factors, making interpretation of the factors difficult. To compensate for this problem, factors can be 'rotated' to a structure in which each feature loads on as few factors as possible, and each factor is characterized by the relatively few features that are most representative of the underlying construct.

Two rotation techniques are commonly used: Varimax and Promax. Varimax maintains orthogonal structure, based on the assumption that the underlying constructs are completely independent, while Promax permits minor correlations among the factors. Because many of the underlying constructs in MD analyses can be inter-related, a Promax rotation is the more appropriate choice. The intercorrelations among factors are generally small. Table 5.17 presents the correlations among factors in the English analysis; the largest inter-factor correlations are between factors 1 and 3 (−0.49), factors 2 and 3 (−0.34), and factors 3 and 5 (0.30). The factor loadings presented in table 5.14 (discussed in section 5.5) show the factorial structure of the Promax-rotated solution.

The interpretations of each dimension presented in chapter 6 are based on tables that include only the salient factor loadings on each dimension. Similar to table 5.15 discussed above, these tables present all features that have loadings greater than $|0.35|$. Features with loadings between $|0.30|$ and $|0.35|$ are included in parentheses; these are relevant for the

Table 5.17 *Inter-factor correlations in the Promax rotation of the factor analysis for English. (Based on Biber 1988: table 5.2)*

	Factor 1	Factor 2	Factor 3	Factor 4	Factor 5	Factor 6	Factor 7
Factor 1	1.00						
Factor 2	0.24	1.00					
Factor 3	−0.49	−0.34	1.00				
Factor 4	0.17	0.12	0.12	1.00			
Factor 5	−0.23	−0.21	0.30	0.16	1.00		
Factor 6	0.16	−0.24	0.01	0.00	0.05	1.00	
Factor 7	−0.01	−0.01	−0.10	0.24	−0.05	−0.09	1.00

factor interpretations, but they are less important than features with larger loadings. Features with loadings of less than $|0.35|$ were not used in the computation of factor scores. In addition, features with a larger loading on another dimension were not used in the computation of factor scores (e.g., present tense verbs on dimension 2, due to the larger loading on dimension 1).[11]

Table 5.14, which presents the complete English factor analysis, shows that the first five factors in this case are well represented, while factors 6 and 7 have enough moderately large loadings to suggest tentative interpretations. Factor 1 is very strong, with 30 features having loadings over $|0.40|$. Factors 2–5 are less well represented than factor 1, but they have sufficient large loadings to make their interpretation straightforward (i.e., 5–6 features with loadings over $|0.40|$ and another 1–2 features with loadings between $|0.35|$ and $|0.40|$. Factors 6 and 7 have fewer large loadings (three over $|0.40|$ on factor 6; none on factor 7), but they each have several moderate loadings between $|0.30|$ and $|0.40|$ (six on factor 6 and five on factor 7). The next chapter will consider the interpretation of each of these dimensions in turn.[12]

5.6.2 Nukulaelae Tuvaluan

Table 5.18 presents the factorial structure used to analyze the relations among registers in Nukulaelae Tuvaluan. Besnier (1988) extracted five factors for analysis, although only the first three are interpreted. (The eigenvalues are not given in this case.) A Varimax rotation was chosen, so the factors in the final solution are uncorrelated.[13]

Table 5.18 shows that the first two factors are well-represented in the factorial structure of Tuvaluan, and factors 3 and 4 are relatively well represented. Factor 1 has 13 features with loadings greater than $|0.40|$,

Table 5.18 *Factorial structure of the Varimax rotation for Nukulaelae Tuvaluan. (Based on Besnier 1988 table 3)*

Features	Factor 1	Factor 2	Factor 3	Factor 4	Factor 5
Adverbs	0.71	−0.02	−0.12	0.06	−0.08
Hedges	0.70	−0.19	0.20	−0.18	0.06
Third-person demonstratives	0.57	0.35	0.24	0.14	0.29
Discourse linkers	0.55	−0.14	−0.26	0.08	−0.09
First-person demonstratives	0.55	0.02	0.01	0.02	−0.06
Second-person demonstratives	0.51	0.13	0.10	0.14	0.30
Intensifying adverbs	0.47	−0.27	0.02	−0.30	0.18
Resultative conjuncts	0.45	−0.04	−0.11	0.07	−0.19
Third-person pronouns	−0.45	0.40	0.11	−0.02	−0.03
Ergative case markers	−0.43	0.01	0.09	0.40	0.13
Nominal focus markers	−0.42	0.41	0.05	0.05	0.05
First-person incl. pronouns	0.42	0.26	−0.22	0.36	−0.10
Possessive noun phrases	−0.15	0.69	−0.14	−0.16	0.05
Definitive noun phrases	−0.30	0.69	0.06	0.14	0.15
Second-person deictic adverbs	0.13	−0.58	−0.20	−0.04	0.05
First-person pronouns	0.01	−0.57	−0.06	−0.03	0.15
Prepositions	0.27	0.56	−0.36	−0.25	0.14
Nominalized verbs	0.11	0.54	−0.12	0.11	0.42
Second-person pronouns	−0.17	−0.53	0.06	0.23	0.00
Co-ordinators	0.04	−0.44	−0.01	−0.12	0.07
Question-word questions	−0.29	0.15	0.65	−0.04	−0.02
Yes–no questions	0.13	−0.11	0.61	−0.18	0.05
Word length	0.03	0.18	−0.57	−0.01	0.08
Direct quotes	−0.46	0.16	0.50	0.00	−0.09
Subordinators	−0.26	−0.36	−0.41	0.09	0.09
Non-past tense markers	−0.27	0.06	0.23	0.62	0.14
Relative clauses	0.12	0.29	−0.15	0.54	−0.17
Raised noun phrases	−0.12	0.03	0.00	0.45	−0.03
Anaphoric nouns	0.13	0.19	0.33	0.41	0.11
Existential verbs	0.06	−0.08	0.04	0.03	0.73
Indefinite noun phrases	−0.26	0.07	−0.05	0.19	0.57
Anaphoric pronouns	−0.30	0.16	0.04	0.17	0.00
First-person deictic adverbs	0.06	−0.33	0.03	−0.20	−0.07
Inchoative aspect markers	0.07	−0.33	0.08	−0.27	−0.24
Speech act verbs	−0.17	0.05	0.33	0.00	0.04
Type-token ratio	0.01	−0.10	0.30	0.17	0.06
Mental process verbs	−0.11	0.08	−0.26	0.34	0.17
Past tense markers	−0.12	0.09	−0.01	−0.33	0.02
Conditional clauses	−0.19	−0.28	0.18	0.30	0.24
Negation	0.06	−0.38	0.19	−0.06	0.38
Absolutive case markers	−0.17	0.16	0.28	0.10	−0.37
'Because' subordinators	−0.27	0.21	−0.30	0.24	0.37

Table 5.19 *Factorial structure of the Promax rotation for Korean (based on Kim 1990 table 3.2). Features are listed in the order used on table 5.9*

	Factor 1	Factor 2	Factor 3	Factor 4	Factor 5	Factor 6
ATTR ADJ	−0.50214	−0.19793	0.26930	0.01361	0.11719	−0.10770
DRV ADJ	−0.16399	−0.35427	0.26237	−0.23079	−0.15287	−0.16070
MANN ADV	0.24408	0.47466	0.19313	0.22423	−0.03193	−0.04721
PLACE ADV	-------DROPPED-------					
TIME ADV	0.26448	−0.26193	0.05215	0.45674	0.01557	0.41597
PLURALS	-------DROPPED-------					
POSSES	−0.39321	−0.40542	−0.05888	−0.28919	0.00771	−0.14128
INFRML PP	0.57266	0.13960	0.16904	0.12549	−0.11882	0.05815
FRML CNJ	−0.00704	−0.22213	−0.19314	−0.39609	0.02851	−0.04519
CONTRACT	0.80135	0.12321	0.25874	−0.06816	−0.05121	−0.13828
TOT NOUN	−0.07804	−0.50866	−0.53682	−0.08390	−0.16511	−0.02624
LONG NEG	-------DROPPED-------					
SHRT NEG	0.67562	0.03397	0.39954	0.00990	0.04679	−0.17135
REL CLS	−0.52800	−0.29465	−0.10475	0.17483	0.07754	−0.16732
NP COMP	−0.41803	0.02627	0.35198	−0.11896	−0.00661	0.02992
VB COMP	−0.02431	−0.00234	0.70416	−0.16792	−0.04517	0.01799
EMBD QUES	0.07196	0.24410	0.39640	0.08682	−0.12416	0.11429
NON FINI	−0.42656	−0.17486	0.32786	−0.05289	−0.04268	0.00733
QUOT CLS	-------DROPPED-------					
S LENGTH	−0.47729	−0.13283	0.07582	−0.13344	−0.47807	0.03267
PASSIVES	−0.22794	−0.39382	0.02158	−0.09625	−0.10695	−0.19261
TOPIC MRK	-------DROPPED-------					
SUBJ MRKR	−0.15732	0.70710	0.11049	−0.03586	0.27345	0.10441
COPULA	−0.08262	0.00640	0.27720	0.03576	0.58877	−0.09217
EXPHR REF	0.42435	0.33588	−0.05670	−0.26872	0.01536	−0.05844
ENPHR REF	0.05363	0.49914	0.29473	−0.08321	−0.09845	−0.07683
1 PRS PRO	0.02257	0.12991	0.36067	0.18117	0.07639	0.39163
2 PRS PRO	-------DROPPED-------					
3 PRS PRO	−0.42475	0.03924	0.13983	0.21125	0.04704	−0.11235
HONORIFIC	0.02287	0.10945	0.05515	−0.10666	0.08797	0.79152
HUMBLE	0.04604	0.04537	0.06990	0.00117	−0.10306	0.78446
FORML END	−0.17162	0.04704	−0.17618	−0.06894	0.49263	0.43419
EXPL CNJ	0.22450	0.67230	0.02996	−0.20572	−0.08086	0.12103
COND CNJ	-------DROPPED-------					
COORD CNJ	-------DROPPED-------					
ADVRS CNJ	−0.21725	−0.15348	0.17596	0.08705	0.35622	−0.02694
DISC CNJ	0.42042	0.32496	0.11238	−0.04774	−0.02683	0.14346
EXPL VB	0.09591	0.79828	−0.10435	0.09505	−0.10803	−0.02191
COND VB	0.23664	0.42855	0.17715	−0.15860	0.25379	−0.11335
CORD VB	−0.26766	0.54196	0.01634	0.02345	−0.11404	0.00768
ADVRS VB	-------DROPPED-------					
DISC VB	0.37493	0.58375	−0.04045	0.03957	−0.10007	−0.08221
ADV SUBRD	−0.17697	0.66364	−0.07606	0.13775	−0.22507	0.10049

Table 5.19 (*cont.*)

	Factor 1	Factor 2	Factor 3	Factor 4	Factor 5	Factor 6
PRES TNS	0.10422	−0.18944	−0.04045	−0.43784	0.68184	0.07758
PAST TNS	−0.14282	0.13299	−0.01250	0.78528	0.00634	0.02314
PROGRESS	-------DROPPED-------					
QUESTION	0.81306	−0.18158	0.27119	−0.02167	0.06699	0.05715
DECLARA	0.24516	−0.14764	−0.09461	0.20327	0.80062	0.04939
S FRAGMENT	0.78071	−0.11383	−0.13101	−0.06070	0.17926	−0.13167
PRV VB	−0.18608	0.00836	0.49723	0.19823	0.14441	0.27399
PUB VB	-------DROPPED-------					
ACT VB	0.19560	0.55429	−0.26286	0.45476	−0.02041	−0.28092
HEDGES	0.34831	0.02293	0.42371	0.05646	−0.03670	0.18307
EMPHATICS	−0.01674	−0.07445	0.69687	0.25227	0.12626	−0.04363
ATTITUDE	−0.07273	−0.01046	0.54907	0.11057	−0.03386	−0.00695
TYP–TOKEN	−0.12946	−0.14032	0.34165	0.73459	−0.03155	−0.09743
PP/CASE	−0.71932	0.47408	0.33062	−0.09633	0.23427	−0.11808

and 15 features with loadings greater than $|0.30|$. Factor 2 is nearly as strong, with 10 features having loadings greater than or equal to $|0.40|$, and 15 features having loadings greater than $|0.30|$. Factors 3 and 4 are represented by fewer features: both have 5 features with loadings over $|0.40|$, and a total of 10 features with loadings over $|0.30|$. In contrast, factor 5 is not well represented, with only 3 features having loadings over $|0.40|$ and a total of 7 features having loadings over $|0.30|$. Besnier (1988) interprets only the first three factors in his analysis, considering only features with loadings greater than $|0.40|$. However, in the following interpretation of Tuvaluan dimensions (in chapters 6 and 7), I extend the analysis to include brief mention of all features having loadings over $|0.30|$ as well as a brief discussion of factor 4.

5.6.3   Korean

The overall factorial structure for the forty-six linguistic features analyzed in Korean is given in table 5.19, with the eigenvalues for the first eleven factors from this analysis being given in table 5.20. Using the same criteria as the analyses for English and Tuvaluan (i.e., consideration of the eigenvalues and ability to interpret the structure for each solution), six factors were extracted as the optimal solution in this case. Together, the six factors account for approximately 58% of the total shared variance. The solution presented in table 5.19 has been rotated using a Promax rotation, although Kim does not present the intercorrelations among factors.

Table 5.20 *First eleven eigenvalues of the unrotated factor analysis for Korean. (Based on Kim 1990: table 3.1)*

Factor number	Eigenvalue	Percentage of shared variance
1	12.06	26.2
2	4.40	9.6
3	3.41	7.4
4	2.64	5.7
5	2.22	4.8
6	2.18	4.7
7	1.55	3.4
8	1.36	3.0
9	1.25	2.7
10	1.20	2.6
11	1.08	2.3

In the factorial structure of the Korean analysis (table 5.19), all six factors are relatively well represented. Factor 1 has fourteen features with loadings over |0.40|, and factor 2 has thirteen features with loadings over |0.40|. Factors 3–6 have successively fewer strong loadings: factor 3 has eight loadings over |0.40|; factor 4 has six strong loadings; factor 5 has five strong loadings; and factor 6 has only four loadings over |0.40|. All of these factors are sufficiently well represented to enable dimension interpretations, however.

5.6.4 Somali

Finally, the factorial structure for Somali is given in table 5.21, and the eigenvalues for the first eleven factors are given in table 5.22. In this case, six factors were extracted for the final analysis; together, these account for approximately 53% of the total shared variance.

The factors were rotated using a Promax rotation, and the inter-factor correlations are given in Table 5.23. The largest correlations are between factors 1 and 2 (−0.545), factors 1 and 5 (0.517), and factors 4 and 5 (0.499).

Similar to the factor structures for the other languages, table 5.21 shows that the first factor in the Somali analysis is very well represented, while all six factors are sufficiently strong to be interpreted. For example, the first factor has twenty-eight features with loadings over |0.40|, but even factor 6 has four loadings over |0.40| and ten features with loadings over |0.30|.

In the Somali analysis, dimension scores were transformed to a common scale, to aid in comparability across dimensions. Following the practice in

Table 5.21 *Factorial structure of the Promax rotation for Somali. (Features are listed in the order used on tables 5.10 and 5.13)*

	Factor 1	Factor 2	Factor 3	Factor 4	Factor 5	Factor 6
DEPND CLS	−0.63135	0.29267	0.30618	0.24753	−0.01609	0.22968
CND CLS	0.42748	0.10976	0.32701	−0.17900	0.27930	0.05943
PRPS CL	−0.29653	0.31295	−0.04506	0.02016	0.09272	0.12251
CNC CLS	−0.13879	0.20755	0.12055	0.29128	−0.04320	−0.02729
TIM CLS	0.06123	−0.01207	−0.01223	0.61202	−0.10291	0.00798
FRM CLS	−0.13082	0.19537	−0.36158	0.17289	−0.17739	0.39161
AH-RELS	−0.57583	−0.06330	0.18160	−0.00537	−0.13870	0.20060
RELS	−0.63458	0.26475	0.29011	0.06238	0.13219	−0.22082
V CMP CLS	−0.45199	0.08833	0.08740	0.05028	0.04192	0.39716
TAAS REL	−0.16312	0.40381	0.06254	−0.10476	−0.03248	−0.09270
AHAAN ADV	−0.27733	0.01514	0.09704	−0.08833	−0.14405	0.12124
MAIN CLS	0.62803	−0.09967	0.03137	0.17022	0.29079	−0.11151
TUNIT LNG	−0.33770	0.17853	−0.22157	−0.31354	−0.28728	0.08335
VRBLS CLS	0.29915	−0.21755	0.38076	−0.01023	−0.00097	−0.17634
IND VB	0.72661	−0.03154	−0.04403	0.04842	0.31760	−0.04108
IMPERATIVE	0.58232	0.10731	−0.15533	−0.08803	0.36461	0.11827
OPT CLS	0.08983	0.14938	0.15950	−0.19727	0.60494	−0.05469
CMPND VB	−0.13702	0.47676	−0.06620	−0.05438	−0.03849	−0.03680
PRES TNS	−0.15477	−0.04850	0.88600	−0.16401	0.08473	0.16736
PAST TNS	0.13914	0.18808	−0.57630	0.68552	0.13870	−0.13636
POS MODAL	−0.07872	0.14808	0.50440	−0.04390	−0.15654	−0.00686
FUT MODAL	−0.20950	−0.09379	−0.32471	−0.04111	−0.01144	0.30556
HAB MODAL	0.05642	0.02107	−0.06953	0.40183	−0.19876	−0.06704
OTHER N	−0.51606	0.02172	0.05507	−0.11304	−0.05498	−0.17296
PROPER N	−0.16294	−0.14516	−0.54496	−0.03012	−0.08920	−0.15199
POSS N	−0.25379	0.17552	0.12091	0.30884	0.32146	0.07226
NOMS	−0.14925	0.54101	−0.04760	−0.14552	−0.06534	−0.15758
VERBAL N	−0.27039	0.35220	−0.02779	−0.30272	−0.20491	0.00801
AGENTV N	−0.32783	−0.12101	−0.45239	−0.29614	−0.21275	0.15039
CMPND N	−0.32506	0.16395	−0.19216	−0.36649	−0.20729	0.03886
EED GENTV	−0.45936	−0.08902	−0.15605	−0.23248	0.05790	−0.35455
PRO1	0.29700	−0.10019	−0.07422	−0.22804	0.54520	0.51540
PRO2	0.41025	0.02528	0.01927	−0.27442	0.59297	0.29620
PRO3	−0.18413	0.14064	−0.08021	0.87256	−0.12106	−0.27606
DRVD ADJ	−0.47600	0.03172	0.37644	0.05086	−0.16500	0.11539
ATTRB ADJ	−0.32185	0.22523	0.38375	0.10653	−0.13962	0.11188
PRED ADJ	0.19217	−0.04509	0.55231	0.09503	−0.11757	−0.07897
STANCE ADJ	0.80565	0.15886	0.11053	0.00988	−0.14975	0.04617
STANCE VB	0.21308	−0.26731	0.16152	0.31373	−0.07645	0.13330
SPCH ACT V	0.19353	−0.21480	−0.28627	0.21550	0.23550	0.11695
TIME ADV	0.68223	0.07526	0.14101	−0.18941	0.12016	−0.01327
PLACE ADV	−0.25597	0.10843	−0.02606	0.03033	0.05987	−0.38672
DOWNTONER	0.58994	0.03244	0.09776	−0.06039	−0.05250	0.02074

Table 5.21 (*cont.*)

	Factor 1	Factor 2	Factor 3	Factor 4	Factor 5	Factor 6
AMPLIFIER	−0.10279	−0.09062	0.01518	−0.21501	0.17425	0.60477
CONC CNJ	0.06349	−0.07674	0.46230	−0.01634	0.08497	−0.00236
REASON CNJ	0.00704	0.15475	0.10442	−0.24823	0.15178	0.45858
WRDLENGTH	−0.53476	0.30288	−0.18938	−0.26168	0.07258	−0.24710
ONCE	0.22963	0.91505	0.08038	0.17201	0.17123	−0.02800
TYPE–TOKEN	0.29687	0.87985	0.05693	0.08072	0.19590	0.02290
CSE PRTCL	−0.34327	0.47172	0.03686	0.22384	0.43111	0.11318
CASE SEQ	−0.44486	0.20505	−0.15491	−0.00002	0.31823	0.06207
IMPERSNL	−0.05395	0.03043	0.37026	−0.07921	−0.09391	−0.08074
LOCATIVE	−0.06446	−0.12921	−0.21965	−0.06875	0.47249	0.08228
CONTRAC	0.73586	−0.02566	−0.00468	0.13984	0.22774	0.03663
Y-N QUES	0.91167	0.01807	0.10786	0.08906	−0.22726	−0.04368
SOO QUES	0.74058	0.13747	0.06485	−0.03250	−0.23444	0.00114
WH QUES	0.47301	−0.01855	0.01611	0.07659	0.16587	−0.09756
RESPONSES	0.96764	0.08712	0.02344	−0.07116	−0.29054	0.02801
OO CORD	−0.54379	−0.28395	0.13318	−0.11215	0.04517	−0.21077
IYO COORD	−0.51750	0.09286	0.05141	−0.31082	0.11253	−0.37626
EH COORD	0.88296	0.17237	0.03353	−0.06330	−0.00787	−0.05147
NA COORD	−0.11663	0.35355	−0.13345	0.21614	0.37754	0.29321
WAA FOCUS	0.66569	−0.10080	0.22707	−0.02609	0.18478	−0.08277
BAA FOCUS	0.59550	−0.10849	−0.13115	0.10063	0.27286	−0.16694
WX CLEFT	−0.59879	−0.13121	0.12844	0.42971	−0.15421	−0.17842

Table 5.22 *First eleven eigenvalues of the unrotated factor analysis for Somali*

Factor number	Eigenvalue	Percentage of shared variance
1	18.05	27.8
2	4.99	7.7
3	3.95	6.1
4	3.32	5.1
5	2.42	3.7
6	1.92	3.0
7	1.73	2.7
8	1.64	2.5
9	1.56	2.4
10	1.49	2.3
11	1.29	2.0

Table 5.23 *Inter-factor correlations among the six factors in the analysis of Somali*

	Factor 1	Factor 2	Factor 3	Factor 4	Factor 5	Factor 6
Factor 1	1.00000					
Factor 2	−0.54511	1.00000				
Factor 3	0.08372	−0.07061	1.00000			
Factor 4	0.31046	−0.23335	0.20939	1.00000		
Factor 5	0.51724	−0.38399	0.11546	0.49937	1.00000	
Factor 6	−0.07336	0.18948	0.14136	0.08526	0.00429	1.00000

Biber (1988), all frequencies are standardized to a mean of 0.0 and a standard deviation of 1.0 before the dimension scores are computed. Subsequently, each dimension score was multiplied by a scaling coefficient so that all dimensions used a scale running from plus to minus 10 (in the synchronic analysis). The scaling coefficients are:

Dimension	Scaling coefficient
1	0.314
2	−1.693
3	1.067
4	1.310
5	1.188
6	1.329

Dimension 2 is inverted (reversing the positive and negative poles) to facilitate comparisons among dimensions 1, 2, and 5; after inversion, conversational registers are at or near the positive pole of all three dimensions, while expository registers are at or near the negative pole.

Dimension scores should not be interpreted in absolute terms; they are rather useful for relative comparisons among texts and registers. The transformations do not alter these relative relations or the strength of each dimension; their purpose is simply to facilitate comparisons across dimensions.

5.7   Theoretical issues relating to the Multi-Dimensional methodological approach

There are a number of theoretical issues associated with the methodological procedures outlined in the above sections. In particular, there are issues relating to the definition of texts and registers, the sampling methods and the representativeness of the corpora, form/function associations and the definition of linguistic feature classes, notions of function, and the reliability, significance, and validity of dimensions (see Biber 1990, 1993a,b; Biber and Finegan 1991).

5.7.1 Representativeness in corpus design

In order to provide comprehensive descriptions of the patterns of register variation, MD analyses must be based on representative corpora of each language. I argue in Biber (1993a, b) that there are two main considerations influencing the representativeness of a corpus: size and diversity. In early corpus designs, these two considerations were given equal weight. For example, at the original planning conference for the Brown Corpus, participants discussed the text categories and subcategories to be used in the corpus as well as the number of text samples to be included in each category (Francis and Kučera 1979: 2–3). The corpus was intended to 'represent a wide range of styles and varieties of prose' in written American English (p.1). Similarly, the LOB Corpus was designed as 'a general representation of text types [in British English] for use in research on a broad range of aspects of the language' (Johansson [with Leech and Goodluck] 1978: 1). To this end, both of these corpora included 1 million words of written text taken from fifteen major text categories.

Due to rapid advances in computing technology and the general availability of on-line text, a million word corpus is no longer 'large.' Further, it has become clear that very large corpora are important for certain kinds of linguistic research; this is especially true of lexicographic research into the collocational associations for individual words. Some researchers have become so impressed with the resources provided by large corpora that they have downplayed the requirements of register diversity, claiming that corpus size alone is sufficient to insure representativeness. (For example, both the Data Collection Initiative and the COBUILD monitor corpus have previously focused on the rapid collection of any available on-line texts, with little consideration of the kinds of text being represented.)

In the social sciences generally, issues of representativeness are dealt with under the rubric of 'external validity', which refers to the extent to which it is possible to generalize from a sample to a larger target population. There are two kinds of error that can threaten external validity: 'random error' and 'bias error'. Random error occurs when the sample is not large enough to accurately estimate the true population; bias error occurs when the selection of a sample is systematically different from the target population. Random error can be minimized by increasing the sample size, and this is the reason that large text corpora are important. In contrast, bias error *cannot* be reduced by increasing the sample size, because it reflects systematic restrictions in selection.

Bias error is a particularly problematic threat when research purposes require generalization to the entire language, as in MD analyses of register variation. That is, regardless of the corpus size, a corpus that is systematically selected from a single register cannot be taken to represent the patterns of variation in an entire language. Rather, in order to make global generalizations about variation in a language, corpora representing the full range of registers are required.

For MD analyses, it is important to design corpora that are representative with respect to both size and diversity. However, given limited resources for a project, representation of diversity is more important for these purposes than representation of size. As Biber (1990, 1993a) shows, it is possible to represent the distributions of many core linguistic features, both within and across registers, based on relatively short text samples (as short as 1,000 words) and relatively few texts from each register (as few as ten texts). These issues are discussed in sections 5.7.2 and 5.7.3 below. Larger corpora are of course more representative, but the MD analyses to date have reliably analyzed the overall patterns of register variation based on corpora that are relatively small (typically less that 1 million words). In contrast, great pains have been taken to represent the range of register diversity in each of these languages, so that texts are collected from as many different spoken and written situations as possible.

5.7.2   Text sampling

There are several issues relating to the sampling of texts in corpus-based studies: What constitutes a 'text'? Must texts be homogeneous linguistically? Is it appropriate to extract 'samples' from texts? If so, what is the optimal text sample length?

In MD studies, texts are simply continuous segments of naturally occurring discourse. Most complete texts are complex in that they extend over numerous topics, purposes and even participants (as in the case of conversation). A typical academic article, for example, reflects a hierarchical structure of sections and paragraphs. The sections may range from description to narration to expository analysis. (An academic book would show an even wider range of variation.) Reflecting a range of purposes and topics, short stories and novels similarly include different kinds of textual material: description, narrative, and embedded texts such as conversations or letters. The same holds for many spoken texts: political speeches typically include narrative, exposition, and exhortation; conversations are often even more complex in that they can involve a continuous transition among participants, topics, and purposes as speakers come and go from a scene.

Different sampling techniques in such cases would enable different kinds of analysis. A sampling that disregards the changing purposes and topics within a text permits overall characterizations of the text or register. On the other hand, a sampling that extracts sections that are homogeneous with regard to purpose and topic (e.g. discussions of methodology in social science papers or descriptions of the setting in novels) would permit linguistic analysis of the distinctive characteristics of specific subregisters. These two approaches yield different perspectives on text variation, and both are valid.

There are few empirical investigations of the patterns of variation within texts and of the related issue of optimal text sample length. Biber (1990) addresses this issue by analyzing the distribution of linguistic features across 1,000-word text samples extracted from larger texts from several registers. With respect to the features examined, 1,000-word samples reliably represent the distribution of features in a text, as indicated by very high correlations among the feature counts in the samples from each text (i.e., high reliability coefficients) and by small difference scores across samples. In most cases, reliability coefficients were greater than 0.80 (and many were greater than 0.90), while nearly all the difference scores were less than 15 percent (and over half were less then 10 percent). In sum, the study indicates that 1,000-word samples reliably represent many of the surface linguistic characteristics of a text, even when considerable internal variation exists.

Text samples in MD studies have ranged from around 1,000 words to around 2,000 words in length. Although longer text samples would obviously be preferable (given adequate financial and human resources), samples of this length enable reliable analysis of the patterns of variation across most surface linguistic features.

5.7.3 Registers and text types

The notions *register* and *text type* are central to MD analyses. As discussed earlier, registers are defined as the text categories readily distinguished by mature speakers of a language (e.g., novels, newspaper articles, sermons), while text types are groupings of texts defined in strictly linguistic terms.

Previous MD studies (e.g., Biber 1989) have argued for the validity of both registers and text types, claiming that they represent complementary text categorizations. Other studies, though, have questioned the usefulness of register (or genre) distinctions (e.g., Oostdijk 1988). Two questions are relevant here: (1) To what extent are register categories linguistically homogeneous? and (2) Does linguistic heterogeneity invalidate a register category?

With regard to the first question, there is considerable evidence that registers are relatively homogeneous linguistically. Biber (1988) shows that the registers of English can be effectively characterized linguistically and that there are large (and statistically significant) differences among them; these findings are summarized in chapter 6 below. Biber (1990) compares the linguistic characteristics of ten-text and five-text subsamples drawn from five registers (face-to-face conversation, public speeches, press reportage, academic prose, general fiction). A comparison of frequency counts for selected linguistic features shows an extremely high degree of stability across subsamples (reliability coefficients greater than 0.95 for the ten-text samples; greater than 0.90 for the five-text samples). These results indicate that there is a high degree of internal linguistic consistency within registers, and that a ten-text sample provides an adequate representation of the register.

Not all registers are equally homogeneous, of course, and a complete linguistic description of a register should include both a characterization of the central tendency (i.e., the average characteristics) and a characterization of the range of variation. Registers can have a relatively wide range of linguistic variation for several reasons.

First of all, some registers include distinguishable subregisters. For example, academic writing includes articles and books from a number of disciplines, ranging from humanities and the arts to engineering and business; newspaper texts include articles covering spot news, society news, sports news, and financial news, as well as reviews and editorials. Academic research articles often include conventional subsections (viz., Introduction, Methodology, Results, Discussion, Conclusion). MD analyses have shown that there are significant linguistic differences among these various kinds of subregister (Biber 1988: 180ff.; Biber and Finegan 1994a).

Second, registers show considerable differences in the extent to which they have a focused norm, even when they lack identifiable subregisters. General fiction in English has a much wider range of variation than science fiction (Biber 1988: 171ff.), possibly reflecting differing degrees of latitude to experiment with styles and perspectives. A wide range of variation can also reflect a transitional period diachronically. Both fiction and essays had an extremely wide range of variation in English during the eighteenth and early nineteenth centuries, in part as a reflection of disagreement concerning the appropriate purposes and audiences for these registers (see Biber and Finegan 1989a). In none of these cases does a wide range of variation invalidate the register category; rather the internal range of variation is simply a descriptive fact about the register that must be accounted for.

5.7.4 Form/function associations and considerations in defining feature classes

As discussed in Biber and Finegan (1991), one of the major issues concerning linguistic features involves the decisions about which forms to group together into feature classes. In particular, two issues arise in defining feature classes: (1) decisions are required concerning the most appropriate level for a given class, since form/function associations can be considered at different levels of generality; and (2) decisions must be made concerning the best feature grouping for those forms having multiple functions, since the feature classes should be exclusive of one another for use in statistical analyses (such as factor analysis).

The pronominal system of English illustrates the first issue. One possibility would be to group all pronouns together as a single feature class, including all persons, personal and impersonal forms, and demonstrative forms; this feature class could be described functionally as marking anaphoric or deictic reference. An alternative grouping would distinguish among personal and impersonal forms, and among the various persons for personal forms. Support for this grouping could be provided from the identifiable functions of these more specific feature classes; for example, first- and second-person pronouns refer to the immediate participants in an interaction, while third-person pronouns can refer to persons or objects not immediately present. This latter grouping would be preferred in MD studies, following the general principle that feature classes should be based on the lowest level of groupings that have distinguishable functions. It is always possible to collapse two feature classes, if it becomes apparent that they are not functionally distinct; but if two classes are combined at the outset, it is not possible to analyze the influence of any functional differences within the larger grouping.

The second issue – how to group features having multiple functions – can be illustrated by past participial adverbial clauses in English. On the one hand, these might be grouped with other adverbial clauses as a type of subordination feature; but they could also be grouped with other passive constructions in a general passive feature class.

Both of these issues were illustrated in chapter 4 by the attempt to find the appropriate level of structure for cross-linguistic comparisons. Thus, relative clauses could be considered as a separate feature class; or they could be combined with participial postnominal modifiers to constitute a class of clausal postnominal modifiers; or they could be further combined with prepositional phrases to constitute the class of all postnominal modifiers; or all of these features could be combined with attributive adjectives to mark the feature class of all nominal modifiers. Any of these groupings could be supported on functional grounds. In addition, some of these constructions could be combined in alternative ways: for example, past participial postnominal clauses can be combined with other passive constructions to mark total passives; prepositional postnominal phrases can be combined with prepositional phrases having adverbial functions to mark the class of all prepositional phrases; attributive adjectives can be combined with predicative adjectives to constitute a class of all adjectives.

As noted in chapter 4, the MD approach provides a solution to this dilemma in that the statistical techniques (viz., factor analysis) identify the functionally salient groupings, that is, those classes having strong co-occurrence associations. However, this approach works only if features are grouped at the lowest level of generality that is likely to be relevant, separating all potentially distinct form/function classes. Taking this approach, each type of pronoun should be considered as a separate linguistic feature. Similarly, past participial adverbial clauses are treated as a distinct feature rather than being grouped with either a general feature class of passive constructions or a general adverbial clause feature class. In the same way, the various types of relative clause, postnominal participial clause, prepositional phrase, attributive adjectives, and predicative adjectives are all analyzed as separate features.[14] If the raw frequency counts are structured at this level, factor analysis will correctly sort features into the functional groupings that are well defined in the language in question, based on the co-occurrence patterns of that language.

Two misunderstandings concerning the form-function relationships assumed by MD analyses have arisen in the past. First, it is *not* the case that a single communicative function is assumed to underlie each grouping of co-occurring linguistic features. Rather, in some cases there are multiple functions associated with the collection of linguistic features on a dimension. English dimension 1, discussed above in section 5.5 (cf. section 6.1.1), is a good example of this type. This dimension combines functions related to the primary purpose of communication (informational versus interactional/ [inter]personal) with functions related to production circumstances (careful production versus on-line production). Dimensions of this type show complex inter-relations among multiple functional domains, which work together to define a single underlying parameter of variation.

Second, it is *not* the case that MD analyses assume that there is a single communicative function associated with each linguistic feature. Rather, in many cases, features can have somewhat differing functions in different kinds of text; further, features can have functions defined at different levels of generality. The MD approach assumes the existence of shared functions underlying groupings of co-occurring features, so that at least some of the functions associated with a given feature will be shared with the other features defining a dimension. As a result, MD analyses sometimes identify functional associations not previously noticed for an individual feature. However, the primary analytical goal of the MD approach is to identify the basic parameters of variation in a language, not to provide detailed functional analyses of the individual features comprising a dimension. As a result, individual features can have particular functions not incorporated into the shared basis of a dimension.

5.7.5 Notions of function

The general approach outlined in the last section is based on the premise that most formal differences reflect functional differences, and thus linguistic variation is typically conditioned by some combination of social, situational, discourse, and processing 'functions.' It is possible to distinguish among four major types of function: (1) the work that a form does in discourse; (2) the situational characteristics that a form reflects; (3) the processing constraints that a form reflects; and (4) a situational or social distinction that a form conventionally indexes.

In the first case, linguistic forms can be said to actually perform particular tasks: for example, relative clauses 'function' to specify or elaborate the identities of discourse referents; some types of adverbial clauses 'function' to set a frame for discourse segments; passive constructions 'function' to rearrange the informational structure of a sentence, to mark informational prominence or discourse continuity.

In the second case, the choice of form directly reflects the speech/writing situation: for example, the use of first- and second-person pronouns reflects the direct participation of oneself (the speaker/writer) and a particular addressee; time and place deictics reflect the actual temporal and physical setting of discourse.

The third type of function is slightly different in that it reflects production circumstances rather than physical setting: for example, contracted forms reflect the pressure of on-line production; generalized content words, such as hedges (*kind of, sort of*) or general nouns (e.g., *thing*) similarly reflect the difficulty of more precise lexical expression under real-time production circumstances (although they can also be used to be deliberately vague or imprecise).

The first type of function above is active, actually performing some task, while the second and third types refer to a passive, but direct, reflection of the setting and production circumstances. Some features can be functional in both senses: for example, a high type–token ratio (representing a high degree of lexical diversity in a text) performs the task of increasing the semantic precision and informational density of a text; at the same time it is a functional reflection of the considerable opportunity for careful production typical in most writing situations, as opposed to the real-time constraints characterizing most speaking situations.

The fourth sense of 'function' listed above refers to the way that forms can conventionally index particular situations or social groups: for example, certain vocabulary items can by themselves mark speakers as members of a social group (e.g., fraternities, professions, genders). Address terms can conventionally mark different role relations, and vocabulary can also be used to index levels of formality. 'Function' in this sense refers to an arbitrary association of particular forms with particular situations or social groups. Many forms, though, can occur in discourse both as conventional indexes and as reflections of the situational or production circumstances. For example, hedges (*kind of, sort of*) index informal, conversational discourse, while the functionally similar class of downtoners (e.g., *barely, mildly, partially*) indexes more formal, written discourse. However, the latter set is more specific than the former, indicating particular aspects or degrees of uncertainty, whereas hedges mark a more generalized uncertainty. The differential distribution of these forms is thus a functional reflection of the greater opportunity for careful word choice in writing situations in addition to a conventional indexing of those situations.

In practice, MD studies have not used feature classes that are purely conventional. In fact, the bias in these studies is to treat most features as functional, in the sense that they serve some discourse task or reflect situational or production circumstances; most conventional or indexical markers can be analyzed as derivative from these more basic functions. (For example, Finegan and Biber [1994] argue that many patterns of social dialect variation can be reanalyzed in these terms.)

The assumption that distributional differences reflect functional differences is a further reason for the relatively fine distinctions among feature classes in MD studies (as with downtoners being treated separately from hedges). A more extreme case concerns *that* complement clauses with and without the complementizer (e.g., *I think [that] he went*). Both structural options are complement clauses, and it might be claimed that the only difference between them is a conventional one, with the deleted *that* arbitrarily indexing speech. The approach taken here would claim instead that this indexing instead reflects a functional difference: that the clauses with deleted *that* reflect the influence of production pressures, and thus they are usually found in spoken registers that are produced on-line.

In sum, the features included in previous MD studies are functional in that they both perform discourse tasks and reflect aspects of the communicative situation and production circumstances. As a result, the dimensions identified from these features show how various functional domains are intertwined in discourse. That is, dimensions are based on groups of linguistic features that co-occur frequently in texts, because of their shared underlying functions, including both their discourse tasks and their associated situational/production circumstances. Thus, as the following chapters show, registers tend to evolve so that their preferred tasks fit the production possibilities of their situation.

5.7.6 The reliability, significance, and validity of dimensions

Before proceeding to the interpretation of the dimensions in each of the four languages, it is important to briefly address issues concerning the trustworthiness of the factor analyses. Three issues are relevant here: (1) Are the factor structures stable and replicable, that is, are they 'reliable'? (2) Are the factors significant and important predictors of register variation? (3) Are the dimensions 'valid', that is, do they actually represent what they are claimed to represent?

Regarding issues of reliability, there are two main concerns. (1) If other representative corpora were used for the analysis, would the factor structure be changed? (2) If additional linguistic features were included in the analysis, would the factor structure be changed?

The first issue has been addressed in Biber (1990), where the corpus of English was split in half, and separate factor analyses were run on each half (about 240 texts each). Both analyses were close replications of the original factor analysis based on 481 texts. Factors 1 and 2 were almost exact replications, while factors 4 and 5 were very close to the original structure (including all original features but adding one or two additional features). Only factor 3 showed any notable difference, in that the negative loadings were not well replicated. (This difference indicates that factor 3 might actually represent two separate underlying dimensions.) Overall, this analysis shows that the factor structure here is quite reliable, being replicated even in corpora half the size of the original. (Similar indications of the stability of this structure have come from previous analyses based on the Brown Corpus, conducted as part of Biber [1986], and previous analyses of related corpora, such as Grabe [1987].)

A related issue is whether the addition of other linguistic features would alter the basic factor structure. In this regard, it should be pointed out that none of the final factor analyses reported here includes the full range of features actually counted for that language. Rather, only those features that have relatively high 'communalities' (usually greater than 0.20) were retained. (Communality scores measure the extent to which the variation of a particular feature overlaps with the total pool of shared variance in a factor analysis.) Dropping features with low communalities results in a cleaner factor structure, in that there are not numerous features having low loadings on all factors. The main point here, though, is that dropping these features does not alter the basic factor structure at all; that is, the features do not rearrange themselves into a different set of factors due to this reduction in the set of features.

This is not to exclude the possibility that the addition of other features might result in the identification of additional dimensions. In fact, Biber (1992b) shows that there are likely additional dimensions in English associated with the marking of reference in discourse. These additional dimensions, however, do not alter or negate the validity of the existing dimensions identified to date. Rather, the original dimensions have been shown to be replicable and quite stable; consideration of additional features from other linguistic domains will probably extend previous analyses, but not contradict them.

There are actually two separate issues that can be discussed regarding the dimensions as predictors of register variation: their statistical significance and their strength (or importance). Significance simply indicates whether the measured differences among registers are likely to be due to chance or not. With a large sample (as in the case of these studies), it is relatively easy to produce significant results (i.e. results that are not due to chance). Strength, on the other hand, measures the importance of observed differences, typically reported in terms of the percentage of variation that can be accounted for. The dimensions in all four languages are consistently significant and usually very strong as well, since they typically account for well over 50% of the variation among registers. This point will become more concrete in the next chapter, where it will be shown that the dimensions are quite powerful in their ability to predict and characterize the differences among registers.

As noted in chapter 1, the dimensions identified in the original MD analysis of speech and writing in English have been successfully used as important predictors of register variation in more specialized discourse domains (such as historical analyses of written and speech-based registers extending over the last four centuries, dialect differences between British and American written registers, and stylistic analyses of particular authors). These studies address the validity of the dimensions by showing that they function as important predictors of register variation in a number of different discourse domains.

A second issue relating to validity, though, is whether the dimensions actually represent the underlying discourse constructs that the interpretations claim for them. Here there are several converging types of evidence. First, it is possible to claim face validity for the interpretations, based on our knowledge of the communicative functions of individual features (from previous research and additional analyses of texts). Second, the distribution of factor scores among registers can be analyzed to test hypothesized interpretations based on the co-occurring linguistic features. If both sets of data support the same interpretation, we can be relatively confident in the validity of that interpretation. These first two criteria have been used in the MD analyses of all four languages.

Third, it is possible to run subsequent factor analyses that include additional linguistic features as a confirmatory test of particular interpretations. That is, for each additional feature, predictions are made concerning the factor that the feature should load on, based on the hypothesized interpretations. To the extent that the new features are distributed as hypothesized, the original interpretations are confirmed. This process was used to compare the factor analyses of Biber (1986) and Biber (1988), supporting the interpretations underlying three of the main dimensions of English (see discussion in Biber 1988: 115–20). Finally, a procedure known as Confirmatory Factor Analysis (using the statistical package known as LISREL) can be used to actually test the relative strengths of competing factorial models hypothesized on the basis of different possible underlying interpretations. Biber (1992a) uses this approach to test several competing models of discourse complexity, building on the functions proposed for each dimension in Biber (1988).

In sum, the reliability, significance/importance, and validity of the dimensions have been investigated empirically. The dimensions have been shown to be stable and replicable, and strong predictors of the differences among registers. The validity of the interpretations has been considered from several different perspectives. In all four languages, the interpretations have strong face validity, being supported by the converging analyses of the linguistic co-occurrence patterns and the relations among registers with respect to their dimension scores. The interpretations in English have further support from confirmatory statistical techniques. The dimensions can thus be considered generally trustworthy, providing confidence in their use for cross-linguistic comparisons.

6   Multi-Dimensional analyses of the four languages

Before undertaking a cross-linguistic comparison of register variation, it is necessary to have a complete description of the distributional patterns within each language. The previous chapter gave the methodological and statistical details of the Multi-Dimensional analyses for English, Nukulaelae Tuvaluan, Korean, and Somali. The present chapter turns to the functional interpretation of the dimensions in each language and analysis of the relations among registers with respect to each of those dimensions.

6.1   English

Six basic dimensions of variation in English are identified and interpreted in Biber (1988). The present section will consider each of these dimensions in turn.

6.1.1   English dimension 1: 'Involved versus Informational Production'

The interpretation of dimension 1 was briefly summarized in section 5.5. As table 6.1 shows, the negative features on this dimension are all associated with an informational focus and a careful integration of information in texts. Nouns are the primary device used to convey referential meaning, and a higher frequency of nouns is one reflection of a greater informational density. Prepositional phrases also integrate information into a text, functioning as postnominal modifiers to explicitly specify and elaborate referential identity (in addition to their function as adverbial modifiers). Word length and type–token ratio also mark a high density of information, by reflecting precise word choice and an exact presentation of informational content. Longer words tend to be rarer and more specific in meaning than shorter words (Zipf 1949). A high type–token ratio reflects the use of many different words in a text (versus extensive repetition of relatively few words), representing a more careful word choice and a more precise presentation of information. Attributive adjectives are used to elaborate nominal referents,

Table 6.1 *Co-occurring linguistic features on English dimension 1: 'Involved versus Informational Production.' (Features in parentheses have lower weights and are not used in the computation of dimension scores)*

Dimension 1	
'Involved Production'	
Positive features:	
Private verbs	0.96
THAT deletion	0.91
Contractions	0.90
Present tense verbs	0.86
Second person pronouns	0.86
DO as pro-verb	0.82
Analytic negation	0.78
Demonstrative pronouns	0.76
General emphatics	0.74
First-person pronouns	0.74
Pronoun IT	0.71
BE as main verb	0.71
Causative subordination	0.66
Discourse particles	0.66
Indefinite pronouns	0.62
General hedges	0.58
Amplifiers	0.56
Sentence relatives	0.55
WH questions	0.52
Possibility modals	0.50
Non-phrasal co-ordination	0.48
WH clauses	0.47
Final prepositions	0.43
(Adverbs)	0.42
'Informational Production'	
Negative features:	
Nouns	−0.80
Word length	−0.58
Prepositions	−0.54
Type−token ratio	−0.54
Attributive adjectives	−0.47
(Place adverbials	−0.42)
(Agentless passives	−0.39)
(Past participial postnominal clauses	−0.38)

but they are highly integrative relative to predicative adjectives or relative clauses, since they pack high amounts of information into relatively few words. Thus these five features can be considered as functioning together to integrate high amounts of information into texts, presenting information in a highly concise and precise manner.

The other three negative features on this dimension are less important but can be interpreted in the same general terms. Agentless passives are associated with a nominal, informational style in which the agent is unspecified (typically because it is recoverable from the discourse context). Postnominal clauses are similar to prepositional phrases and attributive adjectives in being used for integrated referential specification or elaboration. These constructions use few words in comparison to full relative clauses, since the relative pronoun and copula are omitted, and in passive postnominal clauses the agent is often additionally unspecified. (For example, compare *the features grouped on this factor* with the corresponding full relative clause: *the features which the factor analysis grouped on this factor.*) Thus all of these features are used for an integrated packaging of information.[1]

There are a larger number of positive features on dimension 1, and correspondingly a larger number of functions represented, reflecting direct interaction, focus on the immediate circumstance and personal attitudes or feelings, fragmentation or reduction in form, and a less specific, generalized content. Adopting a cover term from Chafe (1982) and Tannen (1982a), many of these features can be considered as reflecting high 'involvement'.

Private verbs, present tense verbs, *do* as a pro-verb, and copula *be* all have a strong co-occurrence relation with the positive features on this dimension, reflecting an active, verbal style. The use of these verbs reflects a high frequency of main clauses, in contrast to the dense (nominal) integration of information into relatively few clauses, associated with the negative features.

In addition, these features are interactive and involved. Present tense verbs often reflect concern with the immediate circumstances. Private verbs (e.g., *think, wish, feel*) are used for the direct expression of personal attitudes and emotions. Several other positive features on dimension 1 are directly interactive or affective. First- and second-person pronouns require the active participation of a specific addressor and addressee, and WH questions typically assume a specific, interacting addressee. Emphatics and amplifiers are used for the heightened expression of attitudes and feelings, and sentence relatives are used for overt attitudinal comments (e.g., *He asked for two servings, which I thought was incredible*). All of these features are thus used for highly involved, interactive discourse with a focus on personal feelings.

Other positive features mark a reduced or fragmented surface form, and a generalized, imprecise presentation of content. Pro-forms and contractions both mark types of surface reduction. Pro-forms include the pro-verb *do*, which substitutes for a fuller (and more explicit) verb phrase or clause, and pronominal forms such as the third-person impersonal pronoun *it*, demonstrative pronouns, and indefinite pronouns, which substitute for fuller (more explicit) noun phrases. Contractions represent a reduction and coalescence of adjacent lexical items (e.g., *won't* for *will not*). Other reductions include the optional deletion of *that* in verb complements (e.g., *I think* [*that*] *I'll go*). Final (stranded) prepositions can also be considered as marking a surface disruption in form–meaning correspondence. A reduced or fragmented surface form often results in a more generalized or ambiguous content. Contractions are often ambiguous; for example, [its] can stand for *it is*, *it has*, or possessive *it*; [ayd] (orthographic *I'd*) can stand for *I would* or *I had*. Pronominal forms, such as *it* and demonstrative pronouns, stand for an unspecified referent that must be inferred from the discourse or situational context. Other features, such as hedges and possibility modals, are a direct expression of uncertainty or lack of precision. Clausal co-ordination represents a joining of main clauses in a loose manner, the polar opposite to a tight integration of information through attributive adjectives, prepositional phrases, etc.

Surprisingly, four subordination features are included among the positive features. This grouping runs counter to the expectations of many previous studies, which have claimed that all dependent clauses are syntactically complex and therefore reflect informational elaboration. This grouping of features supports previous suggestions by Halliday (1979) that certain kinds of subordination represent a relatively fragmented rather than integrated packaging of information, and that subordination can be characteristic of non-informational (spoken) discourse. The functions of dependent clauses in English, and the larger issues relating to structural complexity, require further analysis. For example, the English factor analysis shows dependent clause constructions being associated with all seven factors, performing a number of different functions. Biber (1992a) uses a confirmatory factor analysis to investigate the underlying constructs represented by the various types of dependent clause in English in relation to other types of structural complexity.

The main point here, though, is that some types of dependent clause represent a relatively loose presentation of information, in opposition to the tightly integrated packaging made possible by features such as nouns, attributive adjectives, and prepositional phrases. In addition, certain types of dependent clause are commonly used for affective functions: for example, WH clauses often present the speaker's evaluation or attitude in the associated main clause (e.g., *I believed what he told me*). Causative and conditional adverbial subordination are related to affect or stance in that they set discourse frames for particular propositions; for example, causative clauses present justification for actions or beliefs. Sentence relatives were already mentioned above as direct expressions of the speaker's attitudes. These four types of dependent clause are thus quite similar functionally to the other positive features grouped on dimension 1.

In sum, dimension 1 represents a careful, dense, integration of information (the negative features) versus a fragmented, generalized packaging of content with an affective, interpersonal focus (the positive features). Two major communicative parameters are combined in this dimension: (1) the primary purpose of the speaker/writer: informational versus affective and involved; and (2) the production circumstances: those that enable deliberate production (and even editing), resulting in precise lexical choice and an integrated packaging of information, versus on-line production circumstances, that result in a generalized, reduced, and fragmented presentation of information. Reflecting both of these parameters, the label 'Involved versus Informational Production' is proposed for this dimension.

Figure 6.1, which plots the dimension 1 score for twenty-three spoken and written registers, confirms this general interpretation and enables a better understanding of how purpose and production circumstances are related in this dimension. At the positive extreme are telephone and face-to-face conversations, characterized by very frequent private verbs, *that*-deletions, contractions, first- and second-person pronouns, etc. (the positive group of features) together with markedly few occurrences of nouns, long words, prepositions, varied vocabulary, etc. (the negative group of features). These registers combine a primary affective, interpersonal purpose with the restrictions of on-line production. At the negative extreme of figure 6.1 are registers such as academic prose, press reportage, and official documents, having the opposite linguistic characteristics as conversation: very frequent nouns, long words, prepositions, and varied vocabulary (the negative group of features), combined with the relative absence of private verbs, *that*-deletions, contractions, first- and second-person pronouns, etc. (the positive group of features). These registers also show the combined influence of purpose and production circumstances, having a focused informational purpose together with maximal opportunity for careful production and revision.

Text sample 6.1 illustrates the dimension 1 characteristics of conversation, while text sample 6.2 illustrates the characteristics of informational, expository prose.

Text sample 6.1: Face-to-face conversation (LL:4.3, dinner-table conversation)

    A: Well I must admit # I feel [pause] I mean Edward's mother #
         and his great [pause] and his grandfather #
    B: mm #

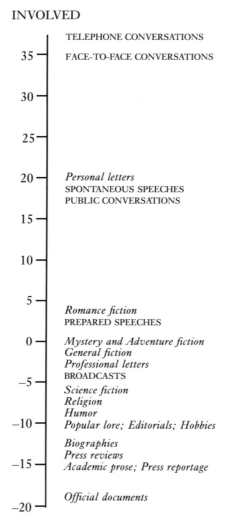

INVOLVED

35 — TELEPHONE CONVERSATIONS
       FACE-TO-FACE CONVERSATIONS

30 —

25 —

20 — *Personal letters*
       SPONTANEOUS SPEECHES
       PUBLIC CONVERSATIONS

15 —

10 —

5 — *Romance fiction*
       PREPARED SPEECHES

0 — *Mystery and Adventure fiction*
       General fiction
       Professional letters
       BROADCASTS
−5 — *Science fiction*
       Religion
       Humor
−10 — *Popular lore; Editorials; Hobbies*

       Biographies
       Press reviews
−15 — *Academic prose; Press reportage*

       Official documents
−20 —

INFORMATIONAL

Figure 6.1 Mean scores of English dimension 1 for twenty-three registers: 'Involved versus Informational Production.' ($F = 111.9$, $p < 0.0001$, $r^2 = 84.3\%$)

A: will come up # on Christmas Day #

B: yes #

A: but I feel somehow # [pause] the sheer fact # of not having
     to have [pause] to have [pause] this [pause] really sort of [long
     pause] it's for one thing it does nark me # that

B: [unintelligible]

A: it's so bloody expensive # that he won't eat anything except the
     largest most splendid pieces of meat # you know #

B: [unintelligible] how annoying #

A: and mm # it upsets me # you know # if he needed it # I
     wouldn't mind # [pause]

B: mm #

D: come to think of it # he's also he's also [pause] an
     extremely greedy individual # who

A: yeah # [pause] so that if you buy enough

D: he isn't satisfied # thank you #

B: does anyone want ham #

A: if you

D: he isn't satisfied with a normal portion #

A: no thank you # if you buy enough

D: oh I don't like this #

A: thing [pause] for cheese for [pause] for three days # if he sees
     it's there # he'll eat it # you know #

D: he simply eats a lot # yeah # [long pause]

Text sample 6.2: Academic prose (LOB: J.34, linguistics)

But while many modern linguists would subscribe to the latter view
there remains still a common core of syntactic terms, common by
definition among those making use of them, not from any content or
semantic meaning, but from the method of establishing them within
each language. Terms like nucleus, expansion, cohesion, endocentric,
and exocentric are general (though not necessarily universal) categories, by reason of the common operations by which sentences in a
language are compared and classed together as regards the formal
inter-relations of their components. These operations and the criteria
employed need not be in detail the same between any two linguists,
but the overall operational similarity in their use is obvious.

Text sample 6.1 is characteristic of informal face-to-face conversation
among friends; it moves freely over numerous topics, and often focuses
on interpersonal relationships as much as particular informational topics.
In addition, the situation requires on-line production, with little opportunity

for preplanning and essentially no opportunity for revision. As a result of these characteristics, sample 6.1 shows frequent private verbs (e.g., *admit, feel, mean, nark, upset, know, think, like*), *that*-deletions (*I must admit* [*that*] *I feel* [*that*] [pause] *I mean* [*that*] *Edward's mother* ..., *he sees* [*that*] *it's there*), contractions (e.g., *it's, he's, isn't*), present tense verbs, first- and second-person pronouns, demonstrative pronouns (*I don't like this*), hedges (*sort of*), emphatics and amplifiers (*really, extremely*), occurrences of *it* as pronoun, *be* as main verb, etc. At the same time, this text sample shows a marked absence of nouns, prepositional phrases, attributive adjectives, long words, and the other negative features grouped on dimension 1. The text has frequent repetitions and therefore a low type–token ratio. This sample is thus strikingly 'involved', shown by the very high frequencies of the positive features on dimension 1, and strikingly non-integrated and non-informational, shown by the very low frequencies of the negative features.

In contrast, text sample 6.2 illustrates the typical linguistic characteristics of text produced with a high informational focus combined with maximal opportunity for careful production: extremely frequent nouns, which are often longer, less common words (e.g., *linguists, definition, nucleus, cohesion, operations, inter-relations*), prepositional phrases (e.g., *the method of establishing them within each language, by reason of the common operations by which sentences in a language* ...), and attributive adjectives (e.g., *modern linguists, syntactic terms, semantic meaning, overall operational similarity*). In addition, this passage shows considerable lexical diversity, reflecting the dense integration of information and careful word choice.

Other registers have intermediate scores on dimension 1 due to different mixes of purpose and production circumstance. For example, public conversations (interviews and panel discussions) are relatively informational in purpose but still interactive and constrained by the limited possibilities of on-line production. Personal letters are affective and interpersonal in purpose, but they can be planned and revised. Fiction combines an entertaining or edifying purpose, maximal opportunity for planning and revision, and deliberate inclusion of fictional dialogue containing some linguistic features characteristic of on-line, affective discourse. Text samples 6.3–6.7 illustrate the linguistic characteristics of these registers.

Text sample 6.3: Public conversation (LL: 5.5, panel discussion)

(A: the discussion monitor; C: Christopher Chataway; B: Lord Boothby

[Question]

A: Do you think that there is any chance that the Labour Party will provide an effective opposition in the forseeable future? ... [responses by several participants]

A: Christopher Chataway # [in reaction to the previous answer]
C: I've seldom heard a string of sentences # that I really do believe # to [pause] contain quite so many # [pause] faulty analyses # of the present situation # [long pause] I don't believe # that this country is swinging to unilateralism # . . .
A: Lord Boothby #
B: Well # [pause] I don't think you know # that Tony Wedgwood Benn can seriously say that personalities [pause] don't matter # [long pause] because I think they do matter tremendously # in [pause] politics today # and especially in the politics of the Left # [long pause] what has happened is . . .

Text sample 6.4: Personal letter (personal corpus, no. 1)

It was so nice to hear from you, and I enjoyed the picture too . . .

I'm glad your life has straightened out for you. I feel the same way about my life. We really lived through a troubled period of history . . .

I hope that if you get to come to Texas that you could visit us . . . I hope we can get together. I would really like to meet your family, and I'd like for you to meet mine . . .

Text sample 6.5: Personal letter (personal corpus, no. 2)

How you doing? I'm here at work waiting for my appointment to get here, it's Friday. Thank goodness, but I still have tomorrow, but this week has flown by, I guess because I've been staying busy, getting ready for Christmas and stuff. Have you done your Christmas shopping yet?

Text sample 6.6: Romance fiction (LOB: P. 24)

But Mike Deegan was boiling mad now. When the inning was over he cursed the Anniston catcher all the way into the dugout . . .

The Anniston manager came right up to the dugout in front of Mike.

His face was flushed. 'Deegan', the manager said, his voice pitched low, quivering, 'That was a rotten thing to do.'

'For God's sake', Mike said, waving the manager away, 'Stop it, will you? Tell your guys not to block the plate!'

'You didn't have to ram him.'

'That's what you say.'

Text sample 6.7: Mystery fiction (LOB: L.12)

I'd finished making the bed by then. As I pushed it back against the wall I heard something drop on the floor.

That was when the percolator in the living-room started making bubbling noises. There was nothing on the floor that I could see. I told myself it must've fallen down between the bed and the wall.

. . . Wasn't urgent anyway. Maybe my cigarette-case . . . or Sonia's powder compact . . . I'd look for it later.

So I got up from my hands and knees, went into the living room and fixed myself a cup of coffee.

Sample 6.3 is from a panel discussion, where a group of discussants interact with one another debating a series of specific issues; this text is thus explicitly informational and interactional/involved at the same time. In addition, the text is marked by features reflecting its on-line production. The interactiveness, involvement, and focus on personal attitudes are reflected by features such as frequent questions (primarily from the moderator), first- and second-person pronouns, emphatics (*quite, really, tremendously*), and private verbs (*think, believe, know*). The on-line production is reflected in the frequent contractions (e.g., *I've, don't*) and *that*-deletions (e.g., *think [that] you know, think [that] they do matter*). At the same time, this sample is shaped by the informational focus of the participants, so that it includes a relatively careful and diverse choice of vocabulary, with relatively frequent nouns, prepositional phrases, and attributive adjectives (e.g., *faulty analyses of the present situation*).

The personal letter has quite different communicative characteristics: a very high focus on the interpersonal relationship and the expression of personal affect, and ample opportunity for careful production, although letter writers often do not take advantage of the planning and revision possibilities offered by the written mode. Thus, in samples 6.4 and 6.5, there are frequent contractions and *that* deletions (*I'm, it's, I've; I'm glad [that] your life has straightened out; I hope [that] we can get together*), plus a generally fragmented style shown by the simple stringing together of (often logically unrelated) main clauses. Both letters are directly interactive, shown for example by the frequent first- and second-person pronouns and questions, and both samples focus on the involved expression of personal feelings rather than expository information (e.g., *It was so nice . . .; I'm glad your life . . .; We really lived . . .; I hope that . . .; I would really like to . . .*).

Finally, fiction can range from quite involved styles to more integrated descriptive and narrative sections. Sample 6.6 illustrates high involvement in fictional dialogue, where there are numerous features characteristic of face-to-face conversation (e.g., contractions, questions, first- and second-person pronouns). Sample 6.7 illustrates many of the same features in a narrative section of a novel. Here there are frequent contractions, references to first person, and a generally fragmented structure, composed primarily of main clauses. If longer portions of these texts were considered, it would be clear that they have a more diverse vocabulary than conversational texts, as well as a more integrated structure. However, the combination of those features with the interactive characteristics of dialogue and the deliberately involved characteristics of many narrative passages results in an intermediate dimension 1 score for fiction.

The distribution of registers seen in figure 6.1 shows that dimension 1 is closely related to the mode difference between speech and writing, with stereotypically spoken registers (conversation) having the largest positive scores, and stereotypically written registers (informational exposition) having the largest negative scores. However, there is also considerable overlap among spoken and written registers. Personal letters have a large positive score, and the fictional registers plus professional letters have intermediate scores, even though these are all written registers. Conversely, prepared speeches and broadcasts are spoken registers with intermediate scores.

Thus highly interactive, affective registers produced under real-time constraints have the linguistic characteristics of 'Involved Production,' regardless of whether they are spoken or written. Conversely, informational registers produced with maximal opportunity for planning and revision have the linguistic characteristics of 'Informational Production'; these are all written registers, because only the written mode enables these careful production circumstances. However, there are several intermediate registers, both written and spoken, that combine different purposes (interpersonal or informational to varying degrees) with different possibilities for careful production.

6.1.2   English dimension 2: 'Narrative versus Non-narrative Discourse'

Dimension 2, summarized in table 6.2, shows a primary opposition between past and present time, with past tense and perfect aspect included among the positive features, and present tense one of the two main negative features. In addition, the positive features include third-person personal pronouns (e.g., *she, he, they*), public verbs (or speech act verbs), synthetic negation, and present participial clauses. The other major negative feature is attributive adjectives, with past participial postnominal clauses and word length having less strong co-occurrence relations.

The positive features on dimension 2 can be interpreted as marking

Table 6.2 *Co-occurring linguistic features on English dimension 2: 'Narrative versus Non-narrative Discourse.' (Features in parentheses are not used in the computation of dimension scores)*

Dimension 2	
'Narrative Discourse'	
Positive features:	
Past tense verbs	0.90
Third-person pronouns	0.73
Perfect aspect verbs	0.48
Public verbs	0.43
Synthetic negation	0.40
Present participial clauses	0.39
'Non-Narrative Discourse'	
Negative features:	
(Present tense verbs	−0.47)
(Attributive adjectives	−0.41)

narrative discourse, and this interpretation is supported by the large positive scores for all fiction registers on figure 6.2 (which plots the mean dimension scores for dimension 2). Past tense verbs and perfect aspect verbs are used to describe the major past events that constitute the backbone of the narrative, while third-person pronouns are used to refer to the animate, typically human, participants in the narrative. Public verbs are used to report the direct and indirect speech acts of these participants, including verbs such as *assert, declare, proclaim, report, say*, and *tell*. In addition, a type of adverbial subordination – present participial clauses – is grouped with the positive features. Thompson (1983) characterizes these forms as being used to create vivid imagery in 'depictive' discourse, and their co-occurrence with these other narrative features apparently reflects their frequent use for descriptive background in narratives.[2]

The narrative characteristics of fiction texts are illustrated by text samples 6.6 and 6.7 in the last section. These samples show the frequent use of past tense and perfect aspect verbs, together with the absence of present tense verbs. They also illustrate the use of speech act verbs, especially for direct dialogue in the case of sample 6.6. Figure 6.2 shows that fictional texts from several subregisters are marked by the frequent use of these narrative features.

In addition, figure 6.2 shows that dimension 2 is fundamentally different from dimension 1 in that the distribution of registers along this dimension has no relation to speech and writing. That is, written registers occupy both

NARRATIVE

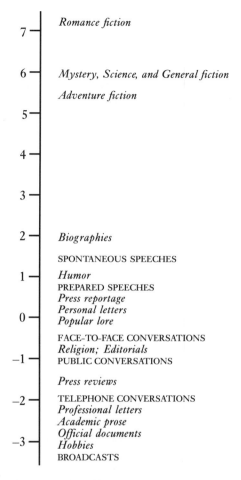

NON-NARRATIVE

Figure 6.2 Mean scores of English dimension 2 for twenty-three registers: 'Narrative versus Non-narrative Discourse.' ($F = 32.3$, $p < 0.0001$, $r^2 = 60.8\%$)

extremes along dimension 2, with the fiction registers being extremely narrative, while registers such as academic prose, official documents, and skills and hobbies prose are extremely non-narrative. Several spoken registers are also markedly non-narrative in nature, including broadcasts (which report events actually in progress) and telephone conversations (which deal primarily with immediate concerns).

Non-narrative discourse can thus have many purposes with different structural organizations; these registers are similar in their dimension 2 characteristics in that they lack a narrative organization, rather than sharing certain communicative concerns. Many of these registers are expository and informational, such as academic prose and official documents. Text sample 6.2 in the last section illustrates the use of present tense verbs and attributive adjectives, combined with the absence of narrative features, in these registers. Hobbies texts are somewhat different in that they are procedural, but they have similar dimension 2 characteristics; sample 6.8 below illustrates this type of discourse. The present time orientation in these texts is used to describe the steps in a process, rather than to focus on the explanation of some phenomenon as in expository prose.

Text sample 6.8: Hobbies (LOB:E, 2, procedural discourse)

> When a leg has a simple taper the procedure of making it is straightforward. The wood is first planed parallel to the largest section, and pencil lines marking the beginning of the taper squared round on to all four sides. At the bottom end the extent of the taper is gauged in, . . .

Conversational texts are also often markedly non-narrative, but for quite different reasons: conversational participants adopt a present-time orientation to focus on the immediate interaction and circumstances. Text sample 6.1 in the last section illustrates these characteristics in a face-to-face conversation.

Figure 6.2 shows, however, that many registers combine narrative and non-narrative concerns, and thus they have intermediate characterizations along dimension 2. This is frequently the case in conversation, which can switch back and forth between narratives and the immediate interaction (see Ochs 1994). Text sample 6.3 in the last section illustrates the combined discussion of past events and present concerns in a public conversation (e.g., *I think they do matter* . . . [long pause] *what has happened is* . . .). Personal letters also often combine present and past concerns, as illustrated by sample 6.4 above (e.g., past: *It was so nice; I enjoyed*; present: *I'm glad; I feel*; past: *We really lived*; present: *I hope*). Similar observations could be made for public speeches, biographies, press reportage, and humor. In all of these registers,

Table 6.3 *Co-occurring linguistic features on English dimension 3: 'Situation-dependent versus Elaborated Reference.' (Polarity reversed – see note 3)*

Dimension 3	
'Situation-dependent Reference'	
Positive features:	
Time adverbials	0.60
Place adverbials	0.49
Adverbs	0.46
- -	
'Elaborated Reference'	
Negative features:	
WH relative clauses on object positions	−0.63
Pied-piping constructions	−0.61
WH relative clauses on subject positions	−0.45
Phrasal co-ordination	−0.36
Nominalizations	−0.36

narrative and non-narrative concerns are combined to support the overall purpose and topic of discourse.

Overall, dimension 2 thus distinguishes between narrative and non-narrative discourse. Fiction registers are the major type of narrative text included in the present study of English, while several types of discourse are non-narrative (expository, procedural, and those focused on the immediate circumstances). In addition, several registers combine narrative and non-narrative concerns, often framing narratives within a larger interactive or expository discourse in support of the overall point.

6.1.3   English dimension 3: 'Situation-dependent versus Elaborated Reference'

As table 6.3 shows, there are three important positive features on dimension 3: time adverbials, place adverbials, and other adverbs.[3] Place and time adverbials are used for locative and temporal reference (e.g., *above, behind; earlier, soon*); these forms typically mark exophoric reference to places and times outside the text itself, often serving as deictics that can be understood only by reference to an external physical and temporal situation. The class of 'other adverbs' includes manner and other adverbials.

Among the negative features on dimension 3 are three different types of relative clauses: WH relative clauses on object positions, WH relative clauses on subject positions, and pied-piping constructions (e.g., *a financial base on which to work*). These features function to explicitly identify referents or to provide elaborating information concerning referents. The co-occurrence of phrasal co-ordination and nominalizations with these relativization features indicates that referentially explicit discourse also tends to be integrated and informational.

Considering both positive and negative features, dimension 3 can be interpreted as distinguishing between 'situation-dependent' reference and highly explicit, 'context-independent' reference. WH relative clauses are used to specify the identity of referents in an explicit and elaborated manner so as to leave no doubt about the intended referent. Time and place adverbials, on the other hand, usually require the addressee to identify the intended referents in the actual physical context of the discourse. Overall, the label 'Situation-dependent versus Elaborated Reference' is suitable for this dimension.

The distribution of registers seen in figure 6.3 fits well with this interpretation. The registers with large positive mean scores, most notably broadcasts but also conversations, fiction, and personal letters, have very frequent time adverbials, place adverbials, and other adverbs, together with markedly few relative clause constructions. Conversely the registers with large negative mean scores, especially official documents and professional letters, have very frequent relative clause constructions (plus phrasal co-ordinators and nominalizations) combined with the marked absence of time and place adverbials. The linguistic characteristics of these two extremes are illustrated by text samples 6.9, 6.10, and 6.11.

Text sample 6.9: Sports broadcast (LL:10.2, soccer match)

as from the hands of Stepney the ball comes out onto this near side # . . . just below us here # . . . Charlton flicking it even more laterally # away from us # . . . down the line now # . . . Curry # on the far side of the field # chips the ball forward # . . . Dunn # down the line # . . . Tom Curry # one of the midfield players ahead of him # [pause] Curry has got the ball # on that far side # chips the ball down the centre #

Text sample 6.10: Sports broadcast (LL:10.2, horse race)

and it's Fire Raiser who's coming up to join Carbon # Fire Raiser on the stand side # and right over on the stand side # is Grange Court # coming to the two furlong from home marker # and it's Carbon over on the far side in the sheepskin noseband # in the centre is Fire Raiser in the check cap # and on the stand side is Grange Court . . . and Fire Raiser's gone to the front now

SITUATION-DEPENDENT

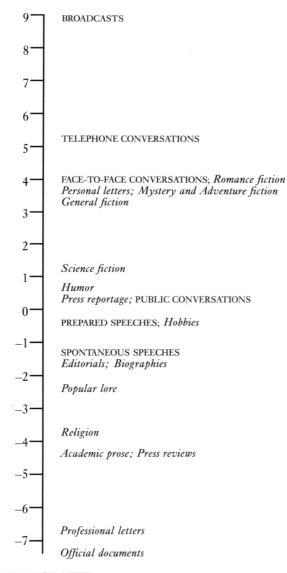

ELABORATED

Figure 6.3 Mean scores of English dimension 3 for twenty-three registers: 'Situation-dependent versus Elaborated Reference' (Polarity reversed). ($F = 31.9$, $p < 0.0001$, $r^2 = 60.5\%$)

Text sample 6.11: Official document (LOB:H.29, university bulletin)

> Students must follow throughout the terms the courses for which they are registered and attend such classes and such examinations as required by the University and by the Heads of the Departments concerned . . . Students must enter on their registration form particulars of any external examinations which they propose to take during the session. University examinations of any kind will in all cases take priority over any other examinations which a student wishes to take.

Samples 6.9 and 6.10 show the extreme use of place and time adverbials common in radio sports broadcasts, which report events actually in progress. These features are used to refer directly to the physical and temporal situation of communication, tracking the sequence of events as they occur. Thus, the soccer broadcast (sample 6.9) is packed with expressions such as *this near side, just below us here, away from us, down the line now, chips the ball forward, ahead of him, on that far side, down the centre*; all of these require direct reference to the playing field and the sporting event in progress for understanding. Similarly the broadcast of the horse race (sample 6.10) shows very frequent referring expressions, such as *right over on the stand side, over on the far side, in the centre, gone to the front now*. The frequent use of these expressions results in the extremely situated characterization of broadcasts on dimension 3.

At the other extreme, sample 6.11 from an official document illustrates the complete absence of such time and place adverbials combined with a dense use of relative clause constructions, phrasal co-ordination, and nominalizations. The relative clauses are used for referential explicitness, leaving no doubt as to the intended reference (e.g., *the courses for which they are registered, any external examinations which they propose to take, any other examinations which a student wishes to take*). Phrasal co-ordination is used for compound referents, again leaving no room for ambiguity (e.g., *attend such classes and such examinations as required by the University and by the Heads of the Departments*). Sports broadcasts and official documents are thus polar opposites in their marking of referents, with broadcasts relying to a very large extent on the physical and temporal situation, and official documents attempting to remove all possible ambiguity.

Other registers, such as telephone and face-to-face conversation, are also situated in reference, although not to the same extent as sports broadcasts. In these registers, participants share temporal and physical situations, addressees can request clarification in case of misunderstanding, and there is a high topical focus on the immediate circumstances and interaction. Sports broadcasts are more situated than conversations since they need to report events actually in progress under severe time constraints. These other registers are similar in showing a marked dependence on direct references to the time and place of communication, however.

Surprisingly, certain written registers are also markedly situated in reference, including personal letters as well as all fiction registers. Personal letters typically assume familiarity with the place and time of writing, even though writer and reader are in fact separated (e.g., from sample 6.5 above, *I'm here at work, I still have tomorrow, this week has flown by*). Fiction is a special case in that it contains situated references to the fictional world created by the author rather than the actual physical and temporal circumstances of writing. For example, in sample 6.7, the references *back against the wall, on the floor, in the living-room*, and *between the bed and the wall* all refer to physical locations within the fictional world of the novel.

Other written registers are quite elaborated in reference, although not to the same extent as official documents and professional letters. Press reviews, academic prose, and religion show extensive use of elaborated reference, while registers such as popular lore, editorials, and biographies show a more moderate use. Among the spoken registers, spontaneous and prepared speeches show a moderate use of elaborated reference (in keeping with their primary informational purposes).

Overall, then, dimension 3 distinguishes among registers according to their reliance on situated versus elaborated reference. As with dimension 1, this dimension is related to the mode distinction between speech and writing, with the most extreme use of situated reference occurring in spoken registers, and an extreme use of elaborated reference occurring in written registers. However, this dimension does not correspond to a spoken/written dichotomy; rather, written registers such as fiction and personal letters are markedly situated in reference, and spoken public speeches are moderately elaborated in reference.

6.1.4   English dimension 4: 'Overt Expression of Argumentation'

Dimension 4 has only positive features: infinitives, prediction modals, suasive verbs, conditional subordination, necessity modals, split auxiliaries, and possibility modals (see table 6.4). Figure 6.4 shows that most registers are unmarked with respect to this dimension, but professional letters and editorials are distinguished by a high frequency of these features, while press reviews and broadcasts are distinguished by the near absence of these features.[4] Text sample 6.12 from a professional letter, and sample 6.13 from an editorial, illustrate the linguistic characteristics of large positive scores on dimension 4.

Table 6.4 *Co-occurring linguistic features on English dimension 4: 'Overt Expression of Argumentation'*

Dimension 4	
Positive features:	
Infinitives	0.76
Prediction modals	0.54
Suasive verbs	0.49
Conditional subordination	0.47
Necessity modals	0.46
Split auxiliaries	0.44
(Possibility modals	0.37)
[No negative features]	

Text sample 6.12: Professional letter (private corpus, Z.1)

Furthermore it really would be inappropriate for me to put words in your mouth. In short, you should really take the format of the resolution and put in your own thoughts . . . the association is already sampling opinion on a number of other matters and it may be possible to add this one. If it is not possible to add your concern this year, it would certainly be possible to add it next year.

Text sample 6.13: Editorial (LOB:B.1, *Daily Herald*, March 6, 1961)

Prime Minister after Prime Minister speaks out in revulsion against the South African Government's policy of apartheid . . .

Will it end with South Africa's exclusion from the Commonwealth? The issue is touch and go.

There is a possibility that it will not be settled at this conference. It may be agreed to wait until South Africa actually becomes a republic later in the year.

But if a final decision is to be faced now, on which side do the strongest arguments lie?

The Archbishop of Capetown has shown that the matter is not clear-cut . . . He must be heard with attention.

On purely practical grounds he holds that it would be a mistake to expel South Africa, weakening the whites who are working for a change of policy. In his view it would also be against the interests of the Africans.

He holds that more pressure can be put on South Africa while she

OVERTLY ARGUMENTATIVE

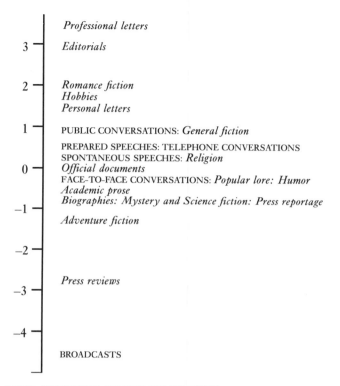

NOT OVERTLY ARGUMENTATIVE

Figure 6.4 Mean scores of English dimension 4 for twenty-three registers: 'Overt Expression of Argumentation.' ($F = 4.2$, $p < 0.0001$, $r^2 = 16.9\%$)

remains in the Commonwealth than could be exercised were she cut off from it

From a consideration of the defining linguistic features together with the distribution of registers, this dimension can be interpreted as reflecting overt argumentation or persuasion. The three modal classes distinguish among different stances that authors (or speakers) take towards their subject, considering various alternatives and then arguing in favor of one of them. Conditional clauses and infinitives can function as part of the same overall scheme of argumentation. Thus, the professional letter (sample 6.12) proceeds as follows: *it really would be inappropriate . . . you should really take . . . it may be possible to add . . . If it is not possible . . ., it would certainly be possible to add it next year.* Split auxiliaries are common in this style of discourse to indicate the author's commitment to the propositions (e.g., *really, certainly*).

These features are even more prominent in the editorial shown in sample 6.13. This text considers various possible future events and possible arguments for and against excluding South Africa from the Commonwealth. Again the overall argument is marked by dimension 4 features: *Will it end . . .? There is a possibility that it will not be settled . . . It may be agreed to wait . . . But if a final decision is to be faced . . .? The Archbishop . . . must be heard . . . he holds that it would be a mistake . . . it would also be against the interests . . . more pressure can be put . . . than could be exercised . . .* The combined use of these features provides the overall structure of the argument in these texts, identifying possible alternatives and the author's stance towards each of them. The large positive scores for editorials and professional letters on dimension 4 reflect the fact that this discourse style is common in those registers.

In contrast, broadcasts and press reviews are marked by the absence of dimension 4 features. Broadcasts are a simple reportage of events in progress, and thus they do not involve argumentation or persuasion (see samples 6.9 and 6.10 above). Press reviews are opinionated, but these opinions are expressed as if they were *the* correct view, and thus reviews have little overt argumentation in support of their position. Samples 6.14 and 6.15 illustrate this direct expression of opinion in press reviews.

Text sample 6.14: Press review (LOB:C.1)

The BBC's dramatised documentary on Florence Nightingale last night cleverly managed to suggest the person behind the legend.

While never minimising the immensity of her work, it lifted the saintly halo which usually surrounds her name to reveal a warm, dedicated person who accomplished most by perseverance and hard work.

Text sample 6.15: Press review (LOB:C.1)

After ten days of intermittent, near fatal ennui, the eleventh Berlin International Film Festival was suddenly jolted back to life by two extraordinary films, Bernhard Wicki's *das Wunder des Malachias* ('The Miracle of Father Malachias') and Michaelangelo Antonioni's *la notte*.

The number of German film directors who have made first rate works in the last 25 years can be counted on the fingers of one hand.

Table 6.5 *Co-occurring linguistic features on English dimension 5: 'Non-abstract versus Abstract Style.' (Polarity reversed – see note 3)*

Dimension 5	
[No positive features]	
Negative features:	
Conjuncts	−0.48
Agentless passives	−0.43
Past participial adverbial clauses	−0.42
BY-passives	−0.41
Past participial postnominal clauses	−0.40
Other adverbial subordinators	−0.39

Both of these samples are typical of press reviews, which express strong opinions without apology or consideration of alternative points of view. Texts from this register thus have very few occurrences of dimension 4 features. Interestingly, the one occurrence of *can* in sample 6.15 connotes the reviewer's ability to describe reality, rather than indicating the existence of different possible points of view (as in samples 6.12 and 6.13).

Figure 6.4 shows that most registers have intermediate scores on dimension 4. Most texts in these registers are not overtly argumentative, but the intermediate score reflects the fact that some of these texts are (see section 9.2.2.6 below).

Dimension 4 is similar to dimension 2 in being unrelated to distinctions between speech and writing. Rather, this dimension reflects an emphasis on overt argumentation, specifying various logical alternatives and arguing for a particular point of view.

6.1.5   English dimension 5: 'Abstract versus Non-abstract Style'

Dimension 5 is similar to dimension 4 in having only negative features. As table 6.5 shows, the features associated with this dimension are conjuncts, agentless passives, past participial (passive) adverbial clauses, *by*-passives, past participial (passive) postnominal clauses (e.g., *the textbook [which was] used in that class*), and other adverbial subordinators.[5] Most of these structures are passive forms, used to present propositions with reduced emphasis on the agent, giving prominence to the 'patient', the entity acted upon. As illustrated by text sample 6.16, the promoted patient is typically a non-animate referent, and it is often an abstract rather than a concrete entity. At the same time, the demoted agent, which is often deleted, is typically an animate referent.

Text sample 6.16 (LOB:J.73, Engineering prose)

> Eventually however fatigue cracks were noticed in the roots of two of the blades and it was suspected that the lack of freedom in the drag hinges was the possible cause. Later, after new blades had been fitted, it was thought better to run with drag hinges free and so reduce root stresses, experience having shown that the possibility of resonance was small. As a further precaution, to eliminate fatigue failure, the new blades of a modified design were run at a reduced top speed of 1200 r.p.m. This question of blade fatigue is more fully discussed in the appendix.

There are numerous passive constructions in this short sample. All of these constructions are main clause agentless passives, which promote an inanimate referent and demote (and delete) the animate agent: *fatigue cracks were noticed* [*by someone*], *it was suspected* [*by someone*], *new blades had been fitted* [*by someone*], *it was thought* [*by someone*], *the new blades . . . were run* [*by someone*], *this question . . . is more fully discussed* [*by someone*]. The animate agents have been demoted to object position and deleted, since the specific agents are not important to the discourse purposes. Rather, inanimate referents, such as *fatigue cracks, new blades*, and *this question* are the focus of discourse here, and these referents have thus been promoted to subject position. Two of these clauses have non-referential *it* as subject, with a *that*-clause in focus; the use of the passive in these constructions similarly demotes the agent of the verb as topically irrelevant. (Sample 6.16 also illustrates the use of conjuncts and adverbial subordinators in this style of discourse, to specify the logical relations among propositions.)

As figure 6.5 shows, academic prose and official documents are the two registers that are most marked by the use of dimension 5 features. The large negative scores for academic prose and official documents reflect very frequent use of conjuncts, main clause passive constructions (agentless and *by*-passives), and dependent clause passive constructions (adverbial clauses and postnominal clauses). These features are especially prominent in the academic subregister of technical and engineering prose, as in text sample 6.16 above. Consideration of the positive extreme of figure 6.5 shows that the distribution of these passive constructions is quite restricted, since all spoken registers as well as written fiction and personal letters are marked by the absence of dimension 5 features. In addition, a number of other written registers, such as biographies, professional letters, and editorials, show only a moderate use of these forms. Overall, then, texts with frequent use of dimension 5 features tend to be abstract and technical in topic and purpose,

NON-ABSTRACT

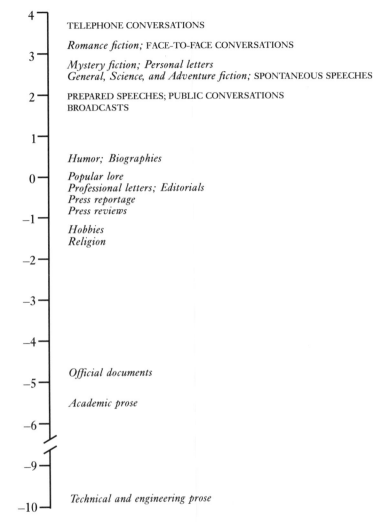

4 — TELEPHONE CONVERSATIONS

Romance fiction; FACE-TO-FACE CONVERSATIONS

3 — *Mystery fiction; Personal letters*
General, Science, and Adventure fiction; SPONTANEOUS SPEECHES

2 — PREPARED SPEECHES; PUBLIC CONVERSATIONS
BROADCASTS

1 —

Humor; Biographies

0 — *Popular lore*
Professional letters; Editorials
Press reportage
Press reviews

−1 — *Hobbies*
Religion

−2 —

−3 —

−4 —

Official documents

−5 —

Academic prose

−6 —

−9 —

Technical and engineering prose

−10 —

ABSTRACT

Figure 6.5 Mean scores of English dimension 5 for twenty-four registers:
'Non-abstract versus Abstract style' (Polarity reversed). ($F = 28.8$,
$p < 0.0001$, $r^2 = 58.0\%$)

Table 6.6 *Co-occurring linguistic features on English dimension 6: 'On-Line Informational Elaboration Marking Stance'*

Dimension 6	
Positive features:	
THAT clauses as verb complements	0.56
Demonstratives	0.55
THAT relative clauses on object positions	0.46
THAT clauses as adjective complements	0.36
(Final prepositions	0.34)
(Existential THERE	0.32)
(Demonstrative pronouns	0.31)
(WH relative clauses on object positions	0.30)
Negative features:	
(Phrasal co-ordination	−0.32)

while several registers (spoken and written) are marked simply by the absence of these features, suggesting the label 'Non-abstract versus Abstract Style'.

6.1.6   English dimension 6: 'On-line Informational Elaboration Marking Stance'

The main features grouped on dimension 6, summarized in table 6.6, are three types of dependent clause: *that*-complement clauses on verbs, *that*-complement clauses on adjectives, and *that*-relative clauses on object positions. Surprisingly, these features co-occur with features such as final ('stranded') prepositions and demonstrative pronouns, which are normally considered to be colloquial. As figure 6.6 shows, this group of features is most common in informational spoken registers: prepared speeches, public conversations (interviews and debates), and spontaneous speeches. Other spoken registers are unmarked for these features or actually show a dispreference for them; these registers include the two conversational registers and broadcasts. Written registers also tend to show only a moderate use of these features (e.g., professional letters and editorials) or to be marked by the absence of dimension 6 features (e.g., fiction, personal letters, press reportage and reviews).

Text sample 6.3 (discussed in section 6.1.1 above) is from a panel discussion and illustrates the frequent use of *that*-complement clauses and relative clauses. These features are typically used to provide informational elaboration while at the same time explicitly presenting the speaker's

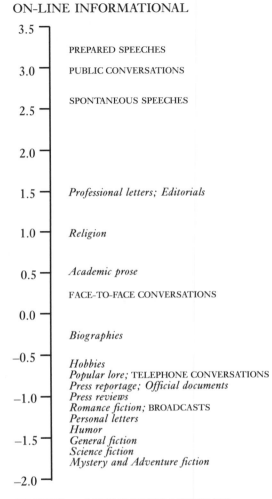

ON-LINE INFORMATIONAL

3.5 ⌐

      PREPARED SPEECHES

3.0 ⌐   PUBLIC CONVERSATIONS

      SPONTANEOUS SPEECHES

2.5 ⌐

2.0 ⌐

1.5 ⌐   *Professional letters; Editorials*

1.0 ⌐   *Religion*

0.5 ⌐   *Academic prose*

      FACE-TO-FACE CONVERSATIONS

0.0 ⌐

      Biographies

−0.5 ⌐

      Hobbies
      Popular lore; TELEPHONE CONVERSATIONS
      Press reportage; Official documents
−1.0 ⌐   *Press reviews*
      Romance fiction; BROADCASTS
      Personal letters
      Humor
−1.5 ⌐   *General fiction*
      Science fiction
      Mystery and Adventure fiction

−2.0 ⌐

EDITED or NOT INFORMATIONAL

Figure 6.6 Mean scores of English dimension 6 for twenty-three registers: 'On-line Informational Elaboration Marking Stance.' ($F = 8.3$, $p < 0.0001$, $r^2 = 28.5\%$)

stance or attitude towards the proposition. For example, the following constructions are illustrated in sample 6.3: *Do you think* [*that there is any chance* . . .], *I've seldom heard a string of sentences* [*that I really do believe* . . .], *I don't believe* [*that this country is* . . .], *I don't think* [*you know* [*that Tony Wedgwood Benn can seriously say* [*that personalities* [*pause*] *don't matter* . . .]]]. In these examples, the speaker's stance is encoded in the verb of the main clause – *think, believe, know* – and the proposition itself is presented in the dependent clause.[6]

Altogether, there seem to be three salient characteristics underlying the extensive use of dimension 6 features: (1) they are used primarily in spoken registers produced under real-time constraints; (2) they are used for informational elaboration in registers having a primary informational (rather than interpersonal) focus; and (3) they are often used to overtly mark the speaker's stance in combination with an informational purpose. These last two characteristics account for the relatively frequent use of these features in professional letters and editorials; as seen from the discussion of dimensions 1, 3, and 4, these two registers are informational as well as overtly argumentative. The characterization of these registers with respect to dimension 6 indicates that they have a moderate marking of stance along with overt argumentation. Thus, although the interpretation of this dimension is more tentative than the others, the defining linguistic features and the distribution of registers both support an underlying function reflecting 'On-line Informational Elaboration Marking Stance.'[7]

6.1.7   English dimension 7 (tentative interpretation: 'Academic Hedging')

Dimension 7 was not interpreted in Biber (1988), because it has no features with factor loadings greater than |0.40|. However, as table 6.7 shows, the features grouped on this dimension are functionally coherent and thus enable a tentative interpretation as reflecting a style of academic argumentation that involves hedging. *Seem* and *appear* are used with *that*-complement clauses to reflect impersonal uncertainty regarding a proposition (e.g., compare *it seems that* with *I think that*). Downtoners similarly express uncertainty, but they enable finer semantic distinctions than hedges, which co-occur with the involved features on dimension 1 (e.g., compare the hedges *sort of, maybe*, and *almost* with downtoners such as *barely, mildly, partially, scarcely*). Concessive adverbial subordination can also function together with these other features, limiting the applicability or validity of one assertion by reference to a second assertion (i.e., *although* ASSERTION 1, ASSERTION 2).

Table 6.7 *Co-occurring linguistic features on English dimension 7. Tentative interpretation: 'Academic Hedging'*

Dimension 7	
Positive features:	
SEEM/APPEAR	0.35
(Downtoners	0.33)
(Adverbs	0.31)
(Concessive adverbial subordination	0.30)
(Attributive adjectives.	0.30)
[No negative features]	

6.2   Nukulaelae Tuvaluan

The analysis of Nukulaelae Tuvaluan is based on Besnier (1988), although additional information and some text samples are taken from Besnier (1986). In the 1988 study, Besnier identifies and interprets three major dimensions of variation in Nukulaelae Tuvaluan. A fourth dimension, which was identified but not interpreted in that study, will also be considered here.

As noted in chapters 3 and 5, Nukulaelae Tuvaluan has a quite restricted range of registers. Nearly all registers can be considered interpersonal in some sense. There are only two written registers: personal letters and sermons. Personal letters are written to specific addressees with the expectation that there will be some response (either an answering letter or a future face-to-face encounter). Sermons are written to be spoken directly to a relatively small, interacting audience; they include religious description and explanation as well as considerable exhortation. The range of registers found in the other three languages is quite different from that found in Nukulaelae Tuvaluan: English, Korean, and Somali all include written registers addressed to large, unbounded audiences, with no expectation of interaction, and highly informational, expository purposes. Since the range of registers in Nukulaelae Tuvaluan is extremely restricted relative to the other three languages, it is likely that the salient dimensions of variation will also be different to some extent.

6.2.1   Nukulaelae Tuvaluan dimension 1: 'Attitudinal versus Authoritative Discourse'

Table 6.8 shows that adverbial forms and pronominal forms account for most of the major positive features on Tuvaluan dimension 1. The adverbial

Table 6.8 *Co-occurring linguistic features on Tuvaluan dimension 1: 'Attitudinal versus Authoritative Discourse'*

Dimension 1	
'Attitudinal'	
Positive features:	
Adverbs	0.71
Hedges	0.70
Third-person demonstratives	0.57
Discourse linkers	0.55
First-person demonstratives	0.55
Second-person demonstratives	0.51
Intensifiers	0.47
Resultative conjuncts	0.45
First-person inclusive pronouns	0.42
'Authoritative'	
Negative features:	
Direct quotes	−0.46
Third-person pronouns	−0.45
Ergative case markers	−0.43
Nominal focus markers	−0.42
(Definite noun phrases	−0.30)
(Anaphoric pronouns	−0.30)

forms – general adverbs, hedges, and intensifiers – indicate the speaker's commitment or attitude towards a proposition. First- and second-person demonstratives are used for noun deixis, identifying a referent in relation to the speaker (first person) or addressee (second person). First-person inclusive pronouns, on the other hand, refer to the speaker together with hearers, indicating solidarity and in-groupness. Discourse linkers and resultative conjuncts are associated with persuasive discourse (Besnier 1988: 722). Together these features are interpreted as marking a careful expression of personal attitudes.

There are fewer negative features: direct quotes, third-person pronouns, ergative case markers, and nominal focus markers. These features are common in authoritative discourse (Besnier 1988: 722), which makes assertions about third-person referents, often marked as being in focus or having high agency (by the ergative case marker). Direct quotes are used as a source of evidence in such discourse.

The interpretation of this dimension as reflecting attitudinal versus authoritative discourse is supported by the distribution of registers, plotted in figure 6.7. The features reflecting attitudinal discourse are most common in the various meetings on Nukulaelae: private-setting speeches, political meetings (*fono*), and maneapa speeches. In these registers, there is an emphasis on the collective activities of the group together with a careful marking and negotiation of personal stance. For example, the following text sample is from the closing of a political meeting:

Text sample 6.17: Political meeting (Besnier 1986: 35)

FAIVA: Kae fakamaaloo fakafetai lasi eiloo moo te . . . Kaati kookoo
            oti taatou, nee? Me koo ppono a te fono a taatou.
OLD MEN: Faafetai! Taai!

Translation
FAIVA: And thank you very much indeed for the . . . Perhaps we
            are done, aren't we? Our meeting is closed.
OLD MEN: Thank you! Thanks!

This short sample illustrates the use of intensifiers (*eiloo* 'very much indeed'), hedges (*kaati* 'perhaps'), tag questions (*nee* 'aren't we?'), and first- and second-person pronouns, including the first-person inclusive pronoun (*taatou*). At the other extreme, sermons are notably authoritative, marked by the absence of features indicating personal attitude, together with a frequent use of nominal and referential features. Text sample 6.18 illustrates several of these features.

Text sample 6.18: Sermon (Besnier 1988: 729)

Ko ia fua toko tasi tou taugaasoa see lavea, e see toko lua, e see toko tolu, e toko tasi eiloa. Ko ia teelaa e fakappula nee ia ou mata faka-te-fakatuanaki kee laeva ei nee koe a ia mo tena kau toko uke, kolaa e tausi kiaa koe mo au mo taatou. Ppula ttonu ou mata kee lavea ei nee koe.

Translation
It is him alone who is your invisible friend, there aren't two of them, there aren't three of them, only one. It is him that makes the eyes of your belief see him and his numerous cohort, those who watch over you and me and us all. Open your eyes so that you can see.

This sample shows the frequent use of sentence-initial focus markers (*ko*), third-person pronouns (*ia*), and ergative case markers (*nee*). These

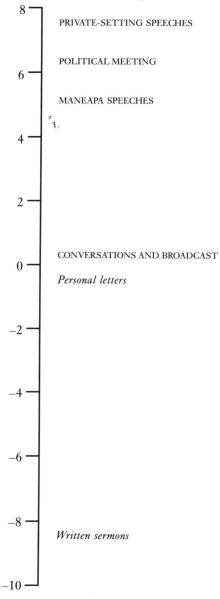

Figure 6.7 Mean scores of Tuvaluan dimension 1 for seven registers: 'Attitudinal versus Authoritative Discourse.' (F = 85.40, p < 0.0001, r² = 70%)

Table 6.9 *Co-occurring linguistic features on Tuvaluan dimension 2: 'Interpersonal versus Informational Reference.' (Polarity reversed)*

Dimension 2	
'Interpersonal Reference'	
Positive features:	
Second-person deictics	0.58
First-person pronouns	0.57
Second-person pronouns	0.53
Co-ordinators	0.44
(Negation	0.38)
(Subordinators	0.36)
(First-person deictics	0.33)
(Inchoative aspect	0.33)
'Informational Reference'	
Negative features:	
Possessive NPs	−0.69
Definite NPs	−0.69
Prepositions	−0.56
Nominalization	−0.54
Nominal focus markers	−0.41
(Third-person pronouns	−0.40)
(Third-person demonstratives	−0.35)

features, together with the absence of features marking personal stance and involvement, result in an authoritative expression of content in sermons.

Interestingly, conversations and personal letters are unmarked on this dimension, apparently because they involve interactions among individual participants, resulting in a less frequent use of inclusive pronouns and a lesser need to specify personal attitudes.

6.2.2   Nukulaelae Tuvaluan dimension 2: 'Interpersonal versus Informational Reference'

Dimension 2 can be considered as reflecting two opposing referential emphases: interpersonal versus informational.[8] The major positive features shown in table 6.9 are referential in that they refer directly to the speaker and hearer: first-and second-person pronouns.[9] Co-ordinators co-occur with these directly interpersonal features, indicating that an interpersonal focus is often associated with a fragmented presentation of information.

The negative features on dimension 2 are also referential, but in this case they reflect an informational rather than interpersonal purpose. Most of these are nominal features: possessive noun phrases, definite noun phrases, nominalizations, and nominal focus markers. These features, together with third-person pronouns, are the major devices used for references to third-person objects or events. Prepositional phrases are used to further elaborate these nominal referents. These features are thus used for informational discourse.

The features on this dimension reflect a basic opposition between interpersonal, fragmented discourse, and informational, integrated discourse. The distribution of registers along dimension 2, seen in figure 6.8, is readily interpreted in these terms. Personal letters, with the largest positive score, have the most frequent occurrence of first- and second-person pronouns and clause co-ordinators (the positive features). Written sermons and broadcasts, which have the largest negative scores, have a dense use of nominal features and prepositional phrases together with the marked absence of interactive features. Sample 6.18 in the last section illustrates the use of these informational features in a sermon.

Other registers, such as maneapa speeches and private-setting speeches, have intermediate scores on this dimension. Conversations also have an intermediate score, reflecting a moderate use of interpersonal reference (and the relative absence of informational referents). The fact that personal letters have a considerably larger positive score than face-to-face conversations supports the interpretation of this dimension as reflecting extensive interpersonal reference rather than direct interaction. That is, personal letters make frequent reference to the author ('I') and receiver ('you'), even though direct interaction through letters is extended over long periods of time due to physical difficulties in communication by mail (Besnier 1986: 45ff.). In fact, letter writers on Nukulaelae sometimes regard letters as a one-sided conversation. For example, consider the following excerpts from letters:

Text sample 6.19 Personal letter extracts (Besnier 1986: 46, 49)

Ia, te ala o te tusi ko te fia sauttala atu fua mo koulua.
'So, the motivation for this letter is my desire to chat with the two of you.'

Fakafetai mo koo fetaui taatou i te lau pepa teenei. Ia, see ko mata, ka ko lau pepa.
'Thanks for the fact that we can meet through this piece of paper. It is not a face-to-face [encounter], but [one that takes place] through a piece of paper.'

Ia, kaati koo gata atu i konaa te sauttalaaga, ia au koo fia moe.
'So, perhaps the conversation will stop here, because I am sleepy.'

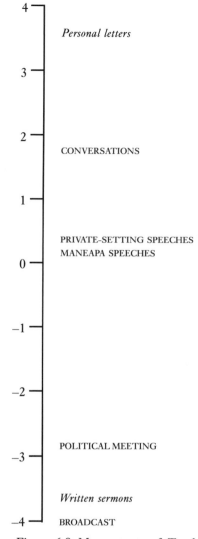

Figure 6.8 Mean scores of Tuvaluan dimension 2 for seven registers: 'Interpersonal versus Informational Reference' (polarity reversed). ($F = 21.77$, $p < 0.0001$, $r^2 = 38\%$)

In addition, one of the main purposes of letters is the expression of personal affect; for example:

Text sample 6.20 Personal letter (Besnier 1986: 49)

> A maaua i taimi katoa e maua ei nee maaua au tusi, e peelaa loa me se aa te mea tafasili koo maua nee maaua i temaa fiaffia mo temaa loto alofa kiaa koe. Teelaa laa, e faitau nee maaua au tusi kae ttagi, ona ko te maafaufau atu moo koe.

Translation
The two of us, every time we get a letter from you, it is like the most joyous thing that happens to the two of us given our love for you in our hearts. Thus, we read them and cry, because we keep thinking about you.

Given these purposes, it is not surprising that letter writers make extensive reference to themselves and the primary addressee. In contrast, since conversations are truly interactive and not openly affective towards the direct participants, they use fewer overt references to the addressor and addressee (who are both physically present). The following discussion of dimension 3 shows, however, that there are other linguistic features associated with direct interactiveness; conversations are marked for the extremely frequent use of these other features, while letters are marked for their absence.

6.2.3   Nukulaelae Tuvaluan dimension 3: 'Multi-party versus Monologic Construction of Text'

dimension 3 can be interpreted as reflecting different ways in which texts are constructed, ranging from truly interactive settings that involve the active participation of several addressors, to monologic production situations.[10] The positive features on dimension 3, summarized in table 6.10, are directly interactive, requiring the participation of more than one addressor. WH questions and direct questions are both direct offers of the floor to another participant, proposing a particular topic for discussion and interactively co-constructing discourse relating to that topic. Direct quotes repeat prior utterances of other participants, and speech act verbs are commonly used with direct quotes.

As figure 6.9 shows, these features are by far most common in conversations, which are the most directly interactive register analyzed for Tuvaluan. Text sample 6.21 illustrates the frequent use of questions in interactive conversation, and sample 6.22 illustrates the combined use of questions and direct quotes in interactive conversational gossip.

Table 6.10 *Co-occurring linguistic features on Tuvaluan dimension 3: 'Multi-party versus Monologic Construction of Text'*

Dimension 3	
'Multi-party Co-Construction of Text'	
Positive features:	
WH questions	0.65
Yes–no questions	0.61
Direct quotes	0.50
(Anaphoric nouns	0.33)
(Speech-act verbs	0.33)
(Type–token ratio	0.30)
'Monologic Construction of Text'	
Negative features:	
Word length	−0.57
Subordinators	−0.41
(Prepositions	−0.36)
(Causative subordination	−0.30)

Text sample 6.21: Conversation (Besnier 1986: 42)

T: Meaa ne mea ppaku? Io, te oso teelaa e ave? Kae aa, kaati teenaa hoki! Me e fai mai me e ave mmata.

V: Koo see fai nee te fenua?

T: Hee iloa atu. Ka ne lavea atu, fakattau mai telotou mea ne fai loo i te ao.

Translation

T: These things are cooked? Oh, [you] are sending that bag of provisions? There, that one too probably! Because they said that it should be sent raw.

V: So the provisions won't be sent as a gift from the whole community?

T: I don't know. I just saw what they said just today.

Text sample 6.22: Conversational gossip (Besnier 1986: 43)

Ta: Konei gaaluega o te kaaiga mo te mea hee ssaga o hai. Te popo mo te uttanu, olo atu o aumai i aso llei, ffoa, ia, maua moo sene, ia, koo kkai. Ko te fale, ko te fale (hoki) teenaa e hai mai.

To: Fakattau koe, a mei i te ffuaaga nei, fakalogo atu nei, koo uga a E mo ko se tino o ssala mai se tamaliki kee tau a te mei. 'Ei! E- e- e fano o aa?' 'Seei, kee tau aka te mei.' 'Sanamapiti! Konei

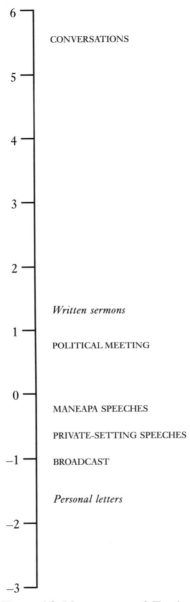

Figure 6.9 Mean scores of Tuvaluan dimension 3 for seven registers: 'Multi-party versus Monologic Construction of Text.' (F = 15.26, p < 0.0001, r² = 30%)

au tama, see maua nee koe o fakatonu, ka iaa ai tama kee fano
koe o- o fai mai?'

Translation
Ta: So here is the work and things that the family is not paying any
attention to. When the weather is nice, [they should] go and get
some copra and some germinated coconuts, then crack them
open, get some cents from it and eat from it. The house, the
house also needs to be built.

To: You just imagine, the breadfruit trees are full of fruit, and
yet what do I hear? She is sending E or someone else to go
and look for some child to harvest the breadfruit tree. 'Hey,
where is she going?' 'Nowhere, just to get the breadfruit tree
harvested.' 'Son of a bitch! Here are your own children, you
don't even know how to give orders to them, and whose child
are you going to ask?'

In contrast to the interactive positive features on dimension 3, the negative
features on this dimension represent types of structural or lexical elaboration:
long words, subordinators, prepositions, and causative subordination. Figure
6.9 shows that these features are most common in the non-interactive
registers, where texts are constructed individually rather than co-constructed
interactively. In addition to the monologic spoken registers – maneapa
speeches, private-setting speeches, and the broadcast – these structural
elaboration features are common in personal letters (which actually has
the largest negative score). This characterization of letters reflects the
distinction between interpersonal reference, which underlies dimension
2, and interactive co-construction of text, which underlies dimension 3.
Letters and conversations are relatively similar with respect to dimension 2,
with letters having an extremely frequent use of interpersonal reference and
conversations showing a moderate use of these features. These two registers
are polar opposites with respect to dimension 3, however; conversations
are extremely interactive, with discourse being co-constructed by multiple
participants, while letters are non-interactive in their production, and thus
require relatively extensive use of these features marking structural and
lexical elaboration.

Several registers (e.g., political meetings, private-setting speeches, and
maneapa speeches) have intermediate scores on dimension 3, reflecting
a certain amount of interaction in combination with extended monologic discourses. Sermons have a moderately large positive score on this
dimension, even though they are not produced interactively. This linguistic
characterization reflects the frequent use of direct quotes (from scripture),

Table 6.11 *Co-occurring linguistic features on Tuvaluan dimension 4. (Tentative interpretation: 'Non-past vs Past Time Orientation')*

Dimension 4	
Positive features:	
Non-past tense markers	0.62
Relative clauses	0.54
Raised noun phrases	0.45
Anaphoric nouns	0.41
(Ergative case markers	0.40)
(First-person inclusive pronoun	0.36)
(Mental process verbs	0.34)
(Conditional clauses	0.30)
Negative features:	
(Past tense markers	−0.33)
(Intensifiers	−0.30)

together with the use of questions for rhetorical effect (e.g., *Fesili: Se aa te taimi o te fakaolataga?* 'Question: What is the time of the resurrection?'; Besnier 1986: 57).

In sum, dimension 3 is interpreted as reflecting 'Multi-party versus Monologic Construction of Text.' Interactional production circumstances involve the active participation of multiple addressors, reflected by frequent questions (and their responses) and the use of direct quotes. Monologic production circumstances, on the other hand, are non-interactive, resulting in a more extensive use of structural and lexical elaboration features.

6.2.4 Nukulaelae Tuvaluan dimension 4 (tentative interpretation: 'Non-past versus Past Time Orientation')

Tuvaluan dimension 4, summarized in table 6.11, was not interpreted in Besnier (1988). It is included here because it represents an opposition between past tense and non-past tense forms, making it important for cross-linguistic comparisons. Some of the other positive features co-occurring with non-past tense forms appear to represent types of structural complexity (e.g., relative clauses, raised noun phrases, conditional clauses). However, without a plot showing the distribution of registers along the dimension, it is difficult to propose a complete interpretation.

All three of the other languages considered here have dimensions reflecting narrative versus non-narrative discourse organizations, marked primarily by the opposition of past and non-past tense forms. The fact that

Nukulaelae Tuvaluan has no written fiction registers, and no exclusively narrative spoken registers, can be used to account for the absence of a strong narrative dimension in that language.[11] However, given this gap in the repertoire of Nukulaelae registers, it is noteworthy that there is still a dimension related to the difference between past and non-past time orientation.

6.3   Korean

The analysis of Korean register variation in based on Kim (1990; cf. Kim and Biber 1994). Although the language and culture of Korea are quite different from the other three language situations considered here, the range of spoken and written registers is similar to that in English. In total, Kim analyzes the relations among twenty-two registers (ten spoken and twelve written) with respect to six dimensions of variation.

6.3.1   Korean dimension 1: 'Informal Interaction vs. Explicit Elaboration'

The co-occurring linguistic features grouped on Korean dimension 1 are presented in table 6.12. Direct questions are the strongest feature on this dimension, indicating that there is an underlying interactive component here. (In Korean, first-person pronouns are often omitted in declarative sentences, and second-person pronouns are often omitted in questions, so these pronominal forms are not strongly associated with the marking of interactiveness or involvement.) Demonstratives are somewhat related to questions in that they mark direct, deictic reference to the situation of communication.

In addition, there are several features that indicate a reduced or fragmented structure. Contracted forms represent a reduction in surface form and a coalescence of morphemes. Fragmentary sentences are structurally incomplete, either missing the required sentence-final speech level marker on the verb or not ending in a verb at all. Discourse conjuncts and discourse verbal connectors are generalized devices for connecting clauses without specifying a particular logical relation between them. Hedges are related to these features in that they mark words or propositions as imprecise.

The positive features on dimension 1 additionally include two features that have conventional associations with colloquial, informal language: short negation and informal postpositions. These forms are considered inappropriate when used in formal written prose or formal spoken situations.

In contrast, the negative features on dimension 1 are associated with an explicit and elaborated presentation of information. Many of these features

Table 6.12 *Co-occurring linguistic features on Korean dimension 1: 'On-line Interaction versus Planned Exposition (Fragmented versus Elaborated Structure)'*

Dimension 1	
'On-line Interaction (Fragmented Structure)'	
Positive features:	
Direct questions	0.81
Contractions	0.80
Fragmentary sentences	0.78
Short negation	0.68
Informal postpositions	0.57
Demonstratives	0.42
Discourse conjuncts	0.42
(Discourse verbal connectors	0.37)
(Hedges	0.35)
'Planned Exposition (Elaborated Structure)'	
Negative features:	
Postposition–noun ratio	−0.72
Relative clauses	−0.53
Attributive adjectives	−0.50
Sentence length	−0.48
Non-finite clauses	−0.43
Third-person pronouns	−0.42
Noun complementation	−0.42
(Possessive NPs	−0.39)

reflect clause complexity and various types of structural embedding: relative clauses, sentence length, non-finite clauses, and noun complementation. Attributive adjectives, relative clauses, noun complementation, and possessive (genitive) noun phrases are all devices for specifying and elaborating the identity of nouns. Postposition–noun ratio indicates the number of nouns that are explicitly marked for their case roles, since postpositions are frequently omitted in Korean. Because third-person pronouns and genitive case markers are recent developments in Korean, they are rarely used; when they do occur, they function to explicitly specify referents.

In sum, the linguistic features defining dimension 1 can be interpreted as reflecting an opposition between reduced, fragmented structures and elaborated, explicit structures. In addition, the positive features show an association between interactiveness and fragmented structure. Figure 6.10 shows that these features are most common in Korean conversation, especially private conversations, but also television drama and public conversations. The large positive scores for these registers also reflect the relative absence of structural elaboration features. These registers are all overtly interactive, plus they are produced on-line, accounting for the fragmented and reduced structure. Text sample 6.23 from a private conversation illustrates some of these characteristics. (The numbers are reference points used below.)

Text sample 6.23: Private conversation (Kim 1990: 111–12)

1   Ppalli wase ancayo.
2   Kamanhi isse.
3   Wuli cejswussi selkeci kkuthnakellang kathi chicako.
4   Ton isseyo, F-ssi?
5   Ton epse. Ton epse.
6   Kulem senpaj-hanthej kkweyaci.
7   Mwe mathkil ke epsna? Sikyej matha, sikyej-na.
8   Sikyej-to an chako osin ke kathaj.
9   Mwe, amukes-to epseyo?
10 Phalcci isse, phalcci.
11 Palcci hoksi ala, palcci?
12 Phalcci isse. Kuke mathkimyen twajci.
13 An twajyo.
14 An twajmyen 'contact lens' mathkitunci.
15 Hahaha.

Translation
1   Come here and sit.
2   Hold on.
3   (Let's) play (cards) after our 'sister-in-law' finishes dish-washing.
4   Do you have money, F?
5   No cash. No cash.
6   Then, borrow from your (senior) alumnus.
7   Do you have collateral? Take a watch, watch.
8   It seems as if she doesn't even have a watch.
9   You don't have anything?
10 Oh, (she) has a bracelet on, bracelet.
11 Do you know about an ankle bracelet, an ankle bracelet?
12 She has a bracelet. That will do.
13 I won't do that.
14 If not, (how about) depositing your contact lenses?
15 Hahaha.

This short sample has four direct questions (lines 4, 7, 9, 11), five fragmentary sentences (lines 3, 7, 10, 11, and 14), short negation forms in lines 8, 13, and 14, and an informal postposition in line 6.

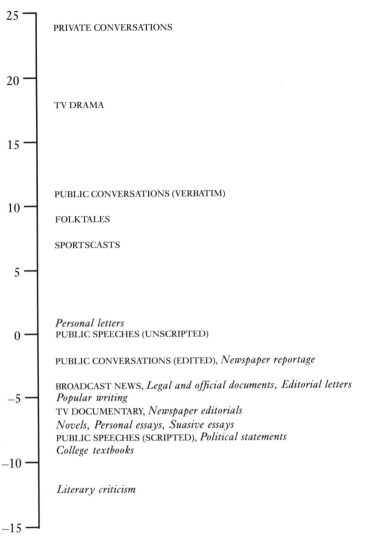

Figure 6.10 Mean scores of Korean dimension 1 for twenty-two registers: 'On-line Interaction versus Planned Exposition (Fragmented versus Elaborated Structure).' (Speech/writing diference: $F = 78.39$, $p < .0001$, $r^2 = 34.69\%$ – see note 13)

At the other extreme on dimension 1 are written expository registers (e.g., literary criticism, college textbooks, essays, editorials) plus informational, spoken monologues (e.g., prepared speeches, television documentaries). The large negative scores for these registers reflect frequent nouns with explicit case marking, relative clauses, attributive adjectives, long sentences, etc. (the negative features), plus markedly infrequent questions, contractions, and fragmentary sentences (the positive features). Text sample 6.24, from literary criticism, exemplifies many of these linguistic characteristics.

Text sample 6.24: Literary criticism (Kim 1990: 113–14)

1   Kule-myen wusen   han-ilanun mal-uj ttus-un
    if-so   first of all han-BE-COMP word-of meaning-TOP

    mues-i-nka?
    what-BE-Q
    'Then, what is the meaning of the word *han*, first of all?'

2   I-ej tajhajse-nun imi   philca-ka   aph-uj   kul-ejse
    this-to-about-TOP already author-SUBJ before-of writing-LOC

    enkuphan   pa-ka   iss-ciman
    mentioned-COMP thing-SUBJ exist-but
    'Although the author (= I) already mentioned about this in the previous article',

3   yeksi kantanhi yoyakhaj poki-lo ha-nta.
    again briefly   summarize to try-as do-DECL
    '(I) will again try to summarize it briefly.'

4   Cuk, han-ilanun mal-un hancae-im-ejnun thullimeps-una,
    i.e., han-BE-COMP word-TOP Chinese-BEING-TOP unmistakable-but
    'I.e., although it is certainly a Sino-Korean word',

5   Cwungkwuk, Ilpon tung talun   hanca sayong
    China   Japan like different Chinese-character-using

    kwukka-ejse ssuiko issnun   kyengwu-ej pihaye,
    country-LOC is being used-COMP case-with   compared
    'compared with the usages in such Chinese character-using countries as China and Japan',

6   hwelssin ku 'connotation'-i nelpko kiphtanun kes.
    by far   the connotation-SUBJ wide   deep-COMP that
    '(it is that) the connotation is by far wider and deeper.'

7   Wenhan, hanthan,   piaj,   hojhan tungtung pucengcekin
      enmity   lamentation sorrow regret etc.   negative

      cengse-lul   phokwalhanun mal-ilanun   cem-ejsenun talun
      emotion-OBJ encompass-REL word-BE-COMP point-LOC   different

      hanca sayong kwukka-uj kyengwu-wa cokumto talul   pa
      Chinese-using countries case-with   not a bit differ-COMP that

      eps-cimanun,
      not-though

      'Although it goes without saying that it expresses such negative
      emotions as enmity, lamentation, sorrow, regret, etc. as with the
      cases in other Chinese character-using countries',

8   tongsiej   kulen pucengcekin cengse-lul   nemesenun
      simultaneously such negative   emotion-OBJ cross-over-REL

      palkun 'connotation'-ul awulle   kancikha-ko isski-to
      bright connotation-OBJ together retain-ING   exist-TO-also

      hatanun kes.
      do-COMP that

      'it also has a bright connotation that can transcend such negative
      sentiments.'

Perhaps the most striking difference between the conversational sample
(6.23) and the prose sample (6.24) is that the latter has much longer
sentences. The prose sample also has several relative clauses (lines 7, 8),
attributive adjectives (lines 5, 7, 8), non-finite clauses (lines 3, 4, 8), and
noun complements (lines 1, 4, 5, 7, 8).

The functional basis of Korean dimension 1 is complex. On the one
hand, it represents a distinction between interactive and non-interactive
discourse. However, this function alone cannot account for the distribution
of registers seen in figure 6.10: for example, folktales and sportscasts are
minimally interactive yet still have relatively large positive scores; edited
public conversations are as interactive as non-edited public conversations,
but the edited versions have moderate negative scores. In addition, many
of the features co-occurring on this dimension are not directly associated
with interactiveness. Rather, several positive features indicate a reduced and
fragmented structure (e.g., contractions, fragmentary sentences, hedges, and
generalized discourse connectors); these features reflect the pressures of
real-time production circumstances. In contrast, the structural elaboration
and explicitness associated with the negative features requires extensive time
during production for planning and revision. The label 'On-line Interaction

versus Planned Exposition' captures the important functional bases of this dimension.[12]

Korean dimension 1 is closely related to the mode difference between speech and writing. Only spoken registers, which are given in small capital letters in figure 6.10, have positive scores reflecting 'on-line interaction.' In contrast, the written registers, which are italicized in figure 6.10, all have negative scores, reflecting their 'planned elaborated exposition.' (Personal letters have a score near 0.) The overall mean score for speech is 6.6, while the mean score for writing is −5.8. The F-score and r^2 value at the bottom of figure 6.10 show that this is a significant and important difference, with 34.6% of the variation among dimension scores being predicted simply by knowing whether a text is spoken or written.[13]

At the same time, there is considerable overlap among some spoken and written registers. In particular, scripted speech − public speeches, television documentaries, and broadcast news − share many of the features of elaborated written exposition. This characterization reflects the fact that these registers originate in writing, even though they are eventually realized in speech.

6.3.2   Korean dimension 2: 'Overt versus Implicit Logical Cohesion'

The positive features on dimension 2, listed in table 6.13, relate primarily to textual cohesion, specifying the relations among propositions. Clause connectors and conjuncts clearly have this function: explanative connectors (translated as 'because'), explanative conjuncts ('therefore'), general 'discourse' connectors ('and', 'but', 'by the way'), co-ordinate connectors ('and-then'), and conditional connectors ('if'). Adverbial subordination similarly specifies a particular relation between the main clause and subordinate clause propositions (e.g., 'when . . .', 'as . . .', 'in order to . . .'). These devices result in an explicit marking of logical cohesion, overtly specifying the logical relations among clauses.

The co-occurrence of co-referential expressions with these positive features shows that there is a high degree of lexical cohesion associated with the explicit marking of logical cohesion; that is, the same referents are referred to repeatedly in these texts. Action verbs, manner adverbs, and subject markers indicate that this is an active, clause-oriented style. (Subject marking, as opposed to topic marking, is the typical case in transitive clauses.) Postposition−noun ratio measures the proportion of nouns that have overt case markers, again explicitly specifying the logical relations among discourse entities. Together, these positive features indicate highly cohesive text, with frequent active, transitive clauses, repeated references

Table 6.13 *Co-occurring linguistic features on Korean dimension 2: 'Overt versus Implicit Logical Cohesion'*

Dimension 2	
'Overt Logical Cohesion'	
Positive features:	
Explanative verbal connectors	0.80
Subject markers	0.71
Explanative conjuncts	0.67
Adverbial subordination	0.66
'Discourse' verbal connectors	0.58
Action verbs	0.55
Co-ordinate verbal connectors	0.54
Co-referential expressions	0.50
Manner adverbs	0.47
Postposition–noun ratio	0.47
Conditional verbal connectors	0.43
- -	- - -
'Implicit Logical Cohesion'	
Negative features:	
Nouns	−0.51
Possessive markers	−0.41
(Passive constructions	−0.39)
(Derivational adjectives	−0.35)

to the same participants, and an overt specification of the logical relations among clauses and phrases.

The negative features are fewer in number, but they show a nominal as opposed to verbal style (frequent nouns, possessives, adjectives), and the frequent use of passive clauses as opposed to active, transitive clauses. Most importantly, though, there are no features that mark logical relations associated with the negative features. This linguistic pattern indicates that highly nominal, passive texts tend to rely on an implicit system of cohesion, requiring readers and listeners to determine the logical relations among discourse entities for themselves.

The distribution of registers along dimension 2, shown in figure 6.11, is somewhat surprising. Spoken folktales have by far the largest positive score, reflecting the most extensive overt marking of logical cohesion. Private conversations also have a relatively large positive score on this dimension, followed by public speeches, television drama, and public conversations with moderately positive scores. Text sample 6.25 illustrates the extensive use of these cohesive devices in a folktale.

At the other extreme are several written expository registers, such as

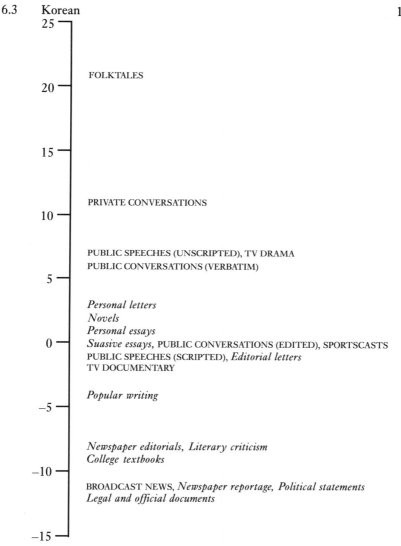

Figure 6.11 Mean scores of Korean dimension 2 for twenty-two registers: 'Overt versus Implicit Logical Cohesion.' (Speech/Writing difference: $F = 61.50$, $p < 0.0001$, $r^2 = 29.4\%$)

legal and official documents, newspaper reportage, and political statements, together with (scripted) broadcast news. It is interesting that the explicit marking of logical and lexical cohesion (as measured by these features) does not correlate with some situational requirements for explicit, unambiguous meaning in Korean: for example, legal and official documents must be maximally clear and unambiguous, so that they can provide the basis for legal and official decisions free from the biases of particular readers. Despite this requirement, the distribution along dimension 2 shows that there is little overt marking of logical cohesion in Korean legal documents, reflecting a reliance on other mechanisms to specify the logical relations among clauses (such as punctuation and the implicit relations underlying adjacent clauses). Sample 6.26 illustrates the absence of cohesive devices in a legal document (an executive order regulating industrial complexes).

Text sample 6.25: Folktale (Kim 1990: 117)
[Folktale of a husband who is trying to find his wife, who was kidnapped by a mountain boar. Capitalized words are either conjuncts or co-references; italicized morphemes are verbal connectors.]

   1 KULAJ, kiphun sancwung-ejl tulekass*nuntej*,
   2 halwu ta mos ka*ko* myechil-inci kwulmeka*mye*, caka*mye*, kunyang tulekass*nuntej*,
   3 kiphun sancwung-ulo tuleka*nikka*,
   4 khun pawi, cipchej-manhan pawi-ka iss*nuntej*,
   5 KU pawi-ka mun-i isse.
   6 KULAJSE kamanhi po*nikka*, cham pancilpancilha*ntej*,
   7 kwul-i isse chachumchachum tulekassketun.
   8 Tuleka*nikka*, acwu, KEKI-se ppallaj soli-to na*ko* kkalkkalkeliko wusnun soli-to na*ko*
   9 tto phulpath-to iss*ko* KU sok-ejnun.
  10 KULAJ, phulpath-ej ka*se* kamanhi anca tulu*nikka*,
  11 kamanhi po*nikka* kunyang ppallajhanun yecatul-i wuski-to ha*ko* tto wulki-to ha*ko* kule*nuntej*,
  12 maak kunyang phi mutun os-to ppal*ko* haketun.
  13 KULAJ kamanhi anca po*nikka*, isanghaketun, KULEN sancwung-ejse.

Translation
   1 So, (he) went deep into (the) mountains.
   2 As (he) couldn't reach (there) in a day, (he) kept on going, sleeping (here and there on the way) without eating.
   3 As (he) continued to go deep into (the) forest,

4 (he) found a big rock, as big as a house.
5 There was a door on the rock.
6 So (he) looked at (it) closely, (the texture of it) was very fine.
7 Through a tunnel (inside the rock, he) went in slowly.
8 As (he) went in, you know, there (he) heard people washing clothes and laughing.
9 There was even a grass patch, inside it.
10 So, (he) crept to (the) grass and tried to hear (them).
11 As (he) closely watched, some people were laughing and some people were weeping.
12 A lady was washing blood-stained clothes.
13 So (he) felt strange because (it) was in such deep mountains.

The words in parentheses are implied but not realized in Korean.

Text sample 6.26: Legal document (Kim 1990: 119–20)
[an executive order regulating facilities in industrial complexes]

1 I yeng-un kongep   tanci   kwanlipep-uj   (iha
   this order-TOP industrial complex maintenance law-of (hence

   pep-ila   hanta) sihajng-ej   kwanhaye philyohan
   the law-as call) implementation-to about   necessary

   sahang-ul   kyucengham-ul mokcek-ulo hanta.
   matters-OBJ regulate-ING-OBJ objective-as do

   'The purpose of this order is to provide ordinances that are necessary for implementing the regulations on industrial complex maintenance.'

2 Pep cej2co   cej2ho-uj   kyuceng-ej ujhan kongep   tanci-uj
   law 2nd article 2nd item-of regulation-by   industrial complex-of

   kwanli   epmu-nun taum   kakho-wa   kathta.
   maintenance duty-TOP   following each item-as same

   'Maintenance responsibilities defined by article 2–2 of the regulation are as follows.'

3 Kongkong sisel-uj   selchi,   wunyeng   mich ku
   public   facilities-of installation management and the

   kyejhojk-uj swulip.
   plan-of   making

   'Installation and maintenance of public facilities and the planning of it.'

4 Ipcwu   kiepchej mich ciwen   kiepchej-uj sisel-uj
   participating business and   supporting business-of facilities-of

   selchi-wa   ku majkak ttonun imtaj.
   installation-and the selling or   lease

   'Installation, marketing, and lease of manufacturing and supporting
   facilities.'

5 Kongep tanci   an-uj   yongci mich sisel-uj   majkak kyejyak
   industrial complex inside-of site   and   facilities-of selling contract

   ttonun imtaj kyejyak-uj chejkyel.
   or   lease contract-of deal-making

   'Selling or leasing contracts for the sites and facilities within the
   boundary of the complex.'

6 Sisel-uj   selchi-wa   yongci mich sisel-uj   yuci,
   facilities-of installation-and site   and   facilities-of maintenance

   poswu ttonun kajlyang-ej   ttalun   iyongca-loputheuj
   repair or   improvement-to accompanying user-from-of

   piyong   cingswu.
   expenses collecting

   'Provisions for collecting expenses and fees for installation, maintenance, and improvement of the facilities.'

7 Sisel-uj   kyengpi.
   facilities-of security

   'Security of the facilities.'

8 Cej1ho   najci   cej5ho-uj   epmu swuhajng-ej   philyohan
   1st article through 5th article-of duty   performance-for necessary

   putaj   epmu.
   auxiliary duty

   'Other responsibilities for implementing articles 1 through 5.'

Text sample 6.25 from a folktale shows extensive use of logical clause connectors, although they are not all transparent from the English translation.
The cohesive devices illustrated here include explanative clause connectors
(-*nikka*, in lines 3, 6, 8, 10, 11, 13), explanative conjuncts (*kulaj*, in lines 1,
6, 10, 13), discourse clause connectors (-(*nu*)*ntej*, in lines 1, 2, 4, 6, 11),
co-ordinate clause connectors (-*ko*, -*mye*, in lines 2, 8, 9, 11, 12). There are
also numerous co-referential expressions and action verbs in this sample.

There are generally few nouns, though, since many nominal references are realized by zero pronouns. In particular, the frequent references to the main character ('he') in subject position consistently have no overt surface realization, since these referents are easily recoverable from the context.

Text sample 6.26 from a legal document illustrates the opposite extreme: no overt markers of logical cohesion, few co-references, few main clauses, and no 'action' verbs, coupled with very frequent nouns. This sample illustrates the linguistic characteristics of expository text having a focus on referential (nominal) information rather than events, resulting in little specification of the relations among clauses.

In sum, dimension 2 represents the overt marking of logical cohesion versus other discourse organizations that rely on implicit relations among propositions; the label 'Overt versus Implicit Logical Cohesion' reflects this interpretation.[14] Extensive use of overt cohesive devices is most common in registers that present a sequence of events, to specify the relations among events (especially in folktales, conversations, television drama). Edited registers use fewer cohesive devices than corresponding unedited registers; thus, compare edited and unedited public conversations, and scripted and unscripted public speeches. Similarly, spoken registers show a much greater tendency to use overt cohesive devices than written registers. Thus, the overall mean score for speech is 5.6, while the overall mean score for writing is -4.8; this is a significant and important difference (F-score $= 61.5$; $r^2 = 29.4\%$). Apparently the careful planning and editing possible in written registers enables a more integrated, implicit specification of relations among clauses, and readers have ample opportunity to infer logical relations when processing a written text; thus writing tends to omit overt surface markers of cohesion. In contrast, many spoken registers show a frequent use of these features, because listeners require an overt specification of logical relations (since they have less time for comprehension), and speakers have less opportunity for an integrated, implicit specification of relations during production.

6.3.3   Korean dimension 3: 'Overt Expression of Personal Stance'

Dimension 3, summarized in table 6.14, comprises several features reflecting the personal attitudes and feelings of speakers and authors. Hedges and emphatics measure the degree of commitment to a proposition: weak commitment in the case of hedges (e.g., *ama* 'perhaps', *keuj* 'almost') and strong commitment in the case of emphatics (e.g., *punmyenghi* 'obviously', *chamulo* 'really'). Although these forms mark opposite attitudes, they co-occur in that they are both overt markers of attitude, in contrast to the absence of any attitudinal markers. Attitudinal expressions, or delimiters, are also

Table 6.14 *Co-occurring linguistic features on Korean dimension 3: 'Overt Expression of Personal Stance'*

Dimension 3	
'Overt Personal Stance'	
Positive features:	
Verbal complementation	0.70
Emphatic expressions	0.70
Attitudinal expressions	0.55
Private verbs	0.50
Hedges	0.42
Short negation	0.40
Indirect questions	0.40
(First-person pronouns	0.36)
(Noun phrase complementation	0.35)
- -	
'Faceless'	
Negative features:	
Nouns	−0.54

grouped on this dimension (e.g., *-(i)ntul* 'even', *-(i)ya* 'as far as'). Private verbs and verb complements often occur together; private verbs are used to express a variety of personal feelings and attitudes (e.g., *ujsimhata* 'doubt', *musewehata* 'fear'), and verb complements present propositions modified by these attitudes. First-person personal pronouns co-occur with these other features to mark attitudinal expressions as belonging personally to the speaker/writer. (The only negative feature on dimension 3 is nouns, apparently reflecting a highly nominal style of informational exposition that has a minimal marking of personal stance.)

As figure 6.12 shows, dimension 3 features are most pronounced in those registers having personal expression as a primary purpose: private conversations, personal letters, and personal essays. Interestingly, these features are even more frequent in television drama than in private conversations; this distribution apparently reflects the dramatic nature of television dialogue, where personal feelings and attitudes are exaggerated to stimulate audience interest, resulting in a style that is even more 'real' than real life!

The negative extreme of this dimension might be characterized as 'faceless,' that is, a presentation of information with no acknowledgment of personal attitude. In fact, legal documents, with the largest negative score, do not even have an acknowledged author, since they are an institutional statement of laws or regulations; these texts thus show no expression of personal attitude. Newspaper reportage, (spoken) news broadcasts, television documentaries, and sportscasts are similar in that they are direct reportage

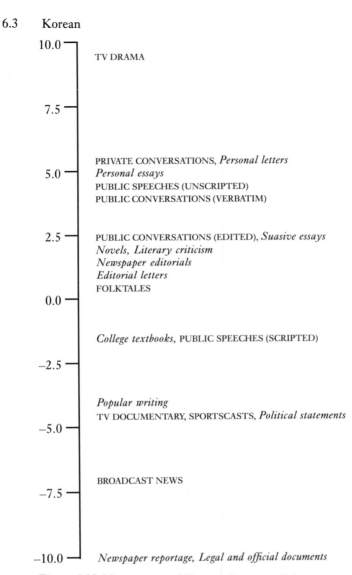

10.0 ┐
         TV DRAMA

7.5 ─

         PRIVATE CONVERSATIONS, *Personal letters*
5.0 ─   *Personal essays*
         PUBLIC SPEECHES (UNSCRIPTED)
         PUBLIC CONVERSATIONS (VERBATIM)

2.5 ─   PUBLIC CONVERSATIONS (EDITED), *Suasive essays*
         Novels, Literary criticism
         Newspaper editorials
         Editorial letters
         FOLKTALES
0.0 ─

         College textbooks, PUBLIC SPEECHES (SCRIPTED)

−2.5 ─

         Popular writing
         TV DOCUMENTARY, SPORTSCASTS, *Political statements*
−5.0 ─

         BROADCAST NEWS

−7.5 ─

−10.0 ┘   *Newspaper reportage, Legal and official documents*

Figure 6.12 Mean scores of Korean dimension 3 for twenty-two registers: 'Overt Expression of Personal Stance.' (Speech/Writing difference: $F = 8.66$, $p < 0.005$, $r^2 = 5.5\%$)

Table 6.15 *Co-occurring linguistic features on Korean dimension 4: 'Narrative versus Non-narrative Discourse'*

Dimension 4	
'Narrative Discourse'	
Positive features:	
Past tense	0.79
Type-token ratio	0.73
Time adverbs	0.46
Action verbs	0.45
'Non-narrative Discourse'	
Negative features:	
Present tense	−0.44
Formal conjuncts	−0.40

of events and situations, purportedly factual rather than reflecting an individual's attitudes. It is interesting that political statements have a relatively large negative score on this dimension; even though these texts express an individual's attitude towards current affairs, they apparently adopt a direct, 'faceless' stance.

In sum, dimension 3 can be interpreted as marking the 'Overt Expression of Personal Stance', depending on the primary purpose of discourse. Although figure 6.12 shows that personal stance is more likely to be expressed in spoken registers than in written registers, it also shows that both speakers and writers can adopt a personal stance when it fits their purposes (as in conversation and letters); similarly, both speakers and writers can suppress overt markers of stance when a 'faceless' style is required (as in broadcast news and press reportage).

6.3.4   Korean dimension 4: 'Narrative versus Non-narrative Discourse'

Only a few features co-occur on Korean dimension 4, and their interpretation is straightforward (see table 6.15). Three of the four positive features are verbal. These features mark a primary focus on the temporal succession of past events, or narrative discourse: past tense reflects a focus on past time; temporal adverbs indicate a temporal ordering among events; and action verbs are used to narrate dynamic events (as opposed to static description or explanation). Type–token ratio co-occurs with these features, indicating that narrative discourse in Korean tends to have more varied vocabulary than non-narrative discourse.

There are only two important negative features on dimension 4: present tense and formal conjuncts. These features are used to provide static descriptions and explanations, emphasizing the logical rather than temporal relations among clauses.

As figure 6.13 shows, novels and folktales have two of the largest positive scores on dimension 4. These registers are primarily narrative, marked by very frequent past tense verbs, time adverbs, and action verbs. Text sample 6.25 (in section 6.3.2) illustrates these features in a folktale, and sample 6.27 illustrates their use in a novel.

Text sample 6.27: Novel (*Yengwung sitaj*' from Kim 1990: 125)
[from a novel on the Korean War]

> Putulewun 'engine' soli-wa hamkkej catongcha-nun yathumakhan entek kil-lo cepetulessta. Kajcen cikhwu Pukhan-ejse tajlyang-ulo nohojkhan chalyangtul-un cinan myech tal tonganej keuj somotojepelintejta twukkepkej ancun hukmenci-man takkanajmyen kumsaj tulenanun santtushan kwukpangsajk chachej-lo poa ujyongkwun-i kajiptojn twi-ej sajlo nohojkhan yenhapkwun-uj 'jeep' cha kathassta.

Translation
> The car approached a road on a hill with a soft engine sound. Cars captured by the North Korean army during the first stage of the war were almost consumed, but this car had a bright brown color right underneath a thin layer of dirt: this jeep must have been captured from the allied forces very recently after the 'voluntary' corps became involved in the war.

In addition to the exclusive use of past tense forms, text sample 6.27 illustrates the extreme lexical diversity typical of Korean fiction. None of the lexical words in this sample is repeated forms; even the word 'car,' which is repeated in the English translation, is referred to as *catongcha*, *chalyangtul*, and *jeep'cha*. In contrast, expository prose in Korean shows extensive lexical repetition (a low type–token ratio) in addition to a nearly exclusive use of present tense and static verb forms. Sample 6.28 illustrates these characteristics from a college textbook on statistics. The short sample shows several repetitions of the technical terms *pyenin* 'variable', *yenkwuca* 'researcher', *yenkwu* 'research', and *toklip* 'independent'. These technical forms tend to be repeated to preserve the exact meaning (as opposed to the alternation among semantically related, but distinct, terms in fiction).

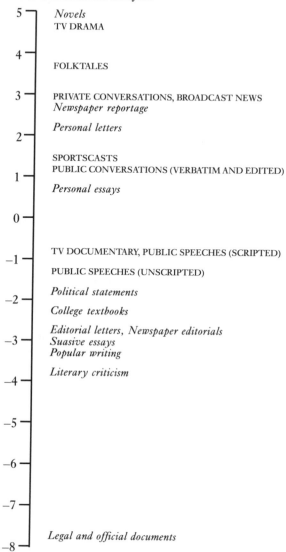

Figure 6.13 Mean scores of Korean dimension 4 for twenty-two registers: 'Narrative versus Non-narrative Discourse.' (Speech/writing difference: $F = 26.32$, $p < 0.0001$, $r^2 = 15.1\%$)

Text sample 6.28: College textbook on statistics (Kim 1990: 126)

Silhem yenkwu-ejse yenkwuca-ka imujlo cocakhanun pyenin-ul toklip
pyenin-ila hako i toklip pyenin-ej yenghyang-ul patnuntako sajngkak-
hanun, yenkwuca-uj kwansim-uj pyenin-ul hunhi congsok pyenin-
ilako pulunta. Kulena kiswulcek yenkwu-ej isseseto pilok yenkwuca-ka
yenkwuhakoca hanun pyenin-ul ujtocekulo cocak thongcejhal swu-nun
epsciman . . .

Translation
In an experimental study, the variable that researchers can manipulate
at will is called independent variable, and the variable that is affected
by the independent variable and that is the focus of the research is
often called dependent variable. But even in a descriptive study, where
researchers cannot manipulate variables at will . . .

Figure 6.13 shows that a number of registers besides novels and folktales
are narrative in orientation. Television drama has a positive score almost as
large as novels, and private conversations also have a quite large positive
score. Public conversations have moderately large positive scores on this
dimension. These characterizations seem to indicate that narration is an
integral part of Korean conversation. The relatively large positive score
for personal letters shows that narration plays a key role in all personal,
interactive discourse in Korean, whether spoken or written. In addition,
news reportage is marked for its reliance on narration, again both spoken
(broadcast news and sportscasts) and written (newspaper reportage).

However, the exclusion of narration appears to be restricted to written
registers in Korean. Thus, Figure 6.13 shows that television documentary
and public speeches are relatively unmarked on this dimension, having a
slight preference for non-narrative over narrative discourse forms, while
several written registers are distinguished by the absence of narrative
forms. These registers represent various types of informational exposition,
for example, textbooks, editorials, literary criticism. The most extreme case
is represented by legal and official documents (see sample 6.26 in section
6.3.2), which show a nearly exclusive reliance on present tense, static verb
forms, together with extensive repetition of technical vocabulary.

In sum, dimension 4 reflects the distinction between narrative and
non-narrative discourse organization. In Korean, this distinction has some
relation to physical mode differences: the frequent use of narrative forms is
common in both spoken and written registers, but the exclusive reliance on
non-narrative forms is found primarily in written, expository registers.

Table 6.16 *Co-occurring linguistic features on Korean dimension 5: Tentative interpretation: 'On-line Reportage of Events'*

Dimension 5	
Positive features:	
Declarative sentences	0.80
Present tense	0.68
Copular verbs	0.59
'Formal' sentence endings	0.49
(Adversative conjuncts	0.36)
Negative features:	
Sentence length	−0.48

6.3.5 Korean dimension 5: 'Tentative Interpretation: On-line Reportage of Events'

The functional basis of dimension 5 is not clear, so only a tentative interpretation will be given here. Table 6.16 presents the co-occurring linguistic features on the dimension, and figure 6.14 plots the distribution of registers. It is clear from this figure that the primary distinction along dimension 5 is between sportscasts and the other registers. The large positive score for sportscasts reflects very frequent occurrences of declarative sentences, present tense verbs, copular verbs, formal sentence endings, adversative conjuncts (translated 'but' or 'however'), and short sentences. The other two sentence types analyzed by Kim (interrogative and imperative) are generally rare in Korean; imperatives were dropped from the factor analysis because they were too infrequent, and interrogatives are restricted primarily to the conversational registers. Thus the frequency of declarative sentences essentially represents the total frequency of sentences in a text, and the complementary distribution of declarative sentences and sentence length represents an opposition between many, short sentences versus relatively few, long sentences. This use of frequent, short sentences is apparently well suited to the on-line reportage of events in progress, as in sportscasts, suggesting the tentative label 'On-line versus Off-line Reportage of Events.'

At the negative extreme on figure 6.14 is newspaper reportage, with registers such as broadcast news, college textbooks, and political statements having moderately large negative scores. Newspaper reportage and broadcast news were shown in the last section to rely on a past tense narration of events, and thus it is not surprising that they should be marked here by the absence of present tense forms. The characterization along dimension

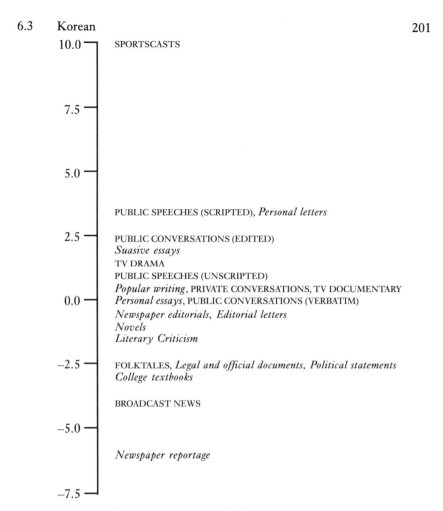

Figure 6.14 Mean scores of Korean dimension 5 for twenty-two registers. Tentative interpretation: 'On-line Reportage of Events.' (Speech/writing difference: $F = 9.68$, $p < 0.005$, $r^2 = 6.1\%$)

5 shows further that these registers have relatively few sentences that are often quite long, and that they rely on lexical rather than copular verbs for their reportage.

Most registers are relatively undistinguished along this dimension, however, and the scores for some registers seem at odds with the interpretation of on-line reportage: for example, it is not clear why suasive essays, personal letters, or scripted public speeches have moderately large positive scores,

Table 6.17 *Co-occurring linguistic features on Korean dimension 6: 'Honorification'*

Dimension 6	
Positive features:	
Honorific expression	0.79
Humble expression	0.78
'Formal' sentence ending	0.43
Time adverb	0.42
(First-person pronoun	0.39)
- -	
[No negative features]	

since they do not describe events in progress and are not produced on-line. A careful analysis of these features in particular texts from these registers is thus needed for a more satisfactory interpretation of dimension 5.

6.3.6   Korean dimension 6: 'Honorification'

Although there are relatively few features co-occurring on dimension 6, they are readily interpretable (see table 6.17). Honorific expressions are used to express deference to the addressee or the person spoken about. Humble expressions are particular forms of the first- and second-person pronouns plus particular verbs that are used with first-person pronouns; these forms also show deference to the addressee relative to the speaker/writer. Speech levels (sentence-final particles) are yet another marker of deference; formal sentence endings, which mark speech level 1, show the greatest deference to the addressee. First-person pronouns are commonly omitted in Korean sentences; when they are expressed, they commonly co-occur with humble forms to mark explicit deference of the speaker/writer to the addressee.

From the distribution of registers seen in figure 6.15, three main considerations seem to be involved in the extensive use of honorification devices: the existence of a particular addressee, the social distance between addressor and addressee, and a public setting. Thus, apart from personal letters, all written registers have negative scores on dimension 6, reflecting the relative absence of honorification devices. This characteristic is apparently due to the lack of a particular addressee in these registers, making the use of honorifics and self-humbling expressions less important. Personal letters are the only written register included in the Korean study that is addressed to an individual reader, and thus letters show extensive use of honorification.

The influence of a specific addressee can also be seen from a comparison

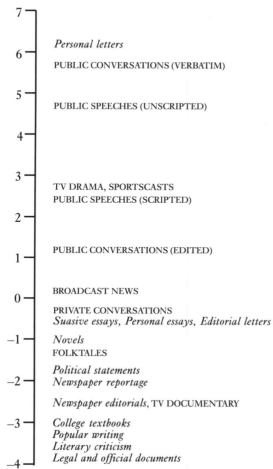

Figure 6.15 Mean scores of Korean dimension 6 for twenty-two registers: 'Honorification'. (Speech/writing difference: $F = 35.42$, $p < 0.0001$, $r^2 = 19.3\%$)

of parallel spoken and written registers: verbatim and edited public conversations, unscripted and scripted public speeches, and broadcasts and newspaper reportage. In each of these comparisons, the spoken register is addressed to a live audience: an individual addressee in public conversations (interviews), a physically present audience in the case of public speeches, and a television audience in the case of broadcasts. As the addressee becomes less identifiable across these three spoken registers, the use of honorification becomes less frequent. Thus, public conversations have one of the largest positive scores here, while broadcast news is essentially unmarked. In addition, the written counterpart in each of these comparisons has considerably less honorification than the spoken counterpart; the honorific and humbling devices have apparently been removed by editors in the written registers, in recognition of the fact that the published version is being addressed to a wider, less specified audience.

Surprisingly, private conversations show much less use of honorific and humbling devices than (written) personal letters or public conversations. Private conversations are by definition not public, and the participants are commonly friends or peers. In contrast, public conversations (such as live interviews, radio talk shows, parliamentary hearings) occur in front of a live audience, and the individual participants are typically unacquainted. The public setting and relatively large social distance seem to be the main factors causing the greater use of honorification in public conversations. The personal letters in this study were addressed primarily to relatives across generational boundaries (e.g., son to mother, son-in-law to mother-in-law, daughter to mother, daughter-in-law to mother-in-law), so that the social distance is relatively large (in comparison to conversations among peers). In addition, a written letter is public in the sense that it is permanent, which apparently also contributes to the careful use of honorific devices in this register.

It is interesting that even television drama shows a considerably greater use of honorification than private conversations. As with dimension 3 ('Stance'), the characterization here identifies a difference between the perception of what conversational interactions *should* be like (viz., television drama) and actual conversations. In addition, this difference reflects the fact that television drama occurs in a public forum; that is, these are 'private' conversations viewed by a wide public audience. For this reason, they show considerably greater use of honorific devices than truly private conversations.

In sum, dimension 6 shows the importance of social relations and setting in the characterization of Korean registers. The honorification system is one of the most studied aspects of the Korean language, and it is one of the most noticeable and problematic areas for foreign learners of the language. The analysis here confirms the importance of this system as a separate dimension of register variation in Korean.

6.4   Somali

The analyses of Somali presented here are based primarily on the published papers by Biber and Hared (1992a, b, 1994), supplemented by further analyses of the Somali corpus. Although Somali has only a very short history of literacy, it has a wide synchronic range of spoken and written registers. The analysis here describes the relations among twenty-nine registers with respect to six dimensions of variation.

6.4.1   Somali dimension 1: 'Structural Elaboration: Involvement versus Exposition'

Somali dimension 1 is represented by a large number of co-occurring linguistic features, presented in table 6.18. The positive features include:

1   non-declarative, interactive, sentence types: yes–no questions, 'what if' questions, imperatives, WH questions;

2   interactive or involved lexical classes: responses (e.g., *haye* 'ok'), stance adjectives (adjectives such as *neceb* 'hate' and *jecel* 'like' functioning in predicative positions as personal expressions of feeling; e.g., *waan jeclahay*... 'I like ...'), time deictics (e.g., *shaley* 'yesterday'), and downtoners (e.g., *waa laga yaabaa* 'maybe');

3   main clause features: contrastive main clause co-ordination (*eh*), independent verbs, main clause focus markers (*waa, baa*), total main clauses, and verbless clauses;

4   other involved or reduced features: contractions, conditional clauses, first- and second-person pronouns.

The negative features on this dimension include:

1   dependent clause features: dependent clauses, full relative clauses, *waxaa* clefts, *ah* relative clauses, *oo* co-ordination (which connects dependent clauses, independent clauses, or verb phrases), and verb complements;

2   nominal elaboration: word length, common nouns, derived adjectives, phrase co-ordination (*iyo*), *-eed* genitives, and attributive adjectives;

3   elaborating phrases in clauses: case particle sequences (marking the inclusion of multiple indirect object case roles in a clause) and single case particles.

Some of the positive features are overtly interactive (e.g., questions, first- and second-person pronouns) or involved (e.g., stance adjectives, downtoners), while other positive features are primarily structural, reflecting a simple co-ordination of clauses. In contrast, the negative features represent structural elaboration (e.g., dependent clauses, relative clauses, clefts) and informational integration (e.g., long words, frequent nouns, and attributive adjectives).

Based on the patterns associated with analogous dimensions in English and Korean, it is possible to anticipate that the distribution of registers along Somali dimension 1 distinguishes between interactive, involved,

Table 6.18 *Co-occurring linguistic features on Somali dimension 1: 'Structural Elaboration: Involvement versus Exposition'*

Dimension 1

'Involvement (+ structurally reduced and fragmented)'
Positive features:

Simple responses	0.97
Yes–no questions	0.91
Contrast clause co-ordination (*eh*)	0.88
Stance adjectives	0.81
Contractions	0.74
Independent verbs	0.73
'What if' questions (*soo*)	0.70
Time deictics	0.68
waa focus markers	0.67
Main clauses	0.63
baa focus markers	0.60
Downtoners	0.59
Imperatives	0.58
WH questions	0.47
Conditional clauses	0.43
Second-person pronouns	0.41
(First-person pronouns	0.30)
(Verbless clauses	0.30)

- -

'Exposition (+ structurally elaborated)'
Negative features:

Dependent clauses	−0.63
Full relative clauses	−0.63
waxaa clefts	−0.60
ah relative clauses	−0.58
Clause co-ordination (*oo*)	−0.54
Word length	−0.53
Common nouns	−0.52
Derived adjectives	−0.52
Phrase co-ordination (*iyo*)	−0.52
-eed genitives	−0.46
Verb complements	−0.45
Case particle sequences	−0.44
(Single case particles	−0.34)
(t-unit length	−0.34)
(Agentive nouns	−0.33)
(Compound nouns	−0.33)
(Attributive adjectives	−0.32)
(Purpose clauses	−0.30)
(*ahaan* adverbials	−0.28)

structurally fragmented registers (with large positive scores) and expository registers having carefully integrated information and extensive structural elaboration (with large negative scores). As figure 6.16 shows, this is the set of distinctions found along this dimension.

The registers with large positive values, such as conversations and family meetings, have high frequencies of yes/no questions, stance adjectives, contractions, main clauses, etc. (the positive features on dimension 1), together with markedly low frequencies of total dependent clauses, relative clauses, nouns, derived adjectives, etc. (the negative features on dimension 1). Registers with large negative values, such as political pamphlets and editorials, have the opposite linguistic characteristics: high frequencies of dependent clauses, nouns, etc., plus low frequencies of yes/no questions, contractions, etc.

The positive extreme of Somali dimension 1 thus characterizes three extremely involved registers: conversations, family meetings, and conversational narratives. In contrast, there is a tight cluster of informational, expository registers at the negative extreme of this dimension (e.g., editorials, political pamphlets, press reportage). In between these two extremes, there are a number of spoken registers and three written registers. These intermediate registers are also distributed according to their focus on personal involvement versus informational exposition. Among the intermediate spoken registers, sermons and conference discussions are relatively involved, while lectures and sports broadcasting are relatively informational. Among the intermediate written registers, folk stories and personal letters are relatively involved, while general fiction is more informational.

Text sample 6.29 illustrates the extremely involved characterization of face-to-face conversations in Somali, while text sample 6.30, from a university lecture, illustrates the mixed informational/involved characterization common in informational spoken registers.

Text sample 6.29: Conversation

[Some young women discussing whether they had meddled in a relationship between a married couple; speaker A feels unjustly accused]

B: Wallaahi   dee way   iska fiicnayd [pause].
    swear to God uh FM-she just was fine [pause]

    Suurahay   taqaan haye.
    coyness-FM-she knew   isn't it

D: Walaal   meherkeedii   [unintelligible words]
    oh sister legal-wedding-her

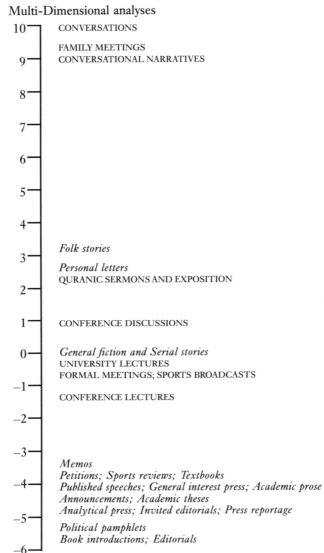

Figure 6.16 Distribution of twenty-nine registers along Somali dimension 1: 'Structural Elaboration: Involvement versus Exposition.' (F = 101.0, p < 0.0001, df = (25,253), r^2 = 90.9%)

A: Waxaa iigu   dambeysayba waa kaas.
what   me-for last-time-was FM   that [time]

Waxay   iigu   darnayd   ayaantay   Aamina ku
what-she me-for was the worst [was] day-the-she Amina   to

tidhi   'ninkayga [pause] ninkayga
she-said man-my   [pause] man-my

B: ninkaygay   igu   dirayaan.'
man-my-FM-they me-against they-set

A: Adduunka kelmaddaasi weli waa xasuustaa ka   warran!
world-the, word-that   still FM-I remember, about report

B: Dee horta   waa runoo   waan ku dirnee.
uh first-the FM   truth-and FM-we to we send-and

Ma og   tahay? Taasi ma been baa?
QM know being That QM lie   FM

A: Kuma dirin.
to-NEG send

B: illaahay baan kugu   dhaarshee ma been baa?
God-my FM-I   from-with swore-and QM lie   FM

Laakiin adaa   adaa   gardarnaa   Sacaado.
but   you-FM you-FM justice-without Sa'ado

Markaan ku idhi ha u sheegin, ha u sheegin, ma tidhi
time-the-I to said OPT to tell-not   OPT to tell-not   QM said

saaxiibaan nahay?
friends-we being

Ma naag   baa iyo ninkeedaa la dhexgalaa?
QM women FM   and man-her-FM IMP middle-enter

Translation
B: I swear, she [i.e., the wife] was just fine. She knew how to be
coy, didn't she?
D: Sister, her legal-wedding . . .
A: The last time that I saw her was that time. What was the worst
thing for me was the day that she said to Amina 'my man,
my man –
B: – they are setting my man against me.'

A: Can you imagine! I still remember that word, what do you
think of that?

B: uhm, first of all it is true and we set her against him, don't you
know? Is that a lie?

A: We didn't set her against him.

B: I swear to you upon God, is it a lie? But you, you were at fault,
Sa'ado. When I said to you 'don't tell (her), don't tell (her),'
didn't you say 'we are friends?' Are a woman and her husband
meddled with? [i.e. isn't it wrong to meddle with a women and
her husband?]

Text sample 6.30: University lecture (economics)

Heerka   3aad wuxuu noqonaayaa   [pause]
level-the third what-it is becoming (is)

isla   maalgelin   ayuu noqonaayaa [pause].
REFLEX-with wealth-enter FM-it is becoming

Laakiin waxa loo   fiirinaa maalgelinta   siday
But   what IMP-for looking wealth-enter-the (is) way-the-it

u saameyn kartaa ama u faragelinaysaa dhismaha   guud   [pause]
affect   can   or   for finger-entering building-the general,

dhismaha   guud   oo dhaqaaalaha
building-the general of economy-the

iyo siday   u   faragelin   kartaa ama u saameyn kartaa qofka
and way-the for finger-enter can   or affect   can   person-the

wax soo saaraaya [pause].
thing from producing

Masalan waxaad   ka   soo qaadaysaa   siday   sawir
example what-you from back are taking (is) way-which-FM-it picture

uga   bixinaysaa   maalgelintani   guud   ahaan
for-from you are giving wealth-enter-this general being

dalka   [pause].
country-the

Translation
The third stage is going to become – it is also going to be investment.
However, investment is considered for the way that it can affect or

interfere with the general structure, the general structure of the
economy, and how it can interfere with or it can affect the person
producing goods. For example, you are going to consider [i.e. if
you were an investment planner, you would consider] how will this
investment give a picture about the country in general?

Sample 6.29 illustrates the high-involvement style common in Somali conversation, marked by frequent questions, first- and second-person pronouns,
and contractions (e.g., *suurahay* = *suuraha* + *ayaa* + *ay* 'coyness-the'
+ FM + 'she'; *runoo* = *run* + *oo* 'truth' + 'and'). This sample is
also quite unelaborated structurally, shown by the preponderance of main
clause constructions and focus markers, together with the relative absence
of relative clauses, WH clefts, and other dependent clauses.

Sample 6.30, on the other hand, illustrates the mixture of involvement
and structural elaboration common in informational spoken registers: for
example, in this sample from a university lecture there are frequent contracted forms (e.g., *siday* = *sidee* + *ayaa* + *ay* 'way-which' + FM +
'it'; *wuxuu* = *waxa* + *uu* 'thing-the' + 'it'), plus a few rhetorical WH
questions and references to *aad* 'you.' Structurally, though, lectures are
quite elaborated, relying on clefts and dependent clause constructions more
than simple main clause constructions. Thus sample 6.30 contains only one
simple main clause, but it has three WH clefts, plus frequent relative clause
and dependent clause constructions (e.g., *qofka wax soo saaraaya* 'the person
who is producing goods'; *siday sawir uga bixinaysaa* 'the way that you are
going to give a picture').

Expository written registers are even more marked with respect to Somali
dimension 1. Thus figure 6.16 shows that all written registers, apart from
letters and the fiction registers, have larger negative scores than any spoken
register. The extremely elaborated linguistic characteristics of these registers
can be illustrated by the following text sample from an editorial.

Text sample 6.31: News editorial (May 11, 1974; *Xiddigta Oktoobar*)

Gobanimadoonka Afrika iyo afgembiga ka dhacay dalka Bortuqiiska
'Independence movements of Africa and the coup d'etat that occurred
in Portugal'

Haddii aan arrintaa   ka   eegno dhinaca dhaqdhaqaaqa
if   we matter-that from look   side-the movement-the

gobanimadoonka   Afrika waxaan oran karnaa   in
independence-search-the Africa what-we say   can   (is) that

isbeddelkaasi   ka   dhacay   Boortuqiiska uu yahay mid
REFLEX-change-that from happened Portugal-the it being one

hore   u wadi doono siyaasadda isticmaariga   ah, hase yeeshee
forward to take will   policy-the colonialism-the is let be-but

waxa dhici   karta   inuu   la   yimaado tabo   cusub uu ula
what happen can (is) that-it with come   tactics new it to-with

jeedo inuu   waqti ku kasbo   markaa kaddibna   bannaanka
mean that-it time   with benefit time-that from-after-and outside-the

uu ula   soo   baxo siyaasaddiisii is-addoonsiga ahayd.
it to-with towards go   policy-its-the REFLEX-slavery was

Translation
If we look at that issue with respect to the liberation movements of Africa, what we could say is that the self-transformation [i.e., the coup] that happened in Portugal is one which will continue the policy which is colonialism. However, what can happen is that it [i.e., the political change] would come with new tactics whose purpose is to gain time and then come out in public with its [old] policy which was enslavement.

Text sample 6.31 has only two main clauses, both structured as WH clefts followed by complement clauses rather than simple independent clauses (i.e., *waxaan oran karnaa in* . . . 'what we can say is that . . .' and *waxa dhici karta inuu* . . . 'what can happen is that it . . .'). The sample also illustrates the extremely dense use of relative clause constructions common in Somali written prose (e.g., *isbeddelkaasi ka dhacay Boortuqiiska* 'the change that happened in Portugal'; *mid hore u wadi doono siyaasadda isticmaariga ah* 'one which will continue the policy which is colonialism'). The only involvement features in this sample are the conditional clause, the use of rhetorical 'we' in the beginning, and a few contractions (i.e., *waxaan = waxa + aan, inuu = in + uu*).[15] Overall, this sample is thus characterized by the very frequent use of structural elaboration features and the near absence of involvement features.

However, even though the poles clearly separate spoken and written registers, it should be emphasized that Somali dimension 1 does not define a spoken/written dichotomy. Rather, folk stories and personal letters are written but have relatively 'involved' characterizations, while lectures, formal meetings, and sports broadcasts are spoken with relatively 'expository' and 'elaborated' characterizations. Similarly, dimension 1 does not clearly

Table 6.19 *Co-occurring linguistic features on Somali dimension 2: 'Lexical Elaboration: On-line versus Planned/Integrated Production' (Polarity reversed; see note 16)*

Dimension 2	
[No positive features]	
Negative features:	
Hapax legomena	−0.92
Type-token ratio	−0.88
Nominalizations	−0.54
Compound verbs	−0.48
Single case particles	−0.47
Demonstrative relatives	−0.40
(Clitic topic co-ordination	−0.35)
(Gerunds	−0.35)
(Purpose clauses	−0.31)
(Word length	−0.30)

distinguish between interactive and non-interactive registers: for example, among the spoken registers, conversational narratives are somewhat less interactive than conversations but just as marked on this dimension. Among the written registers, personal letters are more interactive than folk stories, but they have nearly the same characterization (with folk stories actually being slightly more involved).

Although this dimension is functionally related to mode and interactiveness, the primary underlying parameter here seems to reflect different author/speaker purposes: a cline from personally involved expression to informational exposition. Linguistically, many of the features on dimension 1 relate to structural elaboration (the negative features) versus a fragmented, reduced structure (the positive features). This dimension can thus be labeled 'Structural Elaboration: Involvement versus Exposition.'

6.4.2 Somali dimension 2: 'Lexical Elaboration: On-line versus Planned/Integrated Production'

Table 6.19 shows that Somali dimension 2 has only negative features.[16] The stronger features on this dimension are lexical characteristics: *hapax legomena* (once-occurring words), type-token ratio (the number of different words),[17] nominalizations, and compound verbs. Gerunds and word length also co-occur with these features. This grouping of features can be interpreted as distinguishing between texts having careful and elaborated lexical choice

214 Multi-Dimensional analyses

(lexical diversity, rare words, and derivationally complex words) and texts using frequent repeated lexical forms which are short and derivationally simple.[18]

Figure 6.17 plots the mean dimension scores of Somali registers with respect to dimension 2. Sports broadcasts have the largest positive score, and registers such as lectures, conversations, and family meetings have relatively large positive values; these scores reflect markedly low frequencies of once-occurring words, nominalizations, compound verbs, and gerunds, together with markedly short words and little lexical diversity (type–token ratio). Published political speeches and editorials have the largest negative scores, reflecting extreme lexical diversity and elaboration.

Although both dimension 1 and dimension 2 distinguish between spoken registers at one extreme and written registers at the other extreme, there is a major difference in the overall distribution of registers along the two dimensions: all spoken registers are similar to one another in their lack of lexical elaboration on dimension 2, while there is a relatively wide spread of spoken registers using structural elaboration features to differing extents along dimension 1. The distribution along dimension 2 shows that all spoken registers are marked as having little lexical variety and an absence of elaborated lexical items, regardless of their purpose (e.g., informational versus interpersonal), topic (e.g., academic versus everyday), or interactiveness (monologue and dialogue).[19]

Thus consider text samples 6.29 and 6.30 again. Although they differ markedly in their structural elaboration features, both of these texts have relatively restricted vocabularies and extensive repetitions. Sample 6.29, from a conversation, has almost no lexically complex forms (nominalizations or compound forms), and it relies heavily on repeated occurrences of common words, frequent pronominal forms, and elided references. Often, entire phrases are repeated in conversations (e.g., *ma been baa* 'is it a lie?', *ha u sheegin* 'don't tell [her]'). Sample 6.30, although much more informational in purpose, similarly shows a frequent use of repeated forms (e.g., *noqonaayaa* 'is becoming', *faragelin* 'interfere', *dhismaha guud* 'the general structure'); these repeated words are sometimes relatively technical in meaning (e.g., *maalgelin* 'investment').

In contrast to the restricted range of variation among spoken registers, written registers have many different characterizations along dimension 2. Some written registers, such as editorials, published political speeches, political pamphlets, and analytical press, are very elaborated in their lexical choice, showing extreme lexical diversity and very frequent use of derived words and longer words. Other written registers, such as folk stories, memos, and personal letters, are less informational in purpose and thus have more moderate scores here, although they still show greater lexical diversity and

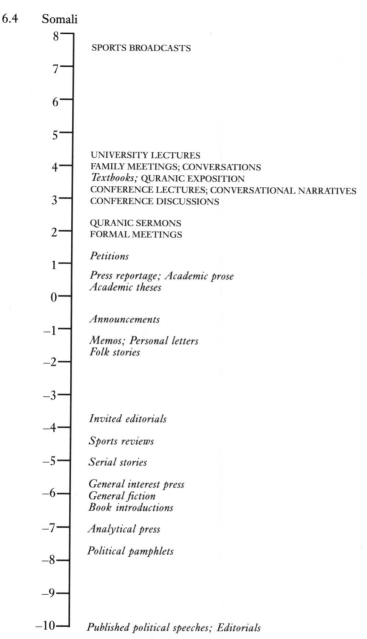

8 ─ SPORTS BROADCASTS

7 ─

6 ─

5 ─

4 ─ UNIVERSITY LECTURES
FAMILY MEETINGS; CONVERSATIONS
Textbooks; QURANIC EXPOSITION
CONFERENCE LECTURES; CONVERSATIONAL NARRATIVES
3 ─ CONFERENCE DISCUSSIONS

QURANIC SERMONS
2 ─ FORMAL MEETINGS

Petitions
1 ─
Press reportage; Academic prose
Academic theses
0 ─

Announcements
−1 ─
Memos; Personal letters
Folk stories
−2 ─

−3 ─

Invited editorials
−4 ─
Sports reviews

−5 ─ *Serial stories*

General interest press
−6 ─ *General fiction*
Book introductions

−7 ─ *Analytical press*

Political pamphlets
−8 ─

−9 ─

−10 ─ *Published political speeches; Editorials*

Figure 6.17 Distribution of twenty-nine registers along Somali dimension 2: 'Lexical Elaboration: On-line versus Planned/Integrated Production' (Polarity reversed). ($F = 13.7$, $p < 0.0001$, $df = (25,253)$, $r^2 = 57.5\%$)

216 Multi-Dimensional analyses

elaboration than the spoken registers. Surprisingly, some informational registers, such as press reportage and academic prose, have intermediate scores on this dimension, while high-school textbooks have a relatively large positive score. These scores reflect the frequent repetition of technical terms, which are often borrowed (from English or Italian) rather than derived from native Somali words. In contrast, editorials and the political registers make frequent use of institutional terms, which are typically created through nominalizing and compounding processes; these forms tend to be longer than borrowed forms, and they are also derivationally complex.[20]

Text sample 6.31 above, from an editorial, shows an extremely different style from both samples 6.29 and 6.30 with respect to its lexical characteristics; there are few lexical repetitions, but a frequent use of long, relatively rare lexical forms, which are frequently compounded or derived (e.g., *dhaqdhaqaaqa* 'the movement', *gobanimadoonka* 'the liberation movements', *isbeddelkaasi* 'that self-transformation', *isticmaariga* 'the colonialism', *siyaasaddiisii* 'its policy', *is-addoonsiga* 'enslavement').

This editorial sample can also be contrasted with text sample 6.32, from a front-page press report.

Text sample 6.32: Press reportage (May 25, 1974; *Xiddigta Oktoobar*)

Jaalle Carte: Wadammada Afrika waxay muujiyeen kalsoonida iyo tixgelinta ay u hayaan dadka Soomaaliyeed

'Comrade Arte: The African countries, what they expressed [is] the confidence and the respect [that] they have for the people of Somalia'

Muqdisho, May, 24 ((SONNA))
Mogadishu, May, 24 ((SONNA))

Xoghayaha Arrimaha Dibadda   ee dalkan   Soomaaliya
Secretary-the affairs-the outside-the of country-this Somalia

Jaalle   Cumar Carte Qaalib shalay   ayuu ku   soo
Comrade Omar Arte Qalib yesterday FM-he with towards

laabtay   magaaladan Muqdisho kaddib markii   uu socdaal
came-back city-this   Mogadishu after   the time [that] he trip
ku   kala   bixiyey   waddamo   ku yaal
with from   each he caused to go out countries [that] in are there

Qaaradda   Afrika iyo Aasiya. Xoghayuhu intii   uu booqashada
continent-the Africa and Asia   secretary-the while he visit-the

ku marayey dalalka   ka   mid ah   Qaaradda Afrika
to going-on countries from one being (is) continent Africa

wuxuu Madaxdooda u gudbiyey dhammbaalo uu uga   siday
what-he heads-theirs to conveyed messages   he from-to brought

Madaxweynaha GSK, Jaalle   Maxamed Siyaad Barre.
President-the   SRC Comrade Mohamed Siad   Barre

Key to abbreviations
GSK = Golaha   Sare   ee Kacaanka
             Council-the Supreme of Revolution-the
SRC = Supreme Revolutionary Council

Translation
Mogadishu, May 24 ((SONNA)) – The Foreign Secretary of this country
of Somalia, Comrade Omar Arte Qalib, came back yesterday to this city
of Mogadishu after having paid visits to countries which are on the
continents of Africa and Asia. While the secretary was visiting these
countries which are part of the African continent, he conveyed to their
heads [i.e. the presidents] messages that he carried from the President
of the SRC, Mohamed Siad Barre.

This sample differs from the editorial sample (sample 6.31) in that the words
tend to be shorter, less complex, and more common. There are also more
repeated lexical forms in the press reportage sample. However, the kinds
and extent of lexical repetition are different from that found in conversations
and lectures. In the spoken registers, it is rare to find synonymous lexical
items used for the same referent, and there is frequent repetition of phrases
due to the constraints of on-line production (as well as the emphatic force
achieved by repetitions). In the case of press reportage, repetitions are used
to give the text a high degree of cohesion; for example, the following lexical
roots are repeated in the two sentences contained in sample 6.32: *xoghaya*
'the secretary', *dal* 'country', *Qaaradda* 'the continent', *Madax* 'head' or
'president'. A longer sample would illustrate additional repetitions of this
type, as well as relatively frequent repetitions of proper nouns. However,
this short sample also illustrates several cases where distinct lexical forms
are used to refer to the same or overlapping referent; for example *maddamo*
and *dalalka* for 'countries', *socdaal* and *booqashada* for 'trip/visit', *bixiyey*
and *marayey* for 'travel through (a place)'. Text sample 6.32 thus illustrates
the intermediate characterization of press reportage with respect to the
lexical elaboration dimension – it has considerably more lexical diversity
and complexity than the most planned and informational spoken registers,
but considerably less lexical elaboration than registers such as editorials.
    Considering the grouping of linguistic features on dimension 2, which
represent lexical diversity and lexical elaboration, together with the distribution

of registers seen in figure 6.17, it is possible to propose the label 'Lexical Elaboration: On-line versus Planned/Integrated Production.' This dimension seems to represent a basic difference between the production possibilities of speech and writing. All spoken registers, regardless of purpose or interactiveness, are produced on-line and thus show little lexical diversity or elaboration. This restriction is most pronounced in sports broadcasts, where broadcasters must describe events in progress. In contrast, writers have extensive opportunity for careful word choice, and thus written registers can show extreme lexical diversity and elaboration. However, writers of registers such as personal letters, folk stories, and announcements can choose not to exploit the production possibilities of the written mode because lexical elaboration is not required for their purposes and topics. Finally, writers of registers such as academic prose and textbooks can deliberately restrict the range of lexical diversity, due to the need for precise, technical vocabulary.

Somali dimensions 1 and 2 show reverse patterns with respect to the range of variation within speech and writing. Both dimensions polarize interactive, interpersonal speech at one extreme and informational exposition at the other. dimension 1, though, shows a quite restricted range of variation among written registers versus a wide range of variation among spoken ones. Apart from folk stories, personal letters, and fiction, all written registers are markedly elaborated in structure, while spoken registers range from the involved, non-elaborated characteristics of conversations and family meetings to the relatively informational and structurally elaborated characteristics of lectures, formal meetings, and sports broadcasts. In contrast, dimension 2 defines an extremely restricted range of variation among spoken registers versus a quite wide range of variation among written ones. Both dimensions reflect differences relating to purpose and topic, but dimension 2 further reflects differences in the production possibilities of speech versus writing – spoken registers are restricted in lexical elaboration due to on-line production constraints, regardless of their purpose.

6.4.3   Somali dimension 3: 'Argumentative versus Reported Presentation of Information'

Table 6.20 shows that dimension 3 defines a basic opposition between present tense and past tense features. However, as indicated by the co-occurrence of past tense verbs and future time modals (both among the negative features), this dimension does not represent a simple dichotomy between present and past events. In addition to present tense, the positive features on dimension 3 are adjectival forms (predicative adjectives, attributive adjectives, and derived adjectives), qualified statements (possibility modals, concession conjuncts, and conditional clauses), impersonal constructions (clauses with

Table 6.20 *Co-occurring linguistic features on Somali dimension 3: 'Argumentative versus Reported Presentation of Information'*

Dimension 3	
'Argumentative presentation of information'	
Positive features:	
Present tense	0.89
Predicative adjectives	0.55
Possibility modals	0.50
Concession conjuncts	0.46
(Verbless clauses	0.38)
(Attributive adjectives	0.38)
(Derived adjectives	0.38)
(Impersonal particles	0.37)
(Conditional clauses	0.33)
(Dependent clauses	0.31)
'Reported presentation of information'	
Negative features:	
Past tense	−0.58
Proper nouns	−0.54
Agentive nouns	−0.45
(Framing clauses	−0.36)
(Future modals	−0.32)
(Speech act verbs	−0.29)

impersonal agents), and other clausal features (verbless clauses and total dependent clauses). The negative features on dimension 3, in addition to past tense, are animate/human references (proper nouns and agentive derived nouns[21]), future modals, framing clauses, and speech act verbs. The negative features represent projected time (past or future) with a focus on specific human referents; the positive features represent present time, with frequent elaborating details and qualifying conditions and concessions.

Figure 6.18 plots the distribution of Somali registers with respect to dimension 3. Family meetings have the largest positive score on this dimension, similar to dimension 1. Conversations, however, differ from family meetings on this dimension in having an intermediate score, while formal meetings are quite similar to family meetings here. There are also several written registers with quite large positive scores on dimension 3, such as general-interest press, analytical press, textbooks, and invited editorials. All registers with large positive scores are characterized by a heavy reliance on present tense forms, frequent adjectives, possibility modals, and concessive conjuncts (the positive features on dimension 3), combined with a marked absence of past tense forms, proper nouns, and agentive nouns (the

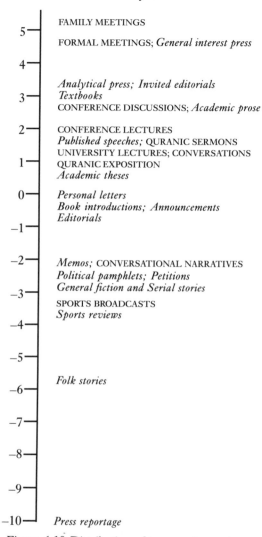

Figure 6.18 Distribution of twenty-nine registers along Somali dimension 3: 'Argumentative versus Reported Presentation of Information.' (F = 11.8, p < 0.0001, df = (25,253), r^2 = 53.8%)

negative features on dimension 3). These characteristics are illustrated by the following two text samples from a family meeting:

Text sample 6.33: Family meeting: plans for the maintenance of the house – building a fence.

A: Adigu waxay ila   tahay konton kun ka   yaraan
    you   what   it-me-with is   50,000   than smaller

    mayso. Hadday oodda   caadiga   ah ay noqoto   laakiin
    not   if it   thorn bush plain [which] is   it becomes but

    tan   kale
    this one other

B: hii
    uhuh

A: lacag   badan iyadu ma leh.   Tan   kale oo   imika
    money much   it   doesn't have this one other which (is) now

    an sheegaynee   gobtii
    we were telling-and (which) 'gob'-tree-the-is

B: hii
    uhuh

A: dhawr dameer   baa ku   filan   baa la   waxaynayaa,
    several donkey (loads) FM   with satisfies FM   IMP is making

    labaatan kun ka   badnaan mayso taa   gobku
    20,000   than more   is not   that-one 'gob'-tree-the

    gobyartu,   laakiin tan   kale lacag   dooray
    small-'gob'-tree-the however this-one other money importance-

              noqoneysaa.
    being-FM-it is becoming

Translation
A: It seems to me that it won't be less than 50,000 (shillings), if we
    use the normal thorn bushes. But the other one
B: uhuh
A: will not cost much money. The other one that we were just now
    talking about, which is the 'Gob' tree,
B: uhuh
A: several donkey loads will be enough, it will be done – the small

'Gob' trees will not be more than 20,000 (shillings). But the other one will become more money.

Text sample 6.34 Family meeting – planning possible business ventures for the family

A: Sigaar   baa la   soo qaadan karaa, alaab kalaa   la soo
    cigarettes FM   IMP DIR take   can   goods other-FM IMP DIR

    qaadan karaa, bariiskan   imminka ay   doontay
    take   can   rice-this (which) now   she looked for

    Xaali   ay keentoo kalaa   la heli karaa [pause]
    Xaali (which) she brought similar-to-FM IMP find can

    betroolka iyo naaftadaasaa la dhex   roori karaa oo   aan
    petrol   and diesel-that-FM IMP middle run   can   and I

    haddaad u amba-baxdo wax   dhulkaa   la kala
    if-you to depart   something country-that IMP away-from

    boobaya   yaad wax   ka   qalaafi kartaa. Haddaanse
    are snatching FM-you something from take   can   if-I-but

    lacag   aan ku   shaqeeyo helo,
    money we with work   find

B: hii
    uhuh

A: waa ka   tegayaa.   Maxaa i   dhigaaya?
    FM-I from am-leaving what   me put down

Translation
A: Cigarettes can be brought back, other goods can be brought back, like this rice which she just looked for now – which Xaali brought – can be found; petrol and diesel can be traded; and (I) if you devote yourself to something, you can get something from the country which is being robbed. But if I get money to work with,
B: uhuh
A: I am leaving (my job). Why am I going to stay?

These two text samples are almost entirely in the present tense, even though future plans are being discussed in both cases. The discussion centers around the relative merits of various plans, and thus there are very frequent possibility modals (*kar-* 'can'), concession conjuncts (e.g., *laakiin* 'although'), and conditional clauses (*haddii-* 'if').[22]

Several other registers, both spoken and written, have moderately large positive scores on dimension 3. These include informational spoken registers, such as conference discussions, conference lectures, university lectures, and sermons, as well as face-to-face conversations. Published political speeches and academic prose also have relatively large positive scores here.

The text samples from a university lecture (6.30) and an editorial (6.31), discussed in the last section, illustrate 'argumentative' styles in informational registers. Both samples show a primary reliance on present tense forms, as well as the use of concessive conjuncts (*hase yeeshee* 'however' in the editorial; *laakiin* 'but, however' in the lecture) and possibility modals (in the editorial: *oran karnaa* 'we could say', *dhici karta* '(what) can happen'; in the lecture: *siday u saameyn kartaa* 'how it can affect', *siday u faragelin kartaa ama u saameyn kartaa* 'how it can interfere with or it can affect'). These forms function to present various possible world views, and to argue for or against a position, rather than to simply report known facts and past events.

At the other extreme, press reportage has by far the largest negative score on dimension 3, followed by folk stories with a relatively large negative score. These registers have the opposite linguistic characteristics: a heavy reliance on past tense forms plus frequent proper nouns and agentive nouns, combined with markedly few present tense forms, adjectives, possibility modals, etc. Text sample 6.32 in the last section and sample 6.35 below, both from press reportage, illustrate these features:

Text sample 6.35 Press reportage (February 25, 1988; *Xiddigta Oktoobar*)

Madaxwaynaha oo Qaabilay Agaasime Goboleedka
president-the   FRM received director   region-of-the (of)

Hay'adda   UNICEF   ugu Qaabilsan Bariga iyo Koonfurta
agency-the (of) UNICEF (who) in   charge of east-the and south-the

    Afrika
(of) Africa

MUQDISHO, FEB. 25 SONNA

Madaxwaynaha   JDS Jaalle   Maxamed Siyaad Barre, waxa
president-the (of) SDR Comrade Mohamed Siad   Barre what

uu habeen hore   ku   qaabilay xarunta   Madaxtooyada
he night   before with received headquarter-the (of) presidency-the

ee Magaaladan Muqdisho Agaasime Gobeleedka
of city-this of   Mogadishu director   province-of-the (of)

224 Multi-Dimensional analyses

Hay'adda UNICEF ugu qaabilsan Bariga iyo Koonfur
agency-the (of) UNICEF who for is in charge east-the and south

Afrika, Dr. Mary Raceles oo baryahanba booqasho ku joogtay
Africa Dr. Mary Raceles who days-these visit in stayed

dalka.
country-the

Translation
'The president, who welcomed the regional director of the agency UNICEF who is in charge of East and West Africa'

MOGADISHU, FEB. 25, Somali National News Agency

The President of Somalia, Comrade Mohamed Siad Barre, [the person] who he received last night at the headquarters of the presidency of this city of Mogadishu was the Regional Director of UNICEF who is in charge of eastern and southern Africa – Dr. Mary Raceles, who these days stayed in the country for a visit.

Both samples from press reportage illustrate the extensive use of past tense verbs together with proper nouns and agentive nouns (e.g., *agaasime* 'director' from *agaasin* 'direct'). These linguistic characteristics are in accordance with the primary purposes of press reportage (typically a direct report of the past activities of 'important' national and community figures).

The interpretive label 'Argumentative versus Reported Presentation of Information' summarizes the functional bases of dimension 3. The term 'argumentative' is used to refer to a qualified presentation of information, considering a number of different possibilities. At the opposite extreme, 'reported' styles simply present the 'facts,' with little consideration of alternative possibilities. The 'reported' presentation of information, as in press reportage, focuses on past events and specific individuals, resulting in high frequencies of past tense forms, proper nouns, and agentive nouns. In contrast, 'argumentative' registers, such as family and formal meetings (spoken), or general interest and analytical press (written), focus on the relative merits of present possibilities, resulting in frequent present tense forms, possibility modals, concessive conjuncts, and conditional clauses.

6.4.4 Somali dimension 4: 'Narrative versus Non-narrative Discourse Organization'

The grouping of features on dimension 4, shown in table 6.21, corresponds closely to the features on the narrative dimensions identified in the analyses of English and Korean. The major features are third-person pronouns, past

Table 6.21 *Co-occurring linguistic features on Somali dimension 4: 'Narrative versus Non-narrative Discourse Organization'*

Dimension 4	
'Narrative discourse organization'	
Positive features:	
Third-person pronouns	0.87
Past tense	0.69
Temporal clauses	0.61
waxaa clefts	0.43
Habitual modals	0.40
(Stance verbs	0.31)
(Possessive nouns	0.31)
(Concession clauses	0.29)
'Non-narrative discourse organization'	
Negative features:	
(Compound nouns	−0.37)
(t-unit length	−0.31)
(Phrase co-ordinator [*iyo*]	−0.31)
(Gerunds	−0.30)
(Agentive nouns	−0.30)

tense verbs, temporal clauses, *waxaa* clefts, and habitual modals.[23] Based on the expectations from these other languages, this co-occurrence pattern can be interpreted as distinguishing between 'Narrative versus Non-narrative Discourse Organization'.

The distribution of registers shown in figure 6.19 supports this interpretation. Folk stories, serial stories (in newspapers), and general fiction have the largest positive scores on dimension 4, reflecting very frequent use of third person pronouns, past tense forms, temporal clauses, *waxaa* clefts, and habitual modals. These features are associated with the discourse development of narrative story lines, consisting of a temporal sequence of past events in relation to several third persons (the characters). This dimension should thus be contrasted with Somali dimension 3, which focuses on the description of past (versus present) events but often does not include sequencing of a series of events. It should also be noted that conversational narratives in Somali do not share these stereotypical narrative characteristics, and thus they have an intermediate score on dimension 4. Although conversational narratives describe a sequence of past events, they often use present (or even future) time verbs, and they include several evaluative comments on the described events.

Folk stories have a complex characterization on dimensions 1–4. They

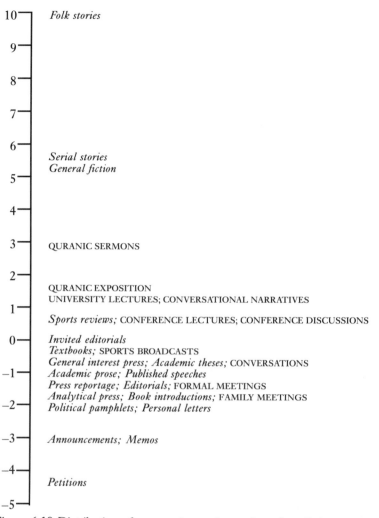

Figure 6.19 Distribution of twenty-nine registers along Somali dimension 4: 'Narrative versus Non-narrative Discourse Organization.' (F = 19.4, p < 0.0001, df = (25,253), r^2 = 65.7%)

make the most extensive use of narrative features (dimension 4), but they are also relatively involved with little structural elaboration (dimension 1), have relatively little lexical diversity and elaboration (dimension 2), and have a generally 'reported' style (dimension 3). This combination of characterizations reflects the fact that these are typically written versions of traditional (spoken) stories, intended for a general audience. They are usually quite short texts that combine a straightforward narration of events with extensive dialogue. Text samples 6.36 and 6.37 illustrate some of these features; sample 6.36 illustrates narrative features, while sample 6.37 illustrates typical dialogue.

Text sample 6.36: Folk story: 'A mouth stuck to a rock'

Af   Sallax Kudheg
mouth rock   with-stuck

Nin baa waa ari   badan lahaa. Arigii   baa
man FM   once sheep-goats many had   sheep-goats-the FM

cudur xumi ka galay, maalin kastana   dhowr neef   baa ka
disease bad   to entered day   every-and several animals FM   from

dhiman jiray.   Goor arigii   sii dabo yar   yahay,
died   used-to time sheep-goats-the DIR tail   small is

buu   laba qaybiyay   oo   yiri: 'Eebbow ariga
FM-he two divided into and said oh God   sheep-goats-the

qaybtaadii   waa taas   ee tayda   ii   nabad geli.'
share-your-the FM   that-one but mine-the me-for peace   enter

Arigii   sidii   buu   u le'anayay, kolkii
sheep-goats-the manner-the FM-the dying-was   time-the

qaybtiisii   neef   ka   dhintana tan Eebbe ayuu mid ka
share-his-the animal from dies-and this of God FM-he one from

gawracayay,   si   uu u aarsado.
slaughtering was manner he to revenge

Markii   ay cadaatay   inuu   muddo gaaban ku   cayrtoobayo,
time-the it clear-became that-he time   short   with poor-become

buu   calaacal   iyo Alla eedeyn   billaabay.
FM-he complaint and God accusing began

Maalintii dambe ayuu . . .
day-the   after   FM-he

Translation
A Mouth Stuck to a Rock

Once a man had many sheep/goats. The sheep/goats got a bad disease, and every day, several animals used to die from it. When the tail of the sheep/goats had become small [i.e., there were few left], he divided them into two groups and said: 'Oh God, there is your share of sheep and goats; and leave mine in peace.' The goats continued dying, and every time that an animal dies from his share, he slaughtered one from God's share, in order to get revenge.

When it became clear that he is going to become poor, he started complaining and accusing God.

The next day, . . .

Text sample 6.37: Folk story: 'A conversation of animals'

Haasaawe   Xoolo
a conversation of animals

Beri   baa waxaa sheekeystay   hal,   sac iyo ri.   Sicii
long ago FM   what   conversed (was) a camel cow and goat cow-the

baa yiri: 'Riyeey, adigu   markaad   daaqeyso maxaad
FM   said goat-oh   you-the time-the-you grazing-are what-FM-you

ka   fekertaa?' 'Berri   caws-weytada igu   dhici   karta
about think   tomorrow grass-missing me-to happen can

baan ka   fekeraa, taa   awgeed baan qaar u   dhaafaa'
FM-I   about think   that-one cause-of FM-I   some for leave

bey   tiri.
she-FM said

Translation
A Conversation of Animals

Long ago, what talked together was a camel, a cow, and a goat.
    The cow said: 'Oh goat, when you are grazing, what do you think about?'
    'I think about the shortage of grass that is going to happen to me tomorrow, and due to that, I leave some', she said.

These texts combine very frequent narrative features, such as past tense verbs, third-person pronouns, temporal clauses (e.g., *goor-*, *mar-*), *waxaa* clefts, and habitual modals (*jir-*), with frequent use of the involved and interactive features of dimension 1 (e.g., questions, contractions, temporal deictics, main clause constructions, first- and second-person pronouns).

Figure 6.19 shows that several other registers mix narrative and non-narrative discourse organizations. Among the spoken registers, sermons, lectures, and conference discussions all show a relatively frequent use of traditional narrative forms; while sports reviews, invited editorials, and textbooks are expository written registers that show moderately frequent use of narrative features. Other registers, such as conversations, formal meetings, family meetings, editorials, and personal letters, are not primarily narrative in purpose but do make use of narrative features to support their primary goals (whether informative or interpersonal). Finally, three written registers are marked for the near total absence of narrative features: announcements, memos, and petitions. These all have extremely restricted purposes and do not typically use narratives even in supporting roles. Announcements and memos are directly informative, with little elaboration of any kind, while petitions are formal requests, which are not typically enhanced by the inclusion of narratives.

The overall pattern on this dimension represents a cline associated with the extent to which registers depend on traditional narrative discourse organizations. Only folk stories and general fiction make extensive use of these features, but most other Somali registers show at least some use of narrative patterns.

6.4.5   Somali dimension 5: 'Distanced, Directive Interaction'

The strongest features on dimension 5 (see table 6.22) are optative clauses, second-person pronouns, first-person pronouns, and directional preverbal particles. Optative clauses function as polite commands or wishes (translated as 'let X do Y'), first-and second-person pronouns are directly interactive, and directional preverbal particles (*soo, sii*) are deictic markers that specify the direction of actions – towards or away from the speaker/writer. Single case particles, -*na* co-ordination (which co-ordinates clauses while topicalizing the preceding noun phrase), and imperatives (direct commands) have a weaker co-occurrence relation on this dimension. These features seem to relate to a type of direct interaction between addressor and addressee.

The strong co-occurrence relation of first- and second-person pronouns with these other features on dimension 5 explains the surprising fact that those pronominal features did not group more strongly with the positive 'involved' features on Somali dimension 1. As discussed in section 6.4.1, the major communicative functions associated with dimension 1 relate to

Table 6.22 *Co-occurring linguistic features on Somali dimension 5: 'Distanced, Directive Interaction'*

Dimension 5	
Positive features:	
Optative clauses	0.60
Second-person pronouns	0.59
First-person pronouns	0.55
Directional preverbal particles	0.47
Single case particles	0.43
(Clitic topic co-ordinator	0.38)
(Imperatives	0.36)
(Independent verbs	0.32)
(Possessive nouns	0.32)
(Case particle sequences	0.32)
[No negative features]	

speaker/writer purpose rather than interactiveness; dimension 5, on the other hand, seems to more directly reflect the requirements of certain types of interaction.

Personal letters have by far the largest positive score on dimension 5, which is plotted in figure 6.20. In addition to frequent first- and second-person pronouns, this score reflects a frequent use of commands (both optative clauses and imperatives) and directional preverbal particles, marking action towards or away from the addressor. Family meetings, conversational narratives, conversations, and sermons all have relatively large positive scores on this dimension. At the other extreme are the expository written registers (e.g., academic prose and political pamphlets), with press reportage and editorials having the largest negative scores; these registers are characterized by the absence of dimension 5 features.

This clustering of features and distribution of registers can be interpreted as reflecting 'Distanced, Directive Interaction'. The communicative needs associated with this type of interaction are most pronounced in personal letters, where there are frequent references to 'I' (the writer) and 'you' (the reader) plus frequent directives of various types. Thus consider the following text sample from a typical letter:

Text sample 6.38: Personal letter

Dhar   aan Xasan u   soo diray iyo alaabo yaryar oo   kale
clothes I   Hassan for DIR sent and goods   small and other

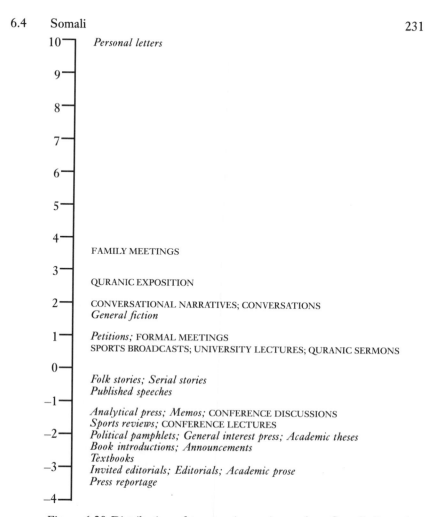

Figure 6.20 Distribution of twenty-nine registers along Somali dimension 5: 'Distanced, Directive Interaction.' (F = 22.9, p < 0.0001, df = (25, 253), r^2 = 69.3%)

siday   inigu   soo gaadheena iiga   soo warama,
manner-the-they you-to DIR   reached-and me-from DIR   inform

umada   ilaahay ee   magaalada ka   imanaysa maxaa
people-the (of) God   who city-the   from coming   what-FM

iniga   xidhxidhay oo war la iniiga   laayahay, ninkana
you-from tied   and news IMP you-from lack-is   man-the-and

adigu   u tegoo sidii   caadigii   ha iigu   soo diraan
you-the to go-and manner-the normal-the let me-to DIR   send

biilka.
money for expenses-the

Translation
Clothes that I sent for Hasan and other small things, let me know
how they reached you. What caused you to be tied from [i.e., to fail
to contact] the people of God who are coming from the city [i.e., the
people who could carry a letter], and why is news not received from
you? And as for the man, you go to him, and in the usual manner, let
them send the money for expenses back to me.

Although this sample illustrates several characteristics of 'involved' discourse (dimension 1), such as questions, contractions, and main clause
constructions, it is even more marked with respect to the features of
distanced, directive interaction (dimension 5). Thus note the frequent
commands, using both optatives (e.g., *ha iigu soo diraan biilka* 'let him
send the money back to me') and imperatives (e.g., *iiga soo warama* 'let
me know back from you'), and the very frequent use of the directional
particle *soo* (marking action towards the writer), together with markedly
frequent occurrences of first- and second-person pronouns. This combination of features reflects the need to be interactive and directive over great
physical distances, where there is no possibility of immediate face-to-face
interaction.

Other registers, such as conversations and family meetings, are face to
face but still directive in many respects, and thus they have relatively large
positive scores here. Fiction and folk stories include dialogue sections that
have many of these characteristics. Conversational narratives are in some
respects directly interactive and directive, and they also include reported
dialogue with these characteristics. Sermons can be considered a type of
distanced interaction: although the addressee cannot ask for clarification, the
addressor (the sheikh) makes frequent reference to 'I' and 'you', and he is
notably directive in exhorting listeners regarding prescribed and proscribed
actions. This dimension thus distinguishes among types of interactions that
are distanced and directive to varying degrees.

6.4.6 Somali dimension 6: 'Personal Persuasion'

Finally, the major positive features on dimension 6 are amplifiers, first-
person pronouns, reason conjuncts, verb complement clauses, and framing
clauses (table 6.23). There are in addition some less important negative

Table 6.23 *Co-occurring linguistic features on Somali dimension 6: 'Personal Persuasion'*

Dimension 6	
'Personal persuasion'	
Positive features:	
Amplifiers	0.60
First-person pronouns	0.52
Reason conjuncts	0.46
Verb complements	0.40
(Framing clauses	0.39)
(Future modals	0.31)
(Second-person pronouns	0.30)
'Non-persuasive discourse'	
Negative features:	
(Place deictics	−0.39)
(Phrase co-ordination	−0.38)
(*-eed* genitives	−0.35)

features: place deictics, phrase co-ordination, and *-eed* genitives. The distribution of registers along this dimension, plotted in figure 6.21, shows that dimension 6 features are common in three personal written registers: petitions, personal letters, and memos. Of these three, petitions show an extremely frequent use of these features, while the other two registers have more moderate characterizations. Considering both the linguistic features on dimension 6 and this distribution of registers, it is possible to propose an interpretation as 'personal persuasion'. This style of discourse focuses on personal requests and their supporting arguments. First-person pronouns reflect the personal nature of the discourse; amplifiers, verb complement clauses, and framing clauses emphasize the writer's commitment and stance to the propositions, and reason conjuncts are used to introduce supporting arguments.

At the negative extreme, figure 6.21 shows that press reportage and sports broadcasts are marked by the near total absence of dimension 6 features. Related registers that are neither persuasive nor personal are marked by the relative absence of dimension 6 features; these include folk stories, announcements, academic theses, book introductions, and academic prose. Other registers are either persuasive or personal, but since they do not combine these characteristics, they are relatively unmarked on this dimension: for example, the registers that are extremely 'argumentative' on dimension 3 are relatively unmarked on dimension 6 (family meetings, formal meetings, general-interest press). Editorials are unmarked on both dimension 3 and

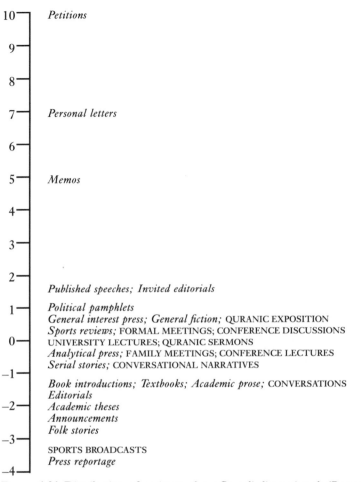

Figure 6.21 Distribution of registers along Somali dimension 6: 'Personal Persuasion.' (F = 15.8, p < 0.0001, df = (25,253), r² = 63.9%)

dimension 6, indicating that Somali editorials are not as argumentative and persuasive as editorials in some languages. Conversations are clearly personal, as shown by their frequent use of the involved, stance-marking features on dimension 1, but they are typically not persuasive in the way that petitions and memos are, and thus they have an unmarked score on dimension 6. Overall, then, dimension 6 represents a relatively specialized parameter, marking highly persuasive discourse arguing for various personal requests.

6.5   Summary

This chapter has presented relatively detailed descriptions of the dimensions of variation in English, Nukulaelae Tuvaluan, Korean, and Somali. Even a quick survey of these dimensions shows that the patterns of variation within each language are quite complex, and that there are striking similarities as well as differences across the languages. The next chapter analyzes these cross-linguistic patterns of variation.

7 Cross-linguistic patterns of register variation: synchronic similarities and differences

7.1 Overview of the cross-linguistic comparisons

Chapters 3–6 present the extensive preliminary analyses required for cross-linguistic MD comparisons of register variation. Chapter 3 describes the four language situations considered in the present study, including the situational characteristics of each register and a brief social history of literacy in each language. The main purpose of chapter 4 is to demonstrate the difficulty of cross-linguistic register comparisons based on individual linguistic features, and to thereby establish the need for an alternative approach. The multidimensional approach is then offered as particularly well suited to the analytical requirements of cross-linguistic register comparisons. Chapter 5 provides a methodological description of the MD approach and presents the technical details of the MD analysis for each language. Finally, chapter 6 gives a fairly detailed description of each dimension in each of the languages, including analysis of: the co-occurring linguistic features on the dimension, the distribution of registers along the dimension, the functions of dimension features in particular text samples, and the overall functional basis of the dimension.

Given this background, it is now possible to proceed to the cross-linguistic analyses. In general terms, the analyses presented in chapter 6 show that the linguistic relations among spoken and written registers in all four languages are quite complex, and that a multidimensional analysis is required because no single dimension by itself adequately captures the similarities and differences among registers. In addition, all four studies failed to find any absolute dichotomies between speech and writing; rather, situational factors such as purpose, topic, and interactiveness work together with the physical mode distinction to define the salient linguistic differences among registers.

Specific cross-linguistic comparisons can be undertaken from two complementary perspectives: first, comparing the dimensions across languages; and second, comparing corresponding registers across languages. Dimensions can be compared with respect to their underlying functions, their defining linguistic characteristics, and their associated relations among registers. It will be shown in section 7.2 that some dimensions have correspondences across all languages, some dimensions have correspondences across two or more languages, and some dimensions are unique to a single language. There are also more complex correspondences; for example, a single dimension in one language might correspond to two dimensions in a second language, indicating that the underlying functions have been merged in the first language. In addition, it will be shown that some functionally similar dimensions define different relations among the registers of two languages, identifying important cross-linguistic differences in 'equivalent' registers.

Cross-linguistic similarities are strongest in relation to the marking of oral/literate distinctions. That is, even though no language has a dimension defining an absolute dichotomy between spoken and written registers, each of the languages has multiple dimensions relating to 'orality' versus 'literacy.' In addition, each language has dimensions that mark personal stance, and some of the languages have related dimensions that mark overt argumentation or persuasion. Finally, each language has a dimension marking narrative versus non-narrative discourse (with the possible exception of Nukulaelae Tuvaluan).

The dimensional structure of each language can also be used to highlight salient cross-linguistic differences. That is, in three of the languages there are idiosyncratic dimensions that reflect the particular functional priorities of that language and culture: Abstract Style in English, Logical Cohesion in Korean, Honorification in Korean, and perhaps Distanced, Directive Interaction in Somali.

These analyses lead to a cross-linguistic comparison of the registers themselves in section 7.3. There are two defining criteria for 'equivalent' registers: they share the same non-linguistic characteristics relating to their communicative situations (e.g., interactiveness, opportunity for careful production, dependence on context); and they have similar linguistic correlates across the languages in terms of their multidimensional characterizations. In some cases, registers with similar physical situations can differ with respect to their typical communicative purposes and topics.[1] The analyses in section 7.3 show that differences associated with communicative purpose can sometimes correspond to notable linguistic differences, even in registers that are otherwise equivalent.

Taken together, the analyses in this chapter provide a general framework for cross-linguistic register analyses. I return to various theoretical considerations in section 7.4.

7.2   Cross-linguistic comparison of dimensions of variation

7.2.1   Overview of oral/literate dimensions

No dimension in any of these languages defines an absolute dichotomy between speech and writing, and MD studies have repeatedly shown that physical mode is not adequate in itself to account for the relations among registers in a language. However, each language has dimensions closely associated with speech and writing. These dimensions typically isolate spoken registers at one extreme and written registers at the other extreme, with registers from both modes overlapping in the middle. In previous analyses of English, I have described these dimensions as marking *oral* versus *literate* distinctions, following Tannen (1982a). The term *oral* refers to stereotypically spoken discourse – that is, conversation – while the term *literate* refers to stereotypically written discourse – that is, informational exposition.

Conversation and informational exposition are stereotypical in the sense that each maximally exploits the resources of its mode, while placing minimal emphasis on the communicative priorities that are better suited to the other mode. First, consider the case of conversation. The communicative focus in conversation is typically on (inter)personal rather than informational concerns, and meaning can be clarified and jointly negotiated by participants. For these reasons, conversational interactions require fast, efficient communication, but they have relatively little need for a precise, dense packaging of information. These communicative priorities match the on-line production circumstances of the spoken mode; on-line production enables fast, easy communication, facilitating direct interaction among participants, but it is less well suited for highly informational or precise communication. (In contrast, writing would be slow and cumbersome for communication in face-to-face interactional situations.) This characterization of conversation as stereotypical speaking is not controversial: all languages and cultures have conversational interactions, and it can be considered the unmarked means of communication universally.

The characterization of informational exposition as stereotypical writing is more controversial. Exposition differs from conversation in that it is not universal. Many speakers and cultures have literate competencies and traditions but lack expository registers. As a result, some researchers have claimed that there is really nothing special about expository registers. For example, authors such as Street (1984, 1993) claim that academic exposition has been regarded as stereotypical writing simply because it is the most highly valued register of the intellectual elite in western societies. According to this view, expository informational prose is not particularly noteworthy in the way that it exploits the linguistic and communicative resources of the written mode; rather, the special status of expository prose is attributed to the fact that western scholars have typically used this form of discourse for their own written communications.

In contrast, it is claimed here that informational exposition is in fact special in both its communicative/situational characteristics and its linguistic characteristics – because it maximally exploits the resources of the written mode. In particular, exposition maximally exploits the opportunities for carefully planned and revised expression made possible by the written mode, and thus it shows extreme characterizations of informational density, elaboration, and precision.

The communicative resources provided by the written mode are not necessarily obvious, to individual speakers or to developing cultures. As Goody (1977, 1986) and Stubbs (1980) point out, exploitation of the written mode is learned gradually over time, in contrast to exploitation of the spoken mode, which appears to be native to all cultures. For example, Stubbs (1980: 102) notes that it took nearly 100 years after the invention of printed books before page numbers were regularly added for the benefit of readers, and modern devices such as a table of contents and indexes came even later. Similarly, it takes time for beginning readers to realize that written materials can be processed in different ways from speech. For example, written materials can be read at different speeds, depending on the difficulty of the material and the purposes of the reader; in addition, written materials can be processed in a non-linear fashion, reading only those parts that are particularly interesting or relevant. Similarly, it takes time for writers to learn to exploit the production opportunities for planning and revision, in order to produce carefully integrated, informational prose.

It is not claimed here that written exposition is in any sense 'better' than other written registers, or that it is desirable for all cultures and speakers to develop proficiency in expository registers. It is claimed, though, that informational exposition is stereotypical writing in that it has the opposite characteristics from conversation: both exposition and conversation make maximal use of the communicative resources provided by their respective modes.

The importance of the distinction between conversation as a stereotypically oral register and exposition as a stereotypically literate register is borne out in the MD analyses of all four languages. English, Korean, and Somali all have multiple oral/literate dimensions, and Nukulaelae Tuvaluan has comparable dimensions, even though it does not have written expository registers. Table 7.1 summarizes the functional bases of the oral/literate dimensions in each language. Spoken registers (usually including conversation) cluster at one pole of these dimensions, and written registers (usually

Table 7.1 *Summary of the functional bases of oral/literate dimensions in each language*

Type A: Interactiveness:
 Dialogue (+ interpersonal focus) versus monologue (+ informational focus)
Type B: Production circumstances:
 On-line versus careful production
Type C: Stance:
 Overt marking of personal stance and involvement versus non-personal
  (and informational)
Type D: Functions particular to each language

ENGLISH

Dimension 1	*Dimension 3*	*Dimension 5*
Types A, B, C	Type B	Type D
Interactive	Situation-dependent	Not abstract
(Inter)personal focus	reference	
Involved	On-line production	
Personal stance		
On-line production		
– – – – – – – – – –	– – – – – – – – – – – –	– – – – – – – – – –
Monologue	Structural elaboration	Abstract style
Informational	Situation-independent	
Integrated	reference	
Careful production	Careful production	

Dimension 6
Type B
On-line production
Informational focus
Personal stance
– – – – – – – – – – –
Not on-line

TUVALUAN

Dimension 1	*Dimension 2*	*Dimension 3*
Type C	Type A	Type A, (B)
Attitudinal	Interactive	Interactive
Personal stance	Interpersonal focus	Multi-party production
– – – – – – – – – –	– – – – – – – – – –	– – – – – – – – – –
Authoritative	Monologue	Monologue production
	Informational	(Careful production)
		(Informational)

exposition) cluster at the other pole. A quick perusal of this table shows, however, that there are a number of different functions represented. That is, orality versus literacy is by no means a unified underlying construct. Rather, within each language there are multiple dimensions that distinguish between stereotypical speaking and writing; each of these dimensions has different

Table 7.1 (*cont.*)

KOREAN		
Dimension 1	*Dimension 2*	*Dimension 3*
Types A, B	Type D	Type C
Interactive	Overt logical cohesion	Personal stance
On-line production		
(Interpersonal focus)		
– – – – – – – – – – –	– – – – – – – – – – –	– – – – – – – – – – –
Monologue	Implicit logical cohesion	Non-personal information
Informational	Informational	
Integrated		
Careful production		
Structural elaboration		
Dimension 4	*Dimension 5*	*Dimension 6*
Type D	Type B, D	Type (C), D
Narrative	On-line reportage of events	Honorification
		Interpersonal
		Public communication
– – – – – – – – – – –	– – – – – – – – – – –	– – – – – – – – – – –
Non-narrative	(Careful production)	Not interpersonal
SOMALI		
Dimension 1	*Dimension 2*	*Dimension 5*
Type A, B, C	Type B	Type A, D
Interactive	On-line	Interactive
(Inter)personal focus	(Situation-dependent)	Distanced
Involved		Directive
Personal stance		
On-line production		
– – – – – – – – – – –	– – – – – – – – – – –	– – – – – – – – – – –
Monologue	Lexical complexity	Non-interactive
Informational	Informational	
Structural elaboration	Integrated	
Faceless	Careful production	
Careful production		

functional underpinnings, and each defines a different set of relations among registers.

For purposes of cross-linguistic comparison, oral/literate dimensions can be grouped into four major types, labeled types A, B, C, and D on table 7.1. Type A dimensions reflect differences in the interactiveness among participants. The oral pole of type A dimensions represents situations having direct interaction among participants, with the focus of communication being on the interpersonal relationship; the literate pole of type A dimensions represents monologue production with an informational focus. Type B dimensions relate to the production circumstances. The oral pole of these dimensions represents on-line production, and the literate pole represents careful, usually edited, written production. Type C dimensions relate to the marking of personal stance. The oral pole of these dimensions represents an overt marking of stance and personal involvement in texts, while the literate pole is marked primarily by the absence of these features. Finally, most languages have idiosyncratic oral/literate dimensions, labeled type D. These clearly distinguish between oral and literate registers but have functions not shared cross-linguistically, such as abstract style and honorification.

An important point of cross-linguistic comparison is that all four languages have at least one complex oral/literate dimension that combines multiple functions, relating at least to both interactiveness and production circumstances. In English, Korean, and Somali, this is the first dimension, which comprises a very large number of co-occurring linguistic features. In English and Somali, this dimension additionally relates to personal stance. These complex co-occurrence patterns show that the functional types distinguished here are often intertwined. That is, situations with extensive interaction and an interpersonal focus often require on-line production, and they are often characterized by extensive overt marking of personal stance. In contrast, monologic situations with an informational focus frequently enable a careful, edited production of text, and they often are not associated with a personalized presentation of attitudes or beliefs. Overall, these patterns indicate that the opposition between oral and literate registers is basic: it is represented in all four languages, and it corresponds to multiple functional differences, which are themselves inter-related in complex ways.

7.2.2 Cross-linguistic comparison of type A oral/literate dimensions: interactiveness

Table 7.2 summarizes the underlying functions, major linguistic features, and distribution of registers for the type A oral/literate dimensions in each language. These dimensions relate to interactiveness, distinguishing between dialogic situations, which tend to have an interpersonal focus, and monologic situations, which tend to be informational in focus. Each of the four languages has at least one dimension reflecting these functions. Linguistically, the oral pole of these dimensions includes directly interactive features, such as first-and second-person pronouns, questions, and imperatives; these features often co-occur with reduced features (e.g., contractions, fragmentary sentences) and stance-marking features (e.g., hedges, emphatics, stance verbs, and adjectives). The literate pole is defined by features used to integrate or elaborate information, including nouns, adjectives, and dependent clauses.

Conversations are at or near the oral pole of these dimensions in all four languages, while informational, expository registers are at the literate pole. (In Tuvaluan, which has no written expository registers, the political broadcast and public speeches are at the literate pole of comparable dimensions.)

English and Korean have only one type A dimension, while Tuvaluan and Somali each have two dimensions relating to interactiveness. In Nukulaelae Tuvaluan, dimension 2 relates to interaction with a specific addressee, while dimension 3 reflects an interactive, multi-party production of discourse. On Tuvaluan dimension 2, first- and second-person pronominal forms are important, and personal letters are the most marked oral register, with conversations also being quite marked; addressors in these registers make frequent reference to self and the addressee, expecting an eventual response. The oral pole of Tuvaluan dimension 3, on the other hand, is defined primarily by questions and direct quotes and characterizes only conversations; here personal letters are similar to public speeches in representing a monologic production, while conversational discourse represents a multi-party co-construction of text.

In Somali, dimension 1 is quite similar to the interactive dimensions in English and Korean, with respect to both the defining linguistic characteristics and relations among registers. Somali dimension 5, on the other hand, is not strictly an oral/literate dimension. The linguistic features associated with this dimension are clearly interactive, including imperatives and first- and second-person pronouns. However, from a functional perspective this dimension combines interactiveness with distanced, directive communication. Letters have by far the most marked characterization with respect to this dimension, while conversations are relatively unmarked.

In sum, each of these four languages has at least one oral/literate dimension relating to interactiveness. Functionally, these dimensions oppose interactive/interpersonal functions to monologic/informational functions; linguistically, these dimensions oppose directly interactive features to features enabling structural integration and elaboration; and with respect to the relations among registers, these dimensions define an opposition between interactive communication (private conversations plus letters and public spoken interactions) and written, informational exposition. Tuvaluan and Somali show further functional discrimination in this area, having two dimensions relating to interactiveness.

7.2.3   Cross-linguistic comparison of type B oral/literate dimensions: production circumstances

Table 7.3 lists the dimensions reflecting differences associated with on-line versus careful production circumstances. Most dimensions that relate to

Table 7.2 *Summary of functions, linguistic features, and characteristic registers for type A oral/literate dimensions: Interactiveness: Dialogue (+ interpersonal focus) versus monologue (+ informational focus)*

Functions	Linguistic features	Characteristic registers
ENGLISH		
Dimension 1		
Interactive	first- and second-person	conversations
(Inter)personal focus	pronouns, questions,	(personal letters)
Involved	reductions, stance verbs,	(public conversations)
Personal stance	hedges, emphatics,	
On-line production	adverbial subordination	
Monologue	nouns, adjectives,	informational exposition
Careful production	prepositional phrases,	e.g., official documents,
Informational	long words	academic prose
Faceless		
TUVALUAN		
Dimension 2		
Interactive	First- and second-person	personal letters
Interpersonal focus	deictics and pronouns	conversations
(Fragmented)	co-ordination	
Monologue	possessive and definite	political broadcast
Informational	noun phrases	written sermons
	prepositions	political meeting
	nominalizations	
Dimension 3		
Interactive	WH and yes/no questions	conversations
Multi-party production	direct quotes	
Monologue production	long words	personal letters
Careful production	subordinators	political broadcast
Structural elaboration		speeches
KOREAN		
Dimension 1		
Interactive	questions, contractions	private conversations
On-line production	fragmentary sentences	TV drama
(Interpersonal focus)	discourse conjuncts	(public conversations)
(Fragmented structure)	clause connectors	(folktales)
	hedges	
Monologue	postposition/noun ratio	literary criticism
Informational	relative clauses	college textbooks
Careful production	attributive adjectives	scripted speeches
(Integrated and	long sentences	exposition
Structural elaboration)	non-finite and noun	(broadcast news and
	complement clauses	TV documentary)

Table 7.2 (*cont.*)

Functions	Linguistic features	Characteristic registers
SOMALI		
Dimension 1		
Interactive	main clause features	conversations
(Inter)personal focus	questions, imperatives	family meetings
Involved	contractions	conversational
Personal stance	stance adjectives	narratives
(On-line production)	downtoners	
	first- and second-person pronouns	
Monologue	dependent clauses	written expository
Informational	relative clauses	registers
Faceless	clefts, verb complements	
(Careful production)	nouns, adjectives	
Dimension 5		
Interactive	optative clauses	personal letters
Distanced and directive communication	first- and second-person pronouns	(family meetings)
	directional particles	(Quranic exposition)
	imperatives	
Non-interactive	[no features]	press reportage and
Non-directive		editorials
		written expository
		registers

interactiveness also relate to production circumstances; the degree of planning and integration possible in face-to-face interactive situations is strikingly different from that possible in monologic writing (with editing and revising). Thus several of the dimensions listed on table 7.2 are also listed on table 7.3: dimension 1 in English, dimension 1 in Korean, dimension 1 in Somali, and dimension 3 in Tuvaluan all show an inter-relation between interactiveness and production circumstances.

However, some interactive registers are not produced in on-line circumstances, and thus some interactive dimensions do not correspond to production differences. In particular, personal letters can be interactive while being carefully produced (relative to conversation). Thus, both Tuvaluan dimension 2 and Somali dimension 5 reflect a type of interactiveness that does not directly relate to differences in production circumstances (see table 7.2).

From the opposite perspective, table 7.3 shows that English, Korean, and Somali all have dimensions related to production circumstances that

Table 7.3 *Summary of functions, linguistic features, and characteristic registers for type B oral/literate dimensions: Production circumstances: On-line versus careful production*

Functions	Linguistic features	Characteristic registers
ENGLISH		
Dimension 1		
Interactive	pronouns, questions,	conversations
(Inter)personal focus	reductions,	(personal letters)
Involved	stance verbs, hedges,	(public conversations)
Personal stance	emphatics,	
On-line production	adverbial subordination	
Careful production	nouns, adjectives,	informational exposition
Informational	prepositional phrases,	e.g., official documents,
Faceless	long words	academic prose
Dimension 3		
Situation-dependent	time and place	broadcasts
reference	adverbials	(conversations)
On-line production		(fiction)
		(personal letters)
Situation-independent	WH relative clauses	official documents
reference	pied-piping constructions	professional letters
(Elaborated)	phrasal co-ordination	(exposition)
Dimension 6		
On-line production	*that*-complement clauses	public speeches
Informational focus	on verbs and adjectives	public conversations
Personal stance	demonstratives	(professional letters)
	that-relative clauses	(editorials)
Not on-line	[no features]	fiction, broadcasts
		personal letters
		edited exposition
TUVALUAN		
Dimension 3		
Interactive	WH and yes/no questions	conversations
Multi-party production	direct quotes	
Monologue	long words	personal letters
Careful production	subordinators	political broadcast
(Informational focus)		speeches

Table 7.3 (*cont.*)

Functions	Linguistic features	Characteristic registers
KOREAN		
Dimension 1		
Interactive	questions, contractions	private conversations
On-line production	fragmentary sentences	TV drama
(Interpersonal focus)	discourse conjuncts	(public conversations)
(Fragmented)	clause connectors, hedges	(folktales)
Monologue	postposition–noun ratio	literary criticism
Informational	relative clauses	college textbooks
Careful production	attributive adjectives	scripted speeches
(Integrated and	long sentences	exposition
Structural elaboration)	non-finite and noun	(broadcast news and
	complement clauses	TV documentary)
Dimension 5		
On-line reportage	declarative sentences	sportscasts
of events	present tense	
	copular verbs	
(Careful production)	long sentences	newspaper reportage
		(broadcast news)
		(textbooks)
SOMALI		
Dimension 1		
Interactive	main clause features	conversations
(Inter)personal focus	questions, imperatives	family meetings
Involved	contractions	conversational
Personal stance	stance adjectives	narratives
(On-line production)	downtoners	
	first- and second-person	
	pronouns	
Monologue	dependent clauses	written expository
Informational	relative clauses	registers
Faceless	clefts, verb complements	
(Careful production)	nouns, adjectives	
Dimension 2		
On-line production	[no features]	sports broadcast
(Situation-dependent)		(other spoken
		registers)
Careful production	once-occurring words	editorials
Informational	high type–token ratio	written political
	nominalizations	speeches and pamphlets
	compound verbs	analytical press

do not represent differences in interactiveness. First, there are dimensions in all three of these languages that mark the reportage of events in progress as being maximally constrained by on-line production, as in broadcasts of sporting events. Dimension 3 in English, dimension 5 in Korean, and dimension 2 in Somali are all of this type, although the defining linguistic features are different in each case. English dimension 3 is interpreted as primarily reflecting elaborated versus situation-dependent reference; elaborated reference requires careful production circumstances, while situated reference is common in on-line production circumstances. Along this dimension, broadcasts are marked as having very frequent references to the immediate situation, while conversations, fiction, and personal letters show a lesser use of these same features. Korean dimension 5 is tentatively interpreted as reflecting an on-line reportage of events, with sportscasts as the most marked register (although the functional basis of this dimension requires further investigation). Somali dimension 2 is the clearest example of a dimension that reflects production circumstances apart from interactiveness. Similar to the analogous dimensions in the other two languages, sports broadcasts are the most marked along Somali dimension 2. However, all spoken registers are characterized by the absence of lexical elaboration features on this dimension, apparently due to the difficulties of precise lexical choice and elaboration in on-line production circumstances.

English dimension 6 also seems to relate to production constraints, reflecting the kinds of structural elaboration possible in spoken informational registers. Conversations and broadcasts are not marked along this dimension, but public speeches and informational public conversations (e.g., interviews, debates) are distinguished by their dependence on verbal and adjectival complementation for informational elaboration, in contrast to the integrated packaging of information possible in written expository registers.

In sum, all four languages have a dimension that reflects both interactiveness and production circumstances; these dimensions have similar linguistic characteristics in all languages, and they define similar relations among spoken and written registers. In addition, English, Korean, and Somali each have a dimension that marks on-line broadcasts as being distinctive due to their production circumstances. These dimensions have different linguistic bases, and they appear to have different functional bases as well. In addition, English has a dimension reflecting the linguistic and functional characteristics of informational registers produced in on-line (spoken) situations. Thus, the four languages are similar in that they all have dimensions relating to production circumstances, and they all have a basic dimension that merges functions associated with interactiveness and production circumstances; the languages are distinct in having additional dimensions that reflect particular aspects of production.

7.2.4   Cross-linguistic comparison of dimensions relating to personal stance (type C)

Table 7.4 presents the dimensions in each language that relate to the marking of *stance*: the linguistic encoding of commitment to a proposition (evidentiality) or of attitudes towards a proposition or other participants (see Biber and Finegan 1988, 1989b). There are two different kinds of stance dimensions distinguished in these languages; the present section discusses stance dimensions that define oral/literate distinctions (summarized in table 7.4); section 7.2.7 below discusses stance dimensions that mark argumentation and persuasion but are unrelated to differences between speech and writing (summarized in table 7.7 below).

A comparison of tables 7.2 and 7.4 shows that the marking of personal stance is frequently an oral/literate characteristic closely related to interactiveness and personal involvement. English dimension 1, Somali dimension 1, and to a lesser extent Korean dimension 1 all have linguistic features reflecting both stance and interactiveness (as well as production circumstances). Stance is marked by linguistic features such as hedges, downtoners, emphatics, and stance verbs and adjectives. These dimensions show that speakers in directly interactive situations, which are often constrained by on-line production, tend to have interpersonal purposes and a high degree of personal involvement, and therefore they tend to overtly mark stance to a high degree.

Korean dimension 3 can also be considered an oral/literate stance dimension, with conversation and informational exposition at opposite poles, but the defining linguistic features in this case relate exclusively to the marking of stance, rather than a combination of features reflecting stance, interactiveness, and production considerations. The features on Korean dimension 3 include emphatics, hedges, attitudinal expressions, first-person pronouns, and verb and noun complement clauses.

In addition, there are several stance dimensions that are related to speech and writing but do not define stereotypical oral/literate distinctions; these are marked by *(O/L)* on table 7.4. Many of these dimensions are composed primarily of stance features, showing that the marking of stance is important in its own right. Tuvaluan dimension 1 falls into this category. The dimension is composed mainly of linguistic features relating to personal stance, such as hedges, intensifiers, other adverbs, and first-person pronouns. This dimension shows a strong relation to speech and writing, with public speeches and political meetings being marked for their extensive use of stance features, and written sermons being marked for the absence of these stance features and an 'authoritative' style. This is not strictly an oral/literate dimension, however, because conversations have an intermediate score.

Table 7.4 *Summary of functions, linguistic features, and characteristic registers for dimensions relating to personal stance (type C)*

Functions	Linguistic features	Characteristic registers
ENGLISH		
Dimension 1 O/L*		
Interactive	pronouns, questions	conversations
(Inter)personal focus	reductions	(personal letters)
Involved	stance verbs, hedges	(public conversations)
Personal stance	emphatics	
On-line production	adverbial subordination	
Careful production	nouns, adjectives	informational exposition
Informational	prepositional phrases	e.g., official documents,
Faceless	long words	academic prose
Dimension 6 (O/L)		
On-line production	*that*-complement clauses	public speeches
Informational focus	on verbs and adjectives	public conversations
Personal stance	demonstratives	(professional letters)
	that-relative clauses	(editorials)
Not on-line	[no features]	fiction, broadcasts
Informational		personal letters
		edited exposition
TUVALUAN		
Dimension 1 (O/L)		
Attitudinal	adverbs, hedges	private-setting and
Personal stance	intensifiers	maneapa speeches
(Persuasive)	first-person inclusive	political meetings
	pronouns	
	personal demonstratives	
Authoritative	direct quotes	written sermons
	third-person pronouns	
	ergative case	
	nominal focus	
KOREAN		
Dimension 3 (O/L)		
Personal stance	verb and NP complements	TV drama
	emphatics, hedges	(private and public
	attitudinal expressions	conversations)
	private verbs	(personal letters)
	first-person pronouns	(personal essays)
Non-personal	nouns	newspaper reportage
information		official documents
		(broadcast news)

Table 7.4 (*cont.*)

Functions	Linguistic features	Characteristic registers
Dimension 6 (O/L) Honorification Self humbling	honorific and humble expressions formal sentence endings first-person pronouns	personal letters public conversations (public speeches)

No overt marking of
  relation to addressee
	[no features]	informational expository
		  registers
		TV documentary

SOMALI *Dimension 1 (O/L)* Interactive (Inter)personal focus Involved Personal stance (On-line production)	main clause features questions, imperatives contractions stance adjectives downtoners first- and second-person pronouns	conversations family meetings conversational narratives
Monologue Informational Faceless (Careful production)	dependent clauses relative clauses clefts, verb complements nouns, adjectives	written expository registers

Dimension 6 (O/L)
Personal persuasion
Personal but
  informational stance
	amplifiers
	first- and second-person
	  pronouns
	reason conjuncts
	verb complements
	framing clauses
		petitions
		personal letters
		(memos)

Non-persuasive Faceless	(place deictics) (phrase co-ordination)	press reportage sports broadcast folk stories announcements

Note: O/L* marks oral/literate dimensions; (O/L) marks a less strong relation to speech and writing.

English dimension 6 similarly identifies public speeches, together with professional letters and editorials, as having an overt presentation of stance in English. The linguistic features on this dimension seem to represent an informational kind of stance; there are no involved evidential markers (e.g., hedges and emphatics), but *that*-complement clauses (on verbs and adjectives) function to encode speaker attitudes. Somali dimension 6 is similar in that it includes structurally complex features that are associated with a more informational presentation of stance – reason conjuncts, verb complements, and framing clauses. This dimension also includes personally involved linguistic features, such as amplifiers, and first- and second-person pronouns. Although Somali dimension 6 characterizes written registers at both poles, it shows that this type of stance and persuasion is common only in personal, often interactive, written registers: petitions, letters, and memos. In contrast, the expository written registers, with no specific addressee and uninvolved (or unacknowledged) authors, are marked for the absence of these stance features. Thus English dimension 6 and Somali dimension 6 are similar in marking a type of informational stance common in persuasive spoken registers or personal written registers.

Korean dimension 6 reflects honorification and self-humbling, aspects of personal stance that are not marked in the other three languages. The major linguistic features on this dimension are special honorific and humbling expressions, plus formal sentence endings and first-person pronouns. This is not a stereotypical oral/literate dimension because private conversations are unmarked, but the distribution of registers is strongly related to speech and writing. Extensive use of honorification is common in registers that have a specific addressor speaking or writing to specific interlocutors in public situations, especially personal letters, public conversations, and public speeches; in contrast, these features are quite rare in informational, expository registers.

7.2.5 Language-specific oral/literate dimensions (type D)

English, Korean, and Somali all have dimensions that define oral/literate relations among registers but have idiosyncratic functions not shared across the languages; these dimensions are summarized in table 7.5. They seem to represent functional parameters that are unique to one of these languages.

English dimension 5, Korean dimensions 2, 5, and 6, and Somali dimension 5 all fall into this category. In some of these cases, comparable linguistic features are well represented in all four languages, but they function together as an underlying parameter in only one language. For example, passives are analyzed in both English and Korean, impersonal constructions are analyzed in Somali, and ergative and absolutive case markers are analyzed in Tuvaluan; however, only English has a dimension distinguishing among abstract and non-abstract styles, defined primarily by the frequent use of passive constructions (dimension 5).

Korean dimension 6 and Somali dimension 5 are somewhat different in that the defining linguistic features exist in only one language, resulting in the possibility of a unique dimension. The honorific/humble expressions and formal sentence endings associated with Korean dimension 6 do not have counterparts in the other languages, and thus Korean is the only language with an honorification dimension. Similarly, optative clauses and directional particles are found only in Somali, resulting in the unique Somali dimension 5 representing 'distanced, directive interaction'.

Korean dimension 4, representing narrative versus non-narrative discourse, is a special case in that comparable dimensions are found in the other three languages (see section 7.2.6 below). Only in the case of Korean, however, is the narrative dimension associated with oral versus literate registers, with television drama having a marked narrative characterization and conversations being moderately narrative, while expository written registers are all markedly non-narrative.

All of the above dimensions are oral/literate in that spoken registers tend towards one pole and written registers tend towards the other pole. They are unique with respect to their structural bases, however. In particular, English dimension 5 ('Abstract versus Non-abstract Style'), Korean dimension 6 ('Honorification'), and Somali dimension 5 ('Distanced, Directive Interaction') represent unique form–function associations (with respect to these four languages), in contrast to the large number of dimensions showing cross-linguistic similarities. These dimensions thus show that in some cases, relatively idiosyncratic communicative functions particular to a culture and language are important enough to be reflected in underlying linguistic dimensions.

7.2.6   Cross-linguistic comparison of narrative dimensions

Besides the oral/literate dimensions described in sections 7.2.2–7.2.5, there are two additional communicative functions shared across these languages: narration and argumentation/persuasion. Narration appears to be the more basic of these two. As table 7.6 shows, English, Korean, and Somali all have strong narrative dimensions, and Nukulaelae Tuvaluan has a weaker, related dimension.

The structural bases of these dimensions are quite similar across the languages, with narrative discourse being marked by past tense verbs,

Table 7.5 *Summary of functions, linguistic features, and characteristic registers for idiosyncratic oral/literate dimensions (type D) in each language.*

Functions	Linguistic features	Characteristic registers
ENGLISH		
Dimension 5		
Non-abstract	[no features]	conversations, fiction personal letters public speeches public conversations broadcasts
Abstract style	agentless passives *by*-passives passive dependent clauses	technical prose (other academic prose) (official documents)
KOREAN		
Dimension 2		

Overt logical
   cohesion
	explanative conjuncts
	explanative, conditional,
	   co-ordinate, and discourse
	   clause connectors
	adverbial subordination
		folktales
		(conversations)
		(speeches)
		(public conversations)

Implicit logical
   cohesion
Informational focus
	nouns
	possessive markers
	passive constructions
		informational
		   expository registers
		broadcast news

Dimension 4		
Narrative discourse	past tense, action verbs type−token ratio time adverbs	novels, TV drama folktales (conversations) (broadcast news) (newspaper reportage)
Non-narrative discourse	present tense formal conjuncts	official documents (literary criticism) (essays, editorials)
Dimension 5		
On-line reportage of events	declarative sentences present tense copular verbs	sportscasts
Careful production	long sentences	newspaper reportage (broadcast news) (textbooks)

Table 7.5 (*cont.*)

Functions	*Linguistic features*	*Characteristic registers*
Dimension 6 Honorification Self-humbling	honorific and humble expressions formal sentence endings first person pronouns	personal letters public conversations (public speeches)

No overt marking of
   relation to addressee
	[no features]	informational expository
		   registers
		TV documentary

SOMALI
Dimension 5
Interactive
Distanced and directive
   communication
	optative clauses
	first- and second-person
	   pronouns
	directional particles
	imperatives
		personal letters
		(family meetings)
		(Quranic exposition)

Non-interactive Non-directive	[no features]	press reportage editorials written expository registers

third-person pronouns, temporal adverbs and clauses, and special verb classes. Non-narrative discourse is marked by the absence of these features together with frequent non-past tense verbs. Written fiction and folktales consistently have the most extreme narrative characterizations. Most written expository registers have non-narrative characterizations, although press reportage shows some narrative characteristics in English, Korean, and Somali. Nukulaelae Tuvaluan lacks written fiction and folktales, as well as press reportage, so this dimension is less well represented in that language. Conversational narratives, which were analyzed separately in Somali, have an intermediate characterization on this dimension, reflecting the mixing of past and present time perspectives.

Somali actually has two dimensions associated with narration. Somali dimension 4 corresponds closely to the narrative dimensions of English and Korean, in both structural characteristics and the distribution of registers. Somali dimension 3, on the other hand, combines a narrative versus non-narrative presentation of information with an argumentative or persuasive stance orientation. This dimension is discussed further in section 7.2.7.

Table 7.6 *Summary of functions, linguistic features, and characteristic registers for narrative dimensions in each language*

Functions	Linguistic features	Characteristic registers
ENGLISH		
Dimension 2		
Narrative discourse	past tense perfect aspect third-person pronouns speech act (public) verbs	fiction
Non-narrative discourse	present tense attributive adjectives	exposition, broadcasts professional letters telephone conversations
TUVALUAN		
Dimension 4		
(Non-narrative)	non-past tense verbs relative clauses raised noun phrases	
(Narrative)	(past tense verbs) (intensifiers)	
KOREAN		
Dimension 4		
Narrative discourse	past tense, action verbs type–token ratio time adverbs	novels, TV drama folktales (conversations) (broadcast news) (newspaper reportage)
Non-narrative discourse	present tense formal conjuncts	official documents (literary criticism) (essays, editorials)
SOMALI		
Dimension 3		

Overt argumentation
Persuasion
	present tense, adjectives
	possibility modals
	concession conjuncts
	conditional clauses
		family and formal
		    meetings
		general interest and
		    analytical press
		(invited editorials)

Reported presentation	past tense proper and agentive nouns future modals	press reportage (folk stories)

Table 7.6 (*cont.*)

Functions	Linguistic features	Characteristic registers
Dimension 4		
Narrative discourse	third-person pronouns past tense verbs temporal clauses clefts, habitual modals	folk stories (serial stories) (general fiction)
Non-narrative discourse	compound nouns gerunds, agentive nouns	petitions announcements memos

7.2.7   Cross-linguistic comparison of dimensions relating to argumentation and persuasion

Finally, there is a type of stance marking, related to argumentation and persuasion, that is represented cross-linguistically. Table 7.7 shows that this communicative function is similar to the narrative/non-narrative distinction in that it is not typically associated with oral/literate dimensions. This function appears to be more specialized than the marking of narration, however, having associated dimensions only in English and Somali.

The present section shows a fundamental opposition between dimensions marking personal stance, described in section 7.2.4 above, and dimensions marking argumentation and persuasion (described here). The marking of personal stance – as on English dimension 1, Tuvaluan dimension 1, Korean dimension 3, and Somali dimension 1 – is associated with a high degree of personal involvement: an active presentation of personal feelings and attitudes by the speaker or writer. The communicative emphasis on personal stance tends to be most common in situations having specific, interactive addressees who provide direct feedback. In contrast, the dimensions described in the present section show that an argumentative and persuasive stance does not require either personal involvement or direct interaction. Rather, these functions can be marked in a distanced, uninvolved manner, and therefore they are not associated with oral/literate dimensions.

The dimensions in English and Somali that mark argumentation and persuasion are summarized in table 7.7. English dimension 4 and Somali dimension 3 are the clearest examples of this type. Both of these dimensions have linguistic features that compare and contrast various alternative points of view, such as possibility modals, conditional subordination, and concession conjuncts. Editorials in both languages are marked as highly argumentative,

Table 7.7 *Summary of functions, linguistic features, and characteristic registers for dimensions relating to argumentation and persuasion*

Functions	Linguistic features	Characteristic registers
ENGLISH		
Dimension 4		
Overt argumentation and persuasion	modals (prediction, necessity, possibility) suasive verbs conditional subordination	professional letters editorials
Not overtly argumentative	[no features]	broadcasts (press reviews)
Dimension 7		
Academic hedging	*seem/appear* (downtoners) (concessive subordination)	
	[no features]	
SOMALI		
Dimension 3		
Overt argumentation Persuasion	present tense, adjectives possibility modals concession conjuncts conditional clauses	family and formal meetings general-interest and analytical press (invited editorials)
Reported presentation	past tense proper and agentive nouns future modals	press reportage (folk stories)

along with professional letters in English, and meetings and analytical press in Somali. Other informational, written registers are marked by the absence of these features (especially press reviews in English and press reportage in Somali). The fact that both poles include types of informational written prose shows that these are not oral/literate dimensions. While it is possible to combine these features of argumentation and persuasion with features marking personal stance and involvement, as in Somali family meetings, argumentative/persuasive discourse is typically presented apart from any acknowledgment of a specific addressor.

English dimension 7 was tentatively interpreted as marking academic hedging (see section 6.1.7), which is also a type of stance unrelated to personal involvement. In its linguistic characteristics, this dimension is similar to the dimensions of argumentation and persuasion; it includes occurrences of *seem* and *appear*, which are quite similar to possibility modals functionally (except that they require a complement clause), as well as concessive subordination. However, since this dimension is defined by very weak co-occurrence relations, its inclusion here is less certain.

7.2.8 Cross-linguistic comparison of the structural bases of dimensions

Sections 7.2.2–7.2.7 have adopted a functional perspective for the comparison of dimensions, showing that certain basic communicative functions are represented repeatedly across these four languages. It is also possible to compare dimensions from a structural perspective, examining the extent to which grammatical resources are exploited in similar ways across the languages.

Reconsidering the structural correlates of each dimension listed in tables 7.2–7.7, it is striking that dimensions that are analogous from a functional perspective also tend to be related in their defining linguistic characteristics. Dimensions reflecting interactiveness are probably the most straightforward of these (table 7.2), since stereotypical interactive discourse universally entails the physical circumstances of a specific addressor and specific addressee(s) sharing the same space and time. Thus, in all four languages the interactive dimensions are defined by features such as first- and second-person pronouns, questions, and imperatives (English D1, Tuvaluan D2 and D3, Korean D1, Somali D1 and D5).

Production circumstances also relate directly to the physical situation and thus have similar structural correlates across the languages: reduced forms (e.g., contractions, deletions, incomplete sentences), a generally fragmented structure (e.g., extensive clause co-ordination), and less precise lexical choice coupled with a greater use of pronominal forms. Table 7.3 shows that English D1, Korean D1, and Somali D1 and D2 all follow this pattern.

There are two major structural correlates of an informational focus: structural integration and structural elaboration. Apparently, there are a limited number of ways to package extensive information into relatively few words, and thus the same kinds of features are used for informational integration in all four languages: frequent nouns, derived nominal forms and nominalizations, attributive adjectives, prepositional or postpositional phrases (case particles in Somali), genitives, and precise lexical choice. English D1, Tuvaluan D2, Korean D1, and Somali D1 and D2 all show this functional/structural association.

The marking of structural elaboration associated with an informational focus, discussed more fully in section 7.2.9 below, is more complex. Relative clause constructions serve this function in English (D3, D5), Korean (D1), and Somali (D1). Further, complement clauses are associated with some types of informational elaboration cross-linguistically (English D6, Korean D1, Somali D1). Other structural correlates of an informational focus are not shared cross-linguistically; these include the passive constructions defining English D5 and the logical cohesion features defining Korean D2.

Personal stance differs from these other functions in that it is not a direct reflection of the physical circumstances. Thus, cultures can choose to express personal stance in different communicative circumstances. However, personal stance is marked in all four languages as a basic function underlying at least one dimension, and the structural correlates of stance are quite similar cross-linguistically: first-person references, various kinds of hedges and emphatics, and private verbs coupled with complement clauses. Dimensions with these characteristics include English D1, Tuvaluan D1, Korean D3, and Somali D1. In addition, Korean overtly marks stance towards the addressee through its dimension of honorification (D6).

The structural correlates of narration include past time verbs, third-person pronouns, and temporal adverbs and clauses. These features are shared as markers of stereotypical story lines, as in novels and folktales, in English (D2), Korean (D4), Somali (D4), and to a lesser extent Tuvaluan (D4). In this style of narration, there is a temporally sequenced presentation of past events, typically occurring in removed circumstances and involving third-person actors. It is not clear whether conversational narratives also have shared structural characteristics cross-linguistically.

Finally, dimensions relating to argumentation/persuasion are represented only in English (D4) and Somali (D3 and D6), but these also share certain structural characteristics: frequent modals (possibility, prediction, necessity), and adverbial clauses or conjuncts (conditional, concessive). These constructions are associated with a non-personal marking of stance and a logical comparison of various arguments.

Some of these structural similarities reflect physical similarities in communicative events cross-culturally. The shared structural correlates of dimensions associated with interaction and production circumstances can be traced to cross-cultural similarities in the physical situations of various types of communicative events. The shared structural correlates of dimensions associated with an informational focus can be traced to the physical characteristics of writing situations and the limited number of ways that information can be integrated or elaborated as writers construct texts. The marking of personal stance, narration, and argumentation/persuasion, however, do not depend on physical considerations. Rather, because of the nature of the communicative purposes associated with these functional domains, similar linguistic structures are used to define the associated dimensions in each language.

7.2.9   The cross-linguistic marking of structural complexity

Numerous studies have posited a basic structural opposition between informal, unplanned, oral registers and formal, planned, literate registers: the oral registers are claimed to have loose, paratactic structures, with extensive co-ordination and fragmentation; the literate registers are claimed to have tight, grammaticalized structures, with greater structural complexity including extensive embedding and a careful integration of structure (e.g., Givón 1979a; Ochs 1979; Chafe 1982). These broad generalizations are supported in part by the four MD analyses presented here.

The first dimension in the analyses of English, Korean, and Somali, which is the strongest dimension in terms of the number of co-occurring features, shows a basic structural opposition of the kind posited in these earlier studies: at one pole there are main clause, co-ordinated, fragmented, and reduced features, characteristic of conversation and other oral registers, while the other pole has structural embedding and integrated features, characteristic of written, informational registers. Nukulaelae Tuvaluan dimension 2 shows a similar pattern, although this dimension is not as strong as the comparable dimensions in the other three languages.

When these analyses are examined in more detail, though, it becomes obvious that a simple structural dichotomy opposing fragmented, paratactic (oral) discourse and integrated, structurally embedded (literate) discourse is not adequate. For example, English and Tuvaluan have separate dimensions marking structural integration and structural embedding. English dimension 1 opposes integration features, such as nouns, attributive adjectives, and prepositional phrases, to fragmented, reduced, and paratactic features, such as clause co-ordination, contractions, and frequent verbs. This dimension does not include structural embedding features co-occurring with the integration features (although some forms of structural embedding occur in a complementary distribution to these integrated features – see discussion below). In contrast, there are some subordination features – specifically relative clause constructions – grouped on English dimension 3, in a complementary distribution to time and place adverbials. Tuvaluan dimension 2 similarly includes integration features apart from structural embedding features – primarily nouns and prepositional phrases, which are opposed to co-ordinators. Some subordinate clauses appear on Tuvaluan dimension 3, opposed to questions and direct quotes.

Korean and Somali show a different pattern, combining integration and structural embedding features on the same dimensions. Thus Korean dimension 1 includes integrated features such as postpositions and attributive adjectives as well as embedding features, such as relative clauses, long sentences, non-finite clauses, and noun complements; these all co-occur in a complementary pattern to involved/fragmented features such as contractions, fragmentary sentences, and simple co-ordination. Somali dimension 1 similarly includes integrated features, such as nouns, adjectives, and case particle sequences, as well as embedded structures, such as relative clauses, clefts, and verb complement clauses; these features are all opposed to involved features, such as simple responses, clause co-ordination, and contractions. Thus, integration and structural embedding features represent different kinds of structural complexity in some languages (English), while these structural domains co-occur to a greater extent in other languages (Korean and Somali). Chapter 8 proposes historical reasons for this difference in the structural organizations of English versus Korean and Somali.

In addition, the analyses of all four languages show that structural embedding can serve a number of different functions, associated with both oral and literate registers (see Biber 1988, 1992a). For example, in English different types of dependent clause are found on all six dimensions:

On dimension 1, causative subordination, sentence relatives, and WH clauses co-occur with interactive and involved features, as opposed to features marking informational integration.

On dimension 2, present participial clauses co-occur with narrative features.

On dimension 3, WH relative clauses function to mark an explicit and elaborated style of reference (as opposed to situated reference).

On dimension 4, infinitive clauses and conditional adverbial clauses co-occur with modals and suasive verbs marking an overtly persuasive and argumentative style.

On dimension 5, past participial postnominal clauses and past participial adverbial clauses co-occur with passive constructions and conjuncts as markers of a technical, abstract style.

On dimension 6, *that*-complement clauses to verbs, *that*-complement clauses to adjectives, and *that*-relative clauses on object position co-occur with demonstratives, final prepositions, and existential *there* reflecting an on-line and personal production of information.

Although there are fewer types of dependent clause in Nukulaelae Tuvaluan, these structures are also distributed across different dimensions:

On dimension 2, general subordinators are grouped co-occurring with features marking interpersonal reference.

On dimension 3, general and causative adverbial subordinators are grouped together with features marking a monologic production of text.

On dimension 4, relative clauses are grouped together with non-past tense, informational features.

Dependent clauses are distributed on each of the first three dimensions in Korean:

On dimension 1, relative clauses, non-finite clauses, and noun complements co-occur with postpositions and attributive adjectives as markers of highly planned, informational discourse.

On dimension 2, temporal adverbial subordination, explanative (causative) subordinators, and conditional subordinators co-occur with various conjuncts and verb classes marking overt logical cohesion; these features are most common in oral registers such as folktales and private conversations.

On dimension 3, verb and noun complement clauses co-occur with hedges, emphatics, private verbs, and other markers of personal stance, commonly found in television drama and private conversations.

Finally, dependent clauses are distributed across five of the dimensions in Somali:

On dimension 1, conditional clauses co-occur with involved and fragmented features, while relative clauses, clefts, and verb complement clauses co-occur with the complementary grouping of integrated features marking informational exposition.

On dimension 2, purpose clauses have a weak co-occurrence relation with lexical elaboration features.

On dimension 3, conditional clauses co-occur with argumentative features, while framing clauses co-occur with features marking a reported presentation of information.

On dimension 4, temporal clauses and clefts co-occur with narrative features.

On dimension 6, verb complement clauses and framing clauses co-occur with other markers of personal persuasion.

Thus, the MD analyses in each language show that dependent clauses can be characteristic of either literate or oral registers, and that they can co-occur with many types of linguistic features serving a wide variety of functions. In addition, there are certain systematic generalizations regarding particular kinds of structural elaboration that hold across the four languages. Relative clauses, and nominal modifiers generally, are characteristic of literate registers, being used for informational elaboration (see English D3, Tuvaluan D4, Korean D1, Somali D1). In contrast, adverbial subordination is used most commonly in oral registers, often to mark some aspect of personal stance; adverbial clauses often co-occur with involved, reduced, or fragmented features (see English D1, D2, D4,; Tuvaluan D2; Korean D2; Somali D1, D3, D4). Complement clauses and infinitives occur frequently in both oral and literate registers, but they frequently co-occur with other features marking personal stance or persuasion (English D4, D6; Korean D3; Somali D6).

Overall, these analyses clearly show that it is not adequate to treat structural complexity as an undifferentiated whole. Rather, there are different kinds of complexities having quite different distributions and functional associations. English (and to a lesser extent Nukulaelae Tuvaluan) shows a fundamental distinction between integrated and embedded structures, while features marking these two kinds of structural complexity co-occur in Korean and Somali. Further, different kinds of embedded structures – relative clauses, adverbial clauses, and complement clauses – function independently in each language, although there are striking cross-linguistic similarities in the distributions and associated functions of each construction type. Although these patterns need further investigation based on a larger sample of languages, they provide strong evidence for the existence of widely shared correspondences between grammatical form and communicative function cross-linguistically.

7.2.10 A cross-linguistic comparison of the multidimensional profile for each language

Because of the strong functional associations underlying each dimension of variation, it is possible to identify important differences in the communicative priorities of each culture through an overall comparison of the multidimensional profiles of each language. While such an analysis is obviously not a substitute for careful ethnographies of communication, it can provide a complementary perspective. That is, an ethnography of communication seeks to analyze the patterns and functions of speaking and writing as a cultural system in a speech community. While such ethnographies are based on a direct observation of social behavior, they often do not include detailed linguistic analysis of the texts produced in different situations. A comprehensive description of communication in a culture, however, must synthesize both behavioral and linguistic analyses (see Bauman and Sherzer 1989: 8).

In the Multi-Dimensional approach, the question of communicative function is approached from a linguistic perspective. That is, MD analyses first identify the patterns of co-occurring features that are linguistically well defined in a language, and then those patterns are interpreted in functional terms. This approach is based on the assumption that the allocation of linguistic resources in a language is functionally motivated, and therefore linguistic co-occurrence reflects communicative function: multiple linguistic features co-occur in texts because they are associated with a common set of underlying communicative goals and functions. Similar generalizations

Table 7.8 *Comparison of the major functional priorities represented in the multidimensional analysis of each language.*

Communicative function	English	Nukulaelae Tuvaluan	Korean	Somali
Oral/literate dimensions	D 1, 3, 5, 6	D 1, 2, 3	D 1, 2, 3, 4, 5, 6	D 1, 2, 5
Interaction	D 1	D *2, *3	D 1	D1, *5
Production circumstances	D 1, *3, 6	D (3)	D 1, *5	D 1, *2
Informational focus	D *1, *3, *5, *6	D *2, (3)	D *1, *2, 3	D *1, *2
Personal stance	D 1, (6)	D *1	D *3, *6	D 1, 6
Argumentation/persuasion	D *4, 7	–	–	D *3, 5, *6
Narration	D *2	D (4)	D *4	D 3, *4

Note: *marks dimensions having the given function as the primary basis.

hold for the overall multidimensional profile of a language: assuming that linguistic resources are preferentially allocated to functions reflecting the communicative priorities of each culture, it follows that a language will have multiple dimensions associated with those same functions. Since each dimension defines a different set of distinctions among registers, the existence of multiple dimensions associated with a single functional domain will result in relatively fine distinctions among related subregisters, such as different kinds of interaction or different kinds of informational discourse. Thus, a global comparison of the multidimensional profile for each language provides an indication of the differing communicative priorities in each culture.

Table 7.8 summarizes the overall multidimensional profiles for the four languages in the present study. For each major communicative function, this table lists the associated dimensions in each language. An asterisk (*) is used to mark those dimensions having a given function as their primary underlying association: for example, the positive features on Tuvaluan dimension 2 relate primarily to interpersonal interaction, and thus this dimension is marked with an asterisk for that function. In contrast, the positive features on English dimension 1 relate to several major functions: interaction, production circumstances, and personal stance. Since none of these can be singled out as the primary function, they are not marked with an asterisk. Thus, an asterisk marks those cases where a dimension is dedicated to a particular function, as an additional reflection of the prominence of that function in the given langauge.

The top line on table 7.8 lists the oral/literate dimensions in each language. Although oral/literate distinctions are important in all four languages, Nukulaelae Tuvaluan and Korean are particularly noteworthy. In Nukulaelae Tuvaluan, all three of the major dimensions show some relation to stereotypical speech and writing (even though these patterns are not uniformly strong, due to the restricted range of registers in the language). The patterns in Korean are even more striking, with spoken and written registers tending to have polar characterizations along all six dimensions.

Three major functions are most strongly associated with these oral/literate dimensions: interactiveness, production circumstances, and informational focus and density. In English and Korean, features that are directly interactive are associated only with dimension 1, which also includes features relating to production circumstances and personal stance. Somali dimension 1 reflects a similar combination of functions, while Somali dimension 5 is related primarily to interaction, reflecting the importance of interactive communication in Somali culture. Interaction is given the greatest prominence in Nukulaelae Tuvaluan, however, where two of the three major dimensions have a primary function marking different aspects of interaction. Along Tuvaluan dimension 2, defined by first- and second-person pronouns, personal letters and conversations are marked as highly interactive and interpersonal in reference, while written sermons and broadcasts are informational. Along Tuvaluan dimension 3, comprising questions and direct quotes, conversations are marked as being highly dependent on a multi-party, interactive construction of text, while personal letters and broadcasts are marked as monologic production. These patterns indicate that direct interaction plays a more important role in the registers of Nukulaelae Tuvaluan than in the other three languages considered here.

In contrast, production circumstances are less important in Nukulaelae Tuvaluan than in the other three languages. In Tuvaluan, only dimension 3 has any relation to production circumstances. Korean and Somali each have two dimensions of this type (Korean D1 and D5; Somali D1 and D2), while English has three such dimensions (1, 3, and 6). All three of these languages have one dimension with a primary association to production circumstances (English D3; Korean D5; Somali D2).

These differences in the importance of dimensions relating to interaction and production circumstances can be tied to the different social histories of the four cultures. By their physical nature, written registers are less interactive and can be more carefully produced than spoken registers. Thus, the more resources a language allocates to careful integrated production and dense informational elaboration (associated with stereotypical writing) the fewer resources it will allocate (proportionally) to the marking of interaction and involvement. Nukulaelae Tuvaluan has by far the least developed repertoire of written registers and thus shows the greatest allocation of resources to interaction and the differentiation of interactive types. Although Somali presently has a wide range of written registers, it has a very short history of literacy and thus also has dimensions dedicated to the marking of interaction. In contrast, English and Korean have long literacy histories and a wide range of written and spoken registers, and thus at present these languages no longer have dimensions dedicated to interaction.

Production circumstances can similarly be related to the range of spoken and written registers. Nukulaelae Tuvaluan, with only two written registers, has relatively little variability in the range of production circumstances, and thus there are no dimensions relating primarily to production differences. In contrast, the registers in English, Korean, and Somali show much greater variability with respect to this parameter, ranging from conversational texts produced on-line to carefully planned written texts which are extensively revised before publication. Thus all three of these languages have multiple dimensions reflecting the different linguistic characteristics possible under different production circumstances.

Informational focus is somewhat related to production circumstances, since it is necessary to have the opportunity for careful production to package information in a dense and elaborated manner. However, given these potential resources of writing, cultures will still differ in the extent to which an informational focus is an important communicative goal in itself. Table 7.8 shows that the packaging of informational content is important in all four languages, since they all have at least one dimension with an informational focus as its primary functional association. However, there are considerable differences in the overall allocation of linguistic resources to this function. At one extreme, Nukulaelae Tuvaluan has only one dimension dedicated to informational integration (dimension 2); this distribution is not surprising given the small range of register variation, and the complete absence of written expository registers, in this language.

Korean and Somali each have two dimensions dedicated to informational integration. The negative pole of Korean dimension 1 combines features for informational integration (e.g., postpositions, attributive adjectives) with features for informational elaboration (e.g., relative clauses, noun complements). The negative pole of Korean dimension 2 is marked by the absence of overt logical cohesion markers and the presence of informational features such as nouns, passives, and derived adjectives. Somali has separate informational dimensions relating to structural integration/elaboration and lexical elaboration. Similar to Korean dimension 1, the negative pole of Somali dimension 1 comprises features for both informational integration (e.g., nouns, genitives, adjectives) and informational elaboration (e.g., relative clauses, clefts, complement clauses). Somali dimension 2 represents precise, and thus informational, word choice (including frequent once-occurring words and a high type–token ratio), representing a kind of lexical elaboration.

English shows by far the greatest allocation of linguistic resources to informational packaging and elaboration. The negative pole of English dimension 1 comprises features for informational integration (e.g., nouns, prepositions, attributive adjectives); all written expository registers are extremely integrated in these terms, while written fiction registers are moderately integrated. English dimension 3 comprises relative clause constructions and phrasal co-ordination, used for informational elaboration. These features are common in highly informational, written registers, such as official documents, professional letters, and academic prose. They are rarely found in prose reportage (e.g., press reportage, biographies), fiction, or spoken registers. Dimension 5 comprises various passive constructions used to focus on an informational proposition rather than an agent performing some action; these features are common only in official or academic prose (especially technical and engineering prose). Dimension 6 includes complement clauses and *that*-relative clauses used for informational elaboration in on-line production circumstances; these features are common in informational, spoken registers, such as public speeches, debates, and interviews. Thus, although English, Korean, and to a lesser extent Somali, have comparable ranges of written registers and comparable literacy traditions, English has allocated the most linguistic resources to this functional domain, enabling a large number of distinctions among various subregisters of informational discourse.

In contrast, Korean shows by far the greatest allocation of resources to the marking of personal stance, with two dimensions dedicated to this function. Both dimensions include first-person pronouns and relate to the presentation of self. Dimension 3 reflects the overt expression of personal attitudes in relation to the message of the text, using features such as complement clauses, emphatics, hedges, attitudinal expressions, and private verbs. Television drama shows the greatest use of these stance features, but they are also common in other spoken registers (private and public conversations, public speeches) and in some written expressive registers (personal letters, personal essays). Korean dimension 6 relates to the marking of honorification and the presentation of self in relation to the addressee. This dimension comprises honorific expressions, humble expressions, and formal sentence endings. Public discourse directed to a specific addressee, including personal letters, public conversations, and public speeches, makes extensive use of these honorific devices; in contrast, these stance features are markedly infrequent in written expository and fiction registers.

Personal stance is also given a prominent role in Nukulaelae Tuvaluan, where one of the three major dimensions (dimension 1) relates directly to attitudinal versus authoritative discourse. Attitudinal discourse is marked by adverbs, hedges, intensifiers, discourse linkers, and first-person pronouns. Speeches and political meetings make the most frequent use of these attitudinal markers, while written sermons are the most authoritative in style.

English and Somali have no dimensions dedicated to the marking of personal stance; rather, both of these languages combine stance features with other markers of interpersonal communication. Both of these languages have dimensions associated with the marking of persuasion and argumentation, however. English dimension 4, relating to the overt expression of argumentation, is defined by infinitives, prediction modals, suasive verbs, conditional clauses, necessity modals, and possibility modals. Professional letters and editorials are marked as the most argumentative in terms of these features. English dimension 7, including features such as *seem/appear*, downtoners, and concessive adverbial clauses, is tentatively interpreted as academic hedging.

Somali has an even greater allocation of linguistic resources to the marking of argumentation and persuasion. Somali dimension 3 opposes an argumentative versus reported presentation of information. Argumentative discourse is marked by frequent possibility modals, concession conjuncts, impersonal particles, and conditional clauses. Registers such as family and formal meetings, analytical press, and invited editorials are marked as highly argumentative in these terms. (Press reportage is marked as extremely reported.) Somali dimension 5 is also related to this functional domain in that it marks highly directive interaction. Somali dimension 6 is dedicated primarily to marking personal persuasion, comprising features such as first-and second-person pronouns, amplifiers, reason conjuncts, verb complements, and framing clauses. Personal petitions, personal letters, and memos are marked as highly persuasive in these terms.

It is interesting that Korean and Nukulaelae Tuvaluan, which do not have argumentation/persuasion dimensions, show the clearest marking of personal stance. Both the personal expression of feelings/evidentiality as well as the impersonal expression of argumentation/persuasion relate to the general expression of attitudes and stance. In these languages, the linguistic co-occurrence patterns associated with personal stance overtly mark attitudes held personally by the speaker/writer, while the linguistic features associated with argumentation/persuasion are used to mark attitudes towards propositions in the abstract, arguing for the superiority of a point of view without identifying those attitudes with a particular addressor.[2] Future research is required to investigate whether this same complementary relationship between personal stance and argumentation holds generally across langauges.

Finally, a distinct narrative dimension is clearly distinguished in English, Korean, and Somali, while Tuvaluan dimension 4 appears to be related to this functional domain. Thus, the marking of traditional narrative story lines, as in fiction and folktales, seems to be carried out by means of similar linguistic characteristics cross-linguistically.

In summary, all four languages have dimensions relating to interaction, production circumstances, informational focus, personal stance, and narration.[3] The functional priorities of the languages differ, however. English shows the greatest allocation of resources to distinguishing among various kinds of informational focus, with dimensions relating to production circumstances and argumentation/persuasion being less important but notable. In Nukulaelae Tuvaluan, the marking of interaction is most important, with personal stance being less important but notable. In Korean, dimensions relating to personal stance have equal importance to those marking an informational focus. This allocation of linguistic resources is particularly noteworthy given the extensive range of written registers in Korean. Finally, in Somali the marking of argumentation/persuasion and informational focus are the two most important functional priorities, while interaction and production circumstances are less important but notable.[4]

7.3   Cross-linguistic comparison of registers

The cross-linguistic analyses to this point have focused on functional and structural comparisons of the underlying dimensions of variation in each language. However, the MD framework can also be used to compare analogous registers cross-linguistically.

Table 7.9 presents multidimensional comparisons for four registers: face-to-face conversations, press editorials, public spontaneous speeches, and personal letters. The characterization of each register in each language is presented in functional terms, using the six major functional categories distinguished in section 7.2. However, the functional similarities identified here have corresponding structural similarities, since the major functions have strikingly similar structural correlates across the four languages (as shown in section 7.2.8 above).

Overall, table 7.9 shows that these four registers are quite similar cross-linguistically in those characteristics associated with the physical situation and global communicative goals, while there are greater differences in those characteristics associated with the specific purpose and/or topic of a register. These patterns reflect the fact that the physical situations and global communicative goals associated with these registers are essentially the same cross-linguistically, while the particular communicative purposes of analogous registers can vary from one culture/language to another. For example, conversation has very similar cross-linguistic characterizations associated with interaction, production circumstances, and informational

Table 7.9 *Comparison of the multidimensional characterizations of equivalent registers across four languages*

Communicative function	English	Nukulaelae Tuvaluan	Korean	Somali
FACE-TO-FACE CONVERSATIONS				
Interaction	interactive D1	interactive D2 multi-party D3	interactive D1	interactive D1 (directive) D5
Production circumstances	on-line D1 situation-dependent D3	(on-line) D3	on-line D1	on-line D1, 2
Informational focus	not integrated D1 not elaborated D3 not abstract D5 not on-line information D6	not integrated D2, (3)	not integrated D1 not elaborated D1 overt cohesion D2	not integrated D1 not elaborated D1, 2
Personal stance	personal stance D1	unmarked D1	personal stance D3 moderate honorification D6	personal stance D1
Argumentation/ persuasion	unmarked D4	—	—	(argumentative) D3 (non-persuasive) D6
Narration	unmarked D2	—	narrative D4	unmarked D4
PRESS EDITORIALS				
Interaction	non-inter-active D1	—	non-interactive D1	non-interactive D1 (non-directive) D5
Production circumstances	careful D1 (elaborated reference) D3	—	careful D1	careful D1, D2

Table 7.9 (*cont.*)

Communicative function	English	Nukulaelae Tuvaluan	Korean	Somali
PRESS EDITORIALS (cont.)				
Informational focus	integrated D1 (elaborated) D3 (abstract style) D5 (on-line information) D6	—	integrated D1 elaborated D1 implicit cohesion D2	integrated D1 elaborated structure D1 elaborated lexical choice D2
Personal stance	not personal stance D1	—	(marked stance) D3 not overt honor- ification D6	not personal stance D1
Argumentation/ persuasion	argumentative D4	—	—	unmarked D3 (non-persuasive) D6
Narration	non-narrative D2	—	non-narrative D4	non-narrative D4
PUBLIC SPONTANEOUS SPEECHES				
Interaction	(interactive and involved) D1	unmarked D2, D3	unmarked D1	(interactive and involved) D1 (directive) D5
Production circumstances	on-line D1 (elaborated reference) D3	unmarked D3	unmarked D1	(on-line) D1, D2
Informational focus	not integrated D1 (elaborated) D3 not abstract style D5 on-line information D6	unmarked D2	unmarked D1 (overt cohe- sion) D2	(not inte- grated) D1 (not elaborated structure) D1 not elaborated lexical choice D2
Personal stance	personal stance D1	attitudinal D1	personal stance D3 overt honori- fication D6	(personal stance) D1
Argumentation/ persuasion	unmarked D4	—	—	(argumentative) D3 unmarked personal persuasion D6

Table 7.9 (*cont.*)

Communicative function	English	Nukulaelae Tuvaluan	Korean	Somali
PUBLIC SPONTANEOUS SPEECHES (cont.)				
Narration	(narrative) D2	—	(non-narrative) D4	(narrative) D4
PERSONAL LETTERS				
Interaction	(interactive and involved) D1	interactive and inter-personal D2 not multi-party D3	unmarked D1	(interactive and involved) D1 directive D5
Production circumstances	(on-line) D1 situated reference D3	careful and monologue D3	unmarked D1	(on-line) D1, D2
Informational focus	not integrated D1 not elaborated D3 not abstract style D5 not on-line information D6	not integrated D2	unmarked D1 (overt cohesion) D2	(not integrated) D1 (not elaborated structure) D1 unmarked lexical elaboration D2
Personal stance	personal stance D1	unmarked D1	personal stance D3 overt honorification D6	(personal stance) D1
Argumentation/persuasion	(argumentative D4	—	—	unmarked D3 personal persuasion D6
Narration	unmarked D2	—	narrative D4	non-narrative D4

Note: Public spontaneous speeches in each language:
English: spontaneous speeches; Nukulaelae Tuvaluan: maneapa speeches; Korean: unscripted public speeches; Somali: Quranic sermons

focus. In each of these four languages, conversation makes extensive use of interactive linguistic features and features reflecting on-line production circumstances, coupled with a lack of structural integration or elaboration features. In contrast, the other three major functions represented by dimensions – personal stance, argumentation/persuasion, and narration – reflect differences in the particular communicative purpose of a given register. For this reason, there are some cross-linguistic differences associated with these parameters. In English, Korean, and Somali, conversational interlocuters tend to reveal their personal stance, but stance is marked to a lesser extent in Tuvaluan conversations. Overt argumentation/persuasion is marked only in English and Somali, and the typical characteristics of conversation differ between these two languages: English conversation tends not to be overtly argumentative, while typical conversations in Somali do tend to be moderately argumentative. Finally, conversations do not have frequent narrative features in English and Somali, but they are typically narrative in Korean. These characterizations reflect the different particular communicative tasks and purposes that tend to shape conversational interactions in the four languages.

This same general pattern holds for press editorials in English, Korean, and Somali. (Nukulaelae Tuvaluan has no comparable register.) In all three languages, editorials have frequent features reflecting careful production circumstances, integrated structure, and elaborated structure, together with an absence of interactive features. However, there are some differences associated with the particular purposes of editorials in each language. Personal stance is not marked in English or Somali editorials, but it is marked to a moderate extent in Korean editorials. English editorials tend to use argumentative/persuasive features, while Somali editorials do not. Editorials are similar across the three languages in being markedly non-narrative. These characterizations indicate that English editorials tend to argue for a point of view by comparing it to alternative points of view, with no overt indication of the author's personal stance. In contrast, Korean editorials directly indicate the author's personal stance but are not overtly argumentative. Somali editorials tend to present an official government position, and thus they are not marked by either personal stance features or argumentative features (see Biber and Hared 1994).

Spontaneous public speeches show more variation, in part because this comparison is based on different kinds of speech events in the four languages. English public speeches were collected from speech events such as court cases, dinner speeches, political speeches, and sermons. Nukulaelae Tuvaluan maneapa speeches are addressed to the entire island community during feasts and dances. Korean unscripted speeches are primarily religious, including sermons and wedding speeches given by a pastor. The Somali speeches used for comparison are also religious: Quranic sermons given in the mosque at the weekly worship service. These situational differences are reflected in some linguistic differences, although the general characterizations are similar cross-linguistically. Public speeches in English and Somali make moderate use of interactive and involved features, and they are marked by features reflecting on-line production circumstances; these features are used to a lesser extent in Tuvaluan and Korean speeches. Public speeches do not have a carefully integrated structure in any of the four languages, but English speeches are elaborated structurally in certain respects. The strongest area of agreement is in the overt expression of personal stance, which is marked in the public speeches of all four languages. In addition, honorification is overtly marked in Korean speeches. English speeches are not uniformly argumentative, although political speeches and some sermons can make frequent use of these features (see Biber and Finegan 1989b). Somali Quranic sermons are more consistent in showing a moderate use of argumentative features. Finally, public speeches in English and Somali are moderately narrative, while those in Korean are marked by a relative absence of narrative features.

With respect to letters, there are cross-linguistic differences that reflect differing communicative purposes as well as the differing register ranges of these languages. That is, letters in English, Korean, and Somali represent the most personal and interactive kind of writing; in Nukulaelae Tuvaluan, on the other hand, letters are the only written register in common use.[5] Letters are interactive and involved in all four languages, although these characteristics are less marked in Korean. Nukulaelae Tuvaluan letters are additionally marked as not representing a multi-party interaction.

In contrast to these similarities in interactiveness, the production circumstances of letters are quite different cross-linguistically. Letters in English and Somali (and Korean to a lesser extent) make extensive use of features reflecting on-line production circumstances (especially in comparison to the expository written registers). However, in Nukulaelae Tuvaluan, letters are among the most carefully produced registers in the language.

Letters are marked to some extent in all four languages for the use of personal stance features. These characterizations of letters can be supplemented by the more detailed analyses of stance and affect features in Besnier (1989a) and Biber and Finegan (1989b). Besnier (1989a) shows that the overt expression of affect is one of the primary functions of Nukulaelae letters, making letters by far the most affective register in that register repertoire. Biber and Finegan (1989b) similarly found personal letters to be one of the most affective registers in English, making extensive use of overtly affective verbs (e.g., *enjoy, dread*), adjectives (e.g., *fortunate, shocked*), and adverbs (e.g., *luckily, alarmingly*).

Letters are not integrated or elaborated structurally in any of the languages. Other characterizations of letters are particular to a single language: letters make extensive use of honorification features in Korean, a moderate use of argumentative features in English, and extensive use of directive and personal persuasion features in Somali. Finally, there are notable differences in the narrative characteristics of letters: they are unmarked in this regard in English, but letters are markedly narrative in Korean, while they are markedly non-narrative in Somali.

Overall, the cross-linguistic comparisons of these four registers reflect the general patterns discussed in section 7.2.8: that major functional similarities tend to be reflected in structural similarities across the languages. Thus, to the extent that registers are similar in their situational characteristics, they will show corresponding structural similarities.

However, the cross-linguistic differences identified in this section show that analogous registers sometimes differ in crucial respects across languages, a fact that can be obscured by referring to them by the same English term. This problem is most notable here with respect to public speeches: the kinds of speeches analyzed in each language are quite different, and correspondingly there are fairly marked cross-linguistic differences for this register. At the other extreme, conversation is quite similar in its situational characteristics cross-linguistically. However, even this register is characterized by differing specific purposes and communicative goals in each culture, and these differences are reflected in different linguistic characterizations.

Letters also have similar situational characteristics across the four languages: in all cases they represent a kind of written interaction produced by a single writer. They have quite different statuses relative to the full range of spoken and written registers, however; they represent the most interactive and interpersonal written register in English, Korean, and Somali, while in Nukulaelae Tuvaluan, they constitute 'the primary purpose of literacy production on Nukulaelae Atoll' (Besnier 1989a: 69). Finally, editorials do not exist in Nukulaelae Tuvaluan, but they are quite similar in the other three languages, representing institutional expressions of opinion. The primary differences cross-linguistically among the editorials relates to the marking of personal stance and overt argumentation. In English, editorials are argumentative but not personal, while Korean editorials tend to have the opposite characteristics. Somali editorials present official government positions and thus are neither personal nor argumentative.

In sum, although all four of these registers represent comparable varieties across the languages, it is important to avoid the assumption that the same specific communicative purposes will be normative in each case. Rather, each culture can attach different primary purposes to a register, resulting in some cross-linguistic structural differences.

7.4   Theoretical discussion

The present chapter has compared the cross-linguistic patterns of register variation from several different perspectives: with respect to the communicative functions represented by the dimensions in each language, with respect to the structural correlates of the dimensions in each language, with respect to the multidimensional profile of each language, and with respect to the MD characterizations of particular registers. These comparisons show that the MD approach provides a principled and empirical framework for cross-linguistic register analysis, in contrast to attempted comparisons based on individual linguistic features. That is, by first analyzing the linguistic co-occurrence patterns within each language, and identifying the underlying dimensions that are well represented in those terms, the MD approach provides a solid basis for cross-linguistic comparisons.

The findings here are not restricted to a simple listing of cross-linguistic similarities and differences. Rather, these MD analyses provide answers to a number of basic theoretical questions, including:

1   Which underlying communicative functions are realized linguistically in all of these languages? Which functions are particular to only some of these languages?

2   Why do these particular functional similarities and differences exist? Specifically, why do all four languages have structural dimensions reflecting interactiveness, production circumstances, informational focus, personal stance (towards content), and narration? Why are dimensions marking stance and argumentation/persuasion particular to selected languages?

3   What are the structural correlates of underlying communicative functions? Which functional dimensions are realized by the same kinds of structural features cross-linguistically? Which dimensions have different structural correlates?

4   Why do these particular structural similarities and differences exist? For example, why do first- and second-person pronouns, questions, and imperatives mark interactiveness cross-linguistically? Why do nouns, adjectives, and other nominal modifiers mark informational integration cross-linguistically? Why are relative clauses associated with informational elaboration cross-linguistically? Why are adverbial clauses associated with the marking of stance in oral registers cross-linguistically?

5   How similar (or different) are analogous registers cross-linguistically?

6   Why do these particular similarities and differences among registers exist? For example, why should editorials be similarly marked for informational integration and the lack of interactiveness in English, Korean, and Somali, while differing with respect to the marking of argumentation?

7   What patterns underlie the overall allocation of linguistic resources within and across languages? To what extent is the overall multi-dimensional profile of each language similar (or different) cross-linguistically?

One of the surprising findings resulting from these comparisons is that the cross-linguistic similarities identified here are far stronger than the cross-linguistic differences. This is especially the case with respect to functional and structural correlates of the physical situation and global communicative goals. Thus, all four languages have multiple dimensions reflecting basic oral/literate differences, the marking of interactiveness, production circumstances, and an informational focus. These dimensions are defined by similar kinds of linguistic features, and analogous registers have quite similar cross-linguistic characterizations along these dimensions. In addition, two functional domains that relate to communicative purpose rather than the physical situation are represented in the dimensional structure of all four languages: personal stance (towards the content) and narration. These dimensions also have similar structural correlates across the languages.

In contrast, there are far fewer major differences in the patterns of register variation. Dimensions relating to argumentation/persuasion are found in only some languages,[6] and there are a few dimensions particular to a single language (such as abstract style in English, and honorification in Korean). Analogous registers also show some differences cross-linguistically with respect to the purpose-related dimensions, including personal stance and narration as well as the more idiosyncratic dimensions such as argumentation/persuasion, abstract style, and honorification.[7]

In addition, there are differences in the overall multi-dimensional profiles of the four languages. That is, while these languages are similar in the range of communicative functions represented by dimensions, and in the structural correlates of analogous dimensions, they differ in the overall allocation of linguistic resources to these various functional domains, depending on the communicative priorities of each culture.

The extent of the cross-linguistic similarities is surprising given the major social, cultural, and linguistic differences represented by the four languages studied here. English and Korean are the most similar socially in that they both have extensive, well-established repertoires of written and spoken registers. Somali also has an extensive range of written and spoken registers, although it is not nearly as well established as in English and

Korean. Nukulaelae Tuvaluan has a much more restricted range of written and spoken registers, in addition to other cultural and linguistic differences, and the patterns of register variation in this language are correspondingly the most different. However, even with respect to Nukulaelae Tuvaluan, the cross-linguistic similarities to the other three languages are more striking than the differences. That is, even though Nukulaelae Tuvaluan has no mass media, no institutional spoken or written registers, and no published (fictional or expository) written registers, its multidimensional profile represents many of the same kinds of underlying functions, with similar kinds of structural correlates, as in the other three languages.

Linguistic and ethnographic descriptions have tended to emphasize the distinctiveness of each language. The analyses here identify several characteristics that are relatively idiosyncratic, reflecting the different linguistic resources and different communicative priorities of each language and culture. However, the most striking, and unexpected, aspect of these cross-linguistic comparisons is the extent to which similar patterns of register variation exist across these four language situations.

These findings are directly relevant to several of the issues raised in recent studies of sublanguages, since similar techniques can be used to specify the linguistic relations among sublanguages both within and across languages. The findings here also support one of the most interesting findings of Kittredge (1982: 108), that 'parallel sublanguages of English and French are much more similar structurally than are dissimilar sublanguages of the same language.' Romaine (1994) discusses similar findings in a comparison of sports reportage in Tok Pisin and English. The present study shows that even when registers are defined at a high level of generality (e.g., conversation, editorials, personal letters), and even when comparisons are across markedly different language families and cultures, parallel registers are indeed more similar cross-linguistically than are disparate registers within a single language.

8 Cross-linguistic patterns of register variation: diachronic similarities and differences

8.1 A register perspective on historical change and the linguistic correlates of literacy

The studies discussed in chapters 6 and 7 have all been synchronic, identifying the dimensions of variation in four languages and describing the systematic similarities and differences among present-day registers in terms of those dimensions. This same analytical framework can be used to study historical change among registers, using the previously identified dimensions of variations to address two major research issues:

1   the linguistic development of an individual register – comparing the linguistic characteristics of a register along multiple dimensions across time periods;

2   historical change in the relative relations among registers – the diachronic patterns of register variation. For example, do spoken and written registers develop in parallel or divergent ways? Over time, do they become more similar or more distinct?

Investigations of this kind are especially important for literacy issues, considering the ways in which a language changes following the introduction of literacy and the early development of written registers. Specific research questions of this type include:

1   What are the linguistic characteristics of written registers when they are first introduced into a language? What linguistic models were used for written registers at that historical stage? Did written registers evolve from pre-existing spoken registers, from similar written registers in other languages, or from other sources?

2   How stable are written registers in the early stages of evolution? In what ways do they develop, and what are the motivating factors influencing change?

3   Do written varieties evolve independently or in shared ways? Do they evolve at a constant or variable rate? Do they evolve over time to become more different from spoken varieties and from one another?

Although a register perspective is obviously required to address literacy issues such as these, there have been few empirical diachronic studies recognizing the importance of register variation. In fact, while there have been numerous studies investigating the social and intellectual consequences of literacy, few studies have investigated its linguistic consequences – that is, the linguistic changes that result from the introduction of written registers in a language.

One such study is Reder's (1981) analysis of spoken and written Vai. Since Vai has an indigeneous literacy that is transmitted apart from formal schooling, Reder could address the question of whether writing itself has any effect on the speech of literate adults. He found that there are systematic differences between speech and writing in Vai (e.g., certain medial consonants are deleted more frequently in speech, and indefinite noun phrases occur more frequently in writing), and that in their speech, literate adults use the forms associated with writing more frequently than non-literate adults.

A second study that directly addresses the linguistic consequences of literacy is Kalmár's (1985) description of Inuktitut (in Canada). He found evidence there that new linguistic forms are developing due to the influence of written language; in particular, true subordinate forms (complement clauses and relative clauses) seem to be developing in the written language at present.

Language-planning studies of language modernization, adaptation, and standardization deal indirectly with the linguistic consequences of literacy, although they are not usually framed in these terms. Ferguson (1968) proposes three stages of 'language development' that a newly literate language can pass through: graphization, standardization, and modernization. Graphization is the process of adopting a writing system, including spelling and orthographic conventions. Standardization is the process by which one variety of a language gains widespread acceptance as the 'best' form of the language. (This stage apparently also includes selection of a norm and codification of standard forms in grammars and dictionaries.) Finally, modernization refers to linguistic extensions that are required to meet the communicative needs of a modern society. Modernization has two aspects: expansion of the lexicon, and 'the development of new styles and forms of discourse'.

Coulmas (1989) discusses related phenomena under the rubric of 'language adaptation', which refers to language change in response to the changing communicative needs of a speech community. These changes can be completely natural or influenced by deliberate intervention (due to language planning). Coulmas notes that, especially in situations where social development proceeds more quickly than language change (due, for example, to war or colonization), the communicative demands of a speech community can exceed the functionality of their language; the language then must either 'adapt' or 'decay'.

Only a few studies have described situations in which a functional expansion of a language has resulted in the addition of new linguistic structures (e.g., Kalmar 1985; Coulmas 1989: 18). Hymes (1974: 73), however, raises another possibility that is probably more typical: that a language can change 'even though the differences may not appear in the structure of the language within the limits of the usual description. The same formal linguistic system, as usually described, may be part of different, let us say, *socio*linguistic systems, whose natures cannot be assumed, but must be investigated.' As noted in chapter 1, Hymes (1984: 44–45) later argues that analysis of the 'change of verbal repertoires in relation to the main processes of societal evolution of our time' is one of the two main tasks currently requiring attention within sociolinguistics. Ure (1982: 7) similarly argues that 'The register range of a language is one of the most immediate ways in which it responds to social change.'

The MD approach is ideally suited to issues such as these, which concern overall shifts within the register repertoire of a language. The present chapter addresses these issues by synthesizing several MD analyses of diachronic register variation and proposing cross-linguistic generalizations. To date, English and Somali have been the only two languages studied from this perspective. The analysis of English is based on Biber and Finegan (1989a, 1992) and Atkinson (1992, 1993). Biber and Finegan (1989a) trace the development of three English registers – fiction, essays, and letters – from 1650 to the present, while Biber and Finegan (1992) add fictional dialogue and dramatic dialogue to the earlier description. Atkinson (1992) focuses on the development of English medical writing from 1735 to the present.[1] Atkinson (1993) analyzes the evolution of scientific research writing in the *Philosophical Transactions of the Royal Society of London* from 1675 to 1975. An analysis of American legal opinions from 1750 to the present is added here to these other previous studies.[2]

The analysis of Somali is based on Biber and Hared (1992b, 1994). The 1992b study compares the range of register variation found before 1973 (when only spoken registers existed) with that found immediately after 1973 (following the introduction of native-language written registers). The 1994 study traces the evolution of seven press registers from 1973 to 1989.

The chapter is organized as follows: sections 8.2 and 8.3 present diachronic analyses of register variation in English and Somali respectively. Both of these sections focus on changes associated with the introduction and evolution of written registers in these two languages. In section 8.4, then, these patterns are compared cross-linguistically as a basis for general hypotheses concerning the kinds of linguistic change resulting from the introduction and subsequent development of written registers in a language.

8.2   Diachronic register variation in English

The social history of written registers in English is complex, with different registers being developed at different times. Thus, while English drama was well established by 1600, many written registers were just beginning to evolve in the 1600s. Registers such as biographies and scientific research articles are generally traced to the late seventeenth century, while the novel and medical research article are usually traced to the early eighteenth century. For the discussion here, the linguistic characteristics of registers produced during the latter part of the seventeenth century are analyzed as indicative of the early history of written registers in English.

The evolution of eight English registers is discussed in the present section: personal essays, medical research articles, science research articles, legal opinions, fiction, personal letters, dialogue from drama, and dialogue from fiction. These registers represent several different communicative situations and purposes, including speech-based as well as written modes; expository/informational, narrative, and personal/involved purposes; differing degrees of careful production and editing; and differing degrees of interactiveness. The texts used for these analyses are summarized in table 5.2.

8.2.1   Multi-Dimensional characterizations of early written registers in English

Figures 8.1–8.3 present the linguistic characterizations of these eight written and speech–based registers at an early stage of their evolution: the seventeenth century for most of these registers, and the early eighteenth century for medical articles and legal prose.[3] These figures plot the relations among registers with respect to English dimension 1 ('Involved versus Informational Production'), dimension 3 ('Situation-dependent versus Elaborated Reference'), and dimension 5 ('Non-abstract versus Abstract Style'). These are the three major oral/literate dimensions identified in the analysis of English (see chapters 6 and 7), and as such they can be used to analyze the linguistic characteristics of early written registers relative to spoken registers, as well as the subsequent evolution of written registers. The dimension scores for twentieth-century conversations and official documents are included on these figures, representing the synchronic oral and literate poles, in order to facilitate comparisons between the analyses in this chapter and those of previous chapters.[4]

INVOLVED

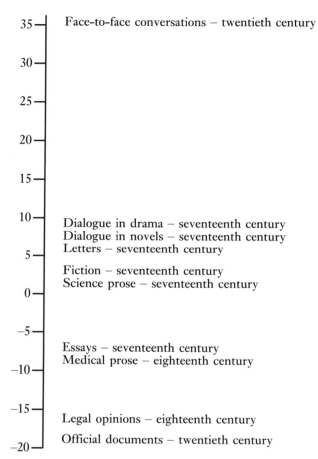

INFORMATIONAL

Figure 8.1 Mean scores of English dimension 1 for six written registers in an early stage of development, compared to two seventeenth-century speech-based registers and twentieth-century conversation and official documents. ('Involved versus Informational Production')

SITUATION DEPENDENT

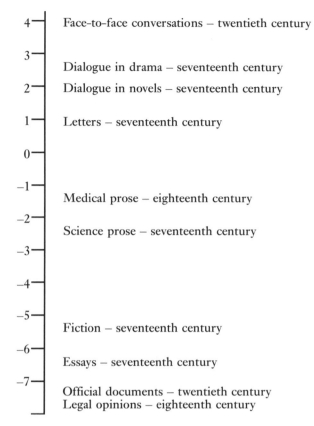

ELABORATED

Figure 8.2 Mean scores of English dimension 3 for six written registers in an early stage of development, compared to two seventeenth-century speech-based registers and twentieth-century conversation and official documents. ('Situation-dependent versus Elaborated Reference')

Figure 8.1 shows that all of these early written registers in English are quite different from present-day conversation in their characterizations along the 'Involved versus Informational' dimension (dimension 1). Although dialogue in drama, dialogue in novels, and letters have moderately involved characterizations, no seventeenth-century written register begins to approach the extremely involved characterization of modern face-to-face

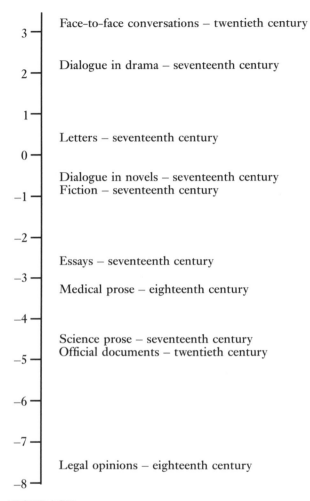

NON-ABSTRACT

3 — Face-to-face conversations – twentieth century

2 — Dialogue in drama – seventeenth century

1 —

Letters – seventeenth century

0 —

Dialogue in novels – seventeenth century
Fiction – seventeenth century

−1 —

−2 —

Essays – seventeenth century

−3 —

Medical prose – eighteenth century

−4 —

Science prose – seventeenth century
Official documents – twentieth century

−5 —

−6 —

−7 —

Legal opinions – eighteenth century

−8 —

ABSTRACT

Figure 8.3 Mean scores of English dimension 5 for six written registers in an early stage of development, compared to two seventeenth-century speech-based registers and twentieth-century conversation and official documents. ('Non-abstract versus Abstract Style')

conversations. In contrast, some early written registers are already quite informational and integrated at this stage. In particular, eighteenth-century legal opinions are nearly as informational as modern official documents along this dimension, while seventeenth-century essays and eighteenth-century medical prose are moderately informational and integrated.

Seventeenth-century registers have an even wider range of variation along the 'Situation-dependent versus Elaborated Reference' dimension (dimension 3). As figure 8.2 shows, seventeenth-century dialogue (in drama and novels) is nearly as situation-dependent as modern face-to-face conversations, while seventeenth-century fiction and essays are nearly as elaborated in reference as modern official documents. Eighteenth-century legal opinions are even more elaborated in reference. Surprisingly, eighteenth-century medical prose and seventeenth-century science prose have intermediate characterizations along this dimension, perhaps because of the predominance of letters and research reports during this period.

Seventeenth-century registers also show a wide range of variation along the 'Abstract Style' dimension (dimension 5), plotted in figure 8.3. Dialogue in drama approaches modern face-to-face conversation in its marked absence of passive constructions, while letters, fiction, and dialogue in novels all have intermediate characterizations. Seventeenth-century essays and eighteenth-century medical articles adopt an abstract style, but not to the extent of modern official documents. Seventeenth-century science articles are quite abstract in style, while eighteenth-century legal opinions are considerably more abstract and passive than modern official documents (which represents a more general register category).

Although there are no first-hand data available from seventeenth-century spoken registers, it is possible to estimate the linguistic characteristics of speech in earlier periods from a consideration of speech-based registers – written dialogue in fiction and drama – in comparison to modern conversation. Such comparisons are especially useful along those dimensions where early written dialogue has very similar linguistic characteristics to modern face-to-face conversation. Thus, along dimensions 3 and 5, seventeenth-century dialogue in fiction and dialogue in drama are quite similar to modern conversation in being markedly situation-dependent in reference and non-abstract in style.[5] Given that it is unlikely that seventeenth-century conversation was more literate than written dialogue from this period, it is probable that early face-to-face conversations had similar characterization to modern conversations on these two dimensions.

The situation is much less clear along dimension 1, where modern face-to-face conversations are much more involved than seventeenth-century written dialogue. Since there are no independent means for assessing the accuracy of early written dialogue with respect to these dimension

1 characteristics, it is not possible to tell whether seventeenth-century conversations were in fact only moderately involved, similar to written dialogue from this period, or whether they were more similar to modern conversations in being quite involved, with written dialogue being an idealized representation.

Overall, these patterns show that the early written prose registers – seventeenth-century letters, fiction, essays, and science prose, plus eighteenth-century medical prose and legal opinions – were already quite different from conversational registers shortly after their introduction into English.[6] That is, these written registers did not simply adopt spoken linguistic conventions when they entered English; rather, from the earliest periods these registers developed distinctive linguistic characteristics in response to their differing communicative purposes and production circumstances.[7]

8.2.2   The evolution of English written registers from 1650 to the present

Figures 8.4–8.6 present the subsequent course of development for six written registers plus dialogue in drama from the seventeenth-century to the present. These figures show that written registers developed to become even more clearly distinguished from spoken registers over the first 100–200 years of their history, although subsequent developments are more complex.

The developments with respect to letters, essays, and fiction are quite similar along all three dimensions: seventeenth-century texts have moderately literate characterizations that are quite different from conversation; eighteenth-century texts become more literate in style; and texts from later periods gradually shift back towards more oral styles. By the modern period, these three registers are usually considerably more oral than their seventeenth-century counterparts. Dialogue in drama follows a similar pattern, although along some dimensions drama shows a steady transition towards more oral characterizations (with no early shift towards more literate styles). In contrast to these other registers, medical prose and legal opinions show a steady progression towards more literate characterizations along all three dimensions.

Figure 8.4 presents these trends along dimension 1 ('Involved versus Informational Production'). Letters can be used to illustrate the development of popular, non-informational registers here. Seventeenth-century letters are quite involved and therefore oral (reflecting frequent private verbs, contractions, first- and second-person pronouns, etc.). Eighteenth- and nineteenth-century letters have shifted to become more literate and less involved, while modern letters shift in the opposite direction to become the most involved of the four periods. To illustrate this development, consider the following two

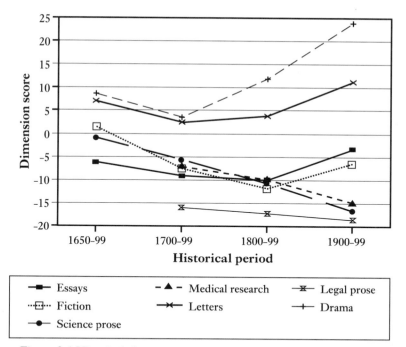

Figure 8.4 Historical change among seven written and speech-based registers along English dimension 1: 'Involved versus Informational Production'

text samples. Sample 8.1 is a nineteenth-century letter by John Keats and sample 8.2 a modern letter by Virginia Woolf. Both are written to personal friends, and both discuss literary concerns.

Text sample 8.1: John Keats, letter (nineteenth century)
[Quoted in Biber and Finegan 1989a: 499]

You say 'I fear there is little chance of anything else in this life.' You seem by that to have been going through with a more painful and acute zest the same labyrinth that I have – I have come to the same conclusion thus far. My Branchings out therefrom have been numerous: one of them is the consideration of Wordsworth's genius and as a help, in the manner of gold being the meridian Line of wordly wealth, – how he differs from Milton. – And here I have nothing but surmises, from an uncertainty whether Milton's apparently less anxiety for Humanity proceeds from his seeing further or no than Wordsworth: ...

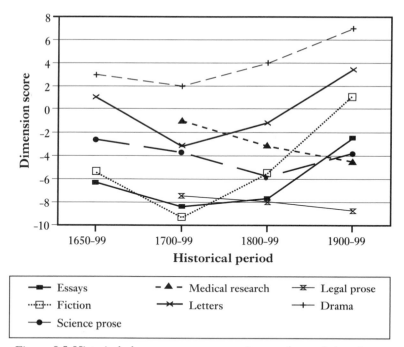

Figure 8.5 Historical change among seven written and speech-based registers along English dimension 3: 'Situation-dependent versus Elaborated Reference'

Text sample 8.2: Virginia Woolf, letter (modern)
[Quoted in Biber and Finegan 1989a: 501]

I'm reading David Copperfield for the sixth time with almost complete satisfaction. I'd forgotten how magnificent it is. What's wrong, I can't help asking myself? Why wasn't he the greatest writer in the world? For alas – no, I won't try to go into my crabbings and diminishings. So enthusiastic am I that I've got a new life of him: which makes me dislike him as a human being. Did you know – you who know everything – the story of the actress? He was an actor, I think; very hard; meretricious? Something had shriveled? And then his velvet suit, and his stupendous genius? But you won't want to be discussing Dickens at the moment.

The difference between these letters is striking. The nineteenth-century letter begins with one of the few direct acknowledgments of the addressee

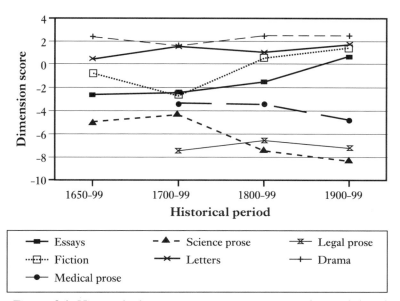

Figure 8.6 Historical change among seven written and speech-based registers along English dimension 5: 'Non-abstract versus Abstract Style'

in the entire text, and then plunges into a detailed, informational exposition of Keat's own thoughts. Although this exposition seems relatively unplanned in its overall organization, it is quite integrated with respect to dimension 1 characteristics: many nouns, prepositions, long words, and a quite varied vocabulary, coupled with very few involved features such as personal pronouns, reduced forms, or hedges. In contrast, the modern letter is extremely involved. Woolf writes as if she were actually having a dialogue, with a series of questions and answers assuming a high degree of shared background knowledge. This sample, which is by no means the most involved section of the letter from which it is taken, illustrates very frequent use of the involved features of dimension 1: first- and second-person pronouns, contractions, private verbs (*You know, I think*), WH questions, etc. These two samples illustrate the transition to a much more involved style that occurred in letters between the nineteenth and twentieth centuries.

Essays and fiction followed a similar pattern along this dimension, although the differences among essays across the periods are relatively small. Eighteenth- and nineteenth-century essays are more informational and integrated than seventeenth-century essays, while modern essays are the most involved. Eighteenth- and nineteenth-century fiction is similarly more integrated than seventeenth-century fiction; modern fiction shows a shift towards more involved styles, although it is not as involved as in the seventeenth century.

Dialogue in drama follows the same basic pattern: a shift in the eighteenth century towards more integrated styles, followed by a steady progression towards more involved styles in the nineteenth and twentieth centuries. The surprisingly integrated style of dramatic dialogue in the eighteenth century can be illustrated by text sample 8.3, from the play *Douglas* by Home (1756):

Text sample 8.3: John Home, *Douglas*
[Quoted in Biber and Finegan 1992: 700]

(Act II, scene i)
- What means this clamour? Stranger speak secure; hast thou been wrong'd? Have these rude men presum'd to vex the weary traveller on his way?
- By us no stranger ever suffer'd wrong: This man with outcry wild has call'd us forth; so sore he cannot speak his fears.
- Not vain the stranger's fears! How fares my lord?
- That it fares well, thanks to this gallant youth, whose valour sav'd me from a wretched death! As down the winding dale I walk'd alone, at the cross way four armed men attack'd me: rovers, I judge, from the licentious camp, who would have quickly laid Lord Randolph low, had not this brave and generous stranger come . . .

This passage shows a high frequency of nouns and prepositional phrases together with an extremely high frequency of attributive adjectives (e.g., *rude, weary, gallant, winding, armed*) and a notably high type–token ratio. In the traveler's narrative, nearly every noun is elaborated with an attributive adjective to provide vivid details: for example, the stranger was not merely saved from death, but from a *wretched* death; the rovers came from a *licentious* camp; the youth who helped was *gallant* and *brave and generous*. Word choice is also varied throughout, resulting in a high type–token ratio. This is reflected in the synonyms chosen for attributive adjectives as well as in the wide variation in other nominal referring expressions: for example, the attackers are referred to as *rude men, armed men*, and *rovers . . . from the licentious camp*; aspects of the attack are referred to as *presum'd to vex, a wretched death, attack'd, would have quickly laid low*; the helper is referred to as *this gallant youth, this brave and generous stranger*, and later in the text as *my good angel* and *master of the bloody field*. This text is thus extremely detailed and informational in its descriptions, and in this respect it is quite unlike modern face-to-face conversation. During the nineteenth and twentieth centuries, dramatic dialogue reversed its earlier course and became much more involved in its dimension 1 characteristics; by the modern period, dialogue in drama is markedly involved, approaching the dimension 1 characterization of true face-to-face conversation.

Medical prose, science prose, and legal opinions show quite different patterns from these other registers in that they follow a steady progression towards more integrated and informational styles. The following introductory sentence from a 1985 medical case report illustrates the extremely dense packaging of information common in medical articles, using extensive nouns, attributive adjectives, prepositional phrases, and careful vocabulary choice.

Text sample 8.4: Medical case report (modern)
[Quoted in Atkinson 1992: 356]

> In a patient with proven chronic duodenal ulceration the development of a metabolic alkalosis due to recurrent vomiting of undigested food suggests a diagnosis of pyloric stenosis or gastric outlet obstruction at the level of the pylorus.

This sentence consists of only a single clause, with one verb (*suggests*). Thus, most of the sentence comprises dense nominal packaging and elaboration: for example, almost every noun is modified by at least one attributive adjective (e.g., *proven chronic duodenal ulceration, metabolic alkalosis, undigested food*). Further, the sentence shows extensive use of prepositional phrase series for nominal elaboration (e.g., *In a patient with proven chronic duodenal ulceration; the development of a metabolic alkalosis due to recurrent vomiting of undigested food*). A similar dense packaging of information is the norm in all three of the specialist, informational registers considered here.

Overall, the developments along dimension 1 represent a considerable diversification. That is, all seven registers had relatively similar dimension 1 characterizations in the seventeenth century, in contrast to the sharp distinctions among these written registers in the modern period. Medical prose, science prose, and legal opinions developed over time to become even more clearly distinguished from spoken registers, while the other registers underwent gradual transitions towards more oral characterizations in recent periods.

Along dimension 3 ('Situation-dependent versus Elaborated Reference'), figure 8.5 shows that all registers except medical prose and legal opinions have followed a single course of development: seventeenth-century texts are relatively elaborated in reference, and eighteenth-century texts are even more elaborated, while nineteenth-century texts have shifted back towards a less elaborated style, and modern texts are relatively situated and unelaborated in reference.

The development of fiction along this dimension is particularly noteworthy. While seventeenth-century and nineteenth-century fiction are both moderately elaborated, a comparison of eighteenth-century fiction with modern fiction shows a radical shift in dimension 3 characteristics: eighteenth-century fiction is the most elaborated of these seven registers, while modern fiction is among the most situated. Text samples 8.5 and 8.6 illustrate these differences. Sample 8.5 is from a story by Samuel Johnson (eighteenth century), and sample 8.6 is from a story by D. H. Lawrence (modern period). Relative clause constructions are capitalized in sample 8.5 to illustrate the extreme use of referential elaboration in eighteenth-century fiction, while time and place adverbials are capitalized in sample 8.6 to illustrate the shift to a situated style of reference in the modern period.

Text sample 8.5: Samuel Johnson, *The History of Rasselas,*
ic*Prince of Abyssinia* (eighteenth century)
[Quoted in Biber and Finegan 1989a: 503]

The place, WHICH the wisdom or policy of antiquity had destined for the residence of the Abyssinian princes, was a spacious valley in the kingdom of Amhara, surrounded on every side by mountains, OF WHICH the summits overhang the middle part. The only passage, BY WHICH it could be entered, was a cavern THAT passed under a rock, OF WHICH it has long been disputed whether it was the work of nature or of human industry. The outlet of the cavern was concealed by a thick wood, and the mouth WHICH opened into the valley was closed with gates of iron, forged by the artificers of ancient days . . .

Text sample 8.6: D. H. Lawrence, *The Fox* (modern)
[Quoted in Biber and Finegan 1989a: 503]

He rose, quietly dressed himself, and crept OUT on to the landing ONCE more. The women were silent. He went softly DOWNSTAIRS and OUT to the kitchen.

THEN he put on his boots and his overcoat and took the gun. He did not think to go AWAY from the farm. No, he only took the gun. As softly as possible he unfastened the door and went OUT into the frosty

December night . . . He went stealthily AWAY DOWN a fence-side, looking
for something to shoot.

Both of these text samples have extremely marked characterizations with
respect to the elaborated reference dimension. In the relatively short
eighteenth-century passage by Johnson (sample 8.5), there are five WH
relative clauses, including three pied-piping constructions. Many of the
descriptive details in this passage are contained in the relative clauses, resulting in a text that is extremely elaborated in reference. The modern passage
from Lawrence (sample 8.7), on the other hand, is markedly unelaborated
in reference while making several direct references to the temporal and
physical context (e.g., *out*, *away*, *down*). These samples illustrate the extreme
shift in fiction norms from the eighteenth to the twentieth centuries along
dimension 3, from a heavily elaborated and nominalized style to a relatively
situated and unelaborated description of referents and events.

Essays and letters follow parallel historical patterns to fiction, although
the extent of the changes are slightly smaller. Science prose shows a slight
shift towards less elaborated reference in the modern period, although
both science prose and essays remain relatively elaborated in all periods.
Dialogue in drama also follows a similar course, although the eighteenth-
century shift towards more elaborated reference is small in this register.

In contrast, the development of medical articles and legal opinions run
counter to the four other registers: rather than following a shift towards more
situated reference in the two most recent periods, medical prose and legal
opinions have continued along a steady progression towards more elaborated
reference.

Figure 8.6 shows that the parallels among registers along dimension
5 ('Non-abstract versus Abstract Style') are less clear than those along
dimensions 1 and 3. However, by the modern period this dimension
defines the most clearly distinguished split between the specialist expository
registers (medical prose, science prose, and legal opinions) and the other
four registers.

In the seventeenth century, there are already relatively sharp differences
among science prose, essays, fiction, letters, and drama in their use of
passive constructions. In the middle periods, these registers develop in
different directions, with fiction becoming more abstract, letters becoming
less abstract, and essays and drama remaining fairly stable. The shift within
fiction to an extremely abstract style can be illustrated by the frequent
occurrence of passive forms in sample 8.5 above, from an eighteenth-century
work by Samuel Johnson; the last two sentences from that sample are
repeated below with the passive constructions italicized:

The only passage, by which it could *be entered*, was a cavern that passed under a rock, of which it has long *been disputed* whether it was the work of nature or of human industry. The outlet of the cavern *was concealed* by a thick wood, and the mouth which opened into the valley *was closed* with gates of iron, *forged* by the artificers of ancient days . . .

By the modern period, though, all four popular registers have developed to become quite similar to one another, and similar to face-to-face conversation, in being markedly non-abstract (with a near total absence of passive constructions). The non-abstract style of modern fiction is illustrated by the D. H. Lawrence passage above (sample 8.6), which is totally devoid of passive constructions.

In contrast to the popular registers, medical research articles, science prose, and legal opinions again follow a quite different course. From their inception in the seventeenth century, science articles are markedly passive in style,[8] and both science articles and medical articles are passive in style in the eighteenth century. As early as the eighteenth century, legal opinions are extremely passive in style. Over subsequent periods, all three of these registers follow a steady progression towards an ever more frequent use of these abstract style features. This shift is most dramatic in science prose, which is by far the most abstract register considered here by the modern period. Text sample 8.7 illustrates these characteristics from a science research article published in 1975 (passive constructions are italicized).

Text sample 8.7: Science research article from the *Philosophical Transactions* (twentieth century)
[Quoted in Atkinson 1993: 212]

> Observations on the muscles and nerves *were made* either from freshly dissected animals or from limbs *fixed* in Bouin's fixative and then *dissected* in 70 percent alcohol. The nerves *were studied* by immersing the preparations in solutions of 5 percent methylene blue *diluted* with sea water (Pantin 1946). Preparations *prepared* in this way *were kept* in a refrigerator

8.2.3 Discussion of the patterns of historical register variation in English

Considering all three dimensions together, the patterns of development described above reflect a fundamental difference between specialist, informational/expository prose, represented here by medical research articles, science prose, and legal opinions, versus other kinds of writing in English. The popular, non-expository registers reflect several different purposes and situations: fiction is carefully produced but written for edification or entertainment; letters are personal and interactive; essays are carefully produced, written from a personal perspective, and descriptive or persuasive in purpose; and dramatic dialogue is modeled after conversational interaction. Despite these important situational differences, these non-expository registers have followed strikingly similar developmental paths, in marked contrast to the developments within medical prose, science prose, and legal opinions.

The generalizations underlying the developments in all seven registers can be summarized as follows:

1 All written prose registers entered English already quite different from the conversational registers, with respect to all three dimensions.

2 Apart from dialogue, most registers evolved to become even more distinct from speech over the first 100–200 years of their history. This generalization holds for all six prose registers (essays, fiction, letters, medical articles, science articles, and legal opinions) along the involved/integrated dimension (D1) and the situated/elaborated dimension (D3), but only fiction, medical articles, and science articles follow this pattern along the abstract style dimension (D5). Although written dialogue underwent some minor fluctuations, it generally followed a steady path towards more oral styles on these three dimensions.[9]

3 In the two most recent periods, all popular, non-expository registers (dialogue, letters, fiction, and essays) have reversed their direction of change and evolved to become more similar to spoken registers, often becoming even more oral in the modern period than in the seventeenth century. These generalizations are clearest along the situated/elaborated dimension (D3). Along the involved/integrated dimension (D1), the reversals are not as dramatic but still evident in all non-expository registers. Along dimension 5, all non-expository registers show a marked shift towards non-abstract styles, but for most registers this development is part of a steady progression rather than a reversal.

4 Medical prose, science prose, and legal opinions follow a different pattern. Rather than evolving towards more oral styles, these expository registers have consistently developed towards more literate styles across all periods: greater integration (D1), greater elaboration of reference (D3), and a more frequent use of passive constructions (D5).

Biber and Finegan (1989a) appeal to both conscious and unconscious motivations to explain these observed developmental patterns for essays, fiction, and letters, including the initial shift towards more literate styles, the reversal of that development, and the overall pattern of 'drift' towards more oral styles. Changes in the overall demographics and purposes of writing across these periods probably had a conscious as well as unconscious influence on the form of written registers. Some of these conscious motivations are explicitly expressed as attitudes in the writings of authors from these periods.

The seventeenth century witnessed the rise of experimental science and a general preference for rationalism over emotionalism in English culture. Writers began to use English almost as much as Latin (Fowler 1987: 124), and new genres such as the scientific expository essay, biography, and history began to appear. To serve these informational purposes, 'plain' expository styles were developed. These styles were quite different from conversational language, but they were not nearly as integrated and elaborated as written prose in the following period.

The eighteenth century witnessed a general, and marked, shift towards more literate styles. It will be argued below (in section 8.4) that this shift is typical of the first stage in the historical development of languages responding to the introduction of written registers. That is, in their early history written registers evolve to become more clearly distinguished from spoken registers, resulting in a general diversification of the register range.

These early developments in written English registers were reinforced by the conscious attitudes of some writers from this period: for example, authors such as Samuel Johnson and Benjamin Franklin argued that writing should be elaborated and 'ornamental' to effectively persuade readers (see discussion in Biber and Finegan 1989a: 514ff.).

However, the eighteenth century was a period of considerable conflict concerning the appropriate styles of written registers; as Biber and Finegan (1989a: 507–12) show, there were large differences among the texts *within* written registers during this period, reflecting different perceptions of the intended audience, the appropriate purposes of prose, and correspondingly the appropriate discourse styles. In fact, many of the texts produced in the eighteenth century are already relatively colloquial and structurally simple.

This conflict in the eighteenth century, and the subsequent shift to more oral styles in the following centuries, can be associated with a number of demographic changes. The eighteenth century witnessed the rise of a popular, middle-class literacy for the first time in British history. The reading public grew throughout this period and came to include upper- and middle-class readers of both sexes. For the first time there were writers like Defoe and Richardson, who were from the middle class themselves and addressed themselves primarily to middle-class readers. Periodicals such as *The Spectator* and *The Tatler* began to appear in the early eighteenth century, and the first modern magazine (*Gentleman's Magazine*) appeared in 1731 (Abrams *et al.* 1979: 1735).

By the nineteenth century, the shift towards a popular literacy began to be widely accepted as the norm. Mass schooling reinforced the already widespread popular literacy (Cook-Gumperz 1986; de Castell and Luke 1986). Fictional genres such as the novel and short story became well established and were widely read by the general public. This widening of the reading public can be associated with the need for more accessible written prose; thus the linguistic norms for the non-expository registers along most dimensions were reversed during this period, and began to shift towards more accessible, oral styles.[10]

These trends continued into the modern period. Literacy became nearly universal in the United States and Britain, so that readers had a wide range of backgrounds and interests, and a large body of literature was written for this general reading public. The shift towards more oral styles in the modern period thus reflects the need for widely accessible written prose.

The same kinds of factors influenced the historical evolution of medical research articles, science articles, and legal opinions, but the direction of those influences and the corresponding linguistic developments are strikingly different. From the earliest periods, these informational registers were quite different from conversational registers in their linguistic characteristics, and over time they evolved to become even more sharply distinguished from typical speech and to exploit the potential resources of the written mode to increasingly greater extents. Thus, all three of these registers became consistently more carefully integrated and informational, more elaborated in reference, and more passive and abstract in style across the last three centuries.

These linguistic developments correspond to the development of a more specialized readership, more specialized purposes, and a fuller exploitation of the written mode. That is, in marked contrast to the general societal trends towards a wider lay readership and the corresponding need for popular written registers, readers of medical research prose, science prose, and legal prose have become increasingly more specialized in their backgrounds and training, and correspondingly these registers have become more specialized in both purpose and linguistic characteristics.

For example, Atkinson (1992) analyzes the changing purposes of typical articles in the *Edinburgh Medical Journal*: early articles were narrative reports of specific medical events witnessed directly by the author, while more recent articles discuss general disease types, building on previous research and presenting statistical findings derived from an impersonal analysis of a large number of cases. Other scholars, such as Bazerman (1984, 1988), describe similar rhetorical developments for scientific research articles; Mellinkoff (1963) provides a critical analysis of the trend towards 'greater precision' in legal language; and Atkinson (1993) discusses similar developments for science prose. It is likely that these patterns hold generally for academic prose as well as for many institutional registers.

Based on these patterns, it is possible to hypothesize three separate stages in the evolution of written registers:

Stage 1: genesis. Written registers enter a language already quite different from typical spoken registers, reflecting their different primary purposes and production circumstances.[11]

Stage 2: early development. Over the course of their early development (100–200 years in English), written registers evolve to become even more sharply distinguished from spoken registers, extending the range of register variation. These developments hold generally for written registers, so that even personal letters and fiction follow the same patterns.

Stage 3: split between popular and specialized registers. Stage 3 is characterized by the development of two sharply distinct trends. Some registers become more popular in purpose, responding to the needs of a widening literate public for accessible reading materials; these registers reverse their earlier course towards more literate styles, developing increasingly more oral characterizations. Other registers become more specialized in purpose, responding to the development of academic, scientific, and institutional fields and the associated need to report current research findings in those areas. The readership for these registers becomes increasingly more specialized, requiring extensive training in the use of texts from these registers. Linguistically, these informational, expository registers continue the earlier general development towards more literate styles, evolving to exploit the resources of the written mode to an even greater extent and becoming even more sharply distinguished from typical spoken registers.

8.3   Diachronic register variation in Somali

The social history of literacy in Somali is quite different from that in English, enabling complementary analyses to those presented above. First, as described in chapter 3, there is a specific date when Somali literacy was initiated (October 21, 1972), and most written registers were created in the months immediately following that date. In addition, several Somali written registers quickly developed to become relatively well established in the language. It is thus possible to clearly identify the initial characteristics of written registers in Somali, and to trace the subsequent development of those registers over small periods of time. It is not possible to analyze longer trends, though, since Somali written registers have been in existence for only twenty years.

Similar to the diachronic analyses of English presented in the last section, two kinds of analysis are presented here to investigate the development of written registers in Somali: description of the initial characteristics of written registers relative to spoken registers, and description of the subsequent evolution of written registers. The first analysis focuses on eleven written registers that quickly became influential following the introduction of Somali literacy; all texts from these registers were written in 1973–74, the first two years after the introduction of literacy. Seven of these are press registers: news reportage, editorial commentary, letters to the editor, commentary articles, analytical articles, announcements, and sports reviews. In addition, three kinds of fiction are included – general fiction, folk stories, and serial stories (published in newspapers) – as well as government memos.

The second analysis focuses on six of these registers: four press registers (news reportage, editorial commentary, letters to the editor, and analytical articles), fiction (represented by serial stories), and government memos. These registers are described in chapter 3, and the sampling of texts for the historical component of the Somali corpus is described in chapter 5.

The diachronic analysis here uses the three oral/literate dimensions identified in Somali: 'Structural Elaboration: Involvement versus Exposition' (dimension 1), 'Lexical Elaboration: On-line versus Planned/Integrated Production' (dimension 2), and 'Distanced, Directive Interaction' (dimension 5). As described in chapters 6 and 7, these dimensions distinguish between stereotypical speech at one extreme and stereotypical writing at the other extreme. However, each dimension comprises a different set of co-occurring linguistic features and defines a different set of relations among the full range of spoken and written registers.

8.3.1 Multi-Dimensional characterizations of early written registers in Somali

Figure 8.7 shows the initial expansion of linguistic variation along the structural elaboration dimension (dimension 1) following the addition of written registers in Somali. Prior to the introduction of writing, there was already a wide range of variation among spoken registers along this dimension.[12] Involved, interactive registers, such as conversations, family meetings, and conversational narratives, have large positive scores, reflecting frequent use of yes/no questions, stance adjectives, contractions, etc. (together with markedly low frequencies of elaborated features). Informational spoken registers such as university lectures, formal meetings, and sports broadcasts have values around 0.0, reflecting a lesser but

INVOLVED

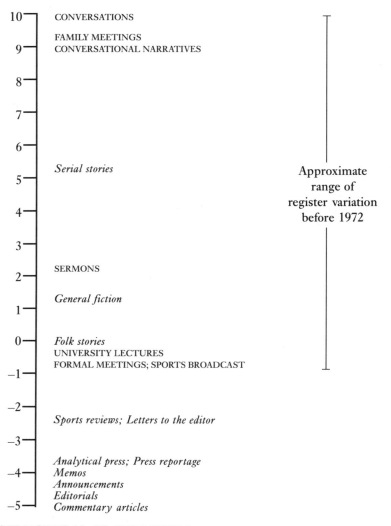

10 — CONVERSATIONS	
FAMILY MEETINGS	
9 — CONVERSATIONAL NARRATIVES	
8 —	
7 —	
6 —	
5 — *Serial stories*	Approximate range of register variation before 1972
4 —	
3 —	
2 — SERMONS	
1 — *General fiction*	
0 — *Folk stories*	
UNIVERSITY LECTURES	
FORMAL MEETINGS; SPORTS BROADCAST	
−1 —	
−2 —	
−3 — *Sports reviews; Letters to the editor*	
−4 — *Analytical press; Press reportage*	
Memos	
Announcements	
Editorials	
−5 — *Commentary articles*	

STRUCTURAL ELABORATION

Figure 8.7 Distribution of spoken and 1972-written registers along Somali dimension 1: 'Structural Elaboration: Involvement versus Exposition'

relatively balanced use of both involved features and structural elaboration features.

When written registers were added to Somali, the dimension 1 range of variation was extended to include styles that use a high concentration of structural elaboration features with essentially no involvement features. Figure 8.7 shows that, in their initial characterizations (i.e., in 1973), all non-fictional press registers and government memos have greater structural elaboration than any spoken register. Somali fiction combines involved and elaborated features in ways similar to some spoken registers. The expository registers, however, have extended the range of variation along this dimension in response to the highly informational purposes and careful production possibilities of these literacy events.

The extension of variation due to the addition of Somali written registers is even more striking on the Lexical Elaboration dimension (dimension 2), plotted in figure 8.8. This dimension is associated primarily with the differing production possibilities of speech and writing; thus, all spoken registers, whether they are informational, involved, planned, or interactive, show very little lexical elaboration on this dimension. The addition of written registers greatly extended this range of variation (by almost a factor of three). Some registers, such as general fiction and press reportage, are relatively unelaborated in their lexical characteristics, although they are still more elaborated than the most elaborated spoken register (formal meetings). Other written registers, such as editorials and general-interest articles, are extremely elaborated in their lexical characteristics, representing a style of discourse completely unlike any of the pre-existing spoken registers.[13] Dimension 2 is the only Somali dimension that nearly defines an absolute dichotomy between spoken and written registers, apparently reflecting the physically different production possibilities of the two modes. It is thus not surprising that the introduction of written registers resulted in an extreme extension of discourse variation along this dimension.

Figure 8.9 shows that the range of variation along the directive interaction dimension (dimension 5) was also greatly extended by the addition of written registers, but not in the expected direction. That is, although the positive pole of dimension 5 reflects the oral function of 'Distanced, Directive Interaction', the discussion in chapters 6 and 7 shows that personal letters (rather than conversation) have by far the largest positive score. Because personal letters in Somali are overtly interactive and directive, often containing considerable task-oriented discussion in addition to affective expression, they have very frequent overt markers of 'directive interaction'. Among the interactive spoken registers, family meetings is the most task-oriented, but due to the face-to-face situation (and the greater threat to face) there are considerably fewer overt directives than in personal letters.

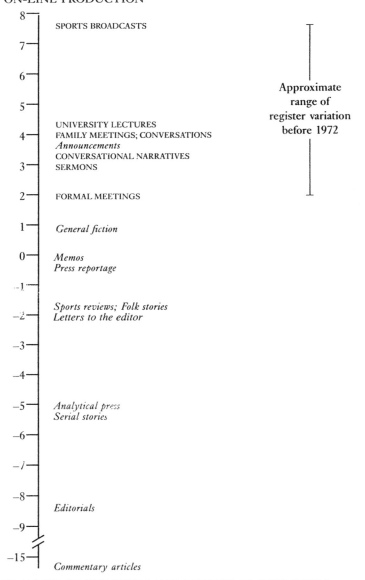

ON-LINE PRODUCTION

8 —

    SPORTS BROADCASTS

7 —

6 —

                  Approximate
                   range of
5 —   register variation
    UNIVERSITY LECTURES   before 1972
4 — FAMILY MEETINGS; CONVERSATIONS
    Announcements
    CONVERSATIONAL NARRATIVES
3 — SERMONS

2 — FORMAL MEETINGS

1 — *General fiction*

0 — *Memos*
    Press reportage

−1 —

    Sports reviews; Folk stories
−2 — *Letters to the editor*

−3 —

−4 —

−5 — *Analytical press*
    Serial stories

−6 —

−7 —

−8 —

    Editorials

−9 —

−15 —
    Commentary articles

PLANNED PRODUCTION AND LEXICAL ELABORATION

Figure 8.8 Distribution of spoken and 1972-written registers along Somali dimension 2: 'Lexical Elaboration: On-line versus Planned/Integrated Production'

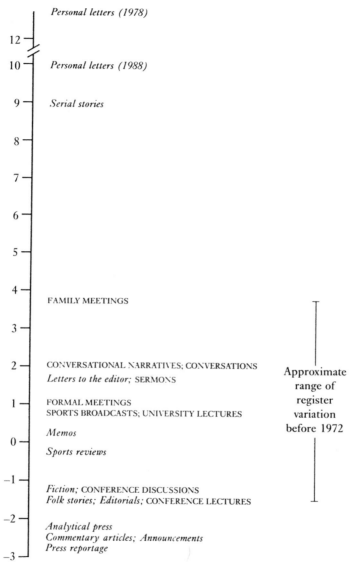

Figure 8.9 Distribution of spoken and 1972-written registers along Somali dimension 5: 'Distanced, Directive Interaction'

The letters plotted on figure 8.9 are from the middle period and most recent period, because Somali letters from the first period were not available.[14] Thus this figure does not necessarily reflect the extent to which the range of variation along dimension 5 was expanded immediately in 1973 due to the addition of letters. However, the introduction of personal letters written in Somali did enable a discourse style that is considerably more directive than that possible in face-to-face interactions, whether this change was abrupt or a more gradual development over several years.

In addition, the range of variation along dimension 5 was extended due to the characteristics of early serial stories. These stories include extensive dialogue – in some cases they are primarily composed of dialogue – and apparently these fictional interactions are more interactive and directive than most actual face-to-face conversations. Finally, the range of variation was extended slightly in the negative direction along dimension 5, with registers such as press reportage, announcements, and analytical press being marked by the near total absence of interactive/directive features.

8.3.2 The evolution of Somali written registers from 1972 to the present

Similar to the analyses in English, it is also possible to trace the early evolution of written registers in Somali. Figure 8.10 plots changes in the mean dimension 1 scores for four press registers, government memos, and serial stories across three time periods: 1973–74, representing the initial creation of written Somali registers; 1977–78, when written registers had become fairly well established in Somali; and 1987–89, representing the most recent period. (Scores for memos are given only in the first and last periods, because no memos from the middle period were available.) Figure 8.10 can be compared to figure 8.7, which presents scores for spoken and 1973 written registers. Most spoken registers, together with serial stories in 1973, have involved characterizations along this dimension; in contrast, all 1973 press registers as well as memos have markedly elaborated characterizations.

With this background, figure 8.10 shows that all of these written registers have undergone a steady progression towards more 'literate' characterizations. That is, all six written registers progressively became more sharply distinguished from spoken registers in having a more frequent use of structural elaboration features and less frequent use of involved features. This shift is most pronounced in serial stories, but the press registers have also undergone shifts in the same direction.[15] These trends indicate that Somali continued to adapt across this timespan, extending the range of structural variation even further as writers developed proficiency and confidence in Somali written discourse styles.

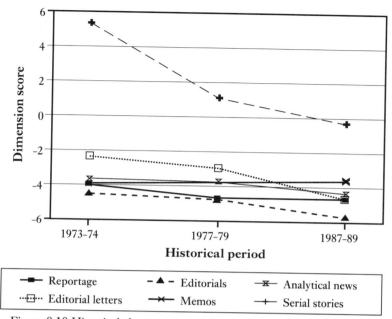

Figure 8.10 Historical change among written registers along Somali dimension 1: 'Structural Elaboration: Involvement versus Exposition'

The historical developments shown on figure 8.11, representing the lexical elaboration dimension (dimension 2), are more complex. Three of the press registers (editorials, editorial letters, and analytical articles) and serial stories show parallel developments here: a sharp shift towards greater lexical elaboration in the middle period, followed by a reversal and smaller shift back towards less elaboration in the most recent period. News reportage follows a different pattern: in 1973, news reportage texts have relatively little lexical elaboration, and they change little over the timespan of the study, actually becoming slightly less elaborated lexically. Overall, though, there has been a general trend towards greater lexical elaboration with respect to dimension 2, with editorial letters, analytical news, institutional editorials, and memos all being more elaborated in the last period than in the first.

Consideration of the development of these written registers relative to typical spoken registers (compare figures 8.8 and 8.11) highlights the extent of the register changes along this dimension. Figure 8.8 shows that the initial addition of written registers greatly extended the pre-existing range of variation with respect to lexical elaboration; figure 8.11 shows that many written registers have evolved to become even more sharply distinguished

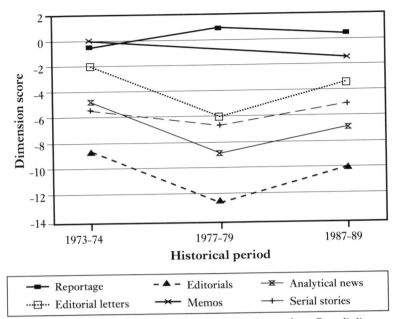

Figure 8.11 Historical change among written registers along Somali dimension 2: 'Lexical Elaboration: On-line versus Planned/Integrated Production'

from spoken registers, continuing to extend the range of lexical variation as writers learn to exploit the production possibilities of the written mode.

The reversal in the development of editorial letters, serial stories, analytical news, and editorials can be interpreted relative to changing social conditions in Somalia: the development of a wider lay readership for Somali newspapers, the corresponding need to make Somali texts more accessible, and changes in the typical production circumstances for these texts.

Somali newspapers in the middle period (1977–78) were more carefully produced than in either of the other two periods: the layout and formatting was professional, daily editions and individual articles were relatively long, and the coverage was more in-depth. Given these differences, it is not surprising that the prose itself was more carefully produced during this period, and the extremely elaborated lexical characteristics of these registers is one reflection of this careful production. At the same time, most writers and readers during the middle period were Somali professionals who had received western educations and made the transition to Somali literacy as adults.

In contrast, newspapers in the most recent period were less carefully edited, the format was less professional,[16] and articles became shorter; these changes accompanied the marked decline in government institutions (and social order in general) in Somalia during the late 1980s and early 1990s. During this time, newspaper staff members frequently had to hold second (and third) jobs to earn enough money for basic needs, hampering their opportunity and motivation for producing carefully written articles. The shift back towards prose with less lexical elaboration in the most recent period is in part a reflection of this less careful production.

In addition, Somali newspapers were at the same time acquiring a broader, less specialized readership, who had been educated entirely in Somali. Thus, the need to write press articles that were accessible to a wider audience dovetailed with the social pressures prohibiting more elaborated production.

Despite the shift towards more oral styles, press registers in the most recent period are still more elaborated lexically than they were in the first period. This overall change apparently reflects a generally increased exploitation of the resources of the written mode, enabling more elaborated and integrated texts.

The historical developments along the directive interaction dimension (dimension 5), plotted in figure 8.12, are more straightforward: all registers except analytical news show a steady progression towards less interactive styles. This change is most marked with respect to serial stories, which shifted from an interactive/directive style in the first period to intermediate characterizations in subsequent periods. Letters to the editor similarly show a notable shift from a moderately interactive/directive style in the first period to a notably non-interactive and non-directive characterization in the most recent period. Memos show a smaller shift in the same direction, while the other press registers change little along this dimension, being non-interactive and non-directive in all periods.

8.3.3   Discussion of the patterns of historical register variation in Somali

Overall, the diachronic register patterns in Somali show several similarities to those in English:

1 From their inception, written registers are markedly different from spoken registers in their linguistic characteristics. This generalization holds for all expository registers as well as memos along the structural elaboration dimension (D1), and it holds for most written registers, including fiction

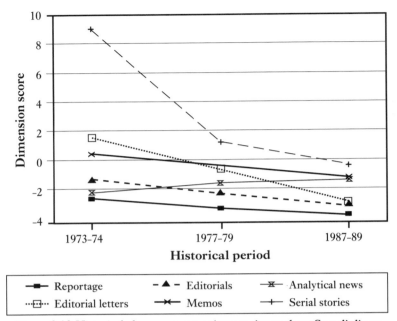

Figure 8.12 Historical change among written registers along Somali dimension 5: 'Distanced, Directive Interaction'

and serial stories, along the lexical elaboration dimension (D2). Along the directive interaction dimension (D5), written registers such as letters and serial stories represent a type of interpersonal communication that was much more directive than the styles considered appropriate in speech; conversely, many press registers were less interactive than previous spoken registers.

2 In the early stages of development, all written registers evolve to become even more sharply distinguished from spoken registers. This pattern holds for the expository press registers as well as memos and serial stories. The pattern is clearest along the structural elaboration dimension (D1) and directive interaction dimension (D5). This trend is also seen in the marked shift towards greater lexical elaboration during the middle period along dimension 2, although that shift is partially reversed during the last period.

3 There is some evidence of a reversal in the development of popular registers – shifting back towards more oral styles in response to less specialized

purposes, a widening literate public, and the need for accessible written texts. This reversal is evident only along the lexical elaboration dimension (D2), but it holds for most press registers as well as serial stories.

8.4   Cross-linguistic patterns of diachronic register variation

Although the analyses in this chapter are based on only two languages, the striking similarities in the observed diachronic patterns provide the basis for several strong hypotheses. These developmental similarities are even more noteworthy given the major situational and social differences between English and Somali. Thus, the following diachronic generalizations are proposed as hypotheses to be tested in the analysis of additional languages:

1 When written registers are first introduced in a language, they are already quite different in their linguistic characteristics from pre-existing spoken registers. These differences reflect the greater opportunity for careful production possible in the written mode, together with more highly informational purposes. Linguistically, these changes reflect greater structural elaboration, lexical elaboration, and informational integration, coupled with a lesser degree of structural reduction and interaction.[17]

2 Over the early periods of evolution, written registers develop linguistically to become more sharply distinguished from typical spoken registers. In part, this trend reflects the developing ability of writers to more fully exploit the potential resources of the written mode, enabling greater elaboration and integration of form. This development might also reflect a conscious awareness of the differing purposes underlying typical spoken and written registers, resulting in a deliberate effort to distinguish between the modes linguistically.

3 In later periods, written registers begin to show a fundamental split between specialized, expository prose, and other more popular kinds of writing (including letters, fiction, and popular non-fictional prose). Specialized expository registers, from scientific, technical, and institutional domains, show a steady progression towards more literate linguistic characteristics, representing an ever greater exploitation of the written mode and an ever sharper distinction from typical spoken registers.[18] In contrast, popular written registers, whether non-fictional, fictional, or interactive, show a reversal of the trend towards more literate characteristics and a marked transition back towards more oral linguistic characteristics, including less structural and lexical elaboration, less dense integration of structure, and greater interactiveness and involvement.

Givón (1979a) discusses similar patterns as typical in the evolution of languages. Of particular interest here, he points out the parallel nature of diachronic processes relating to structure and register repertoire. According to Givón (1979a: 82–83), languages evolve structurally from having predominantly 'loose, paratactic, pragmatic discourse structures' to having 'tight, grammaticalized syntactic structures'. With respect to register repertoires, languages evolve from having registers used primarily for face-to-face, context-dependent communication, to the addition of a wider range of planned, formal spoken registers, to the addition of formal written registers (Givón 1979a: 106). The analyses of both English and Somali support the interdependency of these diachronic processes.

Givón (1979a: 83) further suggests the existence of an additional structural stage, in which 'syntactic structure in time erodes via processes of morphologization and lexicalization'. Using several case studies as a basis (pp. 94–97), Givón argues that the evolution towards tighter syntactic structure involves the simultaneous development of grammatical morphology, so that these are not proposed as distinct stages.

A comparison of the dimensional structure in English and Somali, however, suggests the existence of structural changes accompanying two distinct stages of development. In the first stage, written registers develop distinctive linguistic characterizations through the extremely frequent use of structural elaboration, relying primarily on various kinds of dependent clause. In a later stage, then, structural elaboration becomes more tightly integrated, enabling a denser packaging of information; in this stage, extensive use of dependent clauses is replaced by more integrated kinds of nominal modifiers, such as attributive adjectives and prepositional phrases in English.

Thus, English dimension 1 comprises primarily integrated features used for a dense packaging of information. In comparison to this integrated kind of discourse organization, dependent clauses represent a loose structuring of information. In fact, some types of dependent clause are grouped with the *involved* features on English dimension 1, characteristic of interactive spoken registers rather than informational written registers.

In contrast, Somali, which represents a much earlier stage in the development of written registers, shows structural elaboration features being combined with integration features on dimension 1, with several kinds of dependent clause predominating (relative clauses, clefts, and verb complement clauses). Korean is similar to Somali in having structural elaboration features as the primary markers of informational exposition, and in collapsing dependent clauses and integration features on the same dimension. Thus, Korean dimension 1 includes relative clauses, non-finite clauses, and noun complement clauses, in addition to postposition/noun ratio and attributive adjectives.

These developments do not represent absolute changes in structural organization: for example, English dimension 3 is composed primarily of relative clause constructions, characteristic of highly informational, written registers; English dimension 5 includes passive postnominal clauses, which are characteristic of scientific and technical written registers. There does seem to be a general structural shift operative here, however: written informational registers in languages at earlier stages of literacy (Somali and Korean) rely to a great extent on structural elaboration (especially the frequent use of dependent clauses); written informational registers in languages at later stages of literacy (English) develop to rely more on the dense integration of information. These patterns obviously need further investigation.

In general, the analyses in this chapter have shown notable similarities in the evolution of written registers in English and Somali, indicating the possibility of cross-linguistic generalizations that hold across language situations. The following chapter shows that there are also marked similarities in the linguistically well-defined text types of these two languages.

9   Registers and text types in English and Somali

9.1   Internal variation among texts within registers

The preceding chapters have shown that registers can be described and compared with respect to their linguistic characteristics, from both synchronic and diachronic perspectives. However, registers are identified and defined in situational rather than in linguistic terms. That is, even though register distinctions have strong linguistic correlates, they are defined on the basis of situational characteristics such as the relations among participants, the production circumstances, and the major purposes and goals of communication (see Ferguson 1983; Biber 1994).

Since registers have a primary situational basis, they are not equally well defined in their linguistic characteristics: there are considerable linguistic differences among texts within some registers, while other registers have quite focused norms with relatively small differences among texts. As discussed in section 5.7.3, a wide range of internal variation does not invalidate a register category; rather, this internal range of variation is simply an important descriptive fact about the register. For this reason, a complete quantitative linguistic description of a register must include measures of the variability among texts within the register (e.g., standard deviation or range) as well as measures of the central tendency (the mean).

9.1.1   Internal variation within English registers

Table 9.1 presents descriptive statistics for thirteen English registers, including both the mean and the standard deviation. The analyses in chapter 6 show that the mean dimension scores are important and statistically significant predictors of the differences among registers. The standard deviations listed in table 9.1 show, however, that English registers are not equally well defined linguistically: some registers consistently show a greater range of internal variation, while other registers are more or less well defined on particular dimensions.

The standard deviation is a measure of the variability among scores: 68

percent of the texts in a register have dimension scores that are within the range of plus or minus one standard deviation from the mean score for that register. For example, table 9.1 shows that 68 percent of all press editorial texts have dimension 1 scores falling between -13.8 and -6.2 (i.e., the mean score of -10.0 plus or minus the standard deviation of 3.8). The texts within spontaneous speeches have a much greater range of scores along dimension 1: 68 percent of all spontaneous speeches have dimension 1 scores falling between 5.9 and 30.5 (i.e., the mean score of 18.2 plus or minus the standard deviation of 12.3).

The size of a standard deviation should be interpreted relative to the total range of variability along a dimension. For example, texts can have scores ranging from -26.5 to $+54.1$ along dimension 1, resulting in a total range of 80.6; a standard deviation of 4 or 5 is not large relative to this total spread of scores. In contrast, dimension 2 scores have a much smaller range: from -6.2 to $+15.6$, resulting in a total range of only 21.8. A standard deviation of 4 or 5 thus represents a much larger spread of register-internal variation along dimension 2.

With respect to dimension 1, written expository registers have relatively little internal variation: press reportage has a standard deviation of 4.5; press editorials has a standard deviation of 3.8; official documents has a standard deviation of 4.8; academic prose has a standard deviation of 6.0. The texts in these registers are relatively consistent in having highly integrated structure and few involvement features. In contrast, most spoken registers have relatively large standard deviations on dimension 1: a standard deviation of 9.1 for face-to-face conversations; 10.7 for both interviews and broadcasts; and 12.3 for spontaneous speeches. These scores show that there are relatively large differences within the spoken registers in their dimension 1 characteristics, with some texts being considerably more involved than others. Professional letters have a standard deviation of 13.7 along dimension 1, which is the largest of all these registers. This score reflects the widely differing purposes of professional letters, ranging from an expository presentation of information to a relatively involved and interactive expression of personal views.

Professional letters also have one of the largest standard deviations along dimension 2, reflecting the fact that these letters can range from a complete absence of narrative features to a mixture of narrative and non-narrative discourse. Spontaneous and prepared speeches similarly show a relatively wide range of internal differences in their narrative characteristics. In contrast, registers such as press editorials, official documents, and broadcasts are more well defined in being consistently non-narrative along dimension 2.

A quick perusal of the statistics for dimensions 3, 4, and 5 similarly shows that registers have differing degrees of internal consistency along each

Table 9.1 *Descriptive statistics for selected registers on five English dimensions.*
(Based on Biber 1988: table 7.1)

Register	Mean	Standard deviation
Dimension 1: 'Involved versus Informational Production'		
Press reportage	−15.1	4.5
Press editorials	−10.0	3.8
Official documents	−18.1	4.8
Academic prose	−14.9	6.0
General fiction	−0.8	9.2
Science fiction	−6.1	4.6
Personal letters	19.5	5.4
Professional letters	−3.9	13.7
Face-to-face conversations	35.3	9.1
Interviews	17.1	10.7
Broadcasts	−4.3	10.7
Spontaneous speeches	18.2	12.3
Prepared speeches	2.2	6.7
Dimension 2: 'Narrative versus Non-narrative Discourse'		
Press reportage	0.4	2.1
Press editorials	−0.8	1.4
Official documents	−2.9	1.2
Academic prose	−2.6	2.3
General fiction	5.9	3.2
Science fiction	5.9	2.5
Personal letters	0.3	1.0
Professional letters	−2.2	3.5
Face-to-face conversations	−0.6	2.0
Interviews	−1.1	2.1
Broadcasts	−3.3	1.2
Spontaneous speeches	1.3	3.6
Prepared speeches	0.7	3.3
Dimension 3: 'Situation-dependent versus Elaborated Reference'		
Press reportage	−0.3	2.9
Press editorials	1.9	2.0
Official documents	7.3	3.6
Academic prose	4.2	3.6
General fiction	−3.1	2.3
Science fiction	−1.4	3.7
Personal letters	−3.6	1.8
Professional letters	6.5	4.2
Face-to-face conversations	−3.9	2.1
Interviews	−0.4	4.0
Broadcasts	−9.0	4.4
Spontaneous speeches	1.2	4.3
Prepared speeches	0.3	3.6

Table 9.1 (*cont.*)

Register	Mean	Standard deviation
Dimension 4: 'Overt Expression of Argumentation'		
Press reportage	−0.7	2.6
Press editorials	3.1	3.2
Official documents	−0.2	4.1
Academic prose	−0.5	4.7
General fiction	0.9	2.6
Science fiction	−0.7	1.7
Personal letters	1.5	2.6
Professional letters	3.5	4.7
Face-to-face conversations	−0.3	2.4
Interviews	1.0	2.4
Broadcasts	−4.4	2.0
Spontaneous speeches	0.3	4.4
Prepared speeches	0.4	4.1
Dimension 5: 'Non-abstract versus Abstract Style'		
Press reportage	0.6	2.4
Press editorials	0.3	2.0
Official documents	4.7	2.4
Academic prose	5.5	4.8
General fiction	−2.5	1.6
Science fiction	−2.5	0.8
Personal letters	−2.8	1.9
Professional letters	0.4	2.4
Face-to-face conversations	−3.2	1.1
Interviews	−2.0	1.3
Broadcasts	−1.7	2.8
Spontaneous speeches	−2.6	1.7
Prepared speeches	−1.9	1.4

dimension. Some registers, such as professional letters, have relatively large standard deviations on most dimensions, reflecting the fact that texts in this register can have widely different purposes. Other registers have relatively large standard deviations on some dimensions because they comprise several distinct subregisters: for example, academic prose has relatively large standard deviations on dimension 4 and dimension 5 because it includes texts from a number of academic disciplines, ranging from humanities and the arts to engineering and science. The same techniques used in chapters 5 and 6 to compare registers can be applied to the analysis of these subregisters (see Biber 1988: chapter 8).

Table 9.2 *Descriptive statistics for selected registers on five Somali dimensions*

Register	Mean	Standard deviation
Dimension 1: 'Structural Elaboration: Involvement versus Exposition'		
Press reportage	−4.8	0.7
Press editorials	−5.7	1.0
Press announcements	−4.1	0.8
Academic theses	−4.2	1.2
Serial stories	−0.1	2.8
Folk stories	3.4	0.9
Memos	−3.5	0.5
Personal letters	2.5	1.3
Face-to-face conversations	9.9	2.1
Formal meetings	−0.8	2.0
Quranic sermons	2.5	1.5
University lectures	−0.2	1.5
Dimension 2: 'Lexical Elaboration: On-line versus Planned/Integrated Production'		
Press reportage	0.7	6.1
Press editorials	−9.9	3.5
Press announcements	−0.7	3.8
Academic theses	0.3	3.7
Serial stories	−5.0	3.0
Folk stories	−1.7	2.3
Memos	−1.5	3.4
Personal letters	−1.4	2.2
Face-to-face conversations	4.1	3.8
Formal meetings	4.0	2.5
Quranic sermons	2.5	4.7
University lectures	4.3	6.2
Dimension 3: 'Argumentative versus Reported Presentation of Information'		
Press reportage	−10.0	3.5
Press editorials	−0.7	4.8
Press announcements	−0.5	2.4
Academic theses	0.8	3.8
Serial stories	−2.6	1.8
Folk stories	−5.6	0.8
Memos	−2.0	1.5
Personal letters	0.0	1.5
Face-to-face conversations	1.4	3.4
Formal meetings	4.5	2.5
Quranic sermons	1.7	3.1
University lectures	1.4	5.8

Table 9.2 (*cont.*)

Register	Mean	Standard deviation
Dimension 4: 'Narrative versus Non-narrative Discourse Organization'		
Press reportage	−1.4	1.3
Press editorials	−1.3	1.2
Press announcements	−3.0	0.9
Academic theses	−0.9	1.8
Serial stories	5.8	1.5
Folk stories	10.0	1.5
Memos	−3.0	1.1
Personal letters	−2.1	1.7
Face-to-face conversations	−0.5	2.0
Formal meetings	−1.7	1.9
Quranic sermons	3.0	3.7
University lectures	1.5	2.4
Dimension 5: 'Distanced, Directive Interaction'		
Press reportage	−3.5	0.6
Press editorials	−2.9	0.9
Press announcements	−2.3	1.0
Academic theses	−2.0	1.6
Serial stories	−0.4	1.2
Folk stories	−0.4	1.9
Memos	−1.2	1.4
Personal letters	10.0	2.2
Face-to-face conversations	2.0	2.0
Formal meetings	1.1	2.2
Quranic sermons	0.6	2.8
University lectures	0.8	2.4

9.1.2   Internal variation within Somali registers

Table 9.2 shows that there are similar differences in the degree of internal consistency for Somali registers. All Somali registers have relatively small standard deviations in their dimension 1 scores, reflecting relatively focused norms in their use of involvement versus structural elaboration features. In contrast, there are relatively large standard deviations for some registers with respect to dimension 2 characteristics. In particular, university lectures, press reportage, and Quranic sermons show relatively large internal differences: texts within these registers can range from being fairly elaborated in their lexical characteristics to being notably unelaborated lexically. University lectures also have a fairly large standard deviation along dimension 3, including a variety of argumentative and reported styles.

Quranic sermons have a relatively large standard deviation along dimension 4, showing relatively wide differences in the extent to which they rely on narrative discourse.

In general, though, the standard deviations for the dimension scores of Somali registers are smaller than those for English registers. This difference reflects the fact that the corpus design for Somali defined registers more specifically than the design of the English corpora: for example, several specific press registers are distinguished in Somali, corresponding to the single category of press reportage in English. Somali does not have general categories such as academic prose and professional letters. Somali memos were collected from a single academic department and thus are relatively homogeneous; Somali academic theses were written primarily on aspects of Somali language and literature and thus do not show a wide range of variation similar to English academic prose. These differences reflect the fact that registers which are defined more specifically in their situational characteristics will correspondingly show greater internal homogeneity in their linguistic characteristics.

9.2   Text types in English and Somali

A complementary perspective on textual variation is to identify and analyze the text categories that are *linguistically* well defined; these categories are referred to as *text types* in the present analysis. Text type distinctions have no necessary relation to register distinctions or to their associated situational bases; rather, text types are defined such that the texts within each type are maximally similar in their linguistic characteristics, regardless of their situational characteristics.

Text types and registers thus represent complementary ways to dissect the textual space of a language. Text types and registers are similar in that both can be described with respect to their linguistic characteristics and with respect to their situational/functional characteristics. However, these two constructs differ in their primary bases: registers are defined in terms of situational/functional characteristics, while text types are defined linguistically. The following subsections describe the salient text type distinctions in English and Somali, while cross-linguistic similarities between these typologies are discussed in section 9.3.

9.2.1   Quantitative identification and analysis of text types

Groupings of texts that are similar in their linguistic form – that is, *text types* – can be identified empirically by using a statistical procedure known as cluster analysis. In the present case, the groupings are identified on the basis of similarities among texts with respect to their dimension characteristics. The resulting 'types' thus represent functional as well as formal text classifications. That is, the texts within each type are similar in their characteristic linguistic features, which in turn reflect shared communicative purposes; the types differ from one another in that they have different linguistic characterizations and correspondingly different functional emphases.

Cluster analysis groups texts such that the texts within each cluster are maximally similar to each other in their exploitation of the textual dimensions, while each cluster is maximally distinct from the others.[1] That is, those texts with the most similar dimension scores are grouped into clusters. The resulting clusters can be interpreted as text types by considering their linguistic characterizations with respect to the textual dimensions together with the situational and functional characteristics of the texts grouped in each type.

A cluster analysis produces different solutions for different numbers of clusters (i.e., a one-cluster solution, two-cluster solution, etc.). Therefore, the first task for the researcher is to determine which solution provides the best 'fit' to the data. That is, in which solution are the texts within each cluster maximally similar while the clusters themselves are maximally distinct? The 'fit' of a solution can be assessed by various quantitative indices together with consideration of the interpretability of the resulting clusters; in the analyses of both English and Somali, an eight-cluster solution provides the best fit to the data.[2]

A cluster analysis assigns every text in a study to some cluster. If each text in an analysis is labeled with the number of its cluster, they can be plotted to illustrate the differences among clusters. Figure 9.1 illustrates this notion from the Somali analysis, plotting the distribution of texts with respect to Somali dimension 1 ('Structural Elaboration: Involvement versus Exposition') and Somali dimension 3 ('Argumentative versus Reported Presentation of Information'). This figure represents the distribution of texts according to their exploitation of the linguistic features on these two dimensions: the vertical axis plots the dimension score of each text for dimension 1; the horizontal axis plots the scores for dimension 3. The numbers in the plot represent the cluster number of the texts having the given scores on these two dimensions. For example, the position held by the underscored number 6 on figure 9.1 locates the text that has a score of -5.0 on dimension 1 (the vertical axis) and a score of $+5.5$ on dimension 3 (the horizontal axis), and that belongs to Cluster 6; these dimension scores mark this text as quite elaborated structurally (dimension 1) and argumentative in style (dimension 3).

Dimension 1

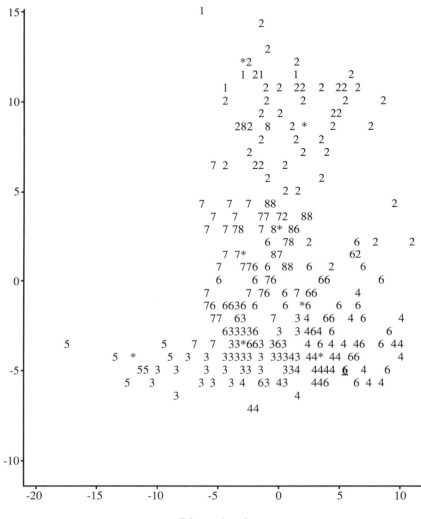

Dimension 3

Figure 9.1 Plot of the classification of Somali texts into text types with respect to Somali dimension 1 ('Structural Elaboration: Involvement versus Exposition') and Somali dimension 3 ('Argumentative versus Reported Presentation of Information'). '*' plots the text type centroids

Figure 9.1 shows relatively distinct groupings for clusters 1, 2, and 5, while the remaining five clusters (3, 4, 6, 7, and 8) are less well distinguished in terms of dimensions 1 and 3. The texts in cluster 1 (marked in the plot by the numeral 1) are characterized by large positive scores on dimension 1 and negative scores on dimension 3. Cluster 2 is similar except it has slightly lower positive scores on dimension 1 and unmarked scores on dimension 3. The texts in cluster 5 have relatively large negative scores on dimension 1 and extremely large negative scores on dimension 3.

The grouping of texts into clusters is determined on the basis of their characterizations with respect to all dimensions in a language. Thus, clusters that appear to be very similar in Figure 9.1 can in fact be quite distinct, due to their characteristics along other dimensions. For example, Somali clusters 4 and 6 are not clearly distinguished in figure 9.1, since they are both structurally elaborated (large negative scores on dimension 1) and argumentative (large positive scores on dimension 3). However, these two clusters are clearly distinguished along dimension 2 (see below).

The asterisks on figure 9.1 plot the 'centroids' (the central characterizations) for each cluster with respect to dimensions 1 and 3. The centroid scores for all dimensions can be plotted to present the complete multidimensional profile of a cluster. For example, figure 9.2 presents the multidimensional profiles for Somali clusters 4 and 6. As this figure shows, these two text types are similar along dimension 1 (with cluster 4 being somewhat more elaborated structurally) and dimension 3 (with cluster 4 being somewhat more argumentative), and they have essentially the same characterizations along dimension 4 (non-narrative) and dimension 5 (not directive or interactive). Consideration of these two clusters with respect to their lexical elaboration characteristics (dimension 2), however, shows that they represent polar opposites: cluster 4 is extremely elaborated lexically while cluster 6 is quite unelaborated lexically. Thus, it is only in terms of the complete multidimensional space that these two clusters are clearly distinguished from one another.

The cluster centroids present the linguistic characteristics of typical texts in each text type. However, texts do not divide neatly into sharply distinct 'types' – instead there is a continuous range of variation in linguistic form and use. The notion of 'text type' developed here is based on the frequent and therefore typical clusterings of texts, which account for the majority of texts in English and Somali. In a sense, these can be considered text 'prototypes'. There are, however, other texts that fall on the periphery of each cluster, grading from one text type into the next. The interpretation of the text types will focus on the core texts in each cluster, but it is also important to recognize the continuous nature of variation among texts.

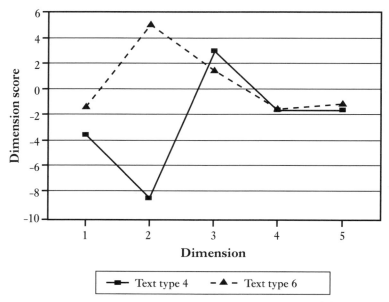

Figure 9.2 Multidimensional profile of Somali text types 4 and 6.
Dimension 1: 'Structural Elaboration: Involvement versus Expostion'
Dimension 2: 'Lexical Elaboration: On-line versus Planned/Integrated
    Production'
Dimension 3: 'Argumentative versus Reported Presentation of Information'
Dimension 4: 'Narrative versus Non-narrative Discourse Organization'
Dimension 5: 'Distanced, Directive Interaction'

9.2.2 Salient text type distinctions in English

An overall summary of the eight clusters identified in the analysis of English
text types is given in table 9.3. This table lists the number of texts in each
cluster, the nearest cluster, and the 'distance' to the nearest cluster. This
distance measure represents the cumulative difference between the cluster
centroids with respect to all five English dimensions. As table 9.3 shows, the
English text types are not equally distinct in their linguistic characterizations.
In particular, clusters 3 and 4 are less distinct than the others, with a distance
of only 8.3 between them.

Figures 9.3 and 9.4 summarize the distinguishing characteristics of the
eight English clusters, plotting the centroid score of each cluster with
respect to each dimension.[3] Figure 9.3 presents clusters 1–4, while figure
9.4 presents clusters 5–8.

On the basis of figures 9.3 and 9.4, it is possible to describe the

Table 9.3 *General summary of the clusters in the analysis of English text types*

Cluster number	Frequency of texts	Nearest cluster	Centroid distance to nearest cluster
1	23	2	15.3
2	73	1	15.3
3	43	4	8.3
4	71	3	8.3
5	60	8	11.0
6	150	4	10.2
7	12	5	15.3
8	49	5	11.0

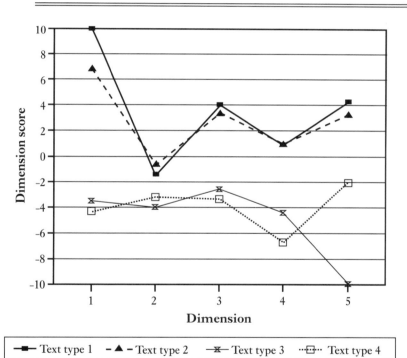

Text type 1   – ▲ – Text type 2   —✕— Text type 3   ⋯⊟⋯ Text type 4

Figure 9.3 Multidimensional profile of English text types 1–4.
Dimension 1: 'Involved versus Informational Production'
Dimension 2: 'Narrative versus Non-narrative Discourse'
Dimension 3: 'Situation-dependent versus Elaborated Reference'
Dimension 4: 'Overt Expression of Argumentation'
Dimension 5: 'Non-Abstract versus Abstract Style'

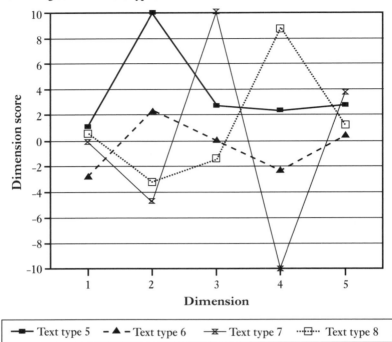

Figure 9.4 Multidimensional profile of English Text Types 5–8.
Dimension 1: 'Involved versus Informational Production'
Dimension 2: 'Narrative versus Non-narrative Discourse'
Dimension 3: 'Situation-Dependent versus Elaborated Reference'
Dimension 4: 'Overt Expression of Argumentation'
Dimension 5: 'Non-abstract versus Abstract Style'

distinguishing linguistic characteristics of each of the eight English text
types (using the interpretive dimension labels presented in chapter 6).
Figure 9.3 shows that text type 1 is extremely involved (D1), and relatively
situated (D3) and non-abstract (D5). It is not marked for narrative concerns
(D2) or persuasion (D4). Text type 2 is similar to text type 1, except it is
less involved (D1). Text types 3 and 4 are also similar to each other: both
are extremely integrated and informational (D1), extremely elaborated in
reference (D3), non-narrative (D2), and non-persuasive (D4). These two
clusters differ primarily with respect to dimension 5, where text type 3 is
extremely abstract in style while text type 4 is only moderately abstract.
    As figure 9.4 shows, text type 5 is extremely narrative (D2), moderately
involved (D1), situated (D3), non-abstract (D5), and not marked for persuasion (D4). Text type 6 combines the distinctive characteristics of text

types 4 and 5: it is informational (D1) as well as narrative (D2), while it is not marked on dimensions 3, 4, and 5. Text type 7 is extremely situated in its reference (D3), in addition to being markedly non-narrative (D2), non-persuasive (D4), and non-abstract (D5). Finally, text type 8 is distinctive in being extremely persuasive (D4), in addition to being moderately involved (D1), non-narrative (D2), and elaborated in reference (D3).[4]

Table 9.4 summarizes the composition and distinguishing characteristics of the eight text types. For each type, this table gives an interpretive label, the total number of texts in the type, the breakdown of texts by register, the percentage of texts from each register that occur in the type (in parentheses), and a summary of the multidimensional characterization of the text type. The asterisks in the table identify cases where a majority of the texts from a single register occur in a single text type (e.g., text type 1 contains 62 percent of all telephone conversations between personal friends included in the analysis). The centroid score of each cluster with respect to each dimension is given in parentheses after the dimension characterizations.

The labels in table 9.4 summarize the interpretations of each cluster as a text type. This interpretation is based on consideration of the predominant linguistic characteristics of each cluster, the communicative characteristics of the texts grouped in each cluster, and micro-analyses of individual texts. I turn now to a detailed consideration of each English text type.

9.2.2.1 English text types 1 and 2: 'Intimate Interpersonal Interaction' and 'Informational Interaction'

As noted above, the multidimensional characterizations of English text types 1 and 2 are quite similar to each other (see figure 9.3). Both are characterized by situated reference (dimension 3), a non-abstract style (dimension 5), and relatively unmarked scores on dimensions 2 and 4. Even on dimension 1, they are both characterized as highly involved; the major difference between these two clusters is that text type 1 has an extreme characterization on dimension 1 while text type 2 has a more moderate characterization.

The texts grouped into text types 1 and 2, summarized on table 9.4, reflect the shared linguistic characteristics of these two clusters as well as the difference between them along dimension 1. Text type 1 comprises strictly 'involved', interpersonal conversations, for the most part face-to-face conversations and telephone conversations between personal friends. Text type 2, on the other hand, comprises person-to-person interactions that have an informational concern, such as interviews, business telephone conversations, and face-to-face conversations in professional contexts. In both of these text types, the interaction is primary – speakers address individual

Table 9.4 *Summary of the English text types. (Table gives the number of texts in each text type, the percentage of texts from each register occurring in that text type, and a multidimensional characterization of the text type. * marks cases where more than 50 percent of a register occurs in a single text type)*

Type 1:   Intimate Interpersonal Interaction (23 texts)

Composition by register

13   Face-to-face conversations (29 percent)
 8   Telephone conversations – Personal friends (62 percent) *
 1   Telephone conversations – Disparates (17 percent)
 1   Telephone conversations – Business associates (13 percent)

Dimension characteristics

Dimension 1:   Extremely involved (+48)
Dimension 2:   Unmarked (−1.0)
Dimension 3:   Situated (+5.5)
Dimension 4:   Unmarked (+0.5)
Dimension 5:   Non-abstract (+4.0)

Type 2:   Informational Interaction (73 texts)

Composition by register

31   Face-to-face conversations (70 percent) *
11   Interviews (50 percent) *
 9   Spontaneous speeches (56 percent) *
 7   Telephone conversations – Business associates (88 percent) *
 5   Telephone conversations – Personal friends (39 percent)
 4   Telephone conversations – Disparates (67 percent) *
 3   Personal letters (50 percent) *
 1   Non-sports broadcasts (13 percent)
 1   Professional letters (10 percent)
 1   General fiction (3 percent)

Dimension characteristics

Dimension 1:   Very involved (+32)
Dimension 2:   Unmarked (−0.5)
Dimension 3:   Situated (+4.5)
Dimension 4:   Unmarked (+0.5)
Dimension 5:   Non-abstract (+3.0)

listeners who are immediately present and personal. The main difference between these types relates to the primary purpose of interaction: to convey information in text type 2 and to maintain the interpersonal relationship in text type 1. This difference can be illustrated by comparison of text sample 9.1, representing text type 1, with text sample 9.2 representing text type 2.

Table 9.4 (*cont.*)

Type 3:   'Scientific' Exposition (43 texts)

Composition by register

35   Academic prose (44 percent)
 4   Official documents (29 percent)
 1   Biographies (7 percent)
 1   Press reviews (6 percent)
 1   Hobbies (7 percent)
 1   Press reportage (2 percent)

Dimension characteristics

Dimension 1:   Very integrated (−17)
Dimension 2:   Non-narrative (−2.5)
Dimension 3:   Elaborated (−3.5)
Dimension 4:   Non-persuasive (−2.0)
Dimension 5:   Extremely abstract (−9.5)

Type 4:   Learned Exposition (71 texts)

Composition by register

25   Academic prose (31 percent)
11   Press reportage (25 percent)
 8   Official documents (57 percent)*
 8   Press reviews (47 percent)
 5   Popular lore (36 percent)
 4   Biographies (29 percent)
 3   Professional letters (30 percent)
 3   Hobbies (21 percent)
 3   Religion (18 percent)
 1   Press editorials (4 percent)

Dimension characteristics

Dimension 1:   Extremely integrated (−20)
Dimension 2:   Non-narrative (−2.0)
Dimension 3:   Very elaborated (−4.5)
Dimension 4:   Non-persuasive (−3.0)
Dimension 5:   Moderately abstract (−2.0)

TEXT TYPE 1
(see also text sample 6.1)

Text sample 9.1 (LL:1.8, informal face-to-face conversation between friends)

A: there are cups # [pause] Nescafe # [pause]
B: shall we have a cup of coffee # [pause]
A: yes certainly # yes certainly # [pause] yes #

Table 9.4 (*cont.*)

Type 5:   Imaginative Narrative (60 texts)

Composition by register

15 General fiction (51 percent) *
12 Romance fiction (92 percent) *
 9 Mystery fiction (70 percent) *
 9 Adventure fiction (70 percent) *
 7 Prepared speeches (50 percent) *
 2 Interviews (9 percent)
 2 Science fiction (33 percent)
 1 Popular lore (7 percent)
 1 Biography (7 percent)
 1 Personal letters (17 percent)
 1 Religion (6 percent)

Dimension characteristics

Dimension 1:   Moderately involved (+5)
Dimension 2:   Extremely narrative (+6.5)
Dimension 3:   Situated (+3.5)
Dimension 4:   Unmarked (+1.0)
Dimension 5:   Non-abstract (+2.5)

Type 6:   General Reported Exposition (150 texts)

Composition by register

32 Press reportage (73 percent) *
23 Press editorials (86 percent) *
13 Academic prose (17 percent)
12 General fiction (41 percent)
10 Religion (59 percent) *
 8 Humor (89 percent) *
 8 Biographies (57 percent) *
 8 Press reviews (47 percent)
 6 Hobbies (43 percent)
 5 Non-sports broadcasts (63 percent) *
 5 Prepared speeches (35 percent)
 4 Adventure fiction (31 percent)
 3 Science fiction (50 percent) *
 3 Mystery fiction (23 percent)
 3 Popular lore (21 percent)
 2 Professional letters (20 percent)
 2 Sports broadcasts (20 percent)
 2 Official documents (14 percent)
 1 Romance fiction (8 percent)

Table 9.4 (*cont.*)

Type 6 (cont.):
        Dimension: characteristics:

        Dimension 1:   Integrated (−12)
        Dimension 2:   Moderately narrative (+1.5)
        Dimension 3:   Unmarked (+0.0)
        Dimension 4:   Unmarked (−1.0)
        Dimension 5:   Unmarked (+0.5)

Type 7:   Situated Reportage (12 texts)

        Composition by register

        8   Sports broadcasts (80 percent) *
        1   Non-sports broadcasts (13 percent)
        1   Science fiction (17 percent)
        1   Mystery fiction (8 percent)
        1   Hobbies (7 percent)

        Dimension characteristics

        Dimension 1:   Unmarked (0)
        Dimension 2:   Non-narrative (−3.0)
        Dimension 3:   Extremely situated (+13.5)
        Dimension 4:   Very non-persuasive (−4.5)
        Dimension 5:   Non-abstract (+3.5)

Type 8:   Involved Persuasion (49 texts)

        Composition by register

        9   Interviews (41 percent)
        7   Spontaneous speeches (44 percent)
        7   Academic prose (9 percent)
        5   Popular lore (36 percent)
        4   Professional letters (40 percent)
        3   Hobbies (21 percent)
        3   Religion (18 percent)
        3   Editorial letters (11 percent)
        2   Personal letters (33 percent)
        2   Prepared speeches (14 percent)
        1   Telephone conversations − Disparates (17 percent)
        1   Non-sports broadcasts (13 percent)
        1   Humor (11 percent)
        1   General fiction (3 percent)

        Dimension characteristics

        Dimension 1:   Unmarked (+3)
        Dimension 2:   Non-narrative (−2.0)
        Dimension 3:   Moderately elaborated (−2.0)
        Dimension 4:   Very persuasive (+4.0)
        Dimension 5:   Unmarked (+1.0)

B: I see # they're all [???] [long pause]
A: some of them are rather large # [pause]
B: mm #
A: some of them are rather large # [pause]

. . . .

B: want any sugar # [pause]
A: yes please Brenda # [pause]
B: one # [pause]
A: that's about right # yes that's enough thank you # [long pause] not yours is it #
B: oh no # those are my scripts # I just saw the note # and I know that's all right # [long pause]
A: just put my glasses on # I can't see a thing without them # [long pause] well after all they're too dark to be inspiriting # aren't they # [pause]
B: I don't want one # I'm afraid #
A: I think I'd rather substitute #
B: yes # I haven't space # I don't want [pause] portraits #
A: no # [pause]

TEXT TYPE 2
(see also text sample 6.3)

Text sample 9.2 (LL:1.1, face-to-face conversation between academic colleagues, concerning student comprehensive exams)

A: well # [pause] may I ask # what goes into that paper now # because I have to advise # [pause] a couple of people who are doing the [mm]
B: well what you do # is to [long pause] this is sort of between the two of us # what you do # is to make sure that your own [pause] candidate [mm] # is [pause] that your [pause] there's something that your own candidate can handle # [long pause]

. . .

A: you mean that the the the papers are more or less set ad hominem # are they # [pause]
B: [mm] [long pause] they shouldn't be # [long pause] but [mm] [pause] I mean one # sets [long pause] one question # now I mean this fellow's doing the language of advertising # [pause] so very well #
A: yeah #
B: give him one on

A: is this a spare paper <change of topic>
B: yeah

Text samples 9.1–9.2 illustrate the shared characteristics of text types 1 and 2, as well as the major difference between these two types. Both samples are interactional, but sample 9.1, which represents text type 1, is nearly exclusive in its interpersonal focus, while sample 9.2, which represents text type 2, has a specific informational purpose in addition to its interpersonal purpose. In sample 9.1, there is no particular topic that is the focus of discussion; rather, the participants change topic freely and place primary emphasis on the interaction itself instead of on the exchange of information. Sample 6.1, discussed in chapter 6, further illustrates these characteristics of text type 1. In contrast, sample 9.2 is from a face-to-face conversation in a professional context, and it thus has an informational as well as interactional focus. These mixed informational and interactive characteristics can also be illustrated by the passage from a panel discussion presented in sample 6.3 (in chapter 6). In a panel discussion, a group of discussants interact with one another debating a series of specific issues; this speech event is thus explicitly informational and interactional at the same time.

The major linguistic difference between text types 1 and 2 relates to their characterization on dimension 1: text type 1 is extremely involved, while text type 2 is more moderately involved. The situational characteristics of the texts grouped into text types 1 and 2, together with this linguistic characterization, lead to the interpretation of text type 1 as highly interpersonal interaction, and text type 2 as informational interaction. The dimension 1 characteristics of text samples 9.1 and 9.2 illustrate this difference. Sample 9.1 thus has very frequent private verbs (e.g., *know*, *think*), *that*-deletions (*I know [that] that's all right*; *I think [that] I'd rather substitute*), contractions (e.g., *they're*, *that's*, *can't*), present tense verbs, first- and second-person pronouns, demonstrative pronouns (e.g., *that's about right, those are my scripts*), occurrences of *it* as pronoun, *be* as main verb, etc. At the same time, this text sample shows a marked absence of nouns, prepositions, attributive adjectives, and long words, and it has relatively little lexical variety. Text sample 9.2 is also involved and interactional, but much less so than sample 9.1. Some positive dimension 1 features occur in this text (e.g., first- and second-person pronouns, contractions, and private verbs). At the same time, sample 9.2 shows more frequent nouns, prepositions, attributive adjectives, and long words than sample 9.1, reflecting its more informational focus.

In summary, text type 1 is a type of interaction that is situated in reference, non-abstract in style, and extremely interpersonal and involved in focus. Text type 2 is also a type of interaction that is situated and non-abstract, but the texts of this type have specific informational as well as interpersonal purposes. The interpretation of these two clusters illustrates the way in which text type categories can cut directly across register classifications. For example, some texts classified as 'spontaneous speeches' are in fact highly interactive and belong to text type 2; texts classified as 'face-to-face conversation' can be either highly interpersonal interaction (text type 1) or relatively informational interaction (text type 2). Text types 3–8 provide other examples of linguistic characterizations that cut across external register classifications.

9.2.2.2 English text types 3 and 4: 'Scientific Exposition' and 'Learned Exposition'

English text types 3 and 4 form a second pair of related types. Figure 9.3 shows that these clusters have very similar characterizations on dimensions 1–4, differing primarily on dimension 5. Both clusters are markedly non-narrative (dimension 2) and non-persuasive (dimension 4), and both are very integrated and informational (dimension 1) and elaborated in reference (dimension 3). On dimension 5, both clusters are characterized by an abstract style; they differ in that text type 3 is extremely abstract in style while text type 4 is only moderately so.

The texts grouped into these text types, listed on table 9.4, show that they both represent types of informational exposition. Text type 3 comprises primarily academic prose texts and a few official documents; the academic prose texts are primarily from natural science, engineering/technology, and medicine. Text type 4, on the other hand, comprises a relatively broad range of texts, including academic prose, press reportage, official documents, press reviews, popular lore, biographies, hobbies, and religion. Academic prose texts make up approximately a third of the texts in this cluster; but unlike text type 3, the academic texts in text type 4 are primarily from the humanities, social sciences, education, and law. Both of these clusters are expository with an informational focus. The difference between them relates to the extreme technical content and abstract style found in text type 3 versus the more 'learned' presentation of information in text type 4. Text samples 9.3 and 9.4 illustrate the shared characteristics of text types 3 and 4 as well as the primary difference between them.

TEXT TYPE 3
(See also sample 6.16 in chapter 6)

Text sample 9.3 (LOB:J.8, physics journal article)

Thus the first few atomic layers deposited during the gettering period are highly oxidized, and when the chamber has been 'cleaned up' the deposit is more metallic. After the evaporation ceases, the deposited film remains open to oxidation. Thus the deposited film is inhomogeneous and approximates to a sandwich layer of oxide/metal/oxide, in which the outer layers are more highly oxidized than the inner layer.

The exact state of oxidation of the deposited film is unknown and a further effect of oxidation can be observed upon baking in air.

TEXT TYPE 4

Text sample 9.4 (LOB:J. 27, sociology text)

Government in Spain continues to rest on the three institutions of an hereditary monarchy (rejected by two short-lived republics), the parliament of the old Castilian Cortes, and an extensive Civil Service, with a permanent staff except for its highest officials. Spain is at the moment a kingdom without a king. The Franco regime has committed itself to the maintenance of the monarchy as an institution by the 1947 Law of Succession and the Referendum of the following year. Meanwhile the regime, in its own words, is a representative, organic democracy in which the individual participates in government through the natural representative organs of the family, the city council and the syndicate.

Both of these samples show the characteristics of dense informational integration and elaborated reference: for example, both have a high concentration of nouns, prepositions, attributive adjectives, long words, and a quite varied vocabulary, together with a near total absence of the involved features associated with dimension 1. On dimension 3, neither text makes direct reference to items in the external situation, and in both cases the full texts make frequent use of WH relative clauses to elaborate intended references (although these samples have only one relative construction each). Both samples are written entirely in the present tense, illustrating their marked non-narrative orientation on dimension 2. Neither sample makes use of the persuasive features associated with dimension 4, resulting in their negative score on that dimension.

The striking difference between these two samples relates to their dimension 5 characteristics. Sample 9.3, representing text type 3, is extremely passive in form, with the agent of predicates being deleted in every case. All of the constructions promote an inanimate referent, while the demoted (and deleted) agents are frequently animate. These forms include main verbs (e.g., *are highly oxidized, has been 'cleaned up', is unknown, can be observed*) as well as postnominal modifying clauses (e.g., *layers deposited during the gettering*). This sample also illustrates the frequent use of conjuncts to mark the logical relations in a text (in this case a repeated use of *thus*). Sample 6.16, discussed in chapter 6, further illustrates these characteristics of text type 3.

Sample 9.4, on the other hand, is consistently in the active voice; the only passive form is in the postnominal clause *monarchy rejected by two short-lived republics*, and even this case is unlike sample 9.3 in that the agent is specified. This sample also illustrates a lesser use of conjuncts, counting on the reader to infer the logical relations among propositions.

In summary, text types 3 and 4 are both expository, extremely informational, integrated, and elaborated in reference. The difference between them relates to their use of an abstract, technical style. This seems to be both a content and a stylistic distinction. On the one hand, the texts in type 3 focus on highly abstract and technical information; they are therefore more concerned with the entities being acted on (the patients) than with active agents. They further depend on a frequent use of conjuncts to specify the logical relations among propositions. Type 4 texts tend to be less technical in content. However, the differences between these types also seem to reflect attitudinal preferences. Thus, the texts in type 3, coming for the most part from engineering and natural sciences, show a stylistic preference for a presentation of information apart from active agents, possibly to give the appearance of scientific rigor. In contrast, the texts in type 4, representing a broad range of 'literate' prose, show a preference for a more active style, perhaps reflecting the influence of prescriptive notions of 'good' style.

As was the case with text types 1 and 2, the classification of texts into types 3 and 4 cuts across register categories: for example, several social science and humanities academic texts are grouped into type 3 because they are relatively technical in content and adopt the abstract and technical style of that type; conversely, a few natural science and engineering academic texts are grouped into type 4, adopting an active, non-abstract style in contrast to the norms for their subregisters.

9.2.2.3 Text type 5: 'Imaginative Narrative'

Figure 9.4 and table 9.4 show that text type 5 is situated in reference (dimension 3), non-abstract in style (dimension 5), and slightly involved (dimension 1), but the primary distinguishing characteristic of this type is its extreme narrative orientation (dimension 2). Not surprisingly, the texts grouped into this cluster are mostly fiction, or 'imaginative narrative'. Text sample 9.5 illustrates the direct narration common in fiction, while sample 9.6 illustrates a non-fictional narrative from a judge's final summary in a court case. Text samples 6.6 and 6.7 (from chapter 6) further illustrate text type 5 characteristics in fiction.

TEXT TYPE 5
(See also samples 6.6 and 6.7 in chapter 6)

Text sample 9.5 (LOB:L.1, mystery fiction)

He did well. He got in touch with the woman Pete was passing off as his mother. Starmouth managed to win her confidence. It seems that she was an honest enough woman, only her mind wasn't as clear as it could have been. She showed him photographs.

Text sample 9.6 (LL:12.4b, prepared speech – court case)

A:
I have to decide in this case # [pause] what # [pause] if any maintenance # [pause] should be paid # [pause] by the husband as I shall call him # [pause] to the wife # [long pause] he's in fact # no longer the husband # [long pause] he was originally petitioner # [pause] because there's been a decree # [pause] absolute # [long pause] and he has remarried # [pause] the decree # [long pause] was pronounced in favour # of the respondent wife # [pause] on the grounds of the husband's admitted adultery # [pause] his charge # of adultery # [pause] against her # with the main correspondent # [long pause] failed # after a [pause] somewhat lengthy [pause] hearing # [pause] her charges of cruelty # against him # [pause] likewise failed # [long pause]

Sample 9.5 is typical of the majority of texts grouped into text type 5, representing simple narration in the past with frequent past tense forms, third-person personal pronouns, and perfect aspect verbs, resulting in a large positive score on dimension 2. Samples 6.6 and 6.7 in chapter 6 illustrate the mixing of involved and narrative characteristics that often occurs in text type 5 texts. Involved features are most common in fiction dialogue, which represents a fictional interaction between characters and thus includes frequent involved features. In addition, fiction texts are often written from a first-person perspective, resulting in the use of many involved characteristics in the narrative as well as dialogue sections (e.g., first-person pronouns, questions, and other features relating to the thought processes of the narrator).

Text sample 9.6 illustrates how non-fictional texts can have a similar mixing of narrative focus and involved presentation. This sample is from a final summation and opinion in a court case. As background to the opinion, the judge summarizes the events that are relevant to the case. This speech event is largely narrative, and sample 9.6 contains many of the features characteristic of a high dimension 2 score, such as frequent past tense verbs, perfect aspect verbs, and third-person pronouns. In addition, this text is moderately involved, with the speaker using features such as first-person pronouns, contractions, and private verbs. There are only a few non-fiction texts grouped in text type 5, but sample 9.6 illustrates how these texts can have a primary narrative focus combined with an involved presentation.

9.2.2.4 Text type 6: 'General Reported Exposition'

Text type 6 is the largest cluster, with 150 total texts. Figure 9.4 shows that this type combines expository/informational and narrative features, making it similar to text types 3 and 4 in some respects and to text type 5 in other respects. With respect to dimension 1, text type 6 is similar to text types 3 and 4 in being markedly integrated, informational, and non-involved; with respect to dimension 2, text type 6 is similar to text type 5 in that it is moderately narrative. On dimensions 3 and 5, text type 6 is unmarked.

The texts grouped into this cluster, listed in table 9.4, likewise combine these two concerns. They are primarily informational and expository, but often use narration and a reported presentation to convey information. Unlike text type 5, the narrative portions in type 6 texts are an integral part of the expository information being conveyed rather than an end in themselves.

Text type 6 is the most general of the English text types. The 150 texts grouped into this type represent nineteen different registers, including press reportage, press editorials, general fiction, biographies, humor, press reviews, academic prose, and religion. This type represents generalized exposition – it is not markedly learned or technical, not markedly elaborated in reference or abstract in style, and it often uses a reported presentation as part of its exposition.

Text samples 9.7 and 9.8 illustrate the distinctive characteristics of this type. Sample 9.7 is from an editorial and illustrates the use of reported forms to convey expository information. Sample 9.8 is from a humor text and is representative of the fictional and biographical types of writing that use the features of this text type for entertainment purposes.

TEXT TYPE 6

Text sample 9.7 (LOB:B.20, editorial letter)

Communism had little or nothing to do with the riots in South Africa or the more recent disorders in Rhodesia. In fact, former leaders of the

Communist Party in the Union have left the country. Some are now in the Rhodesian copper belt and at least one of them is in London.

In contrast, Moscow has embarked upon a special operation in Ruanda-Urundi, which borders on the Belgian Congo. This state of some 21,000 square miles and a population of 4,630,000 has been a United Nations trust territory under the administration of Belgium, but a few days ago she announced that she was giving up the trusteeship.

Text sample 9.8 (LOB:R.2, humor)

He had long sensed injustice in the distinctions drawn between ordinary wage-earners and those self-employed. By the time his monthly salary arrived, the Inland Revenue had already taken their share, and there were precious few reductions in tax except for wives, children, life-insurances or any of the other normal encumbrances which Cecil had so far avoided. He read the film star's sorry story and frowned at the provisions of Schedule D taxation which not only allowed her to claim relief on the most unlikely purchases, but also postponed demanding the tax until her financial year was ended, audited and agreed by the Inspector.

Both of these text samples illustrate the informational features associated with dimension 1: frequent occurrences of nouns, prepositional phrases, attributive adjectives, etc., plus markedly infrequent use of involved features. This is true of the editorial (sample 9.7), which is primarily informational and expository in purpose, as well as the humor text (sample 9.8), which is primarily entertaining in purpose. Despite the different purposes of these texts, they both use narrative forms associated with dimension 2 (e.g., past tense forms, perfect aspect verbs, third-person pronouns). On the other three dimensions, these samples illustrate the unmarked characterization of text type 6: not markedly 'elaborated' or 'situated' in reference, and not marked with respect to persuasion or abstract style.

The text type represented by this cluster has a special place in the typology of English texts: it is the most general and non-distinct of the eight types, in that the linguistic characterization of type 6 tends to be relatively unmarked on all five dimensions. As text samples 9.7 and 9.8 illustrate, the texts in this type can have quite different communicative purposes. In the case of editorials, those purposes relate to analysis of the events and circumstances associated with some political or social situation; in the case of humor (as well as fiction and biography), those purposes include entertainment through a report of events. In the case of other kinds of text, such as press reportage, the primary purposes include informing through a factual reportage of events. These texts all belong to the same text type in their surface linguistic characterizations, but they show considerable variation with respect to their specific purposes.

9.2.2.5 Text type 7: 'Situated On-line Reportage'

Text type 7 is the smallest and most distinct text type identified in the study. Figure 9.4 shows that it is not marked with respect to dimension 1, but it is markedly non-narrative, non-persuasive, and non-abstract (with respect to dimensions 2, 4, and 5). The most distinctive characteristic of this cluster is on dimension 3, where it is marked as extremely situated in reference. The core texts grouped into this cluster are all sports broadcasts. This text type thus represents the on-line reportage of events which are in progress and occurring in a fairly rapid succession. Text sample 9.9, taken from a broadcast of a soccer game, illustrates the distinctive characteristics of this text type. These characteristics are further illustrated by text samples 6.9 and 6.10 in chapter 6; sample 6.9 includes additional material from the same broadcast as sample 9.9.

TEXT TYPE 7
(See also samples 6.9 and 6.10 in chapter 6)

Text sample 9.9 (LL:10.2, sports broadcast – soccer)

A:
Dunn # down the line # a bad one # it's Badger that gets it # he's got time to control it # [pause] he feeds in fact # Tom Curry # one of the midfield players ahead of him # [pause] Curry has got the ball # on that far side # chips the ball down the centre # [pause] again # a harmless one # [pause] no danger # out comes Stepney # [pause] and now left-footed # his clearance # [pause] is again # a long [pause] high # probing ball # down centrefield # onto the head of [long pause] Flynn # Flynn to Badger # Badger on the far side #

Characteristic of text type 7, sample 9.9 is neither involved nor informational; it is markedly non-narrative, non-persuasive, and non-abstract in style; and it is extremely situated in reference. Although these characterizations relate mostly to the absence of certain features, they reflect the very specialized purpose and production circumstances of type 7 texts: situations in which events actually in progress are described to a large audience that is not present. The distant relationship between broadcaster and audience results in the lack of involvement features; the rapid on-line production of text results in the frequent repetition of words and the relative lack of informational integration; and the reportage of events actually in progress results in the non-narrative characterization of these texts. The most distinctive characteristic of type 7 texts is the extremely frequent use of expressions referring directly to the physical and temporal situation of communication. Thus, sample 9.9 contains numerous expressions such as *down the line, ahead of him, on that far side,* and *down the centre,* which require direct reference to the playing field for understanding.

It is somewhat surprising that the texts in this type are much more situated in reference than those in type 1, 'Intimate Interpersonal Interaction'. Both text types are non-informational, and in both types the participants share the same temporal context. In some respects, we might expect type 1 to be more situated in reference than type 7 texts. In type 1 texts, participants actually share the same physical situation, and addressees can request clarification in cases of misunderstanding. In contrast, the speaker (a radio broadcaster) in most type 7 texts does not actually share a physical situation with the listeners, and there is no possibility of clarification. However, there are two other considerations that seem to be instrumental in causing type 7 to be extremely situated in reference relative to type 1. First, the interactive texts in text type 1 do not involve the same informational demands and are not produced under the same time constraints as those in text type 7. That is, the on-line reportage of sports events involves a rapid production of speech describing all relevant events as they occur. In such a situation, there is great demand for situated reference, because there are many different referents to keep track of but little opportunity for elaborated referring expressions. Interpersonal interaction (type 1), on the other hand, involves considerably fewer referents and provides considerably more opportunity for elaborated reference. Second, the expected style of sports broadcasts is one that gives the impression of an extremely rapid and exciting succession of events, even if this is not actually the case. Thus, even in the reportage of baseball games, where events occur much more slowly than in a soccer match, many of the same features seen in sample 9.9 are frequently used (Ferguson 1983). Due to the distinctive linguistic characteristics associated with these unusual communicative demands, sports broadcasts are isolated as a separate text type of 'situated reportage'.

9.2.2.6 *Text type 8: 'Involved Persuasion'*

Type 8 also represents a relatively specialized text type. In their linguistic characteristics, the texts in this cluster are moderately involved, elaborated in reference, and non-abstract in style (figure 9.4). The most distinctive characteristic of text type 8 occurs on dimension 4, where these texts are markedly persuasive in form. The texts grouped into this type (table 9.4) are also characteristically argumentative or persuasive in their primary purpose. The majority of these texts are spoken: some are interactional and informational, such as interviews and the telephone conversation between disparates; others are informational monologues, such as spontaneous and prepared speeches. The remaining texts are written, informational texts, such as popular lore, professional letters, religion, humor, and editorials. Overall, the linguistic characterization of these texts is primarily persuasive and secondarily involved, while the texts themselves are primarily argumentative or persuasive in purpose, leading to the interpretive label 'Involved Persuasion'.

Text sample 9.10, from a session of parliament, illustrates the way in which a text can be persuasive as well as involved. In this sample, a number of MPs are presenting their respective viewpoints and gently arguing with their interlocuters. The complete text contains a number of short interactive monologues, with each speaker attempting to persuade the others. Sample 6.12 in chapter 6 illustrates similar characteristics from a professional letter; that text is moderately interactive in that it responds to a previous letter, but it is persuasive, in that it argues in favor of a specific course of action as opposed to other possible actions.

TEXT TYPE 8
(See also sample 6.12 in chapter 6)

Text sample 9.10 (LL: 11.4, spontaneous speech – MPs in parliament interacting with the Secretary of State)

Q: would he not agree that it is essential at the moment # that more [pause] should be free for exports and less absorbed within our public sector # [long pause]

A: well # I think I would accept on the latter point # that more of our resources must go # into [mm] into the balance of payments # . . .

Q: would he agree that [mm] # [pause] an absence of such a statement # [pause] continues to generate uncertainty in the industry # and perhaps he might like to take this opportunity to [mm] # re-emphasize his support # for the second force airline # [long pause]

A: well I would certainly # [pause] regret it if # [pause] parts or # or or indeed the whole of the [mm] review # [pause] was to

> dribble out # that's not my intention at all # [pause] we shall of
> course # [pause] indeed we are # [pause] studying it [pause]
> very carefully # [pause] . . .

In sample 9.10, there is a high frequency of the 'persuasive' features
associated with dimension 4: prediction modals (*would, shall*), necessity
modals (*should, must*), possibility modals (*might*), suasive verbs (*agree*), and
conditional subordination. It is interesting that most texts from this type
are fairly uniform in adopting an involved presentation rather than a
strictly informational presentation. That is, these texts use both overt
persuasive markers (dimension 4) as well as a personal identification with
the listener/reader and an involved, colloquial style (dimension 1) to make
their point.

In contrast, some other texts in this type are strictly informational while
being overtly argumentative and persuasive. Text sample 9.11, from a
philosophy journal, illustrates this type of text:

Text sample 9.11 (LOB:J.54, academic prose – philosophy)

> . . . the impression must be describable without reference to any
> event or object distinct from it. It must be possible to characterize
> that internal impression without invoking any reference to the so-called
> object of the desire . . . The supposition, then, that desiring or wanting
> is a Humean cause, some sort of internal tension or uneasiness,
> involves the following contradiction: As Humean cause or internal
> impression, it must be describable without reference to anything
> else. . .; but as desire this is impossible. Any description of the desire
> involves a logically necessary connection with the thing desired. No
> internal impression could possibly have this logical property. Hence,
> a desire cannot possibly be an internal impression.

This text is directly persuasive; it overtly considers arguments and counter-
arguments, and forcefully argues in favor of a point of view. In the above
sample, this is shown principally by an extremely frequent use of modals
(*must, could, can*). At the same time, this text has an integrated and
informational characterization with respect to dimension 1 (frequent nouns,
prepositional phrases, etc.). Texts like sample 9.11 are grouped into text type
8 because they are overtly argumentative, but they are relatively peripheral to
this text type because they do not combine the typical use of persuasive and
involved features.[5]

In summary, the texts in type 8 are primarily distinguished by their persuasive and argumentative emphases. This orientation is typically combined

Table 9.5 *General summary of the clusters in the analysis of Somali text types*

Cluster number	Frequency of texts	Nearest cluster	Centroid distance to nearest cluster
1	5	2	9.0
2	54	1	9.0
3	57	4	8.1
4	40	3	8.1
5	8	3	12.3
6	69	3	9.8
7	33	3	9.3
8	13	2	10.3

with an involved, often interactive, style, which aids the persuasive force of the argument by developing a sense of solidarity with the listener or reader. In some cases, though, these texts can be overtly argumentative while having a marked informational focus, as in text sample 9.11.

9.2.3   Salient text type distinctions in Somali

As table 9.5 shows, text types in Somali differ in the extent to which they are specialized and clearly distinguished (similar to the patterns in English). First, some Somali text types are quite specialized: type 1 has only 5 texts; type 5 has 8 texts; type 8 has 13 texts. In contrast, other Somali types are quite general: type 6 has 69 texts, and types 2 and 3 each have over 50 texts. The types are also not equally distinguished from one another: types 3 and 4 are the least clearly distinguished (having the smallest distance measure from one another), while type 5, with only 8 texts, is the most sharply distinct.

Figures 9.5 and 9.6 plot the multidimensional profiles of each Somali text type.[6] Type 1 is extremely involved (dimension 1) and unelaborated structurally (dimension 2) but moderately reported (dimension 3), narrative (dimension 4), and directive/interactive (dimension 5). Type 2 is similarly involved, unelaborated lexically, and directive/interactive, but these characterizations are not as extreme as in type 1. Further, type 2 is moderately argumentative (dimension 3) and unmarked along the narrative dimension. Types 3 and 4 have opposite characteristics to types 1 and 2: they are both elaborated structurally (dimension 1), elaborated lexically (dimension 2), non-narrative (D4), and not directive/interactive (D5). These two types differ from one another in that text type 4 is extremely elaborated lexically (D2) and quite argumentative (D3), while type 3 is less elaborated lexically (D2) and reported rather than argumentative

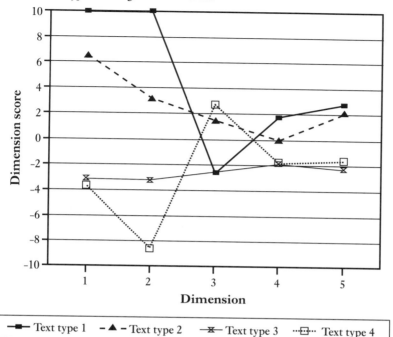

Figure 9.5 Multidimensional profile of Somali text types 1–4.
Dimension 1: 'Structural Elaboration: Involvement versus Exposition'
Dimension 2: 'Lexical Elaboration: On-line versus Planned/Integrated Production'
Dimension 3: 'Argumentative versus Reported Presentation of Information'
Dimension 4: 'Narrative versus Non-narrative Discourse Organization'
Dimension 5: 'Distanced, Directive Interaction'

(D3). Text type 5, plotted on figure 9.6, is most marked in being extremely reported (D3); this text type is additionally quite elaborated structurally, unelaborated lexically, non-narrative, and not directive/interactive. Type 6 is the least marked type in the Somali analysis: it is moderately elaborated structurally, argumentative, non-narrative, and not directive/interactive; the only distinctive characteristic of type 6 is that it is quite unelaborated lexically (D2). Somali text type 7 is unmarked along dimensions 1 and 5, it is moderately elaborated lexically and reported, but it is marked as being extremely narrative on dimension 4. Finally, text type 8 is moderately involved and non-narrative, but it is marked as extremely directive and interactive along dimension 5.

The composition of each Somali text type is summarized in table 9.6,

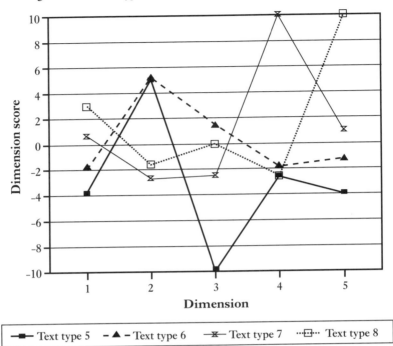

Figure 9.6 Multidimensional profile of Somali text types 5–8.
Dimension 1: 'Structural Elaboration: Involvement versus Exposition'
Dimension 2: 'Lexical Elaboration: On-line versus Planned/Integrated Production'
Dimension 3: 'Argumentative versus Reported Presentation of Information'
Dimension 4: 'Narrative versus Non-narrative Discourse Organization'
Dimension 5: 'Distanced, Directive Interaction'

which also includes functional labels. With this background, we can proceed to a more detailed interpretation of these types.

9.2.3.1 Somali text types 1 and 2: 'Interpersonal versus Informational Interaction'

As noted above, Somali text types 1 and 2 are similar in being involved, non-elaborated lexically, and moderately directive/interactive. Text type 1 is distinguished from type 2 in that it has extreme characterizations on dimensions 1 and 2, reflecting a very frequent use of involved features with little structural elaboration (dimension 1) and extensive vocabulary repetition coupled with little lexical elaboration (dimension 2). Table 9.6 shows that there are only five texts grouped in text type 1, and that they are all conversational (three direct conversations and two conversational narratives). This text type can thus be interpreted as a kind of direct interaction which focuses on the interpersonal relationship and the expression of personal feelings and attitudes.

In contrast, Somali text type 2 can be interpreted as a kind of interaction having an informational focus. Linguistically, this type is less involved than type 1, and it is considerably more elaborated lexically than type 1 (although it is still unelaborated lexically relative to other text types); type 2 is also moderately argumentative, as opposed to the reported orientation of text type 1. Table 9.6 shows that this type comprises a wider range of texts and registers, including most of the face-to-face conversations and conversational narratives, all of the family meetings, as well as conference discussions, Quranic sermons, and Quranic expositions. These are all spoken texts, in which the speaker shows a high degree of involvement and is eager to express personal opinions. Type 2 is more informational in focus than type 1, though. In family meetings, the focus is directed towards solving short-term financial needs and developing long-term plans for the family (see samples 6.33 and 6.34 in chapter 6). In conference discussions, that focus is directed towards a particular academic issue. In conversations and conversational narratives, the informational focus can range over a wide range of topics, including gossip concerning particular individuals (see sample 6.29) or narration and discussion of past events. These are all in contrast to the marked interpersonal focus of interactions grouped in type 1, reflecting a distinction between these two basic kinds of interaction similar to that distinguishing between English text types 1 and 2.

9.2.3.2 Somali text types 3, 4, and 5: 'Non-fictional Prose Types'

A look at the composition of Somali text types 3, 4, and 5 (table 9.6) shows that the texts in all three types are almost entirely from written, non-fictional registers. There are notable differences among the three types, however. Type 3 comprises a majority of the texts from government memos, press announcements, sports reviews, and official petitions, as well as several texts from press reportage, letters to the editor, and book introductions. Text type 4 shows a quite different composition by register, having a majority of the texts from analytical and general press articles, editorials, (published) political speeches, book introductions, and propaganda pamphlets. Text type 5 includes only press reportage articles from the front page of the daily newspaper. Linguistically, figures 9.5 and 9.6 show that all three of these text types are elaborated structurally (dimension 1), non-narrative (dimension 4), and

Table 9.6 *Summary of the Somali text types. (Table gives the number of texts in each text type, the percentage of texts from each register occurring in that text type, and a multi-dimensional characterization of the text type. * marks cases where more than 50 percent of a register occurs in a single text type)*

Type 1:   Intimate Interpersonal Interaction (5 texts)

Composition by register

3   Face-to-face conversations (14 percent)
2   Conversational narratives (10 percent)

Dimension characteristics

Dimension 1:   Extremely involved (+12.0)
Dimension 2:   Extremely unelaborated lexically (+9.5)
Dimension 3:   Moderately reported (−3.0)
Dimension 4:   Moderately narrative (+1.0)
Dimension 5:   Directive and interactive (+2.5)

Type 2:   Informational Interaction (54 texts)

Composition by register

18   Face-to-face conversations (86 percent) *
15   Conversational narratives (75 percent) *
 9   Family meetings (100 percent) *
 4   Conference discussions (40 percent)
 3   Quranic sermons (30 percent)
 3   Quranic expositions (30 percent)
 1   University lectures (10 percent)
 1   Formal meeting (9 percent)

Dimension Characteristics

Dimension 1:   Very involved (+8.0)
Dimension 2:   Unelaborated lexically (+3.0)
Dimension 3:   Argumentative (+2.0)
Dimension 4:   Unmarked (0.0)
Dimension 5:   Moderately directive & interactive (+2.0)

Type 3:   Specialized Reported Prose (57 texts)

Composition by register

8   Memos (80 percent) *
8   Press announcements (80 percent) *
7   Sports reviews (88 percent) *
6   Academic theses (60 percent) *
6   Press reportage (43 percent)
5   Petitions (63 percent) *
4   Editorials (40 percent)
2   Book introductions (40 percent)

Table 9.6 (*Cont.*)

Type 3 (cont.)
    2 Letters to the editor (40 percent)
    2 Textbooks (20 percent)
    2 Academic essays (20 percent)
    1 Political speech (20 percent)
    1 General press article (17 percent)
    1 Conference lecture (10 percent)
    1 Analytical press article (9 percent)
    1 Fictional story (8 percent)

Dimension characteristics

Dimension 1: Very elaborated structurally (−4.0)
Dimension 2: Elaborated lexically (−3.0)
Dimension 3: Reported (−3.0)
Dimension 4: Non-narrative (−1.0)
Dimension 5: Not directive and interactive (−2.0)

Type 4: Specialized Argumentative and Informational Prose (40 texts)

Composition by register

    10 Analytical press articles (91 percent) *
     6 Editorials (60 percent) *
     5 General press articles (83 percent) *
     4 Political speeches (80 percent) *
     3 Book introductions (60 percent) *
     2 Propaganda pamphlets (67 percent) *
     2 Letters to the editor (40 percent)
     2 Academic essays (20 percent)
     2 Formal meetings (18 percent)
     1 Press announcement (10 percent)
     1 Academic thesis (10 percent)
     1 Quranic exposition (10 percent)
     1 Fictional story (8 percent)

Dimension characteristics

Dimension 1: Very elaborated structurally (−4.5)
Dimension 2: Extremely elaborated lexically (−8.0)
Dimension 3: Very argumentative (+3.5)
Dimension 4: Non-narrative (−1.0)
Dimension 5: Not directive and interactive (−1.5)

not directive/interactive (dimension 5). They show striking differences with respect to dimensions 2 and 3, though. Text type 3 is elaborated lexically and has a marked reported characterization; text type 4 is extremely elaborated lexically and quite argumentative rather than reported; text type 5 is very *un*elaborated lexically and has an extremely reported characterization. Text

Table 9.6 (*cont.*)

Type 5: Popular Reported Prose (8 texts)

Composition by register

8 Press reportage (57 percent) *

Dimension characteristics

Dimension 1: Very elaborated structurally (−4.5)
Dimension 2: Very unelaborated lexically (+5.0)
Dimension 3: Extremely reported (−12.0)
Dimension 4: Non-narrative (−1.5)
Dimension 5: Strongly not directive and interactive (−3.5)

Type 6: General Argumentative (Spoken) Exposition (69 texts)

Composition by register

10 Sports broadcasts (100 percent) *
9 Conference lectures (90 percent) *
8 Textbooks (80 percent) *
8 Formal meetings (73 percent) *
6 University lectures (60 percent) *
6 Academic essays (60 percent) *
5 Conference discussions (50 percent) *
4 Quranic expositions (40 percent)
3 Petitions (38 percent)
3 Academic theses (30 percent)
2 Quranic sermons (20 percent)
2 Memos (20 percent)
1 Propaganda pamphlet (33 percent)
1 Letter to the editor (20 percent)
1 Press announcement (10 percent)

Dimension characteristics

Dimension 1: Elaborated structurally (−2.0)
Dimension 2: Very unelaborated lexically (+5.0)
Dimension 3: Argumentative (+2.0)
Dimension 4: Non-narrative (−1.0)
Dimension 5: Not directive and interactive (−1.0)

---

type 4 characteristics are illustrated by text sample 6.31 (from an editorial) in chapter 6, while text type 5 characteristics are illustrated by samples 6.32 and 6.35 (both from front-page press reportage).

Text type 5, which can be interpreted as 'Popular Reported Prose', represents a straight reportage of past events, with no discussion of alternative possibilities or logical implications. These texts are quite unelaborated lexically, having a restricted vocabulary with few derived forms. They appear

Table 9.6 (cont.)

Type 7:   Imaginative Narrative (33 texts)

Composition by register

10 Fictional stories (83 percent) *
 7 Serial stories (100 percent) *
 4 Folk stories (100 percent) *
 4 Quranic sermons (40 percent)
 3 University lectures (30 percent)
 2 Quranic expositions (20 percent)
 1 Sports review (13 percent)
 1 Conference discussion (10 percent)
 1 Conversational narrative (5 percent)

Dimension characteristics

Dimension 1: Moderately involved (+1.0)
Dimension 2: Elaborated lexically (−2.5)
Dimension 3: Reported (−3.0)
Dimension 4: Extremely narrative (+6.0)
Dimension 5: Moderately directive and interactive (+1.0)

Type 8:   Distanced Directive Interaction (13 texts)

Composition by register

10 Personal letters (100 percent) *
 2 Conversational narratives (10 percent)
 1 Quranic sermon (10 percent)

Dimension characteristics

Dimension 1: Involved (+3.5)
Dimension 2: Moderately elaborated lexically (−1.5)
Dimension 3: Unmarked (0.0)
Dimension 4: Non-narrative (−1.5)
Dimension 5: Extremely directive and interactive (+9.0)

on the front page of the daily newspaper (*Xiddigta Oktoobar*) and include only articles written by the local Somali news agency (SONNA). Thus, type 5 texts are intended to be accessible to a wide, popular readership.

Longer articles appearing on the inside pages of the same newspaper, which constitute many of the texts grouped in type 4, have the opposite linguistic characterizations with respect to dimensions 2 and 3: they are extremely elaborated lexically, and they are quite argumentative rather than reported. The texts in type 4 are thus much more specialized in their intended audience and purpose, much more informational in focus, and overtly argumentative rather than reported. Reflecting these linguistic and situational characteristics, type 4 is labeled 'Specialized Argumentative and Informational Prose.'

Type 3 texts are also specialized, although to a lesser extent than type 4. This type includes many texts from newspaper registers such as press announcements and sports reviews, which are intended for a wider audience than the highly specialized analytical articles and editorials grouped on type 4. Similarly, government memos are generally intended to have a wide circulation. Reflecting these purposes, type 3 texts are less elaborated lexically than type 4 texts, although they are much more elaborated than the press reportage texts grouped in type 5. The main difference between types 3 and 4 is an argumentative versus reported stance. Type 3 texts simply report information: policy statements in memos; announcements of current events in press announcements; or simple descriptions in sports reviews, academic theses, press reports, and editorials. The interpretive label 'Specialized Reported Prose' reflects these characteristics of type 3.

Types 3, 4, and 5 are all composed of written, non-fictional prose texts. Linguistically, these three types are distinguished from the other Somali text types by being very elaborated structurally, reflecting the importance of careful production circumstances and a primary informational focus. At the same time, this section has discussed important distinctions among these three text types, showing that the intended audience and primary purpose of communication can be powerful determinants of systematic linguistic differences among texts, apart from physical mode considerations.

9.2.3.3 Somali text type 6: 'General Argumentative (Spoken) Exposition'

Linguistically, text type 6 shows some similarities to types 3–5 (see figure 9.6). It is not involved, non-narrative, and not directive/interactive. It is elaborated structurally but to a lesser extent than types 3–5. It is very unelaborated lexically, similar to the popular reportage in type 5, but it is argumentative in orientation, similar to the texts grouped in type 4.

Table 9.6 shows that the texts grouped into type 6 are mostly produced in the spoken mode but with various informational emphases: sports broadcasts report events in progress; conference lectures, university lectures, and conference discussions focus on academic topics; formal meetings deal with institutional and social issues; Quranic expositions and sermons focus on religious topics. In addition, there are informational texts from written registers grouped on this text type: a majority of the texts from school textbooks and academic essays, plus some petitions, academic theses, and memos. Considering both the linguistic characteristics and the composition by register, text type 6 can be interpreted as a general type of informational and argumentative exposition. This type includes nearly all informational exposition in the spoken mode, indicating a very strong association between a spoken presentation of information and an argumentative orientation in Somali.[7] Text sample 6.30, in chapter 6, illustrates these characteristics from a university lecture. In addition, various types of academic writing show similar linguistic characteristics. In particular, school textbooks and academic essays show a high degree of lexical repetition and an argumentative orientation: technical terms are often repeated in these registers, resulting in relatively little lexical diversity, while the argumentative orientation reflects a deliberate comparison of various logical possibilities (similar to text type 4). Some academic theses have similar characteristics, although most theses in Somali tend to be more elaborated lexically and more reported in orientation, resulting in their being grouped on text type 3.

In sum, type 6 reflects the kinds of informational exposition typical of the spoken mode, while showing that similar linguistic characteristics can be common in certain kinds of written exposition as well.

9.2.3.4 Somali text type 7: 'Imaginative Narrative'

The interpretation of text type 7 is straightforward: as table 9.6 shows, all serial stories and folk stories, as well as the large majority of general fiction stories, are grouped into this type. Linguistically, figure 9.6 shows that the texts in this type are moderately involved, elaborated lexically, reported in orientation, and directive/interactive, but they are most marked by being extremely narrative along dimension 4. Thus, these are texts that rely on a narrative discourse organization, primarily various kinds of imaginative fiction. The characteristics of this type are illustrated in text samples 6.36 and 6.37 from folk stories (in chapter 6). In addition, there are some more informational, spoken texts grouped in this type: Quranic sermons and expositions, and university lectures. These groupings show that it is possible to adopt narration as an effective means of spoken instruction, using stories to convey various lessons and morals in non-fictional texts.

It is interesting to contrast types 3, 5, and 7, since all three of these text types are reported in orientation (along dimension 3). However, types 3 and 5 are similar to one another, and different from type 7, in adopting a non-narrative discourse organization and being elaborated structurally; in contrast, type 7 texts are extremely narrative, and moderately involved rather than elaborated structurally. With respect to lexical elaboration, type 7 is similar to type 3 in being relatively elaborated, in contrast to the notable lack of lexical elaboration characterizing type 5. Type 7 demonstrates again the importance of purpose – in this case the narration of past events in stories – in defining the linguistically determined text types of Somali.

9.2.3.5 Somali text type 8: 'Distanced Directive Interaction'

All personal letters are grouped into text type 8, representing interactive communication carried out in the written mode over great distance. Linguistically, these texts are involved, moderately elaborated in their lexical characteristics, non-narrative, and extremely directive/interactive. These characteristics are illustrated by text sample 6.38 in chapter 6. Text type 8 thus represents distanced, directive interaction, reflecting the task-oriented nature of interpersonal communication in letters, as well as the fact that addressors separated physically from their addressees can be overtly directive without threatening face or being considered impolite.[8]

9.3   Cross-linguistic comparison of the text typologies of English and Somali

The salient text type distinctions in a language reflect the underlying multidimensional profile of the language. That is, text types are distinguished from one another by their linguistic characteristics, as represented in their multidimensional characterizations. For this reason, the salient text type distinctions in a language also reflect the underlying functional priorities of the language (see section 7.1.10). For example, English and Somali both have multiple dimensions distinguishing among various kinds of informational discourse, and correspondingly they each have multiple text types that are in some way informational. Similarly, English and Somali both have a dimension relating to persuasion and argumentation, and at least one text type in each language is marked for these characteristics. English has an idiosyncratic dimension relating to abstract style (D5), and 'Scientific Exposition', text type 3, is marked for the frequent use of these features. Somali has an idiosyncratic dimension relating to distanced, directive interaction (D5), and Somali text type 8 is marked with respect to that dimension. Korean and Nukulaelae Tuvaluan would probably have a somewhat different set of text types: for example, Korean would likely have text types differing in their personal stance, reflecting the extensive allocation of linguistic resources to the marking of stance and honorification in that language.

Although the text types of a language reflect the underlying multidimensional profile, there is no one-to-one correspondence between text types and dimensions. Some dimensions are instrumental in distinguishing among multiple text types, while others are important only in relation to a single type. For example, dimension 1 in English distinguishes between two types of interactive discourse (interpersonal and informational), and it further distinguishes both of these text types from other informational, expository text types. Dimension 1 in Somali is instrumental in defining a similar set of text type distinctions. Dimension 3 in Somali ('Argumentative versus Reported Presentation') is important in distinguishing among all four Somali expository text types, which are marked as either argumentative or reported. In contrast, the functionally similar dimension 4 in English ('Overt Expression of Argumentation') is instrumental only in marking English text type 8 as being extremely persuasive; the other English types are unmarked or simply non-persuasive with respect to this dimension.

In fact, there is a multitude of text types that could be distinguished in terms of five underlying dimensions: for example, even if we used only three values along each dimension – large positive, unmarked, and large negative – there would be 243 logically possible text types that could be distinguished by five underlying dimensions.[9] The fact that there are far fewer underlying salient text types in these languages, and that there are striking similarities in the text types distinguished within English and Somali, reinforces the conclusions of earlier chapters that there are powerful communicative factors functioning to constrain the patterns of variation among texts.

The typologies developed here are relatively complex, and sometimes the resulting text types are surprising. For the most part, however, similar distinctions are made within English and Somali. For example, in both English and Somali there is no single interactive or dialogue text type. In English, there are two major interactive types: Intimate Interpersonal Interaction (type 1) and Informational Interaction (type 2). In Somali, there are three major interactive types: Intimate Interpersonal Interaction (type 1), which is similar to English type 1; Informational Interaction (type 2), which is similar to English type 2; and Distanced Directive Interaction (type 8), which is a kind of distanced interaction across time and space represented primarily by personal letters.

English and Somali are also similar in showing the importance of multiple expository text types. The analysis of English identifies three expository types: 'Scientific' Exposition (type 3), Learned Exposition (type 4), and General Reported Exposition (type 6). There are four expository types distinguished in Somali: Specialized Reported Prose (type 3), Specialized Argumentative and Informational Prose (type 4), Popular Reported Prose (type 5), and General Argumentative (Spoken) Exposition (type 6).

In the same way, there is no single narrative text type in English, and characterizations as 'reported' and 'narrative' show a complex interaction in Somali. English has two narrative text types: General Reported Exposition (type 6), which combines an expository, informational focus with narrative discourse organizations, and Imaginative Narrative (type 5), which is a relatively involved text type having a primary narrative orientation. In Somali, there are two expository text types having a reported orientation but not marked for the use of narrative features (text types 3 and 5); these are distinct from Imaginative Narrative (type 7), which is marked as reported in orientation as well as extremely narrative.

The marking of persuasion/argumentation is also important in the text type distinctions of both languages. English text type 8 is labeled 'Involved Persuasion'; these are texts with a primary argumentative and persuasive purpose, which are typically involved in presentation. In Somali, most text types are marked as either argumentative or reported: Intimate Interpersonal Interaction (type 1) is reported, while Informational Interaction (type 2) is argumentative; types 3 and 5 are reported kinds of exposition, while types 4 and 6 are argumentative types of exposition; Imaginative Narrative (type 7) is reported and fictional.

Surprisingly, both English and Somali have only one idiosyncratic text type with no counterpart in the other language. In English, text type 7 is labeled 'Situated Reportage' and includes texts that report events actually in progress. In Somali, text type 8 is labeled 'Distanced Directive Interaction', representing the distinctive kind of communication common in Somali letters. The other text types have corresponding types in the typologies of English and Somali, suggesting that a relatively closed set of communicative functions are well represented linguistically across languages.

In earlier chapters, it was noted that text typologies are needed as a theoretical basis for discourse and register studies. The typologies developed here are immediately useful in this regard. For instance, numerous studies have described discourse characteristics of 'narrative' or 'exposition' – but the typologies of both English and Somali show that there is no single narrative or expository type. Rather, there are multiple narrative types and multiple expository types in both languages; these have different linguistic and communicative characteristics, and each deserves study on its own terms.

These typologies also show that the relationship between registers and text types is not straightforward, but they do not invalidate register distinctions. Register and text type categorizations have different theoretical bases; they are both valid but distinct constructs. As noted in earlier chapters, registers correspond directly to the text distinctions recognized by mature adult speakers, reflecting important differences in the situation of use; they are defined on the basis of systematic non-linguistic criteria, and they are valid in those terms. Text types, on the other hand, are defined on the basis of strictly linguistic criteria. Text types often cut across register categorizations. For example, in both English and Somali, face-to-face conversations are grouped into text types 1 and 2. In English, academic prose texts are split among types 3, 4, 6, and 8. In Somali, press reportage texts are split between types 3 and 5; academic essays are split among types 3, 4, and 6. Although the texts in these registers are similar in their non-linguistic characteristics, they belong to different 'types' in terms of their linguistic characteristics. The two perspectives are thus complementary.

By focusing on linguistic co-occurrence patterns, rather than the distribution of individual features, these typologies identify some surprisingly subtle functional distinctions among texts. For instance, relative differences in the use of dimension 1 features, in both English and Somali, correspond to the subtle functional differences between type 1 and type 2 in the two languages: both types are interactional, but type 1 is strictly interpersonal while type 2 is more informational. In English, differences in the use of dimension 5 features reflect the specialized functional distinction between type 3 and type 4: both types are informational and expository, but type 3 is abstract in style and represents technical specializations while type 4 is non-abstract in style and represents specializations in humanities and the social sciences. In Somali, differences with respect to the lexical elaboration dimension (dimension 2) correspond to degrees of specialization in purpose and audience: types 3 and 4 are specialized and elaborated lexically; types 5 and 6 are more general in audience and purpose and not elaborated lexically.

The text types identified here might be more accurately referred to as 'prototypes.' That is, these types represent the 'typical' text forms (and corresponding functions) that are well defined linguistically in English and Somali. However, these text types do not represent absolute distinctions among texts. That is, the linguistic variation among the texts of a language constitutes a continuous multidimensional space, and text types are dense concentrations of texts within that space. It is theoretically possible for a text to have any score on each dimension, defining a continuous, multidimensional space of variation. It turns out, though, that there are regions that have very high concentrations of texts within that space, and these regions are identified as the text prototypes of a language. In between these prototypes, there are particular texts that combine functional emphases and linguistic forms in complex and relatively idiosyncratic ways. These texts are not aberrations; rather, they reflect the fact that speakers and writers exploit the linguistic resources of their language in a continuous manner.

There are thus three complementary perspectives on linguistic variation among texts. The first perspective compares the linguistic characteristics of registers, which are defined in terms of non-linguistic characteristics. The second perspective focuses on the continuous nature of text variation – showing how it is theoretically possible for a text to represent any combination of linguistic characteristics from multiple dimensions. Finally, the third perspective, which forms the basis of the present chapter, identifies the relatively few distinct text types that are well represented linguistically within a language and across languages.

In theory, texts could be evenly distributed across possible linguistic and functional characterizations. This turns out not to be the case, however. Rather, the majority of texts are distributed across a few well-defined form/function groupings, and these marked concentrations of texts are interpreted as the major text types of a language. Further, it turns out that very similar kinds of text types are well defined in both English and Somali, raising the possibility of a universal text typology that will hold cross-linguistically. This finding echoes the suggestion raised within comparative sublanguage research on English and French, that 'parallel sublanguages ... [across languages] ... are much more similar structurally than are dissimilar sublanguages of the same language' (Kittredge 1982: 108). The analyses here indicate that these generalizations hold at a high level of generality, and that they hold for interpersonal, conversational text types as well as for more informational, expository types. That is, the text types identified here reflect strong tendencies for speakers and writers to construct texts around a limited set of functions and co-occurring linguistic forms. These typologies thus give structure to the multidimensional space of textual variation, even though they do not negate the continuous nature of that space.

10 Towards cross-linguistic universals of register variation

The preceding chapters have shown that the patterns of linguistic variation among texts are strikingly similar across languages. These cross-linguistic similarities hold at several levels:

1. for the co-occurrence patterns among linguistic features, and the ways in which features function together as underlying dimensions;
2. for the synchronic relations among registers within a language, including the multidimensional characteristics of particular registers, and the patterns of variation among registers;
3. for the diachronic patterns of change within and among registers, in response to changing communicative needs and circumstances following the introduction of written registers in a society;
4. for the text types that are well defined linguistically.

Given the strength of these patterns, it is reasonable to hold out the possibility of cross-linguistic universals governing the patterns of discourse variation across registers and text types. However, considerable additional research is required to determine which of the cross-linguistic generalizations identified in the present study are valid as universals, and to formulate more precise statements of those relationships.

One of the most important issues requiring further investigation is the role of literacy in defining the synchronic and diachronic patterns of register variation. From a synchronic perspective, differences in the repertoire of written registers correspond to different multidimensional profiles across languages: for example, the register and text type analyses of English, Korean, and Somali show that written registers – informational and expository registers as well as fiction and letters – vary systematically along several underlying dimensions. Further, the different kinds of writing show different relations to different kinds of speaking along each dimension. In contrast, the patterns of variation are somewhat restricted in Nukulaelae Tuvaluan, apparently due to the restricted repertoire of written and spoken registers. It is thus possible that there will be some cross-linguistic generalizations that hold only for languages with a relatively developed repertoire of registers, while other generalizations hold for register variation in all languages. To investigate this possibility, we need studies of additional languages from all stages of literacy development, including languages with an extensive repertoire of written registers, languages with minimally developed written traditions, and languages with no written registers at all.

The influence of literacy from a diachronic perspective also needs further investigation. The historical patterns documented for English and Somali show that the initial introduction of written registers in a language is accompanied by an extension in the range of linguistic variation along several dimensions; the subsequent development of written registers continues to extend that range of variation. At present, we do not know the ways in which spoken registers develop in response to the functional pressures associated with literacy, although the comparison of dramatic dialogue from earlier periods to present-day conversation suggests that at least some spoken registers are quite stable in their linguistic characteristics.

In addition, we do not know to what extent spoken registers change in oral cultures. There are several different language situations to be investigated in this regard. First, we need studies of register variation in oral cultures that are completely isolated from the social/communicative pressures associated with literacy. A related situation involves speech communities that use a first language for spoken, primarily interactional, purposes, and a second language for institutional and written purposes. These situations are typically regarded as diglossic (see Hudson 1994); diachronically the first language is often 'dying' and is thus associated with a reduction rather than expansion in the range of register variation (see Dorian 1994).

At the other extreme are oral cultures in the process of adding institutional spoken registers, such as radio broadcasts and debates in parliament; these spoken registers often precede the introduction of expository written registers in a language. One important question in these situations is the extent to which the changes accompanying the introduction of institutional spoken registers parallel those that accompany the introduction of institutional written registers. (Chapter 8 indicates that written registers are already quite different from institutional spoken registers when they first enter a language.)

One of the most pressing issues associated with literacy concerns the influence of foreign models. Two separate kinds of analysis are required here: empirical investigations of register variation in contact languages, and analyses of register variation in languages that have not been influenced by contact with other literate traditions.

First, we need empirical investigations of the extent to which the early development of written registers in a language is shaped by the functional and linguistic characteristics of pre-existing foreign models. When written registers enter a language having a pre-existing literate tradition, they can build upon the linguistic and functional bases provided by foreign models; this social history can explain in part why written registers in English and Somali are already quite different from typical spoken registers in the earliest periods of their development. For English, this issue could be investigated through a comparative analysis of academic and institutional registers in Latin and French in historical periods preceding the eighteenth century. Similar analyses of register variation in Arabic, Italian, and English would provide the required basis of comparison for Somali.

In addition, we need both synchronic and diachronic analyses of register variation in cultures that do not already have a well-established literate tradition based on foreign models. Given the current ease of travel and international communication, it is unlikely that languages in the future will develop written registers without being influenced by the literate tradition in some other language. However, classical languages such as Greek and Chinese represent quite different situations. In these cases, written registers without foreign precedents were developed for the first time. Further, in both of these cases the repertoire of written registers continued to expand over time to include a wide range of registers used for different purposes and addressed to different audiences. It is thus possible that the introduction and subsequent development of written registers in such situations depended to a greater extent on pre-existing spoken registers than in modern-day language situations influenced by contact with foreign models.

A final question relating to the influence of literacy is the extent to which individual development parallels the patterns of societal development. Several studies have discussed children's acquisition of register distinctions and the ways in which students develop control of written registers in school (e.g., Britton *et al.* 1975; Perera 1984; Romaine 1984; Andersen 1990). More recently, Reppen (1994) uses the MD approach to provide a comprehensive analysis of variation among students' spoken and written registers. The first step in that study was to identify and interpret the underlying dimensions of variation distinguishing among fifth grade registers. This step is based on analysis of a large corpus of student texts, including spoken registers (dialogue and monologue), written registers (school-related writing tasks), and school registers such as science textbooks, social science textbooks, basal readers, and children's literature. Five basic dimensions are identified: 'Edited Informational Discourse versus On-line Informational Discourse', 'Lexically Elaborated Narrative versus Non-narrative Discourse', 'Involved Personal Opinion versus Non-personal, Uninvolved Discourse', 'Projected Scenario', and 'Other-directed Idea Justification/Explanation'. These dimensions are then used to address a number of developmental issues relating to the acquisition of register knowledge, including: a comparison of fifth grade and adult patterns of register variation; a comparison of student written registers across grades 3, 5, and 6; and a developmental comparison of student written registers produced by different demographic groups (e.g., middle class versus working class, L1 versus L2, male versus female).

A comparison of the major findings of Reppen (1994) with chapters 6–8 of the present study indicates that there are important parallels as well as important differences between the evolution of written registers within a language/society and the acquisition of written registers by elementary students. First, both the adult and the student MD analyses have major dimensions relating to edited versus on-line production circumstances, involvement, personal stance, and narrative discourse. Both analyses also have idiosyncratic dimensions: relating to 'abstract style' for the adults, and relating to 'projected scenario' and 'other-directed idea justification' for the fifth graders. Developmentally, registers that have evolved historically towards more popular 'oral' styles (e.g., narrative registers such as fiction, and registers of personal expression such as letters and diaries) correspond to the kinds of writing that students learn to control relatively early (i.e., narrative tasks). Conversely, those registers that have evolved towards more specialist 'literate' styles (e.g., science prose) have counterparts in expository or explanatory registers that are acquired relatively late by students (see Reppen and Biber 1994 for a fuller discussion).

The MD framework presented here can additionally be used to investigate several other kinds of variation. One of the most important of these other areas of research is the analysis of social dialect variation. Most previous variationist studies in sociolinguistics have been restricted to consideration of a few individual linguistic features (usually phonetic characteristics). To date, there have been few comprehensive descriptions of a social dialect, and few macroscopic analyses of the relations among dialects. In addition, most previous studies of social variation consider only a restricted range of register (or 'style') variation. Because of these restrictions, it has been difficult to empirically assess the inter-relations among the patterns of dialect variation and register variation.

In contrast, the MD approach could be used for comprehensive descriptions of social dialects, including multidimensional characterizations of the range of spoken and written registers within and across dialects. Such analyses would be based on the full range of linguistic variation in a language (represented by the dimensions of variation), and they would encompass the full range of social and situational variation. Previous research comparing the distribution of linguistic features across registers and dialects has shown that the differences among registers are more extensive than the differences among social dialects. This finding, coupled with the fact that the patterns of register variation are functionally motivated, suggests that the patterns of social variation are derivative from the patterns of register variation (see Finegan and Biber 1994). By providing comprehensive linguistic descriptions of the range of social dialects and registers in a speech community, MD analyses would provide the empirical foundation required to fully investigate theoretical issues of this type.

Finally, Multi-Dimensional analyses should prove to be useful for sublanguage research in computational linguistics. For example, previous researchers have posited the existence of distinctive grammars for different sublanguages (e.g., Grishman and Kittredge 1986 ix), and they have shown how prior analysis of these grammars can facilitate natural-language processing applications (e.g., Sager 1986). Such research leads to the question of whether the sublanguage of a text can be automatically identified (Slocum 1986: 195). Further, while some sublanguage studies have recognized the importance of linguistic co-occurrence patterns, they have not to date developed a comprehensive methodology for the analysis of such relations. The Multi-Dimensional framework provides the tools needed for such analyses. For example, Biber (1993b) shows how the text type of a text can be predicted automatically based on the MD profile of the text. In addition, the cross-linguistic investigations presented in chapters 7–9 show that there are systematic regularities in the patterns of register variation across languages, when they are analyzed from a multidimensional perspective. These generalizations raise the likelihood that the Multi-Dimensional framework will prove useful in text categorization for automated translation projects.

The analyses presented here can be extended in several ways. Additional registers in all of these languages could be included. For example, analysis of verse registers, which have been systematically excluded here, would provide a complementary perspective on the early history of written (and spoken) registers in these languages. Analysis of registers such as e-mail would enable consideration of the functional and linguistic characteristics associated with new communication technologies. Additional linguistic features could also be included in future analyses. For example, features relating to information structure, cohesion, coherence, and rhetorical organization could be added to the multidimensional analyses of all of these languages, possibly resulting in the identification of additional dimensions.

Most importantly, there is need for MD analyses of additional languages, representing different spoken and written repertoires, different literacy traditions, different language types, etc. Such analyses are required to investigate the extent to which the synchronic and diachronic patterns found in the present study hold generally across languages. The analyses presented here, however, firmly establish the importance of the Multi-Dimensional research framework, and hold out the possibility of universal patterns of register variation across languages.

Appendix I
Grammatical description of linguistic features in Korean

Yong-Jin Kim

For the sake of presentation, the features of Korean are grouped under nine major categories: lexical elaboration, syntactic complexity, information structure, situation markers, sociolinguistic indicators, cohesion markers, tense-aspect markers, sentence type, and stance markers. This grouping has no influence on the factorial structure and underlying dimensions of Korean discussed in chapters 5–6.

A.   Lexical elaboration (1–11)

1   Attributive adjectives
The grammatical category of adjective is more complex in Korean than in English. In Korean, the predicate form is different from the attributive form and behaves like a copula.

1   Ce ai-nun   meli-ka   *cohta.*
that child-TOP head-SUBJ good
'That child is smart.'

versus

2   meli-ka   *cohun* ai
head-SUBJ good   child
'A child who is smart ← A child whose head is good.'

When used attributively, adjectives behave in a similar way to English adjectives modifying head nouns. Thus, the total number of attributive adjectives indicates the degree of nominal modification.

2   Derived adjectives
This is a special type of attributive adjective. Derived adjectives are derived from nouns with the suffixation of *-uj* 'of +' or *-cek(in)* '-tic/-ish'.

3   Manner or degree adverbs

As the total number of attributive adjectives indicates the degree of nominal modification, so the total number of manner and degree adverbs reflects verbal modification. There are lexical and derived adverbs included in this type. The derivational morphemes for adverbs are: -hakej, -hi, -(cek)ulo.

4   Place adverbs and nouns

Except for a few lexical adverbs such as *yeki* 'here', most place expressions are marked by nouns combined with the locative particles *ej* or *ejse*, meaning 'to', 'in', 'at', or 'on'; for example:

wi-*ej* 'above, over'
aph-*ej* 'front'

The place nouns analyzed are:

wi(ccok)	'above'
alaj(ccok)	'below'
yeph(ccok)	'beside'
twi(ccok)	'behind'
aph(ccok)	'before'
cwuwi	'around'
kunche	'near'
kyeth	'by'
pukccok	'north'
namccok	'south'
seccok	'west'
tongccok	'east'
an(ccok)	'inside'
pakk	'outside'
eti	'where'
kos	'place'
yaoj	'outside'
silnaj	'indoors'
hajoj	'overseas'
kwuknaj	'in the nation'
sok	'inside'
keth	'outside'

The lexical place adverbs are:

melli	'far'
kakkai	'near'
ili(lo)	'hither'
celi(lo)	'thither'

kuli(lo)	'thither'
yeki	'here'
ceki	'over there'
keki	'there'
koskosi	'here and there'
cipcipi	'from house to house'

5   Time adverbs or nouns

As in the case of place adverbs, some time expressions are marked by lexical adverbs, but most of these forms are nouns with the locative particle -*ej*. The following is a list of time-denoting nouns:

hwu	'afterward'
cen	'beforehand'
tocwung	'during'
cwungkan	'in the middle of'
si	'o'clock'

The number of lexical time adverbs is greater than that of place adverbs:

ilcciki	'early'
imi	'yet'
pelsse	'already'
ecej	'yesterday'
kucej	'the day before yesterday'
icej/incej	'now'
pangkum/kumpang	'just now'
onul	'today'
najil	'tomorrow'
chacha	'by and by'
taum	'next'
hwusnal	'in the future'
nul/hangsang	'always'
camsi/camk(k)an	'momentarily'
olaj/kot	'long'
elphis	'short'
yengkwuhi	'quickly'
yengyeng	'permanently/for ever'
mence	'first of all'
ilccik	'early'
kathi	'together'
hamkkej	'all at once'
hankkepenej	'afterward'
nacwung	'next'

taum kakkum	'sometimes'
majil	'everyday'
majpen	'each time'
majyang	'always'
cacwu	'often'
piloso cheum	'for the first time'
penpeni	'each time'

6   Plural marker: -tul

In Korean, there is no grammatical agreement in number or person; but
there is a way of distinguishing singular from plural: the suffix -tul is
attached to nouns and expresses plurality. It is used mainly for nouns
denoting animate objects, most typically human beings. The attachment
of the plural marker -tul is not obligatory; whereas those nouns with -tul
are unequivocally plurals, those without it can be interpreted as singular or
plural depending on the context of the sentence. For instance:

> Ku *chajk*-i   tosekwan-ej isseyo?
> that book-SUBJ library-LOC   exist
> 'Is that *book* in the library?'

> Tosekwan-ejnun Hankwuk-mal   *chajk*-i   isseyo?
> library-LOC/TOP   Korean-language book-SUBJ exist
> 'Does the library have Korean *books*?'

In some cases, sentences are ambiguous as to whether singular or plural is
meant; for example:

> Pang-ej *kulim*-i   isseyo?
> room-LOC picture-SUBJ exist
> 'Is/Are there *a picture/pictures* in the room?'

Some plural pronouns also have the plural marker -tul. In general, -tul is
used only when it is necessary to explicitly distinguish plural from singular.

7   Possessive marker: -uj

The Korean possessive marker is -uj, which is also used to mark genitive
relations. As this feature is not well established in the grammar, it sometimes
sounds unnatural in casual speech.

8   'Informal' postpositions

The postnominal particle *hako* has the same meaning as *wa/kwa* 'and.' While
wa/kwa is mode-neutral, *hako* is primarily a speech form. *Hanthej/hanthejse*
'to/from' (as dative) are other cases of speech-oriented forms. The neutral
forms are *ejkej/ejkejse*.

9   Formal conjuncts
Some conjuncts are rarely used in speech while they are very common
in writing:

kulena	'but'
mich	'and'
ttonun	'or'
kot	'that is, i.e.'
kulemulo	'therefore'

10   Contracted forms
Contracted forms of words are used in less formal situations, especially in
speech. The words that have contracted morphemes are all common words
such as *hata* 'to do.' The following is a list of such words:

Verbs

Citation	Present	Past
hata	hayeyo/hajyo	hayesseyo/hajsseyo
'to do'		
tojta	tojeyo/twajyo	tojesseyo/twajsseyo
'to become'		

(Since *hata* can be productively attached after nouns to make them verbs,
the number of contracted verbs is quite large.)

Particles

i/j	SUBJ marker
(l)ul/l	OBJ marker
(n)un/n	TOP marker
ejse/se	LOC marker 'in'
ejtaka/ejta	LOC marker 'onto'

Pronouns

ikes/ike	'this'
cekes/ceke	'that'
kukes/kuke	'it'
nwukwu/nwu	'who'
mues/mwes, mwe, mue	'what'
ce-uj/cej	'I' (humble)

Conjuncts

kulenikka/kunikka	'therefore'
kulenkolo/kolo	'therefore'
kuleh(a)cimanun/kuleh(a)ciman	'although'

Other
kes/ke   'thing'
tako hanta/tanta ⎫
tako hajyo/tajyo ⎪
lako hanta/lanta ⎬ 'say that —'
lako hajyo/lajyo ⎭
haci aniha/chi aniha   'not that —'

11   Total nouns
All nouns except derived and dependent forms are included here.

B.   Syntactic complexity (12–20)

12–13 'Long' negation and 'short' negation
There are three different negation markers in Korean (Nam and Ko 1988):
an(i), *mos*, and *mal*. Roughly, they mean 'is not', 'cannot', and 'do not'
(the negative imperative). The first two types of negation have two reflexes:
so-called long negation and short negation, or postverbal and preverbal
negation.

The negation marker *an(i)*, for example, can be used either preverbally
or postverbally, as shown below:

Na-nun hakkyo-ej ka-*ci ani* hayessta.
I-TOP   school-LOC go   NEG do-PST
'I didn't go to school.'

Na-nun hakkyo-ej *an* ka-ssta.
I-TOP   school-LOC NEG go-PST
'I didn't go to school.'

Although preverbal (or short) and postverbal (or long) negation have usually
been treated as synonyms, some linguists have found a scope difference
between them. The claim, not without controversy, is that preverbal negation
negates the VP (verb phrase), while the postverbal counterpart negates the
clausal proposition.

While these two negations are often treated as optional, it is not the case
that both forms are possible in any given context: long negation is always
acceptable whereas short negation is not. In this sense, long negation is the
default form.

14   Relative constructions
Korean does not have relative pronouns: instead, it has relative clause
markers that are added at the end of the relative clause as shown below:

[[naj-ka salangha]-*nun*] salam
I-SUBJ   love-REL   person
'the person who I love'

The kinds of relative marker are as follows:

-(u)n: past tense
-nun: non-past (present) tense
-(u)l: imperfective (future) aspect
-ten: perfective (past) aspect

15   Noun complementation

Noun complementation differs from relativization in that there is no gap or trace of the head noun inside the embedded clause; for example:

Na-nun [naj-ka cikcep ku-lul manna-*n*] *kiek*-i   epsta.
I-TOP   I-SUBJ directly he-OBJ meet-PST memory-SUBJ NOT
'I don't have *the memory that* I personally met him.'

Another notable difference is that only abstract nouns can be heads in noun complement constructions. Those nouns are:

somun 'rumor'   nangsel 'rumor'   sosik 'news'
yenlak 'message'   cilmun 'question'   poto 'report'
myenglyeng 'order'   kopajk 'confession'

16   Verbal complementation

Verbal complementation corresponds to English constructions such as *I know that his father quit the job*. In Korean, the *that*-complementizer is realized as a so-called 'dependent noun' such as *ke(s)*, *li*, *ppun*, *cwul*, *ci*, *the*, *swu*, and *nawi*.

17   Embedded question or indirect question

Another type of clausal complementation involves an interrogative complementizer: *-nunya/(u)nya*, *-nunka/(u)nka*, *-nunci/(u)nci*. These forms are similar to English 'whether' or 'if'. For example:

Emeni-ka   na-ejkej [mues-ul mekko siph*unci*]   mulessta.
mother-SUBJ I-DAT   what-OBJ to-eat want-INTERR ask-PST

18   Non-finite complementation

There are three ways for a clause to become nominalized in Korean: adding *-(u)m*, *-ki*, or *-(nu)n kes* after the clause. The last option is treated as a kind of verb complementation. The first two options represent nominalization with non-finite verbs, because tense is not obligatory in these cases. In many respects, these forms resemble English gerunds and *to*-infinitives respectively.

19   *Quotative complementation*

Quotative complementation involves a non-factive complementizer: *-ko* or *-lako*. Speech act verbs, or public verbs, are often used together with this complementizer.

20   *Sentence length*

Sentence length is measured in terms of the number of words per sentence, averaged over a text.

C.   Information structure (21–24)

21   *Passive constructions*

Passives are not as well developed in Korean as in English. There is more than one way of making basic (transitive) sentences into their passive counterparts. One of them is through the use of the infix *-hi-* (or *i/li/ki*).

capta/cap*hi*ta	'catch'/'be caught'
mekta/mek*hi*ta	'eat'/'be eaten'

This process is restricted to a limited set of verbs, which can be regarded as lexical intransitives.

Another method is to use the affix *ci* as follows:

makta/maka*ci*ta   'block'/'be blocked'

This process is relatively productive.

Finally, there are three verbs that intrinsically convey a certain extent of passiveness: *tanghata* 'adversely take the effect of,' *patta* 'receive the effect of,' and *tojta* 'become.' The verb *tojta* is often referred to as a paraphrased passive as opposed to grammatical passive.

22   *Topic marker*

Sentences may be introduced by a word or phrase specifying the topic (what the sentence is going to comment on), marked by the suffix *-(n)un*. This topic marker has thematic and contrastive functions:

Thematic use

> L.A.-*nun* kwukcej   tosi-ita.
> L.A.-TOP international city-BE
> 'Los Angeles is an international city.'

Contrastive use

> L.A.-*nun* Mikwuk-ej   issko   Seoul-*un* Hankwuk-ej issta.
> L.A.-TOP America-LOC exists-and Seoul-TOP Korea-LOC   exists
> 'LA is in America and/but Seoul is in Korea.'

23   Subject markers
In contrast to topic markers, subject markers signal the focus of information. While topic markers are the unmarked forms for copular 'be' sentences, subject markers are the unmarked forms for transitive sentences.

24   Copular construction: -ita
Sentences with the copular verb *-ita* 'be' are typically descriptive.

D.   Situation and pronominal markers (25–29)

25–26 Demonstrative or exophoric co-reference, and co-referential expression or endophoric co-reference

A large number of deictic forms are formed by combinations of a demonstrative with a noun denoting person, place, or time.

Whereas English has a two-way distinction in demonstratives, *this/these* and *that/those*, Korean has a three-way distinction. The following list shows this difference:

English	Korean
this/these	i
that/those	ce/ku

Here, Korean *i* is very much like English *this*, but English *that* has two Korean counterparts: *ce* and *ku*. Cho (1982: 18) summarizes the traditional view on this three-way distinction as follows: 'We will follow the traditional distinction among *i*, *ku*, and *ce* which is based on the concept of 'distance': *i* denotes a person or a thing proximal to the speaker, *ku* one proximal to the addressee, and *ce* one proximal neither to the speaker nor to the addressee.' Cho points out, however, that the notion of distance can be spatial, temporal, or psychological. Indeed, a psychological explanation is more appropriate for the use of *ku*. When the referent is present in the addressee's consciousness at the time of utterance (or, at least the speaker believes so), *ku* is used regardless of the physical distance. A referent can be in the addressee's consciousness if it has been previously mentioned, or if it is somehow identifiable/activatable at the time of utterance. Thus, a two-way opposition exists for these features: *ku*, marking endophoric co-reference associated with text-oriented discourse, and *i* or *ce* marking exophoric co-reference associated with situation-dependent discourse. Both of these features can be combined with place expressions (place deixis), time expressions (time deixis), or person expressions (person deixis).

27   First-person pronouns

First-person pronouns are markers of ego-involvement. In Korean, they are often omitted when they are recoverable from the context. Thus, if they are used at all, they emphasize the involvement of the speaker/author. There are two variants of each pronoun – neutral and humble:

na/naj   'I'; neutral
ce/cej   'I'; humble
wuli   'we'; neutral
cehuj   'we'; humble

28   Second-person pronouns

Second-person pronouns refer to a specific addressee and indicate a high degree of involvement with that addressee. They are frequently omitted in direct questions as first-person pronouns are in declarations. Thus, the explicit use of second-person pronouns signals an emphatic, explicit focus on the addressee. This is especially the case because there are distinctions among second-person pronouns in the extent to which they are deferential or condescending:

ne/nej   'you'; neutral
tangsin(tul) 'you'; honorific
canej(tul)   'you'; to inferior
kutaj   'you'; literate

29   Third-person pronouns

Third-person pronouns in Korean are related to demonstratives in their forms as shown below:

ku/ku i/ku pun 'he'
kunye   'she'
kutul   'they (personal)'
kukes/kukestul 'it/they (impersonal)'

The form *ku* in this series corresponds to the demonstrative form that refers to a psychologically identifiable referent (as opposed to a physically present one).

E.   Sociolinguistic indicators (30–32)

30   Honorifics

Honorifics are forms that function to express 'the speaker's deference to the referent, i.e., the person spoken of' (J. Hwang 1975: 132). Since the addressee can also be a referent, honorifics can be used to defer to either the addressee or a third person. There are several kinds of honorifics: the verbal infix -*si*-; case markers, such as the honorific subject marker -*kkejse*; the honorific nominal suffix -*nim* 'sir/ma'am'; and lexical nouns, verbs, and adjectives.

Honorific case markers are used when the speaker wants to express deference to the subject or indirect object (dative case) of a clause; direct objects cannot take an honorific case marker. The honorific verbal infix, -*si*-, is used only for subjects. The following examples illustrate these forms:

> Tajthonglyeng-*i* onul   Kimpo konghang-ej tochakha-jsssupnita.
> president-SUBJ   today Kimpo airport-LOC   arrived
> 'The president arrived at Kimpo Airport today.'

> Tajthonglyeng-*kkejse* cikum wuli cip-ej   tochakha-*sy*-esssupnita.
> president-SUBJ/HON   now   our   home-LOC arrived/HON
> 'The president arrived at my home now.'

While the first section about the president is a business-like statement, the second one is a personal account. Thus, only the second sentence uses honorific expressions: the subject marker -*kkejse* and the verbal infix -*sy*- (a variant of -*si*-). Most verbs become honorific with this infix, but a limited number of basic, frequently used verbs have lexical honorific counterparts. There are also a limited number of honorific nouns. The following chart shows examples of lexical honorific verbs and nouns:

	Meaning	*Basic*	*Honorific*
Verbs			
	'to eat'	mek-ta	capswu-si-ta
	'to sleep'	ca-ta	cwumu-si-ta
	'to exist'	iss-ta	kyej-si-ta
Nouns			
	'meal'	pap	cinci
	'age'	nai	yensej
	'talk'	mal	malssum

31   Humble expressions, or indirect honorification

With first person as the subject of a sentence, the use of 'humble verbs' shows additional deference to the addressee or to a third-person referent. Examples include *tulita* 'to give,' *mosita* 'to take care of', *pojpta* 'to see/meet,' *yeccwupta* 'to ask of/to tell.' First- and second-person pronouns also have humble reflexes.

32 Formal sentence ending or speech level 1
The term 'speech level' refers to the different grammatical expressions that a speaker can use to show different degrees of deference towards the addressee. These forms are realized as suffixes on the sentence-final verb. When a sentence has several clauses, only the last clause gets marked with a speech level. Whereas honorifics are optional in a sentence, speech level markers are obligatory. (See also J. Hwang [1975] for a fuller discussion.)

Among the various speech level markers, only level 1, or the highest deference marker, is counted as a marked form. It can signal deference or formality or both. Reflexes include *-supnita, -upnita, -pnita, -supnikka.*

F. Cohesion markers (33–43)

Two types of clause combining devices are included as cohesion markers: sentence introducers and clause connectors. Examples are given below:

Con-un   hakkyo-ej kassta. *Kulajse* Mejli-lul mannassta.
John-TOP school-to went   and-*so* Mary-OBJ met

Con-un hakkyo-ej ka*se*   Mejli-lul mannassta.
        go-and-(*so*)
'John went to school and (he) met Mary.'

Both examples have the same two clauses; in the first example, these are expressed as two separate sentences, while in the second example, the two clauses are conjoined in a single sentence. There are certain functional differences between these two constructions. The first example, with a sentence introducer, shows a more explicit clausal relationship than the second example, with a clause connector. The construction with the clause connector, on the other hand, is more conducive to the smooth flow of information: that is, for cohesion.

(33–37) Sentence introducers
Sentence introducers or conjuncts can be subdivided semantically into five categories: explanative, conditional, co-ordinative, adversative, and unspecified discourse relations.

33 Explanative conjuncts
These forms are similar in function to the conjuncts *therefore* and *thus* in English. The following words are counted:

kule(ha)ni	kule(ha)maj	kule(ha)mulo
kule(ha)ncuk	hancuk	kule(ha)nikka
hanikka	kunikka	(kulen)kolo
ttala(se)	kulajse	kule(h)ki ttajmunej

34   Conditional conjuncts

These forms mark conditional ('if . . . then') relations:
kule(ha)myen, kuleh(a)ketun, kulajya(man), kulelcintaj.

35   Co-ordinative conjuncts

These forms mark simple additive relations:

kuliko	'and'	tto	'in addition'
ku ppun anila	'not only that'	tekwuna	'moreover'
hamulmye	'still more/still less'		
kulemyense	'in so doing'	kuleca	'thereupon'
kuletaka	'in the course of that/ after that'		

36   Adversative conjunct

The adversative conjuncts (corresponding to English *however*) are *kuleh(a)ciman(un)*, *haciman(un), hana(ma), kule(ha)na, kule(ha)toj, kule(ha)lcilato, kulentej, kulelmangceng, kulelcienceng, kulajto.*

37   Unspecified discourse conjunct

The conjunct *kulentej* is peculiar in that it can mean 'and,' 'but,' or 'by the way' depending on the flow of the discourse. For this reason, this word is used commonly in most discourse situations, both in speech and in writing. Its contracted form is *kuntej* and casual form is *hantej*.

(38–43)   Clause connectors: verbal connectives

Clause connectors have the same semantic distinctions as sentence introducers; in addition, these can mark temporal relations.

38   Explanative verbal connector: 'because'
-uni, -(u)nikka, -ese, -(u)mulo, -(u)ncila, -nuncila, -kiej

39   Conditional verbal connector: 'if . . . then'
-(u)myen, -(u)l kes kathumyen, -ketun, -eya(man)

40   Co-ordinative verbal connector: 'and–then'
-ko(se), -e(se), -(u)myense, -(u)mye.

41   Adversative verbal connector: 'although'

-telato	-(u)lcilato	-(u)lmangceng	-(u)lcienceng
-ciman(un)	-kenman(un)	-keniwa	-eto
-(u)lyeniwa	-(u)lyenman(un)	-nuntej	-(u)ltoj

42   Unspecified discourse verbal connector: 'and'/'but'/'by the way'
-(n)untej.

43 Adverbial subordination: 'when . . .'/'as . . .'/'in order that'

This type of verbal connector does not have a corresponding lexical conjunct. While all the other verbal connectors are logically oriented, these connectors represent temporal relationships between clauses. Since this is a semantic characterization, paraphrased temporal connectors such as *-ul ttaj* 'when . . .' are also included here. The following list shows the connectors and their meanings:

-myense	'as . . .'/'while . . .'	-lul halyeko 'in order to/that'	
-haca	'as soon as'	-teni	'after . . .'
-n hwuej	'after . . .'	-n swunkan	'the moment when . . .'

G.   Tense-aspect markers (44–46)

44 Present or non-past tense

Present tense verbs are used to deal with topics and situations of immediate relevance. They are also used for informational presentation. In narratives, present tense is used in place of past tense to mark a change in discourse progression (Lukoff 1986).

Only matrix present tense verbs are counted. The forms are marked by *-nun* or *-n* for activity verbs and the absence of any marker for descriptive verbs.

45 Past tense

Past tense forms are most naturally associated with narratives. This tense is marked by *-ess-/-ass-/-ss-*. The so-called double past is also included here. In many cases, past tense additionally functions to mark perfective or resultative aspect in Korean.

46 Progressive constructions

The progressive form, *-ko issta*, is used for situation descriptions. There are other expressions that look like progressives but are in fact *Aktionsart* (*en*), as discussed by Comrie (1976: 6n.). The progressive *Aktionsart*, *-e/-a/-∅ kata*, is not included here.

H.   Sentence types (47–49)

47 (Direct) questions

Questions are, by nature, interpersonal since they normally require an addressee. In addition, they are used for seeking new information with the use of WH words, which are normally pronounced with stress.

48   Imperative sentences
Imperatives also presuppose an addressee. The time orientation in imperatives is either present or future.

49   Declarative sentences
This is the most unmarked, basic sentence type.

I.   Verb types (50–52)

50   Private verbs
Also called psychological verbs, this type of verb expresses human inner
thoughts and feelings; for example:

kitajhata	'expect'	kotajhata	'anticipate'
mitta	'believe'	kyelloncista	'conclude'
kyelcenghata	'decide'	ujsimhata	'doubt'
chwuchukhata/cimcakhata	'estimate'	musewehata	'fear'
nukkita	'feel'	icta/icepelita	'forget'

51   Public verb/speech act verb
A second set of verbs describes speech acts; for example:

cwucanghata 'assert'   kociphata 'insist'
pulphyenghata 'complain'   senenhata 'declare'

Other speech act verbs include: puinhata / selmyenghata / amsihata /
enkuphata / palphyohata / senphohata / yaksok hata / hangujhata / malhata /
/ tajtaphata / pokohata / iyakihata / cejanhata / cejujhata / majngsejhata

52   Action verbs or dynamic verbs
Verbs that are typically associated with dynamic action or movement are
included here.

J.   Stance markers (53–55)

Stance markers indicate the speaker's or writer's attitudes towards the
proposition or the addressee.

53   Hedging expressions
These are lexical and phrasal expressions that make propositions fuzzy or
softened. There are two main types: lexical hedges and syntactic hedges.

Lexical hedges

kkwaj	'quite/pretty'	keuj	'almost'
ama	'perhaps'	ilcong-uj	'sort of'
malhacamyen	'so to speak'	ettehkej pomyen	'in a sense'

Syntactic hedges (from J. Hwang 1975)

-iciyo	'I would say . . .'
-ikejssciyo	'I presume . . .'
-phyen-ita	'more on the side of/it is rather that . . .'
-lako hal swu issta	'we can say that . . .'
-lako pol swu issta	'it can be regarded as . . .'
-lako sajngkaktojnta	'it can be thought of as . . .'

54   *Emphatic or amplifying expressions*

Amplifiers or emphasizers have the opposite effect of hedges.

Lexical emphasizers

punmyenghi	'obviously'	mucoken	'without reservation'
hwaksilhi	'surely'	pantusi	'without fail'
thullimepsi	'definitely'	celtajcekulo	'absolutely'

Syntactic emphasizers

-imej thullimepsta	'it must be the case that . . .'
-eya hanta	'(one) must do . . .'
-eya hanun kes-ita	'it must be the case that one must do . . .'

55   *Attitude expressions*

Attitude expressions are postnominal particles that are neither hedges nor emphasizers. These particles have traditionally been called auxiliary case markers (H. Choi 1971: 653) or delimiters.

-(i)ntul/(i)lato	'even'	-(i)nama	'even'
-(i)na	'no more than'	-(i)ya	'as far as'

For example

> Cip-ej*na*   kaca.
> house-to-*only* go
> 'Let's *just* go home.'

K.   Other features (56–58)

56   *Fragmentary sentences*

In standard Korean, verbs are sentence-final, and complete sentences end with a speech level marker on the verb. Some sentences, however, end with other forms, sometimes because the sentence is simply interrupted (in speaking), and sometimes because the author chooses to do so. This latter case is relatively common in literary writing, especially poems, in which sentences can end with a noun. (Interjections are not counted as fragmentary sentences.)

57   Type–token ratio
Type–token ratio is computed by dividing the number of different words (the word types) by the total number of words (the tokens). The ratio is multiplied by 100 to make a percentage. Since this variable is not a linear function, it is computed over the number of words contained in the shortest text in the Korean corpus. Type–token ratio is interpreted as showing the degree of lexical variety.

58   Postposition/case-receivable noun ratio
The subject markers -i/-ka and object markers -ul/-lul are frequently deleted in speech. Lee and Thompson (1987) attribute the deletion of object markers in speech to the 'sharedness between communicators.'

It is not possible to directly identify these deleted elements because the computer is used to analyze most features automatically. Instead, the ratio of case markers (plus postpositional particles) to case-receivable nouns is measured. This ratio does not directly represent the deletion of case markers because noun compounding does not involve a case marker or a postpositional particle. Nonetheless, this ratio provides a good estimate of postposition deletion. Since this feature measures the occurrence of case markers (rather than deletions), a higher ratio represents more specific grammatical relations and less 'sharedness' between speaker and hearer.

Appendix II
Grammatical description of linguistic features in Somali

With Mohamed Hared

The features of Somali are grouped under eleven major categories: dependent clauses, main clause and verbal features, nominal features, pronouns, adjectival features, lexical classes, lexical choice, preverbal particles, reduced and interactive features, co-ordination, focus constructions. As with the other languages, this grouping has no influence on the factorial structure or the underlying dimensions of Somali (discussed in chapters 5–6).

The following descriptions are intended only as a brief introduction to the linguistic structure of each feature; readers are referred to Saeed (1987) for a much fuller treatment.

A.   *Dependent clauses* (1–11)

1   Total dependent clauses
The sum of all dependent clauses.

2   Conditional clauses
Adverbial clauses headed by *haddii* + subject pronoun. For example:

> Haddaan [haddii+ann] lacag   helo, waa ka   tegayaa.
> if-I   money find FM-I from am-leaving
> 'If I find money, I will leave it [i.e., I will quit my job].'

3   Purpose clauses
Complement clauses with adverbial functions, constructed as *u* + VERB + *in* . . . For example:

> Waxay   wax   u baranaysaa in   ay   hesho shahaadad.
> what-she something for is studying that she get   qualifications
> 'She is studying in order to get qualifications.'   (Saeed 1987.247)

4   Concessive clauses

These are adverbial clauses headed by *in kasta oo* (spoken and often written as *inkastoo*). For example:

> INKASTOO ay sababaan nabaad-guurka arrimo fara badan, haddana waxaa loo aaneeyaa nabaad-guurka ka dhaca Afrika dadka oo iskugu yimaadda meelaha ay barwaaqdu ka jirto iyagoo dhirta goonaya una isticmaalaya xaabo . . .

> 'EVEN THOUGH (*inkastoo*) many things cause soil-erosion, however what the soil-erosion which happens in Africa is blamed on is the people who come together at the places where green vegetation is available while cutting trees and using them for firewood . . .'

Concession can be marked by several other devices in Somali, including clitic particles (*-se*) and conjuncts (e.g., *laakiin, hase yeeshee, haddana*).

5   Temporal clauses

These are adverbial clauses headed by *markii* + pronoun, or *intii* + pronoun. For example:

> Markii   ay cadaatay   inuu   muddo gaaban ku
> time-the it   clear-became that-he time   short   with
>
> cayrtoobayo, buu   calaacal   iyo Alla eedeyn   billaabay.
> poor-become, FM-he complaint and God accusing began.
>
> 'When it (*markii ay*) became clear that he was going to become poor, he started complaining and accusing God.'

6–9   Relative clauses: full relative clauses, ah-relative clauses, framing relative clauses, demonstrative relative clauses

Relative clauses, which are extremely productive in Somali, are described more fully in chapter 4 (section 4.4.3). The analysis here distinguishes between restrictive and 'framing' relative clauses. Restrictive relatives have no overt relative pronoun; they function to specify the identity of intended referents as well as adding elaborating details; for example:

> Xaalidii   *deriskeena   ahayd* buugta   *ay*
> Hali-the (who) neighbor-our was   books-the (that) she
>
> *sheegaysaa*   waa buugtii   Cali.
> is talking about are   books-the Ali
>
> 'The Hali [a proper name] who was our neighbor, the books that she is talking about are the books of Ali.'

'Framing' relative clauses, on the other hand, set a discourse frame for the following proposition. These clauses are marked by the conjunction *oo*. When they have a pronominal head, these are typically temporal in nature, as in the following example:

> Isag*oo quraacanaya*   ayey   u timid.
> he   eating-breakfast FOC-she to came
> 'While he was eating breakfast, she came to him.'

For the analysis here, *oo* clauses with pronominal heads are counted as framing relatives, but all relative clauses with lexical heads are combined.

It is further possible to distinguish between two categories of restrictive relative clause. The first category consists only of a head noun phrase followed by an identificatory noun phrase and the verb *ah* 'to be,' whereas the second category has a full embedded clause. For example:

NP NP ah *relatives*
> siyaasadda *hantiwadaagga ahi*
> politics-the socialism   being
> 'the politics which is socialism'

Full clause relatives
> buugta   *ay sheegaysaa*
> books-the she is talking about
> 'the books that she is talking about'

Finally, demonstrative relative clauses have a demonstrative pronoun as the head NP, followed by the conjunction *oo* (i.e., *taasoo, kaasoo, tuwaasoo, kuwaasoo*). These forms are considered separately because they typically conclude and summarize a series of relative clauses. For example, the following sentence shows a series of three relative clauses, followed by a demonstrative relative clause making the main point:

> dhibaatooyinka ka jira waxaa ka mid ah daawo boorso lagu sido oo aan la ogeyn waxa ay ka sameysan tahay, cidda sameysay iyo waxa ay tarto toona, oo si xaaraan ah dalka u soo galeysa, TAASOO aynnu ognahay khasaarooyinka wax-yeellada caafimaad leh ee bulshadeenna ka soo gaara.
> 'the problems that exist include medicine which is carried in a purse [i.e. sold on the blackmarket], which it is not known what it is made of, the people who made it, or what it does, and which enters the country in a forbidden way, THAT ONE (*TAASOO*) [i.e. the medicine] which we know the losses that include the health damages which come from it to our society.'

(Cf. the fuller translation and discussion of this passage in chapter 4.)

10   *Verb complements*
These are complement clauses headed by *in* + pronoun, which follow the verb in the independent clause; for example:

> Markii   ay cadaatay   inuu   [in + uu] muddo gaaban ku
> time-the it clear-became that-he   time   short   with
>
> cayrtoobayo, . . .
> poor-become
> 'When it became clear that he (*in + uu*) was going to become
> poor, . . .'

11   *Ahaan* adverbials
These are a special class of relative clause construction comprising only the verb *ahaan* 'being.' *Ahaan* adverbials function as sentence adverbials. For example:

> guud ahaan 'general being' = 'generally, in general'
> gaar ahaan 'special being' = 'especially'
> run ahaan 'truth being' = 'truthfully, in fact'
> tusaale ahaan 'for example'
> gebogebo ahaan 'in conclusion'

B.   Main clause and verbal features (12–23)

12   *Total main clauses*

13   *Average t-unit length*
A t-unit is the length, in number of words, of each main clause plus all associated dependent clauses. All t-units for a text are averaged for this count.

14   *Verbless clauses*
These are declarative clauses having the focus marker *waa*, with the copula deleted; for instance:

> Waa been.
> FOC lie
> '(That is) a lie.'
>
> Waa taas.
> FOC that one
> '(It is) that one.'

15   Independent verbs
The count of all main-clause independent verbs.

16, 17 Commands: imperatives and optative clauses
Imperatives are bald commands, with no overt subject and often no surface object. They are marked by the lack of any overt verb inflections. Optative clauses are considered a more polite and indirect form of command. They often include both a subject and object. They take the form of *ha* + VERB-*o/aan*, and are typically translated as 'let X do Y'; for example:

> Ha iigu   soo diraan biilka.
> let me-to DIR send   money for expenses-the
> 'Let them send the money for expenses back to me.'

18   Compound verbs
A combination of a lexical root (usually a noun) with a verb root, to form a compound verb form; for example:

> faragelinaysaa 'interfere'
> *fara*   + *gal*   + inflections
> 'fingers' + 'enter'
>
> dhexgalaa 'meddle'
> *dhex*   + *gal*   + inflections
> 'middle' + 'enter'

19   Present tense
This is marked by the inflectional suffix -*aa*; for instance:

> wuu tagaa   'he goes'   (*tag* + inflections)
> wuu tageyaa 'he is going'

Predicative adjectives can also be considered as being marked for tense. In the present tense, the copula *yahay* carries this information; for instance:

> wuu wanaagsan yahay
> he/it good   is

20   Past tense
This is marked by the inflectional suffix -*ay*; for example:

> wuu tagay 'he went' (*tag* + inflections)
> wuu tageyay 'he was going'

Predicative adjectives marking past time are also inflected for tense (or they can be analyzed as undergoing obligatory contraction with a following copula); for example:

> wuu wanaagsanaa
> he/it was good

21–23 Modals: possibility, future, and habitual
Modals follow the main verb and carry the verb inflections; the main verb in these constructions takes the 'infinitival' form of VERB + *i*; for example:

> wuu tegi [teg+i] karaa [kar+aa]
> he   go   can
> 'he can go'

It is possible to distinguish three semantic classes of modals:
Possibility modals: *kar-* 'can', *lah-* 'conditional.'
Future modals: *doon-* 'will.'
Habitual modals: *jir-* 'used to.'

C.   Nominal features (24–31)

24   Common nouns

A total count of all nouns, excluding derived, compound, and proper forms.

25   Proper nouns
Names of persons or places.

26   Possessive nouns
Possessives are marked by nominal suffixes:

Masculine	Feminine	
kayga	tayda	'my'
kaaga	taada	'your'
kiisa	tiisa	'his'
keeda	teeda	'her'
keenna	teenna	'our'
kiinna	tiinna	'your (pl.)'
kooda	tooda	'their'

27 *Nominalizations*

Nominalizations include all nominal forms derived from nouns or adjectives, as well as non-gerundive nominal derivations from verbs. The derivational suffixes for nouns are *-nimo* and *-tooyo*; for adjectives they are *-aan* and *-ay-*; and for verbs they are *-i*, *-sho*, *-ad*. These forms differ from verbal nouns in having primarily abstract, stative meanings. They are often used for technical concepts or institutions. Examples of this category follow:

Base form		Nominalization	
aqoonso	'to recognize' (V)	aqoonsi	'recognition'
aamusan	'silent' (ADJ)	aamusnaan	'silence'
mid	'one' (N)	midnimo	'unity'
boqor	'king' (N)	boqornimo	'kingship'
		boqortooyo	'kingdom'

28 *Verbal nouns*

Verbal nouns are derived from verbs by addition of the suffixes *-in*, *-id*, *-is*, *-si*, *-aan*, or *-aad*. These forms are typically direct expressions of the 'act of VERB-ing' and thus might be considered gerunds; they tend to be relatively concrete and active in their meanings (see Saeed 1987: 146–47). Some examples of verbal nouns are:

Verb form		Verbal noun	
dhis	'to build'	dhisid	'(the process of) building'
kac	'stand'	kicid	'standing up, uprising'
kici	'to wake up'	kicin	'waking up'
qaad	'to take'	qaadid	'taking'
qaybi	'to divide'	qaybin	'distributing'
qor	'to write'	qoris	'(the process of) writing'
qorshee	'to plan'	qorsheyn	'planning'
xooji	'to strengthen'	xoojin	'strengthening'

29 *Agentive nouns (-e, -te, -to, -so)*

Agentive nominalizations are derived from a verb by addition of the suffixes *-e*, *-te*, or *-to*, to form nouns meaning 'one who does V.' For example:

Verb form		Agentive noun	
bar	'to teach'	bare	'teacher'
duuli	'cause to fly'	duuliye	'pilot'
maamul	'to administer'	maamule	'administrator'
xoogsad	'working'	xoogsato	'workers, proletariat'

30   Compound nouns

Nominal compounds in Somali are similar to nominalizations in that they are
frequently used for abstract concepts or institutions. There is considerable
variation in the orthographic representation of these forms; they can be
written as a single word, a hyphenated word, or separate words (see Hared
1992). They are marked as nominal compounds by the fact that they take
a single inflectional suffix and, in speech, have only one accent. Nominal
compounds can be formed out of many different word classes, and they
often also take a derivational suffix. (Compound forms functioning as proper
names were excluded from the counts.) Following are typical examples:

N + N + (DRV)
magaalo+madax 'city+head' ⇒ magaalo-madax 'capital city'
af+miishaar+nimo 'mouth+saw+DRV' ⇒ afmiisharnimo 'the state/
quality of being an orator who spreads propaganda'

N + (DRV) + V + (DRV)
hanti+wadaag 'wealth+share' ⇒ hantiwadaag 'socialism'
waayo+arag+nimo 'times+see+DRV' ⇒ waayoaragnimo 'experience'
goba+nimo+doon 'prestige+DRV+look for' ⇒ gobannimodoon
'liberation movement'

N + ADJ + (DRV)
aqoon+daran 'knowledge+bad' ⇒ aqoondaro 'ignorance'
madax+weyn+e 'head+big+DRV ⇒ madaxweyne 'president'

Particle + V + (DRV)
wada+jir 'together+exist' ⇒ wadajir 'solidarity'
is+kaasho+i 'self+support+DRV' ⇒ iskaashi 'cooperation'

N + Particle + V + (DRV)
hor+u+socod 'forward+toward+walk' ⇒ horosocod 'progress'
hor+u+socod+nimo 'forward+toward+walk+DRV' ⇒ horoso-
codnimo 'progressiveness'
midab+ka+la+sooc 'color+from+with+separate' ⇒ midab-kala-
sooc 'racial segregation'

31   -eed genitives

The genitive construction for most nouns in Somali has no surface marker; the
genitive is represented simply by the juxtaposition of the two nouns involved, as in

magaaladan Muqdisho
city-this   Mogadishu
'this city of Mogadishu'

These forms were not counted separately from the general noun count in
the analysis of Somali, because there is no semi-automatic way to distinguish
between noun-noun sequences and genitive constructions.

Many feminine nouns, however, take overt suffixes in genitive constructions: -*eed* or -*aad* for singular nouns, and -*ood* or -*aad* for plural nouns; for example:

> dadka   Soomaaliyeed
> people-the Somalia-of
> 'the people of Somalia'
>
> hilib riyaad
> meat goats-of
> 'meat of goats'

D.   Pronouns (32–34)

Pronouns can occur in three different forms: independent pronouns, which are usually emphatic; dependent subject pronouns, which are typically contracted with a preceding focus marker or adverbial subordinator; and dependent object pronouns, which occur as preverbal clitics. Independent subject pronouns frequently take a definite article (-*ka*). Examples of each type are:

Independent subject pronouns
> Laakiin adaa   [*adi* + *ayaa*] adaa   gardarnaa   Sacaado.
> but   you-FM   you-FM justice-without Sa'ado
> 'But you, you were at fault, Sa'ado.'

Dependent subject pronouns
> haddaad [*haddi-aad*] u amba-baxdo wax
> if-you   to devote   something
> 'if you devote (yourself) to something'
>
> Way   [*waa-ay*] iska fiicnayd.
> FM-she   just was fine
> 'She was just fine.'

Dependent preverbal object pronouns
> Maxaa i   dhigaaya?
> what me put down
> 'What will stop me?'

32   First-person pronouns

	Independent	Dependent/subject	Dependent/object
Singular	ani(ga)	aan	i
Plural (excl.)	anna(ga)	aan(nu)	na
Plural (incl.)	inna(ga)	aynu	ina

33   Second-person pronouns

	Independent	Dependent/subject	Dependent/object
Singular	adi(ga)	aad	ku
Plural	idin(ka)	aad/aydin	idin

34   Third-person pronouns

	Independent	Dependent/subject	Dependent/object
Singular			
Masculine	isa(ga)	uu	–
Feminine	iya(da)	ay	–
Plural	iya(ga)	ay	–

Third-person objects are understood if no other overt object occurs in a clause.

E.   Adjectival features (35–37)

35   Derived adjectives
These are formed from nouns and verbs by the addition of the derivational suffix -(s)an; for instance: *gaaban* 'short,' *wanaagsan* 'good.'

36   Attributive adjectives
These forms are similar to relative clauses in that they occur in postnominal position; for example:

halgan   adag
struggle difficult
'a difficult struggle'

ur   qudhmuun
odor rotten
'a rotten odor'

37   Predicative adjectives
As noted in sections 19–20 above, predicative adjectives are followed by a copula (*yahay*) in the present tense, or inflected for tense if they occur in the past tense; for example:

wuu wanaagsan yahay
he/it good   is

wuu wanaagsanaa
he/it was good

F. Lexical classes (38–46)

38 Stance adjectives

These are predicative adjectives functioning as verbs of cognition; they are usually derived forms (having the suffix -*san*). Following is a list of all adjectives identified in this class:

rumeysan	'believe'
og, ogsoon	'know, be aware'
garwaaqsan	'become aware, realize'
tuhunsan	'suspect'
shakisan	'suspect, doubt'
illowsan	'forget'
hilmaansan	'forget'
xusuusan, xasuusan	'remember'
dareensan	'feel'
fahansan	'understand'
cadheysan, cadhaysan, careysan, caraysan	'be angry'
aqoonsan	'recognize, acknowledge'
aaminsan	'trust'
xanaaqsan	'become angry'
dhirifsan	'become angry'
faraxsan	'be happy'
naxsan	'be astonished'
yaabsan	'be surprised'
wareersan	'be confused'
jec(e)l-, jecesh-	'love, think'
nec(e)b-	'hate'

39 Stance verbs

These are verbs marking states of cognition, belief, attitude, or emotion. (The counts include all inflected forms.)

fikir, fikr-	'think'
malee	'think'
fil	'hope'
rumee, rumeyso	'believe'
ogow, ogaa-	'know'
oqow, aq-, yaq-, taq-, naq-, iq-, yiq-, tiq-, niq-	'know'
garo	'understand'
hub	'be certain'
hubso	'ascertain'
garwaaqso	'become aware, realize'

go'aanso	'decide'
gooso	'decide'
kuurgal	'inspect, analyze'
tuhun, tuhm-	'suspect'
shaki	'suspect, doubt'
kas	'understand'
illow	'forget'
hilmaan	'forget'
xusuuso, xasuuso	'remember'
arag-, ark-	'see'
dareen	'feel'
maqal, maql-, maqash-	'hear'
dhageyso, dhegeyso	'listen'
dhadhanso	'infer, deduce'
dhugo	'see, be aware'
fiiri, fiirso	'look'
riyoo	'dream'
fahan, fahm-	'understand'
baq	'become afraid'
cabso	'become afraid'
cadhoo, caroo	'be angry'
aqoonso	'recognize, acknowledge'
bandhig	'demonstrate'
baro	'learn'
u qaado	'understand, think'
u hayso	'think, believe'
malaawaal, mala-awaal	'imagine'
hami	'imagine'
uga jeed	'to mean'
aamin	'trust'
eeg	'look'
xanaaq	'become angry'
dhirif, dhirf-	'be angry'
farax, farx-	'be happy'
nax	'be astonished'
yaab	'be surprised'
wareer	'be confused'
mood	'think'
welwel	'worry'
ciish-	'resent'
doon	'want'
rab	'want'

40   Speech act verbs

These are verbs marking public speech acts. (The counts include all inflected forms.)

hadal, hadl-	'talk'
dhah, dheh, ir-, tir-, yir-, nir-, idh-, tidh-, yidh-, nidh-, ye, te, suye, sayte, oran, odhan	'say'
weydii	'ask'
u sheeg	'tell'
sheeg	'say'
nuuxnuuxso	'emphasize'
isu, isku, ku raac	'agree together'
oggolow	'agree'
diid	'refuse'
bari	'beg, pray'
ducee	'pray in public'
is(ku) tus	'show each other'
dood	'exchange ideas'
taabo	'briefly discuss'
muuji	'express'
qiro	'admit'
cabo	'complain'
amar	'command'
ogeysii	'notify'
codso	'request'
ballan(qaad)	'promise'
dhawaaq	'announce'
baaq	'request in public'
weri	'report'
warran	'give news'
jawaab	'answer'
dhaaro	'swear'
magacow, magow	'nominate'
faafi	'spread news'
dig	'warn'
amaan	'praise'
guubaabi	'encourage'
baraaruji	'call upon, bring to consciousness'
dardaaran	'give parting instructions'
mahadi	'give thanks'
afgaro	'agree'
caddee	'prove'

sharax, sharx-	'explain'
fasir	'explain, expound'
faahfaahi	'elaborate'
balbalaari	'elaborate'
tilmaan	'mention'
soo jeedi	'propose, suggest'
yeedh, yeer	'call'
wac	'call'
canbaaree	'accuse'
dhaleecee	'criticize'
qayli	'shout'
waani	'advise (to younger)'
wacdi	'preach'
war(ay)so	'ask'
dhiirigali, dhiiri gali	'encourage'
canaan	'scold'
cay	'insult'

41   Time deictics
These are forms (usually nouns) marking temporal relations:

markaas-	'then'
goortaas-	'then'
kolkaas-	'then'
weli	'yet'
weli + possessive	'not yet, never'
caawa/caawo	'tonight'
maanta	'today'
berri, berrito, berritoole	'tomorrow'
saaka, saakadan	'this morning'
duhur + k-	'noon prayer time'
casar + k-	'afternoon prayer time'
makhrib + k-	'dusk prayer time'
cishe/cisha + h-	'night prayer time'
saa kuun	'three days from now'
saan dambe	'the day after tomorrow'
shaley	'yesterday'
darraad, dorraad	'the day before yesterday'
xaley	'last night'
had, hadda-, haddeer-	'now'
im(m)i(n)ka	'now'
ka dib, kad(d)ib	'after'
ka hor, kahor	'before'

In addition, the following words followed by *hore* 'previous'
or *dambe* 'next' were counted in this category:

mar + k-	'time'
goor + t-	'time'
kol + k-	'time'
xilli	'time'
maalin + t-	'day'
maalmo/maalma + h-	'days'
habeen + k-	'night'
habeeno/a + d-	'nights'
cawo/cawa + d-	'night'
tod(d)obaad, + k-	'week'
toddobaada + d-	'weeks'
wiig + g-	'week'
bil, bisha, bishii, bishan, bishaas	'month'
bilo/a + ha, hii, han, haas	'months'
san(n)ad + k-	'year'
san(n)ado + d-	'years'
cisho/cisha + da, dii	'day'
saq + d-	'time'
saac	'hour'
subax + d-	'morning'

42   Place deictics

These are forms (usually nouns) marking locative relations:

kor + k-	'above'
hoos + t-	'under'
ag + t-	'beside'
dhinac, dhinaca	'the side of'
barbar + k-	'side'
baal + k-	'side'
dibedda	'outside'
banaanka	'outside'
daba + d-	'back, behind'
gadaal + k-	'behind'
dib + (case particle) + VERB	'backwards, behind'
hor(e) + (case particle) + VERB	'before, in front of'
dib + FOCUS MARKER	'backwards, behind'
hor(e) + FOCUS MARKER	'before, in front of'
dib + POSSESSIVE	'backwards, behind'
hor + POSSESSIVE	'before, in front of'

gude, guda + h-	'inside'
dhex + d-	'inside'
bartamo, bartama + h-	'center'
gees + k-	'corner'
agagaar + k-	'around'
bari + g-	'east'
galbeed + k-	'west'
waqooyi, woqooyi + g-	'north'
koo(n)fur + t-	'south'
midig + t-	'right'
bidix + d-	'left'
xaggaas, xag(g)eer, xag(g)oor	'over there'
meesha(a)n, meeshatan	'here'
meeshaas	'there'
halka(a)n	'here'
halkaas	'there'

43 Downtoners

These are forms that function adverbially to reduce or hedge the certainty or force of a verb:

malaha	'perhaps'
uun	'just, only'
yara	'just, a little'
ayuun	'just'
laga yaabaa	'perhaps'
la arkaa	'perhaps – it might be seen'
waxa suurta-gal	'it is possible'
suurtow	'become possible'
insha(a) al(l)a(a)	'if God wills'
haddu al(l)a/il(l) aahay yiraahdo/yidhaahdo	'if God says/wills'
marar	'sometimes'
marmar	'seldom'
dhif	'seldom'

44 Amplifiers

These are forms that function adverbially to boost or emphasize the certainty or force of a verb:

aad	'really, very'
oo dhan	'all, altogether'
oo idil	'all, altogether'
kulli + g-	'all'

gebi + g-	'all'
dhammaan + t-	'all'
giddi + g-	'all'
runtii	'truth, in fact'
dhabtii	'truth, in fact'here 4 lines
run ahaan(tii)	'in truth'
dhab ahaan(tii)	'in truth'
sida runta/dhabta	'in truth'
hubanti, hubaal	'certainty'
shaki ku jirin	'without doubt'
shaki la'aan	'without doubt'
waxa muran-ma-doonto ah	'does not need argument – i.e., obvious'
badanaa	'often'

45   Concession/contrast/addition conjuncts

These forms join independent clauses while marking a concessive or contrastive logical relation between the clauses.

ha/hase/haba yeeshee	'however'
ha/hase/haba ahaatee	'however'
ha/hase/haba yaraatee	'however'
illowse	'however'
laakiin(se)	'however'
haddii kale	'else'
waxaa kaloo	'also, furthermore'
sid(aas)oo kale	'likewise, similarly'
midda kale	'on the other hand'
mooyi, mooye(e)	'except'

46   Reason conjuncts

These forms join independent clauses while marking a causative logical relation between the clauses.

waayo	'the reason (is)'
haddaba	'hence, therefore'
sidaas awgeed	
sidaas darteed	'as a result, as a consequence, due to'
sidaas daradeed	

G.   Lexical choice (47–49)

47   Word length

This is measured as number of letters per word, averaged over all words in a text.

48   Hapax legomena
The number of once-occurring words. (Because the number of once-
occurring words does not increase linearly as the text length becomes
longer, this characteristic was computed over the first 500 words in all
texts, rather than being normalized to total text length.)

49   Type–token ratio
The number of different word forms. (Because the number of different words
does not increase linearly as the text length becomes longer, this characteristic
was computed over the first 500 words in all texts, rather than being normalized
to total text length. This count is based on all word forms, rather than word lem-
mas; that is, each different inflected form is counted as a different word type.)

H.   Preverbal particles (50–53)

50–51 Single preverbal case particles and case particle sequences
In Somali there are no prepositions or postpositions; rather, all case relations
are marked by a series of preverbal case particles (see Biber 1984a, 1992c;
Saeed 1987). For example:

Cali geela buu   guriga   Faduma u-ga   eriyey.
Ali camels FOC-he house-the Faduma for-from chased
'Ali chased some camels away from the house for Faduma.'

The number of case particles reflects the density of nominal arguments in a
clause, and therefore it can be taken as a reflection of informational density.
Single case particles are counted separately from case particle sequences.
    The single case particles are:

u 'to, for'
ku 'in, into, on, at, with (by means of)'
ka 'from, away from, out of'
la '(together) with'

These particles can occur in sequence, such as *uga* (*u+ka*) or *kaga* (which
can correspond to *ku+ku*, *ku+ka*, or *ka+ka*).

52   Impersonal particles: la
Somali does not have a passive construction, but it does have an impersonal
subject pronoun, *la*, which appears in preverbal position and functions to
demote the agent; for instance:

Waxaa *la*   yidhi beri buu   raacay   geel.
what   'they' said once FOC-he looked after camels
'It was said that he once looked after camels.'

These constructions are discussed in more detail in chapter 4 (section 4.4.2).

53   Locative/directional particles: sii, soo
These particles mark the action of a verb as occurring either in the direction towards (*soo*) or away from (*sii*) the speaker or writer; for example:

> Sigaar   baa la soo qaadan karaa.
> cigarettes FM   IMP DIR   take   can
> 'Cigarettes can be brought back.'

I.   Reduced and interactive features (54–58)

54   Contractions
Contracted and reduced forms are extremely common in Somali speech and writing. Hared (1992) analyzes the distribution and standardization of these forms, identifying two major types of contraction:

Type 1: Cleft/subordinator/complementizer + subject pronoun

> waxaan = wax + aan   'what I'
> hadday = haddii + ay   'if they'
> inuu = in + uu   'that he'

Type 2: Subject pronoun/demonstrative pronoun + co-ordinator *oo*

> isagoo = isaga + oo   'he and'
> taasoo = taas + oo   'that-one and'

55   Yes/no questions
These are formed by the preverbal particle *ma*; in speech, there is also a marked question accentual pattern. For example:

> Ma og   tahay?
> QM know being
> 'Do you know?'

56   'What if' questions
These are formed with the preverbal particles *soo* or *sow*. These constructions often indicate the expectation of an affirmative response; for example:

> Sow Cabdi ma tegin?
> 'Didn't Abdi go?'

> Sow ma aha?
> 'Isn't it so?'

57   WH questions

There are a number of question words used to form WH questions.
These include:

maxaa-	'what'
meeqa	'how many, how much'
immisa	'how many, how much'
sidee	'how, in what manner'
xaggee	'where'
intee	'where'
goorma	'when'
yaa	'who'

58   Simple responses

There are a number of forms that frequently occur by themselves as simple
responses. Two of the counted forms have a negative force (*maya* and *mayee*),
while the other responses are affirmative conversational fillers. A few of
these forms have specific lexical content: *haa* is translated 'yes'; *nacam* is
translated as 'truth'; *kow* means 'one.' The other forms would be translated
something akin to American English 'ok': *haye(e)*, *haahey*, *hee(y)*, *a(a)ha*, *aah*,
hii, *i(i)hi*. The differing discourse functions of these various forms requires
further analysis.

J.   Co-ordination (59–62)

There are a large number of co-ordinating devices available in Somali, and
their differing discourse functions need further investigation. For the analysis here, four major types are distinguished: clause/phrase co-ordination
(*oo*), phrase co-ordination (*iyo*, *ama*), contrastive clause co-ordination (*eh*),
and contrastive topic clausal coordination (*-na*, *-se*).

59   Clause/phrase co-ordination (oo)

These forms can connect main clauses, dependent clauses, or phrases. (The
same form is also used to introduce framing relative clauses; see sections 6–9
above.) For example:

Dee horta   waa runoo   [run + oo] waan ku dirnee.
uh   first-the FM   truth-and   FM-we to we send
'Uh, first of all it is true and we set her against him.'

60   Phrase co-ordination

Phrases are typically co-ordinated by *iyo* 'and,' or *ama* 'or'; as in

> gobanimadoonka   Afrika iyo afgembiga
> independence movements (of) Africa and the coup d'etat (that)
> ka dhacay dalka   Bortuqiiska
> occurred in the country (of) Portugal
>
> 'Independence movements of Africa and (*iyo*) the coup d'etat
> that occurred in Portugal'
>
> (In some cases, these forms also connect full clauses.)

*61, 62 Contrastive clause co-ordination (*eh*) and contrastive topic clausal
co-ordination (-na, -se)*
These are clitic particles that attach to the first noun phrase in a clause. They
function to co-ordinate two clauses while topicalizing the noun phrase; for
example:

> ninkana   [*ninka-na*] adigu   u tegoo sidii
> man-the-and   you-the to go-and manner-the
> caadigii   ha iigu   soo diraan biilka.
> normal-the let me-to DIR send   money for expenses-the
>
> 'And as for the man, you go to him, and in the usual manner, let
> them send the money for expenses back to me.'

K.   Focus constructions (63–65)

Every main clause in Somali must have a focus marker, although question
and negation markers can also function as focus markers. There have been
numerous treatments of focus in Somali; Saeed (1984) provides the most
complete description.

We distinguish among three main types of declarative, affirmative focus
constructions: *waa* clauses, *baa/ayaa* clauses, and *waxaa* clefts. All three types
are frequently contracted with a following subject pronoun.

63   Waa focus markers
These are normally treated as unmarked focus on the verb or the entire
clause. Saeed (1987) regards these as clauses with no focus. Examples are:

> Waan [*waa + aan*] jeclahay
> FM-I   like
> 'I like something.'
>
> Dee horta   waa runoo   waan [*waa + aan*] ku dirnee.
> uh first-the FM   truth-and FM-we   to we send
> 'Uh, first of all it is true and we set her against him.'

64   Baa focus markers

These function to mark the immediately preceding noun phrase as new or contrastive information. (The focus marker *ayaa* is normally treated as equivalent to *baa*, but some Somali speakers feel that they have slightly different discourse functions.)

> Nin baa waa ari   badan lahaa. Arigii   baa
> man FM   once sheep-goats many had   sheep-goats-the FM
>
> cudur   xumi ka galay,   maalin kastana   dhowr neef   baa
> disease bad   to entered day   every-and several animals FM
>
> ka   dhiman jiray.
> from died   used-to
>
> 'Once a man [FOC] had many sheep/goats. The sheep/goats [FOC] got a bad disease, and every day, several animals [FOC] used to die from it.'

65   Waxaa clefts

These are analogous to clefts in English, fronting a highlighted element to the position immediately following *waxaa*, as in

> Waxay   iigu   darnayd   ayaantay Aamina ku
> what-she me-for was the worst [was] day-the-she Amina   to
>
> tidhi . . .
> she-said
>
> 'What was the worst thing for me was the day that she said to Amina . . .'

Notes

1 Introduction

1 In addition, there are factors in the linguistic context that can influence structural choices: for example, thematic considerations and noun phrase status as given/new information influence the choice between active and passive constructions.

2 Biber (1994) develops a preliminary analytical framework to analyze register variation in continuous rather than discrete terms.

3 These authors also raise the important research question of whether sublanguage characteristics can be discovered in a (semi-)automatic manner for a new domain. One possible solution to this problem growing out of the present study would be to approach it from a top-down perspective, first identifying the general register category on the basis of its characteristic surface linguistic features and then identifying the various linguistically well-defined *text types* within that register category (see chapter 9).

4 However, the present study contributes little to further understanding of variation associated with particular topics.

5 There are a number of related discourse studies that can be used as background research on these three languages. Korean has been the best studied in these terms: for example, S. Hwang (1981) discusses aspects of discourse structure in written narratives such as folktales and fiction; Lukoff (1986) studies tense variation in written narratives; H. Lee and Thompson (1987) study the variable deletion of accusative markers in spoken dialogues and narratives; J.-R. Hwang (1975) studies the language use patterns associated with Korean terms of address and levels of deference; Y. Choi (1988) investigates textual coherence features in English and Korean argumentative essays; and W. Lee (1989) analyzes referential choices in conversations and personal letters.

There are fewer relevant discourse studies for Nukulaelae Tuvaluan and Somali. Besnier (1989a, 1991) focuses on the marking of affect in Nukulaelae letters, and Besnier (1989c) describes discourse strategies used in Nukulaelae gossip. Although the marking of focus and topic are important issues in Somali, most studies have considered only sentences in isolation to analyze these structures (e.g., Hetzron 1965; Antinucci and Puglielli 1980; Saeed 1984). Biber (1984b) approaches these issues from a discourse perspective, studying focus and topic constructions in Central Somali folktales.

6 Crystal (1991: 225) similarly calls for comprehensive 'profiling procedures'

because 'A major aim of any theory of style *must* be to explicate the notion of distinctiveness – and not only within a single language, but across languages.'
7 The present study additionally includes some previously unpublished analyses of English and Somali.

2   The comprehensive analysis of register variation

1 This grammatical routine could occur in fiction or drama as well, but it would likely be part of a fictional sports broadcast embedded in a larger text.
2 Similar multivariate statistical techniques were first used in text studies by researchers such as Carroll (1960) and Marckworth and Baker (1974).
3 This generalization holds for quantitative social dialect studies as well as register studies.

3   Sociocultural description of the four language situations

1 This description should not be taken as making the naive claim that all English readers are equally literate or literate in the same ways. Rather, it is simply making the point that relative to the other three languages/cultures considered here, English has a long, well-established history of literacy, and a very wide and diverse readership.
2 In part, the striking differences between the Somali and Tuvaluan situations are due to a different scope of analysis: the Somali study is based on the full range of registers in use in the country of Somalia, while the study of Tuvaluan focuses exclusively on the island of Nukulaelae. A broader range of Tuvaluan registers are used nationally, associated with central government, the press, etc.
3 There were a few early indigenous scripts used for personal communication within Somali clans. The best known of these is Cismaaniya, a script created by Cismaan Yuusuf around 1920. This script was used primarily for personal letters within the Majeerteen clan of the Daarood clan family. Another indigenous script was developed by Sheekh Cabduraxmaan Sheekh Nuur of the Gudabiirsi clan in 1933; and a third was developed by Xuseen Sheekh Axmed Kaddare, from the Abgaal clan of the Hawiya clan family, in 1952. The best published information on these scripts is in Laitin (1977), who indicates that all of them were used primarily for personal communication within their immediate clan. A thorough investigation is needed concerning the range of language uses associated with these scripts, as well as linguistic analyses of the written texts themselves (which are currently scattered across private collections).
4 The social situation in Somalia has obviously changed dramatically between 1989, when the corpus of Somali texts was collected, and the present time (1993).

4   The linguistic bases of cross-linguistic register comparisons: a detailed quantitative comparison of English and Somali registers

1 The Somali analyses presented in this chapter were carried out in collaboration with Mohamed Hared. Some of these results were presented earlier in a

co-authored talk entitled 'Linguistic differences among Somali written genres: elaboration and integration of information in press commentaries, fiction, and personal letters', at the Fourth International Congress of Somali Studies (June 1989), in Mogadishu, Somalia.

2 In addition, other linguistic characteristics can be considered purely conventional, apparently having no functional associations (see Atkinson 1991). In many cases, conventional associations develop out of functional trends – as with the near total avoidance of first-person pronouns in some types of academic writing.

3 The Somali names for these registers are used to emphasize that they are not completely equivalent to corresponding English registers. The singular form of the names is used for consistency, even though a plural sense is sometimes intended. After their initial introduction, these terms are used without quotes or other qualification.

4 The term *sheeko* actually means 'story' and can refer to any spoken or written narrative.

5 The analyses of English linguistic features not included in Biber (1988), such as non-restrictive versus restrictive relative clauses, and prepositional phrases modifying nouns versus verbs, are based on a subset of the English texts.

6 Text counts are normalized by dividing the raw frequency of a feature in a text by the actual number of words in the text, and then multiplying by 1,000. For example, if a 2,000-word text had 30 adjectives, the normalized frequency of adjectives per 1,000 words of text would be 15:

$$(30/2,000) \times 1,000 = 15$$

7 It should be noted that the English editorials analyzed here were written in the early 1960s, and thus it is possible that a similar shift has occurred over the last thirty years in English.

8 The conjunction *oo* is also used to co-ordinate an attributive adjective and relative clause modifying the same head noun.

9 There are other preverbal particles in Somali, such as the impersonal marker *la* discussed in section 4.4.2, that do not mark case.

10 Genitives are excluded from consideration here, since they are a special type of nominal modifier. A complete comparative analysis would additionally include these constructions, however.

5   Methodology

1 Biber (1987), however, compares several American and British written registers from the Brown and LOB Corpora using the MD framework.

2 As noted in chapter 3, several of the text categories in the LOB and LL Corpora include subregisters (e.g., political, sports, and society news within press reportage; natural science, social science, and humanities within academic prose). For the most part, these subregisters are not considered in the present study, although Biber (1988: chapter 8) shows that there are interesting linguistic differences among them.

3 Biber and Finegan are currently collaborating on an NSF-sponsored analysis

of historical change in written and speech-based registers of English from 1650 to the present. The ARCHER Corpus was constructed for the purposes of this project (Biber, Finegan, and Atkinson 1994; Biber *et al.* 1994). This corpus comprises eleven major register categories sampled in fifty-year periods from 1650 to the present. Altogether, the complete corpus includes about 1,000 texts and about 1.7 million words. Among the written registers, the corpus includes personal communication (journals/diaries and personal letters), fiction prose, popular exposition represented by news reportage, and specialist expository registers, represented by legal opinions, medical prose, and scientific prose. It similarly includes several different kinds of speech-based registers: dialogue in drama and dialogue in fiction as reflections of casual face-to-face conversation, courtroom testimony as a reflection of informational conversation, and sermons as a reflection of planned monologue styles.

4 No historical books or general-knowledge books were published in Somali during the most recent period.

5 Each of these programs is interactive and works as follows. Taking raw text as input, it first isolates words and searches the dictionary for their associated grammatical tags. If a word is already in the dictionary and unambiguous (i.e., there is only one entry in the dictionary), it is directly tagged at this point. If the word is not already in the dictionary, the program makes an initial assessment of the grammatical category for the word based on inflectional morphology. The program then displays the word, its hypothesized grammatical tags, and its textual context on the screen, and the analyst can make any needed corrections. If there is a spelling error, the analyst enters the correct spelling, and the program then recycles by looking up the new spelling in the dictionary. When any needed spelling or grammatical editing is completed, the analyst returns control to the program, which enters the new word and its associated tags in the output 'tagged' version of the text and in the dictionary; the next time this word is encountered in a text, it will be automatically analyzed.

Ambiguous forms must be treated differently. For Somali, these include most verbs, since the tagging distinguishes between dependent and independent clauses, a distinction that is not marked in the verb morphology. These ambiguities can often be resolved by reference to the grammatical context, but many occurrences must be brought to the screen for interactive editing. For example, there is no relative pronoun in Somali, so typically there are no overt surface contextual differences between relative clauses and main clauses – these forms thus must be interactively tagged to insure accurate identification.

More recently, an additional tagging program has been developed by Biber for English, as part of the ARCHER project. Similar to the programs for Korean and Somali, this program runs on desktop computers and uses an on-line dictionary, in this case derived from a sorted version of the previously tagged LOB Corpus. However, while earlier programs used in MD analyses depended exclusively on a series of context-sensitive algorithms to resolve grammatical ambiguities, this more recent program exploits probabilistic information, following the approach developed for the CLAWS tagging system by Garside, Leech, and Sampson (1987). Thus, the program compares the probabilities for the grammatical categories of ambiguous lexical items: for example, *book* and *runs* are both noun-verb ambiguities, but *book* has a very high likelihood of being a noun (99 percent in the LOB expository genres), while *runs* has a high likelihood of being a verb (74 percent). When disambiguating forms, the probabilities of tag pairs are also compared. This program is described more fully in Biber (1993c).

6 This difference in the basis of norming has no influence on the cross-linguistic comparisons. The factor analyses in each language, which are based on the correlations among features, would produce the same results regardless of the norming basis. Subsequently, all frequency counts are standardized to a mean score of 0.0 and a standard deviation of 1.0 before factor scores are computed. Because a standardized frequency represents the magnitude of a score relative to other scores in the same language, it is not influenced by the norming basis – each language would have the same standardized scores for each feature, regardless of the norming basis.

7 If a feature has little variation that is shared with the total pool of variation underlying a factor analysis, it will have a small loading on all factors. In extreme cases, these features are dropped from the final factor analysis. Split infinitives in the English analysis is a feature of this type.

8 There are techniques used to determine the required magnitude for statistical significance of factor loadings, based on the number of observations (see, e.g., Gorsuch 1983: 208ff.). However, even though loadings smaller than 0.30 might be considered significant, they are not large enough to be considered important.

9 These statistics actually represent the statistical differences among all twenty-three English registers, rather than just the six registers plotted in figure 5.1.

10 Factor analyses of textual patterns typically account for about 50 percent of the total variance. The remaining patterns of variation are more idiosyncratic, representing the particular ways that individual features vary in association with less fundamental communicative functions.

11 In the following chapters, the polarity of English dimensions 3 and 5 is reversed to facilitate comparisons across dimensions. After this inversion, conversational registers are at or near the positive pole of dimensions 1, 3, and 5 while expository registers are at or near the negative pole.

12 Four additional dimensions relating to lexical cohesion are identified in Biber (1992b). Because that study is exploratory, being based on a relatively small corpus of texts, it is not incorporated into the present cross-linguistic investigation.

13 In general, there are only minor differences between the Varimax and Promax rotations of a given factor analysis. Thus, the use of Varimax rotation in the Tuvaluan factor analysis is not likely to have had much influence on its comparability to the factor analyses of the other three languages.

14 Prepositional phrases as nominal versus verbal modifiers were not distinguished in earlier multidimensional analyses of English. However, the analyses in chapter 4 show that this is a distinction that should be made in future research.

6   Multi-Dimensional analyses of the four languages

1 The co-occurrence of place adverbials with these other features is somewhat surprising, but it is probably due to the use of these features for text deixis (e.g., *It was shown above*).

2 Although Tottie (1983) characterizes synthetic negation as more literary than

analytic negation, the reasons for the co-occurrence of this feature with other narrative features needs further investigation.

3 The polarity of English dimensions 3 and 5 have been reversed from the original factor analysis (presented in table 5.14) to facilitate later comparisons across dimensions. This transformation has no influence on the reported results, since positive versus negative sign is used only to distinguish between two opposing poles, with no necessary association to greater-than or lesser-than relations.

4 Although dimension 4 is a significant predictor of register differences, the r^2 value of 16.9 percent shows that it is relatively weak in comparison to the other English dimensions.

5 The polarity of this dimension has been reversed from the original factor analysis of English (table 5.14) – see note 3.

6 This sample also shows the use of a noun complement clause for similar purposes: *any chance that the Labour Party will* . . .; these features were not counted in the present analysis.

7 See Biber and Finegan (1988, 1989b) for more detailed discussion of the various stance styles in English.

8 Besnier (1988) proposes the interpretive label 'Interactional versus Informational Focus' for dimension 2.

9 Similar to the presentation of English dimensions 3 and 5, the polarity of Tuvaluan dimension 2 has been reversed from the original factor analysis; see note 3.

10 This dimension was labeled 'Rhetorical Manipulation versus Structural Complexity' in Besnier (1988).

11 Personal narratives are regularly incorporated into Nukulaelae Tuvaluan conversations (Besnier, personal communication). None of Besnier's studies indicates the presence of folktales in Nukulaelae culture, however.

12 Kim (1990) proposes the label 'Informal Interaction versus Explicit Elaboration' for this dimension, emphasizing the interactiveness over the production circumstances.

13 Note that the F-scores and r^2 values for Korean differ from those reported for the other three languages. That is, the Korean results report a test of the average difference between all spoken texts and all written texts; this is thus a test of the physical mode differences with respect to the dimension in question. In the other three languages, on the other hand, these statistics are used to test for differences among all registers, regardless of their status as speech or writing.

14 Kim (1990) proposes the label 'Discourse Chaining versus Discourse Fragmentation' for Korean dimension 2.

15 These contracted forms seem to be in the process of being reanalyzed as inflected forms, since they almost never occur separately (see Hared 1992).

16 Similar to some dimensions in the other languages, the polarity of this dimension has been reversed; see note 3.

17 *Hapax legomena* and type–token ratio are both based on the first 500 words in a text.

18 These forms also show weaker correlations with certain structural elaboration features: single case particles, demonstrative relatives (relative clauses with a demonstrative pronoun as head, which conclude a series of relative clauses), clitic topic co-ordination, and purpose clauses.

19 Although poetry has been deliberately excluded from MD analyses to date, oral poetry in Somali is particularly relevant here since it represents a spoken register with extremely careful word choice, containing a wide variety of archaic forms to fit the alliterative patterns of a given poem.

20 The large positive score for textbooks might also reflect a conscious attempt to increase the comprehensibility of difficult subject matter for high-school students by restricting word choice.

21 Agentive nouns are similar to nouns derived by the suffix -er in English.

22 These samples also illustrate the involved nature of family meetings with respect to dimension 1 features; for example, frequent questions and responses, main clause features, contractions, time deictics (e.g., *imika*, *imminka* 'now'), negatives, and second-person pronouns.

23 Dimension 4 has a few weaker positive features, including stance verbs (e.g., *u malee* 'think,' *fil* 'hope'), possessive nouns, and concession clauses. There are also several relatively weak negative features: compound nouns, gerunds, agentive nouns, t-unit length, and phrasal co-ordination.

7 Cross-linguistic patterns of register variation: synchronic similarities and differences

1 I have referred to all non-linguistic characteristics as 'situational' in earlier chapters, whether they relate to the physical situation or typical purposes and topics.

2 In languages that have both personal stance and argumentation dimensions (such as English and Somali), it is possible for a particular text to use features from both domains (as in some English professional letters and interviews). The more typical case, however, is for a register to rely primarily on one or the other domain. Thus, most English editorials and professional letters have informational characterizations on dimension 1, reflecting the general lack of personal stance features, but they have very argumentative characterizations on dimension 4.

3 Reppen (1994) shows that similar underlying functions are represented in the multidimensional profile of elementary students acquiring an extended range of spoken and written registers in English. This study is based on an MD analysis of fifth-grade school registers, including multiple speaking tasks and multiple writing tasks, as well as textbooks and children's literature. Specifically, Reppen's study identifies basic dimensions associated with differing production circumstances, informational focus, degree of involvement and personal stance, and narration. In addition, fifth-grade students have two relatively idiosyncratic dimensions, relating to 'projected scenario' and 'other-directed idea justification'; these dimensions reflect the special kinds of writing tasks that students perform in school.

4 The multidimensional profile of a language represents the basic communicative functions that are systematically distinguished by sets of pervasive, co-occurring linguistic features. Other communicative functions can be served by individual register *markers* (see the discussion in chapter 2 that distinguishes between *register markers* and *register features*). Register features are common, core linguistic features, which are pervasive in the texts of a language and are distributed in

systematic co-occurrence relations. In contrast, register markers are relatively rare linguistic forms that function as isolated conventional indicators of a register; register markers are too rare to participate in systematic co-occurrence relationships.

Those functions that are marked by co-occurring register features and corresponding underlying dimensions are central to a given language and culture. That is, due to the pervasive nature of register features and the co-occurrence patterns underlying dimensions, all texts will have some characterization with respect to each underlying dimension. In contrast, functions marked by register markers are more peripheral; it is possible, and in many cases common, to produce texts that have no characterization with respect to register markers.

In Korean, for example, role relations and the stance of the addressor towards the addressee are an integral part of the underlying multidimensional profile; register features associated with these functions are pervasive in Korean, and it is not possible to produce texts without some characterization along the associated dimensions. In English, on the other hand, similar communicative functions are marked by relatively rare register markers, using devices such as different address terms and different forms of directives. Most English texts have no overt indication of the stance towards the addressee. Thus, although it is possible to mark role relations in both Korean and English, this is a basic communicative function in Korean culture that is therefore realized as an underlying dimension of variation, while this function is less central in English and is therefore marked only by relatively rare register markers.

5 Written sermon notes are produced by a smaller number of lay preachers.

6 It is interesting to note that even here there are notable cross-linguistic similarities, in that the same kinds of structural features are used to mark argumentation/persuasion in the two languages having a separate dimension with this function (English and Somali).

7 These analyses show that the four traditional 'rhetorical modes' – narration, description, exposition, and argumentation – are not equally well represented. Dimensions relating to narration and exposition are clearly represented in English, Korean, and Somali; and analogous dimensions are represented in Nukulaelae Tuvaluan, even though there are no fictional or expository registers. Argumentation is well represented in English and Somali, but there are no corresponding dimensions in Korean or Tuvaluan. In contrast, description is not functionally associated with any dimension in any of these languages (although features marking informational integration might reflect both expository as well as descriptive purposes).

8   **Cross-linguistic patterns of register variation: diachronic similarities and differences**

1 Atkinson (1992) analyzes medical articles from seven different periods, separated by approximately forty years. Similarly, legal opinions have been collected from fifty-year periods. These results have been combined in the present discussion to produce average characterizations of medical articles and legal opinions in each century, which can be compared to the patterns of variation found in Biber and Finegan (1989a, 1992).

2 The legal opinions are taken from the ARCHER corpus (*A Representative Corpus of Historical English Registers*), compiled as part of an on-going investigation of historical register variation in English (see Biber, Finegan, and Atkinson 1994).

3 Medical research articles and American legal opinions from the eighteenth rather than seventeenth century are described in these figures, since these are the earliest texts available for this register.

4 Diachronic register comparisons can be undertaken from two different perspectives. The first, used in the present chapter, analyzes change in terms of the present-day dimensions of variation, which can be considered the 'target' that registers from earlier periods are evolving towards. A complementary perspective is to compute a separate factor analysis based on the patterns of variation among registers from earlier historical periods, identifying the salient dimensions that were well defined in those periods. It would then be possible to compare the modern multidimensional profile to the MD analyses of earlier periods, similar to the cross-linguistic comparisons described in chapter 7. Analyses of this type are currently underway for English, as part of the ARCHER project.

5 Along dimension 5, seventeenth-century dialogue in drama is quite similar to modern conversation, while dialogue in novels shows a greater use of passive constructions.

6 There are no data available to assess the extent to which these registers were also different from formal spoken registers (such as sermons and public speeches).

7 These registers have quite different textual histories preceding the earliest periods considered here. For example, certain kinds of legal prose had been written in English for centuries before the development of American court opinions in the middle eighteenth century. In contrast, medical research endeavors, and the associated research articles, were just beginning to develop in the late seventeenth century, so the sampling of this register more accurately represents the first stages of evolution.

8 This initial characterization of science prose in the seventeenth century is probably due in large part to the influence of pre-existing models for academic and institutional registers in Latin and French. This possibility could be investigated empirically through a MD analysis of Latin and French registers from that period.

9 Although the scores are not plotted here, Biber and Finegan (1992) show that dialogue in fiction follows a very similar developmental course to dialogue in drama.

10 This trend was reinforced by an overt interest in nature and a philosophical preference for naturalness and utility, which found expression in Romantic art, music, and literature. For many writers of the Romantic period, natural prose meant a colloquial style, reflecting conversation's place as the most basic mode of communication (Biber and Finegan 1989a: 514–15). This preference for colloquial, 'natural' language was found on both sides of the Atlantic and characterized grammatical as well as literary discussions (Finegan 1980, 1992).

11 The initial characteristics of written registers in English were obviously influenced to some extent by the pre-existing characteristics of analogous registers in other languages (Latin and French). The influence of foreign models on the early development of written registers is discussed further in chapter 10.

12 The spoken texts in the Somali corpus do not truly represent the range of

412   Notes to pages 303–11

spoken variation as it existed in 1972, because they were collected in 1988–89. The comparison to earlier written texts is thus based on the assumption that spoken registers have changed relatively little since 1972. However, to the extent that they have changed, it is likely that spoken registers have become more similar to written registers (as found by Reder [1981] for Vai), resulting in an *under*assessment of the changes caused by the addition of written registers. That is, it is fairly certain that the addition of written registers expanded the range of register variation in Somali by at least the extent shown in figures 8.7–8.9.

13 Consideration of Somali oral poetry shows that the extension of variation along dimension 2 due to the addition of written registers is less dramatic than it appears from figure 8.8. According to Andrzejewski and Lewis (1964: 45), a Somali poet can spend days working on a single poem. Somali oral poetry is governed by strict rules of alliteration, so that every hemistich must include at least one content word beginning with the chosen sound (a consonant or vowel). Further, there is a strong preference to avoid repetitions of words. To meet these demands, Somali poets use numerous archaic terms and create new words (Andrzejewski and Lewis 1964: 43). Thus, the best Somali poems can have greater lexical diversity than informational written registers. For example, in two of the famous classical poems composed by Maxamed Cabdille Xasan, the type–token ratio is between 67 and 69 percent, and the frequency of once-occurring words is 59–60 per 100 words of text in the first 500 words. Thus, in a poem of 500 words, there would be approximately 350 different words used, and 295 of those words would occur only once. In contrast, institutional editorials have an average type–token ratio of 59 percent and an average of 46 once-occurring words per 100 words of text (in the first 500 words). Thus, oral poetry represents a highly specialized spoken register that exhibited extremely careful word choice before the introduction of writing.

14 The score for letters in the middle period is tentative, since it is based on a sample of only two letters.

15 Memos have actually become slightly less integrated, although the change is very small.

16 There were frequent typographical errors in the articles from this period, and the general layout of the newspapers became much less professional in appearance: for example, articles were set using characters from different fonts, and it was not uncommon for individual characters to be set askew.

17 This finding is particularly noteworthy in that it runs directly counter to the traditional view espoused by many linguists that writing is simply derivative from speech – a view that has been widely accepted as an obvious truth. For example, Bloomfield (1933: 21) confidently asserts that 'writing is not language, but merely a way of recording language by visible marks'. Hall (1964: 8–9) characterizes writing as 'only a secondary derivative'. Aronoff (1985: 28) characterizes this view as an 'undoubtedly correct observation', claiming that 'spoken language is "true" language, while written language is an artifact'. (See Biber 1988: 6 for discussion of other linguists advocating this position.)

  This traditional view is an accurate characterization of the chronology of language development: nearly all children speak before they write, and societies develop spoken register repertoires before they develop written registers.

However, the assumed logical consequence of this chronological sequencing – that writing is derivative from speech – does not hold up to empirical investigation. Rather, the MD analyses described in chapters 6–7 show that written registers can differ in important ways from spoken registers, with respect to both functional and linguistic characteristics. Further, the analyses in the present chapter show that many written registers differ from spoken registers even in their earliest stages of evolution.

18 This trend will presumably level out as specialist written registers approach a ceiling effect on the extent to which information can be integrated and elaborated in a text. However, that development has apparently not yet occurred in English (after several hundred years).

9   Registers and text types in English and Somali

1 Only the first five dimensions in English and Somali were used to identify the text types in the respective languages. In both cases, these constituted the strongest dimensions, having straightforward interpretations.

2 The FASTCLUS procedure from SAS was used for the clustering in both languages. Disjoint clusters were produced since there was no theoretical reason to expect a hierarchical structure. Peaks in the Cubic Clustering Criterion and the Pseudo F Statistic, both produced by the FASTCLUS procedure, were used to determine the number of clusters to extract for analysis. These statistics provide a measure of the similarities among texts within each cluster in relation to the differences between the clusters. In the present case, both measures showed peaks for eight cluster solutions, indicating that they provided the best fit to the data.

3 For the sake of comparison on figures 9.3 and 9.4, the English dimension scores were transformed to a scale having plus or minus 10 as the maximum score. These transformations do not alter the relative comparisons across text types and across dimensions. The scaling coefficients used were as follows:

Dimension	Coefficient
1	0.21
2	1.54
3	0.74
4	2.22
5	1.05

The original dimension scores are used in table 9.4, to enable comparison to the dimension scores for registers presented in chapter 6.

4 Clusters can have intermediate mean dimension scores for two reasons: the cluster is characterized by frequent occurrences of both positive and negative linguistic features on that dimension, or the cluster is characterized by the marked absence of both positive and negative features. Either distribution of features results in an unmarked characterization with respect to the dimension in question.

5 The peripheral nature of such texts can be assessed quantitatively by computing the distance between the five-dimensional characterization of a text and the text

type centroid. Texts with informational characterizations, such as sample 9.11, have distance measures greater than 10 from the centroid of text type 8.

6 Similar to the English dimension scores, the Somali dimension scores for text types were transformed to a scale having plus or minus 10 as the maximum score. The scaling coefficients used were as follows:

Dimension	Coefficient
1	0.83
2	1.05
3	0.83
4	1.67
5	1.11

The original dimension scores are used in table 9.6, to enable comparison to the dimension scores for Somali registers presented in chapter 6.

7 The only Somali spoken register that is informational and reported (rather than argumentative) is radio news broadcasts. These are simply read from scripted news reports (often the same articles published in the newspaper), and thus they have similar characteristics to text type 5.

8 It would be interesting to compare long-distance telephone conversations to letters in this regard; both are task-oriented, with interlocutors being separated by great distance, but letters provide further distancing due to the written mode and the time delay needed to send and receive a letter.

9 That is, $3 \times 3 \times 3 \times 3 \times 3 = 243$.

References

Abrams, M. H. 1979. *The Norton anthology of English literature*, Vol. I. New York: W.W. Norton.

Aijmer, Karin, and Bengt Altenberg (eds.). 1991. *English corpus linguistics: studies in honour of Jan Svartvik*. London: Longman.

Ali, Issa H., and Mohamed S. Gees. 1979. The Somali language in science context. In Hussein M. Adam (ed.), *Somalia and the world*, 84–94. Mogadishu: Halgan.

Altenberg, Bengt. 1984. Causal linking in spoken and written English. *Studia Linguistica* 38: 20–69.

1991. A bibliography of publications relating to English language corpora. In Johansson and Stenström (eds.), 355–96.

Andersen, Elaine S. 1990. *Speaking with style: the sociolinguistic skills of children*. London: Routledge and Kegan Paul.

Andrzejewski, B.W. 1974. The introduction of a national orthography for Somali. *African Language Studies* 15: 199–203.

1978. The development of a national orthography in Somalia and the modernization of the Somali language. *Horn of Africa* 1: 39–46.

1979. The use of Somali in mathematics and the sciences. In Hussein M. Adam (ed.), *Somalia and the world*, 57–83. Mogadishu: Halgan.

Andrzejewski, B.W., and I.M. Lewis. 1964. *Somali poetry: an introduction*. Oxford University Press.

Antinucci, Francesco, and Annarita Puglielli. 1980. The syntax of indicator particles in Somali. Part one: Relative clause construction. *Afroasiatic Linguistics* 7.3: 85–102.

Aronoff, Mark. 1985. Orthography and linguistic theory. *Language* 61: 28–72.

Atkinson, Dwight. 1991. Discourse analysis and written discourse conventions. *Annual Review of Applied Linguistics* 11: 57–76.

1992. The evolution of medical research writing from 1735 to 1985: the case of the *Edinburgh Medical Journal. Applied Linguistics* 13: 337–74.

1993. A historical discourse analysis of scientific research writing from 1675 to 1975: The case of the *Philosophical Transactions of the Royal Society of London*. Ph.D. dissertation, Department of Linguistics, University of Southern California.

Atkinson, Dwight and Douglas Biber. 1994. Register: a review of empirical research. In Biber and Finegan (eds.), 351–85.

Baron, Dennis E. 1982. *Grammar and good taste: reforming the American language*. New Haven: Yale University Press.

Basso, Keith H. 1974. The ethnography of writing. In R. Bauman and J. Sherzer (eds.), *Explorations in the ethnography of speaking*, 425–32. Cambridge University Press.

Bauman, Richard, and Joel Sherzer (eds.). 1989. *Explorations in the ethnography of speaking*. Cambridge University Press.

Bazerman, Charles. 1984. Modern evolution of the experimental report in physics. *Social Studies of Science* 14: 163–96.

  1988. *Shaping written knowledge: the genre and activity of the experimental article in science*. Madison: University of Wisconsin Press.

Bennett, James R. 1971. *Prose style: a historical approach through studies*. San Francisco: Chandler.

Bernstein, Basil. 1970. *Class, codes, and control*. Vol. I: *Theoretical studies towards a sociology of language*. London: Routledge.

Besnier, Niko. 1986. Spoken and written registers in a restricted-literacy setting. Ph.D. dissertation, Department of Linguistics, University of Southern California.

  1988. The linguistic relationships of spoken and written Nukulaelae registers. *Language* 64: 707–36.

  1989a. Literacy and feelings: the encoding of affect in Nukulaelae letters. *Text* 9: 69–91.

  1989b. *Tuvaluan: the Southern dialects*. (Croom Helm Descriptive Grammar Series.) London: Croom Helm.

  1989c. Information withholding as a manipulative and collusive strategy in Nukulaelae gossip. *Language in Society* 18: 315–41.

  1991. Literacy and the notion of person on Nukulaelae atoll. *American Anthropologist* 93: 570–87.

Biber, Douglas. 1984a. The diachronic development of preverbal case markers in Somali. *Journal of African Languages and Linguistics* 6: 47–61.

  1984b. Pragmatic roles in Central Somali narrative discourse. *Studies in African Linguistics* 15: 1–26.

  1984c. A model of textual relations within the written and spoken modes. Ph.D. dissertation, Department of Linguistics, University of Southern California.

  1985. Investigating macroscopic textual variation through multi-feature/multi-dimensional analyses. *Linguistics* 23: 337–60.

  1986. Spoken and written textual dimensions in English: resolving the contradictory findings. *Language* 62: 384–414.

  1987. A textual comparison of British and American writing. *American Speech* 62: 99–119.

  1988. *Variation across speech and writing*. Cambridge University Press.

  1989. A typology of English texts. *Linguistics* 27: 3–43.

  1990. Methodological issues regarding corpus-based analyses of linguistic variation. *Literary and Linguistic Computing* 5: 257–69.

  1991. Oral and literate characteristics of selected primary school reading materials. *Text* 11: 73–96.

  1992a. On the complexity of discourse complexity: a multidimensional analysis. *Discourse Processes* 15: 133–63.

  1992b. Using computer-based text corpora to analyze the referential strategies of spoken and written texts. In Svartvik (ed.), 213–52.

1992c. Somali. *Oxford International Encyclopedia of Linguistics* 4: 25–27.

1993a. Representativeness in corpus design. *Literary and Linguistic Computing* 8: 1–15.

1993b. Using register-diversified corpora for general language studies. *Computational Linguistics* 19: 219–41.

1993c. The multi-dimensional approach to linguistic analyses of genre variation: an overview of methodology and findings. *Computers and the Humanities* 26: 331–45.

1994. An analytical framework for register studies. In Biber and Finegan (eds.), 31–56.

Biber, Douglas and Edward Finegan. 1986. An initial typology of English text types. In Jan Aarts and Willem Meijs (eds.), *Corpus linguistics*. Vol. II: *New studies in the analysis and exploitation of computer corpora*, 19–46. Amsterdam: Rodopi.

1988. Adverbial stance types in English. *Discourse Processes* 11: 1–34.

1989a. Drift and the evolution of English style: a history of three genres. *Language* 65: 487–517.

1989b. Styles of stance in English: lexical and grammatical marking of evidentiality and affect. *Text* 9: 93–124.

1991. On the exploitation of computerized corpora in variation studies. In K. Aijmer and B. Altenberg (eds.), *English corpus linguistics: studies in honour of Jan Svartvik*, 204–20. London: Longman.

1992. The linguistic evolution of five written and speech-based English genres from the seventeenth to the twentieth centuries. In M. Rissanen, O. Ihalainen, T. Nevalainen, and I. Taavitsainen (eds.), *History of Englishes: new methods and interpretations in historical linguistics*. 688–704. Berlin: Mouton.

1994a. Intra-textual variation within medical research articles. In N. Oostdijk and P. de Haan (eds.), *Corpus-based research into language*, 201–22. Amsterdam: Rodopi.

1994b. Multi-dimensional analyses of author's style: some case studies from the eighteenth century. In S. Hockey and N. Ide (eds.) *Research in Humanities Computing*, vol. III. Oxford University Press.

(eds.). 1994c. *Sociolinguistic perspectives on register*. New York: Oxford University Press.

Biber, Douglas, and Mohamed Hared. 1992a. Dimensions of register variation in Somali. *Language Variation and Change* 4: 41–75.

1992b. Literacy in Somali: linguistic consequences. *Annual Review of Applied Linguistics* 12: 260–82.

1994. Linguistic correlates of the transition to literacy in Somali: language adaptation in six press registers. In Biber and Finegan (eds.), 182–216.

Biber, Douglas, Edward Finegan, and Dwight Atkinson. 1994. ARCHER and its challenges: compiling and exploring A Representative Corpus of Historical English Registers. In U. Fries, G. Tottie and P. Schneider (eds.), *Creating and using English language corpora*, 1–14. Amsterdam: Rodopi.

Biber, Douglas, Edward Finegan, Dwight Atkinson, Ann Beck, Dennis Burges, and Jená Burges. 1994. The design and analysis of the ARCHER corpus: a progress report. In M. Kytö, M. Rissanen, and S. Wright (eds.), *Corpora across the centuries*, 3–6. Amsterdam: Rodopi.

Blankenship, Jane. 1962. A linguistic analysis of oral and written style. *Quarterly Journal of Speech* 48: 419–22.

1974. The influence of mode, submode, and speaker predilection on style. *Speech Monographs* 41: 85–118.

Bloomfield, Leonard. 1933. *Language.* New York: Holt, Rinehart and Winston.

Britton, James, Tony Burgess, Nancy Martin, Alex McLeod, and Harold Rosen. 1975. *The development of writing abilities (11–18).* London: Macmillan Education.

Brown, Penelope, and Colin Fraser. 1979. Speech as a marker of situation. In Klaus R. Scherer and Howard Giles (eds.), *Social markers in speech*, 33–62. Cambridge University Press.

Bruthiaux, Paul. 1994. Me Tarzan, you Jane: linguistic simplification in 'personal ads' register. In Biber and Finegan (eds.), 136–54.

Carroll, John B. 1960. Vectors of prose style. In Thomas A. Sebeok (ed.), *Style in language*, 283–92. Cambridge, MA: MIT Press.

Celce-Murcia, Marianne, and Diane Larsen-Freeman. 1983. *The grammar book.* Newbury House.

Chafe, Wallace L. 1982. Integration and involvement in speaking, writing, and oral literature. In Tannen (ed.), 35–54.

Chafe, Wallace L., and Jane Danielewicz. 1986. Properties of spoken and written language. In Rosalind Horowitz and S. J. Samuels (eds.), *Comprehending oral and written language*, 82–113. New York: Academic Press.

Chafe, Wallace L., and Deborah Tannen. 1987. The relation between written and spoken language. *Annual Review of Anthropology* 16: 383–407.

Cho, Choon-Hok. 1982. A study of Korean Pragmatics: Deixis and Politeness. PhD dissertation, University of Hawaii.

Choi, Hyunpae. 1971. *Wuli malpon* [Our grammar]. Seoul: Cengumsa.

Choi, Yeon Hee. 1988. Textual coherence in English and Korean: an analysis of argumentative writing by American and Korean students. Ph.D. dissertation, University of Illinois at Urbana-Champaign.

Clancy, Patricia M. 1982. Written and spoken style in Japanese narratives. In Tannen (ed.), 55–76.

Clifford, Geraldine J. 1984. Buch und lesen: historical perspectives on literacy and schooling. *Review of Educational Research* 54: 472–500.

Comrie, Bernard. 1976. *Aspect.* Cambridge University Press.

Cook-Gumperz, Jenny. 1986. Literacy and schooling: an unchanging equation? In Jenny Cook-Gumperz (ed.), *The social construction of literacy*, 16–44. Cambridge University Press.

Coulmas, Florian. 1989. Language adaptation. In Florian Coulmas (ed.), *Language adaptation*, 1–25. Cambridge University Press.

Couture, Barbara. 1986. Effective ideation in written text: a functional approach to clarity and exigence. In Barbara Couture (ed.), *Functional approaches to writing research perspectives*, 69–91. Norwood, NJ: Ablex.

Crystal, David. 1991. Stylistic profiling. In Karin Aijmer and Bengt Altenberg (eds.), *English corpus linguistics*, 221–38. London: Longman.

Crystal, David and Derek Davy. 1969. *Investigating English style.* London: Longman.

De Castell, Suzanne, and Allan Luke. 1986. Models of literacy in North American schools: social and historical conditions and consequences. In de Castell, Luke, and Egan (eds.), 87–109.

De Castell, Suzanne, Allan Luke, and Kieran Egan (eds.). 1986. *Literacy, society, and schooling.* Cambridge University Press.

Deibler, Ellis W., Jr. 1976. Differences between written and oral styles in languages near Goroka. *Read* 11: 77–79.

Devitt, Amy J. 1989a. *Standardizing written English: diffusion in the case of Scotland, 1520–1659.* Cambridge University Press.

1989b. Genre as textual variable: some historical evidence from Scots and American English. *American Speech* 64: 291–303.

Dorian, Nancy C. 1994. Stylistic variation in a language restricted to private-sphere use. In Biber and Finegan (eds.). 217–32.

Duff, Martha. 1973. Contrastive features of oral and written texts in Amuesha. *Notes on Translation* 50: 2–13.

Duranti, Alessandro. 1985. Sociocultural dimensions of discourse. In Teun van Dijk (ed.), *Handbook of discourse analysis*, vol. I, 193–230. New York: Academic Press.

Engwall, Gunnel. 1992. Comments on Gellerstam (1992). In Svartvik (ed.), 164–69.

Ervin-Tripp, Susan. 1972. On sociolinguistic rules: Alternation and co-occurrence. In John J. Gumperz and Dell Hymes (eds.), *Directions in sociolinguistics*, 213–50. New York: Holt.

Faber, Dorrit, and Karen M. Lauridsen. 1991. The compilation of a Danish-English-French corpus in contract law. In Johansson and Stenström (eds.), 235–43.

Ferguson, Charles A. 1959. Diglossia. *Word* 15: 325–40.

1964. Baby talk in six languages. In John J. Gumperz and Dell Hymes (eds.), *The ethnography of communication*, 103–14. Washington, DC: American Anthropological Association.

1968. Language development. In J. A. Fishman, C. A. Ferguson, and J. D. Gupta (eds.), *Language problems of developing nations*, 27–35. New York: John Wiley.

1983. Sports announcer talk: syntactic aspects of register variation. *Language in Society* 12: 153–72.

1994. Dialect, register, and genre: working assumptions about conventionalization. In Biber and Finegan (eds.), 15–30.

Finegan, Edward. 1980. *Attitudes towards English usage: the history of a war of words.* New York: Teachers College Press.

1982. Form and function in testament language. In *Linguistics and the professions*, ed. by Robert J. Di Pietro, 113–20. Norwood, NJ: Ablex.

1992. Style and standardization in England: 1700–1900. In Tim W. Machan and Charles T. Scott (eds.), *English in its social contexts: essays in historical sociolinguistics*, 102–30. New York: Oxford University Press.

Finegan, Edward and Douglas Biber. 1994. Register variation and social dialects: toward an integrated view. In Biber and Finegan (eds.), 315–47.

Firth, J. R. 1935. The technique of semantics. *Transactions of the Philological Society*, 36–72.

Fitzpatrick, Eileen, Joan Bachenko, and Don Hindle. 1986. The status of telegraphic sublanguages. In Grishman and Kittredge (eds.), 39–52.

Fowler, Alastair. 1987. *A history of English literature.* Cambridge, MA: Harvard University Press.

Francis, W. N., and H. Kučera. 1979. *Manual of information to accompany A*

Standard Corpus of Present-Day American English, for use with Digital Computers.
Providence, RI: Department of Linguistics, Brown University.

1982. *Frequency analysis of English usage: lexicon and grammar.* Boston: Houghton Mifflin.

Galeb, Mohamed H. 1979. Brief reflections on the modernization of the Somali language. In Hussein M. Adam (ed.), *Somalia and the world,* 53–56. Mogadishu: Halgan.

Garside, Roger, Geoffrey Leech, and Geoffrey Sampson (eds.). 1987. *The computational analysis of English: a corpus-based approach.* London: Longman.

Gellerstam, Martin. 1992. Modern Swedish text corpora. In Svartvik (ed.), 149–63.

Geshekter, Charles L. 1978. Language, politics, and university teaching in Somalia. *Horn of Africa* 1: 11–17.

Ghadessy, Mohsen (ed.). 1988. *Registers of written English: situational factors and linguistic features.* London: Pinter.

Giglioli, Pier Paolo (ed.). 1972. *Language and social context.* New York: Penguin.

Givón, Talmy. 1979a. From discourse to syntax: grammar as a processing strategy. In Givón (ed.), 81–112.

(ed.). 1979b. *Discourse and syntax.* (Syntax and Semantics, vol. XII). New York: Academic Press.

Goody, Jack. 1977. *The domestication of the savage mind.* Cambridge University Press.

1986. *The logic of writing and the organization of society.* Cambridge University Press.

Gordon, Ian A. 1966. *The movement of English prose.* Bloomington: Indiana University Press.

Gorsuch, Richard L. 1983. *Factor analysis.* Hillsdale, NJ: Lawrence Erlbaum.

Grabe, William. 1987. Contrastive rhetoric and text-type research. In Ulla Connor and Robert B. Kaplan (eds.), *Writing across languages: analysis of L$_2$ text,* 115–37. Reading, MA: Addison-Wesley.

Gregory, M., and S. Carroll. 1978. *Language and situation: language varieties and their social contexts.* London: Routledge and Kegan Paul.

Grishman, Ralph and Richard Kittredge (eds.). 1986. *Analyzing language in restricted domains: sublanguage description and processing.* Hillsdale, NJ: Lawrence Erlbaum.

Hall, Robert A. 1964. *Introductory linguistics.* Philadelphia: Chilton.

Halliday, M. A. K. 1979. Differences between spoken and written language: Some implications for literacy teaching. In Glenda Page, John Elkins, and Barrie O'Connor (eds.), *Communication through reading: proceedings of the 4th Australian Reading Conference,* vol. II, 37–52. Adelaide: Australian Reading Association.

1988. On the language of physical science. In Ghadessy (ed.), 162–78.

1989. *Spoken and written language.* Oxford University Press.

Hared, Mohamed. 1992. Modernization and standardization in Somali press writing. Ph.D. dissertation, Department of Linguistics, University of Southern California.

Heath, Shirley Brice, and Juliet Langman. 1994. Shared thinking and the register of coaching. In Biber and Finegan (eds.), 82–105.

Hetzron, Robert. 1965. The particle *baa* in northern Somali. *Journal of African Linguistics* 4: 118–30.

Hiltunen, Risto. 1990. *Chapters on legal English: aspects past and present of the language of the law.* (Annals of the Finnish Academy of Science ser. B 251.) Helsinki: Finnish Academy of Science.

Hudson, Alan. 1994. Diglossia as a special case of register variation. In Biber and Finegan (eds.), 294–314.

Hurd, Conrad. 1979. A study of oral versus written Nasioi discourse. *Read* 14: 84–86.

Hwang, Juck-Ryun. 1975. The role of sociolinguistics in foreign language education with special reference to Korean and English terms of address and levels of deference. Ph.D. dissertation, University of Texas at Austin.

Hwang, Shin Ja Joo. 1981. Aspects of Korean narration. Ph.D. dissertation, University of Texas at Arlington.

Hymes, Dell (ed.). 1964. *Language in culture and society.* New York: Harper and Row.

   1974. *Foundations in sociolinguistics: an ethnographic approach.* Philadelphia: University of Pennsylvania Press.

   1984. Sociolinguistics: stability and consolidation. *International Journal of the Sociology of Language* 45: 39–45.

Irvine, Judith. 1979/1984. Formality and informality in communicative events. In John Baugh and Joel Sherzer (eds.), *Language in use: readings in sociolinguistics,* 211–28. Englewood Cliffs, NJ: Prentice-Hall.

Janda, Richard D. 1985. Note-taking as a simplified register. *Discourse Processes* 8: 437–54.

Johansson, Stig (with G. N. Leech and H. Goodluck). 1978. *Manual of information to accompany the Lancaster-Oslo/Bergen Corpus of British English, for use with digital computers.* Department of English, University of Oslo.

Johansson, Stig and Knut Hofland. 1989. *Frequency analysis of English vocabulary and grammar, Based on the LOB Corpus.* 2 vols. Oxford: Clarendon.

Johansson, Stig and Anna-Brita Stenström (eds.). 1991. *English computer corpora: selected papers and research guide.* Berlin: Mouton.

Joos, Martin. 1961. *The five clocks.* New York: Harcourt, Brace and World.

Jucker, Andreas H. 1992. *Social stylistics: syntactic variation in British newspapers.* Berlin: Mouton.

Kalmár, Ivan. 1985. Are there really no primitive languages? In D. R. Olson, N. Torrance, and A. Hildyard (eds.), *Literacy, language, and learning: the nature and consequences of reading and writing,* 148–66. Cambridge University Press.

Kim, Yong-Jin. 1990. Register variation in Korean: a corpus-based study. Ph.D. dissertation, Department of Linguistics, University of Southern California.

Kim, Yong-Jin and Douglas Biber. 1994. A corpus-based analysis of register variation in Korean. In Biber and Finegan (eds.), 157–81.

Kittredge, Richard. 1982. Variation and homogeneity of sublanguages. In Kittredge and Lehrberger (eds.), 107–37.

Kittredge, Richard and John Lehrberger (eds.). 1982. *Sublanguage: studies of language in restricted semantic domains.* Berlin: De Gruyter.

Kytö, Merja. 1986. On the use of the modal auxiliaries *can* and *may* in American English. In Sankoff (ed.), 123–38.

   1991. *Variation and diachrony, with Early American English in focus.* Frankfurt: Peter Lang.

Kytö, Merja, and Matti Rissanen. 1983. The syntactic study of Early American

English: the variationist at the mercy of his corpus? *Neuphilologische Mitteilungen* 84: 470–90.

Labov, William. 1972. *Sociolinguistic patterns*. Philadelphia: University of Pennsylvania Press.

Laitin, David D. 1977. *Politics, language, and thought: the Somali experience*. University of Chicago Press.

Laqueur, T. 1976. The cultural origins of popular literacy in England: 1500–1850. *Oxford Review of Education* 2: 255–75.

Lee, Hyo Sang, and Sandra A. Thompson. 1987. A discourse account of the Korean accusative marker. In Hyo Sang Lee and Sandra A. Thompson (eds.), *Santa Barbara papers in linguistics*. Vol. I: Korean: papers and discourse data, 23–49. University of California at Santa Barbara.

Lee, Hyun Bok. 1989. *Korean grammar*. Oxford University Press.

Lee, Won-Pyo. 1989. Referential choice in Korean discourse: cognitive and social perspective. Ph.D. dissertation, Department of Linguistics, University of Southern California.

Leech, Geoffrey N. 1966. *English in advertising*. London: Longman.

Leech, Geoffrey N. and Michael H. Short. 1981. *Style in fiction: a linguistic introduction to English fictional prose*. London: Longman.

Lehrberger, John. 1982. Automatic translation and the concept of sublanguage. In Kittredge and Lehrberger (eds.), 81–106.

Li, Charles N., and Sandra A. Thompson. 1982. The gulf between spoken and written language: a case study in Chinese. In Tannen (ed.), 77–88.

Longacre, Robert. 1976. *An anatomy of speech notions*. Lisse: Peter de Ridder Press.

Lukoff, Fred. 1986. The use of tenses in Korean written narrative. In Nam-Kil Kim (ed.), *Studies in Korean language and linguistics*, 1–36. Los Angeles: East Asian Study Center, University of Southern California.

Malinowski, Bronislaw. 1923. The problem of meaning in primitive languages. Supplementary essay in C. K. Ogden and I. A. Richards, *The meaning of meaning*, 296–336. New York: Harcourt, Brace.

Marckworth, Mary L., and William J. Baker. 1974. A discriminant function analysis of co-variation of a number of syntactic devices in five prose genres. *American Journal of Computational Linguistics*, Microfiche 11.

Martin, J. R. 1985. Process and text: two aspects of human semiosis. In James D. Benson and William S. Greaves (eds.), *Systemic perspectives on discourse*, vol. I, 248–74. Norwood, NJ: Ablex.

Mellinkoff, David. 1963. *The language of the law*. Boston: Little, Brown and Co.

Mezei, Regina. 1989. Somali language and literacy. *Language Problems and Language Planning* 13: 211–21.

Mulkay, Michael. 1985. Agreement and disagreement in conversations and letters. *Text* 5: 201–27.

Nam, Kishim, and Youngunkun Ko. 1988. *Phyocwun Kwuke Munpeplon*. [Standard Korean Grammar.] Seoul: Tower Press.

Nelson, Harold D. (ed.). 1982. *Somalia: a country study*. Washington, DC: U. S. Government.

Nevalainen, Terttu. 1986. The development of preverbal *only* in Early Modern English. In Sankoff (ed.), 111–21.

Nevalainen, Terttu and Helena Raumolin-Brunberg. 1989. A corpus of Early

Modern Standard English in a socio-historical perspective. *Neuphilologische Mitteilungen* 90: 67–110.

Nuyts, Jan. 1988. *IPrA survey of research in progress.* Wilrijk, Belgium: International Pragmatics Association.

Ochs, Elinor. 1979. Planned and unplanned discourse. In Givón (ed.), 51–80.

1994. Stories that step into the future. In Biber and Finegan (eds.), 106–35.

Oostdijk, N. 1988. A corpus linguistic approach to linguistic variation. *Literary and Linguistic Computing* 3: 12–25.

Perera, Katharine. 1984. *Children's writing and reading: analysing classroom language.* Oxford: Basil Blackwell.

Poole, Millicent E., and T. W. Field. 1976. A comparison of oral and written code elaboration. *Language and Speech* 19: 305–11.

Pride, J. B., and Janet Holmes (eds.). 1972. *Sociolinguistics.* New York: Penguin.

Quirk, Randolph, Sidney Greenbaum, Geoffrey Leech, and Jan Svartvik. 1985. *A comprehensive grammar of the English language.* London: Longman.

Redeker, Gisela. 1984. On differences between spoken and written language. *Discourse Processes* 7: 43–55.

Reder, Stephen. 1981. The written and the spoken word: influence of Vai literacy on Vai speech. In Scribner and Cole, 187–99.

Reppen, Randi. 1994. Variation in elementary student writing. Ph.D. dissertation, Department of English, Northern Arizona University.

Reppen, Randi and Douglas Biber. 1994. A multi-dimensional comparison of elementary student spoken and written registers. Conference presentation, American Association of Applied Linguistics.

Rissanen, Matti. 1986. Variation and the study of English historical syntax. In Sankoff (ed.), 97–109.

Romaine, Suzanne. 1980. The relative clause marker in Scots English: diffusion, complexity, and style as dimensions of syntactic change. *Language in Society* 9: 221–47.

1982. *Socio-historical linguistics: its status and methodology.* Cambridge University Press.

1984. *The language of children and adolescents.* Oxford: Basil Blackwell.

1994. On the creation and expansion of registers: sports reporting in Tok Pisin. In Biber and Finegan (eds.), 59–81.

Rushton, James, and George Young. 1975. Context and complexity in working class language. *Language and Speech* 18: 366–87.

Saeed, John Ibrahim. 1984. *The syntax of focus and topic in Somali.* Hamburg: Helmut Buske.

1987. *Somali reference grammar.* Wheaton, MD: Dunwoody Press.

Sager, Naomi. 1986. Sublanguage: linguistic phenomenon, computational tool. In Grishman and Kittredge (eds.), 1–18.

Sankoff, David (ed.). 1986. *Diversity and diachrony.* Amsterdam: Benjamins.

Schafer, John C. 1981. The linguistic analysis of spoken and written texts. In Barry M. Kroll and Roberta J. Vann (eds.), *Exploring speaking-writing relationships: connections and contrasts*, 1–31. Urbana, IL: National Council of Teachers of English.

Scribner, Sylvia, and Michael Cole. 1981. *The psychology of literacy.* Cambridge, MA: Harvard University Press.

Slocum, Jonathan. 1986. How one might automatically identify and adapt to a sublanguage: an initial exploration. In Grishman and Kittredge (eds.), 195–210.

Smith, Edward L. 1985. Text type and discourse framework. *Text* 5: 229–47.

Smith, Jeremy J. 1992. The use of English: Language, contact, dialect variation, and written standardisation during the Middle English period. In Tim W. Machan and Charles T. Scott (eds.), *English in its social contexts: essays in historical sociolinguistics*, 47–68. New York: Oxford University Press.

Street, Brain V. 1984. *Literacy in theory and practice.* Cambridge University Press.

(ed.). 1993. *Cross-cultural approaches to literacy.* Cambridge University Press.

Stubbs, Michael. 1980. *Language and literacy: the sociolinguistics of reading and writing.* London: Routledge Kegan Paul.

Svartvik, Jan (ed.). 1990. *The London-Lund Corpus of Spoken English: description and research.* (Lund Studies in English 82.) Lund University Press.

(ed.). 1992. *Directions in corpus linguistics.* (Proceedings of Nobel Symposium 82.) Berlin: Mouton.

Svartvik, Jan and Randolph Quirk (eds.). 1980. *A corpus of English conversation.* (Lund Studies in English 56). Lund University Press.

Tannen, Deborah. 1982a. Oral and literate strategies in spoken and written narratives. *Language* 58: 1–21.

(ed.). 1982b. *Spoken and written language: exploring orality and literacy.* Norwood, NJ: Ablex.

1984a. Spoken and written narrative in English and Greek. In Tannen (ed.), 21–41.

1984b. *Conversational style: analyzing talk among friends.* Norwood, NJ: Ablex.

(ed.). 1984c. *Coherence in spoken and written discourse.* Norwood, NJ: Ablex.

Taylor, Lita, Geoffrey Leech, and Steven Fligelstone. 1991. A survey of English machine-readable corpora. In Johansson and Stenström (eds.), 319–54.

Thompson, Sandra A. 1983. Grammar and discourse: the English detached participial clause. In Flora Klein-Andreu (ed.), *Discourse perspectives on syntax*, 43–65. New York: Academic Press.

Tottie, Gunnel. 1983. *Much about* not *and* nothing: *a study of the variation between analytic and synthetic negation in contemporary American English.* Lund: CWK Gleerup.

Trudgill, Peter. 1974. *Sociolinguistics: an introduction.* New York: Penguin.

Ure, Jean. 1982. Introduction: approaches to the study of register range. *International Journal of the Sociology of Language* 35: 5–23.

Vallins, G. H. 1956. *The pattern of English.* London: Andre Deutsch.

Ventola, Eija. 1984. Orientation to social semiotics in foreign language teaching. *Applied Linguistics* 5: 275–86.

Wardaugh, Ronald. 1986. *An introduction to sociolinguistics.* Oxford: Basil Blackwell.

Zipf, G. K. 1949. *Human behavior and the principle of least effort.* Cambridge, MA: Addison-Wesley.

Zwicky, Ann D., and Arnold M. Zwicky. 1980. America's national dish: the style of restaurant menus. *American Speech* 55: 83–92.

Index